A HOOSIER HOLIDAY

THE WARSAW HOME
The Mecca of this trip
Frontispiece

A HOOSIER HOLIDAY

with Illustrations by FRANKLIN BOOTH
and a New Introduction by DOUGLAS BRINKLEY

THEODORE DREISER

INDIANA UNIVERSITY PRESS
Bloomington and Indianapolis

This book is a publication of

Indiana University Press
601 North Morton Street
Bloomington, IN 47404-3797 USA

http://www.indiana.edu/~iupress

Telephone orders 800-842-6796
Fax orders 812-855-7931
Orders by e-mail iuporder@indiana.edu

This version of *A Hoosier Holiday* was originally published in 1916.
Introduction © 1997 by Douglas Brinkley
First reprinted in paperback in 1998.

The paper used in this publication meets the minimum requirements of
American National Standard for Information Sciences—Permanence of Paper
for Printed Library Materials, ANSI Z39.48-1984.

Manufactured in the United States of America

Library of Congress Cataloging-in-Publication Data

Dreiser, Theodore, 1871–1945.
    A Hoosier Holiday / Theodore Dreiser ; with illustrations by Franklin
Booth and a new introduction by Douglas Brinkley.
        p. cm.
    ISBN 0-253-33283-4 (alk. paper). — ISBN 0-253-21121-2 (alk. paper. : pbk.)
    1. Indiana—Description and travel. 2. Pennsylvania—Description and
travel. 3. Ohio—Description and travel. 4. New York (State)—Description
and travel. 5. Dreiser, Theodore, 1871–1945—Journeys. 6. Booth, Franklin,
1874–1948—Journeys. I. Title.
E169.D77 1997
917.7204'41—dc21   96-51687

3 4 5 6 7 03 02 01 00 99 98

TO
MY MOTHER

CONTENTS

CONTENTS

ILLUSTRATIONS

ILLUSTRATIONS

A HOOSIER HOLIDAY

INTRODUCTION

Theodore Dreiser and the Birth of the Road Book

DOUGLAS BRINKLEY

A HOOSIER HOLIDAY (1916) grew out of an August 1915 party given by novelist Theodore Dreiser, the author of *Sister Carrie* (1900), in uptown Manhattan to honor Edgar Lee Masters, who that spring had awakened the literary community with the publication of *Spoon River Anthology*, a best-selling volume of poetry. New York reporters covered the convivial gathering as if it were a glitzy bohemian ball, noting that the eclectic guest list included "parlor socialists, artists, bobbed hair models, temperamental pianists, girls in smocks and sandals and a corporation lawyer in a soft-boiled shirt." And, most importantly for Dreiser, the respected *Masses* illustrator and native Indianan Franklin Booth was in attendance, his brand-new automobile parked outside.

All evening long, even as Masters read from *Spoon River Anthology*, Booth boasted about his sixty-horsepower Pathfinder touring car. "How would you like to go out to Indiana in my car?" Booth asked Dreiser, a fellow Hoosier who hadn't visited the towns of his youth—Terre Haute, Vincennes, Sullivan, Warsaw, and Bloomington—in twenty-seven years. It took Dreiser all of a second to seize the opportunity and a collaborative deal was struck: Dreiser would write a book about their motorized pilgrimage from New York to Indiana,

3

and Booth would illustrate it. Two weeks later, the artistic duo chugged out of bustling Manhattan in the Pathfinder, destined for the lazy blue hills of Pennsylvania and beyond.

Although they didn't realize it at the time, a literary subgenre—the American automobile road book—was about to be born. The motorized trek resulted in Theodore Dreiser's 500-page *A Hoosier Holiday*, a narrative brimming with detail and the text singularly responsible for bringing the automobile to the forefront of American literature. It also marks the first time a serious writer captured the euphoric freedom to be found behind the wheel of a car: "We clambered up the bank on the farther side, the car making great noise. In this sweet twilight with fireflies and spirals of gnats and 'pinchin' bugs ... we tore the remainder of the distance, the eyes of the car glowing like great flames." As H. L. Mencken perceptively noted in *The Smart Set* (October 1916), *A Hoosier Holiday*— along with certain outstanding sections of *The Titan* (1917)— marked "the high tide of Dreiser's writing"—high praise indeed.

The Western tradition of travel writing can be traced back at least to thirteenth-century Icelandic and Norwegian epic narratives, but it wasn't until the mid-nineteenth century and the emergence of Walt Whitman, Ralph Waldo Emerson, and Henry David Thoreau that "the journey" took on a decidedly introspective, self-reflective dimension. "Every walk is a sort of crusade," Thoreau proclaimed, "preached by some Peter the Hermit in us, to go forth and reconquer this Holy Land from the Hands of the Infidels."

Ironically, Thoreau's infidels—the industrialists who preached the gospel of unfettered commerce—would ultimately make the modern genre of "highway literature" or "road books" possible by inventing the automobile. Motorized travel gave the generation entering Henry Luce's "American Century" something transcendental indeed: "Thoreau at 29 cents a gallon," as one commentator put it.

No sooner had the automobile been created than a flood of public relations stunts, from races to marathon drives, was unleashed to promote the novel mechanical horse. Highway billboards became an effective way for the auto industry to make new buyers realize that "Even You Can Afford a Ford," and the arrival of "horseless carriages" in cities such as Omaha and Denver was an event as big as a Billy Sunday evangelical revival or a Buffalo Bill Wild West show. By the time Theodore Roosevelt became president in 1901, the Tin Pan Alley jingle "In My Merry Oldsmobile" was being hummed down almost every Main Street in America. One of the manufacturers' favorite ploys to promote their shiny new product was to stage long-distance treks to prove the durability of the automobile—and then distribute a written account of the heroics far and wide. These publications, along with manufacturers' promotional pamphlets, song-sheets, and racing books, can be considered the seeds of highway literature, all designed to stir consumers' imaginations and open their wallets.

With the number of cars registered in the United States growing from a few thousand to almost half a million it was clear the rage was on, full throttle. "Within only two or three years, every one of you will have yielded to the horseless craze and be a boastful owner of a metal demon," predicted Indiana novelist Booth Tarkington, who fretted that automobiles would transform America's dirtways from Walt Whitman's spiritual paths of transcendental enlightenment into William Blake's apocalyptic avenues of industrial angst. As Tarkington saw it, Whitman's self-celebrating "Open Road" had become a noisy bumper-to-bumper nightmare. By 1913, when companies such as Texaco and Standard Oil began constructing "filling stations" on city corners and rural roads, the process was complete: Tarkington's "metal demon" had forever tarnished America's pristine landscape.

But not every "serious" writer shared that view. As Henry Ford's Highland Park assembly line began punching out

Model Ts at an astonishing rate, Theodore Dreiser, who had been living in New York City and writing his controversial novels *The Financier* (1912), *The Titan* (1914), and *The Genius* (1915), found his imagination piqued by the automobile's indisputable advantages over other means of leisure travel. Unlike those confined to trains and trolleys, the owner of a car could go whenever and wherever he pleased. A factory worker shackled to a time clock would no longer waste his weekend leisure hours waiting in stuffy train depots or riding in the back of smelly horse-drawn wagons. In Dreiser's eyes the automobile, far from being a "metal demon," could, if mass-marketed properly, have a liberating effect on America's bulging middle class. As for Dreiser, writing three long novels in succession had made him eager to travel—with a purpose, of course.

A Hoosier Holiday's storyline is quite simple. Dreiser, born in Terre Haute, hadn't been back to the Indiana towns of his youth in nearly three decades, not since the time when he had been a sixteen-year-old kid yearning to become a big-city reporter. "It had been one of my clearly cherished ideas," Dreiser wrote, "that some day, when I had the time and money to spare, I was going to pay a return visit to Indiana." His reasons for the 2,000-mile, two-week pilgrimage were myriad: nostalgia, a social realist's penchant for taking the pulse of the nation, a middle-aged yearning for episodic adventure, and the authorial impulse to write a travelogue laced with his philosophical musings on democracy. "Motoring was a new experience for Dreiser," noted biographer Richard Lingeman about the trip to Indiana, "and venturing into the interior on unpaved roads was akin to African safari."

Dreiser was not the only writer contemplating car travel. Just six months before Dreiser's departure in August 1915, *Scribner's*, in its February issue, published two articles side by side: L. Freeston's "Motor in Warfare," which detailed how France was using cars to great effect against the Germans in World War I, and J. Belden's "Motoring in the High Sierras," about his real-life adventure touring John Muir's high country in a Model T. That same year the indomitable Emily Post made a cross-country jaunt by auto through forbidding Rocky Mountain terrain, causing a swirl of attention wherever she went. The automobile was clearly the story of the age, and Dreiser knew it.

With his trusty Automobile Association of America "scenic route" map in hand, Dreiser, the self-designated trailblazer, headed out to see America with Booth, who had charcoal always at hand to sketch the countryside, and the chauffeur named Speed, "a blonde, little, gangling youth with an eerie farmer-like look." Speed's real name is never revealed, nor need it be: he is Everymechanic, a gifted autohead who can fix a flat tire in seconds. "He can take a car anywhere she'll go," Booth assured Dreiser, bragging that Speed had been "one of the chauffeurs who led the procession of cars from New York over the Alleghenies and Rockies to the coast, laying out the Lincoln Highway"—as if that made him the equivalent of Daniel Boone leading pioneer families through the Cumberland Gap.

For two weeks, Dreiser, Booth, and Speed together celebrated the transcendental freedom of motorized travel. "I can think of nothing more suited to my temperament than automobiling," Drieser wrote. "It supplies just that mixture of change in fixity which satisfies me—leaves me mentally poised in inquiry, which is always delightful." *A Hoosier Holiday* details the hours Dreiser, Booth, and Speed "idled together" down the "poor, undernourished routes which the dull, imitative rabble shun, and where, because of this very fact, you have some peace and quiet." Although in no real hurry, Dreiser did enjoy the rush when Speed took him racing over drawbridges and down steep hills, laughing in the wind without a care in the world. "It was the first opportunity that Speed had to show what the machine could do," Dreiser wrote (foreshadowing Jack Kerouac's portrait of Neal Cassidy as

Dean Moriarty in *On the Road* forty years later), "and instantly, though various signs read 'Speed Limit: 25 miles an hour,' I saw the speedometer climb to thirty-five and then forty and then to forty-five. It was a smooth-running machine which, at its best (or worst), gave vent to a t-r-r-r-r which after a while sounded like a croon."

Throughout *A Hoosier Holiday* Dreiser ruminated on everything from Slavic immigration to women's fashions, a modern-day Alexis de Toqueville careening through the heartland at 40 m.p.h. He mused on 'tinsel tourists' at the Delaware Water Gap, where New York finally sheds its grip; the drowsy hill villages where "ordinariness" is a coveted way of life; delectable roadside breakfasts and rotten egg lunches; the giant coal pits of western Pennsylvania and the dull sidewalks of Scranton; the sandy beaches of Lake Erie and the fallow cornfields of Indiana—a chant of Middle America. Deploring the narrow provincialism he encountered in unpaved towns, he nevertheless marveled at the nature of raw Midwest democracy, which produced the likes of Abraham Lincoln and William Jennings Bryan: "America is so great, the people so brisk. Everywhere they are fiddling with machinery & production & having a good time of it." H. L. Mencken, an acerbic curmudgeon, surprisingly applauded Dreiser's sentimental observations about the Midwest at a time when most eyes were fixated on the Great War in Europe: "I know, indeed, of no book which better describes the American hinterland. Here we have no idle spying by a stranger, but a full-length representation by one who knows the things he describes intimately, and is himself a part of it."

There is no mistaking Dreiser's cultural nationalism in *A Hoosier Holiday*: he got a thrill just from filling his notebook with the names of towns such as Tobyhanna, Meshoppen, Blossburg, and Roaring Branch. As he admitted, his pilgrimage by car through the Midwest made Dreiser "enamored of our American country life once more." On the other hand, he fumed about the brute ugliness of uninviting industrial cities such as Cleveland, Buffalo, and Indianapolis, all intent on building cheap skyscrapers at the expense of architectural integrity. "Destroy the old, the different, and let's be like New York!" Dreiser lamented of these misguided downtowns. "Every time I see one of these tenth-rate imitations, copying these great whales, I want to swear." If Dreiser's auto jag to Indiana did not alter the essence of his being, it did afford him a fresh perspective on himself and his country.

The author's Hoosier homecoming was more than a picaresque frolic. Pangs of nostalgia gripped Dreiser as he peered into his Indiana boyhood home and spied on an exhausted lad asleep in what once was *his* bedroom. In Terre Haute he scoured the grim streets in earnest looking for his birthplace, in vain, as it turned out, because he had the wrong address. Celebrating his forty-fourth birthday in Bloomington, his old college haunt, Dreiser felt old and out of place. "New life. New age. A rich town, instead of a poor one," he jotted down in his notebook with a distinct tone of despair. In the end, the notebook may have served a cathartic function. With a handful of exceptions, when composing *A Hoosier Holiday* in a Savannah, Georgia, boarding house in early 1916, Dreiser shied away from stories about himself, preferring to tell about his mother and father instead.

Because Dreiser was creating a new genre, not a single review called *A Hoosier Holiday* a "road book"; the term did not become popular until the mid-1950s. But Dreiser's contemporaries—at least those who could stomach his anti-British asides (which crippled book sales)—quickly understood that the pioneer of literary naturalism had in effect brought Whitmanesque joy for the open road into the modern era. Suddenly, Dreiser had revealed, courtesy of the automobile, common city folk could come into "intimate contact with woodland silences" and "grassy slopes" and escape the humdrum of their urban lives.

As Detroit continued to churn out pulp motorcar tracts, serious writers began taking Dreiser's lead and crafting their own road books, both fiction and nonfiction. Some budding writers—Hart Crane, e. e. cummings, Ernest Hemingway, John Dos Passos, and others—put their experiences driving ambulances in Europe during World War II to good use. Sinclair Lewis published his own highway romance novel, *Free Air* (1919), a clever hybrid of the dime Western and gothic romance. Although *Free Air* is considered fiction, Lewis based it on his own cross-country jaunt in a Model T Ford as a newlywed in 1916, escaping from Minneapolis–St. Paul to Seattle with his new bride, Grace Hegger Lewis, who appears as socialite Claire Boltwood in the book. As Claire navigates behind the wheel on the deep-rutted rural roads of Minnesota, she declares their adventure together a "voyage into democracy." Following in the footsteps of Dreiser and Lewis, much memorable fiction of the 1920s and 1930s prominently features the automobile, from F. Scott Fitzgerald's *The Great Gatsby* (1925) and William Faulkner's *The Sound and the Fury* (1929) to Erskine Caldwell's *Tobacco Road* (1932) and John Steinbeck's *The Grapes of Wrath* (1939). Each of these quintessentially American writers, in one story or another, portrayed driving a car down what Steinbeck called "roads of flight" as the ultimate escape routes from institutional racism, stark poverty, a regimented life, or whatever else ailed you.

But Theodore Dreiser's *A Hoosier Holiday* was the first to satisfy the public's newfound hunger to learn about their nation by reading automobile adventures written from the Great American Road. It is without question a classic literary contribution to our national canon. As Dreiser biographer Richard Lingeman surmised: "*A Hoosier Holiday* is perhaps

Dreiser's most accessible book, philosophical in parts and pessimistic in outlook, yet steeped in the sights, sounds, and talk of the Middle West and leavened by his rather ponderous humor." *A Hoosier Holiday* is Dreiser at his best—and that is as good as it gets in the annals of American literature.

Douglas Brinkley
New Orleans
October 10, 1996

A HOOSIER HOLIDAY

CHAPTER I

THE ROSE WINDOW

It was at a modest evening reception I happened to be giving to a new poet of renown that the idea of the holiday was first conceived. I had not seen Franklin, subsequent companion of this pilgrimage, in all of eight or nine months, his work calling him in one direction, mine in another. He is an illustrator of repute, a master of pen and ink, what you would call a really successful artist. He has a studio in New York, another in Indiana—his home town—a car, a chauffeur, and so on.

I first met Franklin ten years before, when he was fresh from Indiana and working on the Sunday supplement of a now defunct New York paper. I was doing the same. I was drawn to him then because he had such an air of unsophisticated and genial simplicity while looking so much the artist. I liked his long, strong aquiline nose, and his hair of a fine black and silver, though he was then only twenty-seven or eight. It is now white—a soft, artistic shock of it, glistening white. Franklin is a Christian Scientist, or dreamy metaphysician, a fact which may not commend him in the eyes of many, though one would do better to await a full metaphysical interpretation of his belief. It would do almost as well to call him a Buddhist or a follower of the Bhagavad Gita. He has no hard and fast Christian dogmas in mind. In fact, he is not a Christian at all, in the accepted sense, but a genial, liberal, platonic metaphysician. I know of no better way to describe him. Socalled sin, as something wherewith to reproach one, does not exist for him. He has few complaints to make concerning people's weaknesses or errors. Nearly everything is well. He lives happily along, sketching landscapes and trees and drawing many fine simplicities and perfections. There is about him a soothing repose which is not religious but human, which I felt, during all the two thousand miles we subsequently idled together. Franklin is also a very liberal liver, one who does not believe in stinting himself of the good things of the world as he goes—a very excellent conclusion, I take it.

At the beginning of this particular evening nothing was farther from my mind than the idea of going back to Indiana. Twentyeight years before, at the age of sixteen, I had left Warsaw, the last place in the state where I had resided. I had not been in the town of my birth, Terre Haute, Indiana, since I was seven. I had not returned since I was twelve to Sullivan or Evansville on the Ohio River, each of which towns had been my home for two years. The State University of Indiana at Bloomington, in the south central portion of the state, which had known me for one year when I was eighteen, had been free of my presence for twentysix years.

And in that time what illusions had I not built up in connection with my native state! Who does not allow fancy to color his primary experiences in the world? Terre Haute! A small city in which, during my first seven years, we lived in four houses. Sullivan, where we had lived from my seventh to my tenth year, in one house, a picturesque white frame on the edge of the town. In Evansville, at 1413 East Franklin Street, in a small brick, we had lived one year, and in Warsaw, in the northern part of the state, in a comparatively large brick house set in a grove of pines, we had spent four years. My mother's relatives were all residents of this northern section. There had been three months, between the time we left Evansville and the time we settled in Warsaw, Kosciusko County, which we spent in Chicago —my mother and nearly all of the children; also six weeks, between the time we left Terre Haute and the time we settled in Sullivan, which we spent in Vincennes, Indiana, visiting a kindly friend.

We were very poor in those days. My father had only comparatively recently suffered severe reverses, from which he really never recovered. My mother, a dreamy, poetic, impractical soul, was serving to the best of her ability as the captain of the family ship. Most of the ten children had achieved comparative maturity and had departed, or were preparing to depart, to shift for themselves. Before us—us little ones—were all our lives. At home, in a kind of intimacy which did not seem to concern the others because we were the youngest, were my brother Ed, two years younger than myself; my sister Claire (or Tillie), two years older, and occasionally my brother Albert, two years older than Claire, or my sister Sylvia, four years older, alternating as it were in the family home life. At other times they were out in the world working. Sometimes there appeared on the scene, usually one at a time, my elder brothers, Mark and Paul, and my elder sisters, Emma, Theresa, and Mary, each named in the order of their ascending ages. As I have said, there were ten all told—a restless, determined, halfeducated family who, had each been properly trained according to his or her capacities, I have always thought might have made a considerable stir in the world. As it was—but I will try not to become too technical.

But in regard to all this and the material and spiritual character of our life at that time, and what I had done and said, and what others had done and said, what notions had not arisen! They were highly colored ones, which might or might not have some relationship to the character of the country out there as I had known it. I did not know. Anyhow, it had been one of my dearly cherished ideas that some day, when I had the time and the money to spare, I was going to pay a return visit to Indiana. My father had once owned a woolen mill at Sullivan, still standing, I understood (or its duplicate built after a fire), and he also had managed another at Terre Haute. I had a vague recollection of seeing him at work in this one at Terre Haute, and of being shown about, having a spinning jenny and a carder and a weaver explained to me. I had fished in the Busseron near Sullivan, nearly lost my life in the Ohio at Evansville in the dead of winter, fallen in love with the first girls I ever loved at Warsaw. The first girl who ever kissed me and the first girl I ever ventured to kiss were at Warsaw. Would not that cast a celestial light over any midwestern village, however homely?

Well, be that as it may, I had this illusion. Someday I was going back, only in my plans I saw myself taking a train and loafing around in each village and hamlet hours or days, or weeks if necessary. At Warsaw I would try to find out about all the people I had ever known, particularly the boys and girls who went to school with me. At Terre Haute I would look up the house where I was born and our old house in Seventh Street, somewhere near a lumber yard and some railroad tracks, where, in a cool, roomy, musty cellar, I had swung in a swing hung from one of the rafters. Also in this lumber yard and among these tracks where the cars were, I had played with Al and Ed and other boys. Also in Thirteenth Street, Terre Haute, somewhere there was a small house (those were the darkest days of our poverty), where I had been sick with the measles. My father was an ardent Catholic. For the first fifteen years of my life I was horrified by the grim spiritual punishments enunciated by that faith. In this house in Thirteenth Street I had been visited by a long, lank priest in black, who held a silver crucifix to my lips to be kissed. That little house remains the apotheosis of earthly gloom to me even now.

At Sullivan I intended to go out to the Basler House, where we lived, several blocks from the local or old Evansville and Terre Haute depot. This house, as I recalled, was a charming thing of six or seven rooms with a large lawn, in which roses flourished, and with a truck garden north of it and a wonderful clover field to the rear (or east) of it. This clover field—how shall I describe it?—but I can't. It wasn't a clover field at all as I had come to think of it, but a honey trove in Arcady. An army of humble bees came here to gather honey. In those early dawns of spring, summer and autumn, when, for some reason not clear to me now, I was given to rising at dawn, it was canopied by a wonderful veil of clouds (tinted cirrus and nimbus effects), which seemed, as I looked at them, too wonderful for words. Across the fields was a grove of maples concealing a sugar camp (not ours), where I would go in the early dawn to bring home a bucket of maple sap. And directly to the north of us was a large, bare Gethsemane of a field, in the weedy hollows of which were endless whitening bones, for here stood a small village slaughter house, the sacrificial altar of one local butcher. It was not so gruesome as it sounds—only dramatic.

But this field and the atmosphere of that home! I shall have to tell you about them or the import of returning there will be as nothing. It was between my seventh and my tenth year that we lived there, among the most impressionable of all my youth. We were very hard pressed, as I understood it later, but I was too young and too dreamy to feel the pinch of poverty. This lower Wabash valley is an Egyptian realm—not very cold in winter, and drowsy with heat in summer. Corn and wheat and hay and melons grow here in heavy, plethoric fashion. Rains come infrequently, then only in deluging storms. The spring comes early, the autumn lingers until quite New Year's time. In the beech and ash and hickory groves are many turtle doves. Great hawks and buzzards and eagles soar high in the air. House and barn martins circle in covies. The bluejay and scarlet tanager flash and cry. In the eaves of our cottage were bluebirds and wrens, and to our trumpet vines and purple clematis came wondrous humming birds to poise and glitter, tropic in their radiance. In old Kirkwood's orchard, a quarter of a mile away over the clover field, I can still hear the guinea fowls and the peacocks "calling for rain."

Sometimes the experiences of delicious years make a stained glass window—the rose window of the west—in the cathedral of our life. These three years in "dirty old Sullivan," as one of my sisters once called it (with a lip-curl of contempt thrown in for good measure), form such a flower of stained glass in mine. They are my rose window. In symphonies of leaded glass, blue, violet, gold and rose are the sweet harmonies of memory with all the ills of youth discarded. A bare-foot boy is sitting astride a high board fence at dawn. Above him are the tinted fleeces of heaven, those golden argosies of youthful seas of dream. Over the blooming clover are scudding the swallows, "my heart remembers how." I look, and in a fence corner is a spider web impearled with dew, a great yellow spider somewhere on its surface is repairing a strand. At a window commanding the field, a window in the kitchen, is my mother. My brother Ed has not risen yet, nor my sister Tillie. The boy looks at the sky. He loves the feel of the dawn. He knows nothing of whence he is coming or where he is going, only all is sensuously, deliriously gay and beautiful. Youth is his: the tingle and response of a new body; the bloom and fragrance of the clover in the air; the sense of the mystery of flying. He sits and sings some tuneless tune. Of such is the kingdom of heaven.

Or it is a great tree, say, a hundred yards from the house. In its thick leaves and widespreading branches the wind is stirring. Under its shade Ed and Tillie and I are playing house. What am I? Oh, a son, a husband, or indeed anything that the occasion requires. We play at duties—getting breakfast, or going to work, or coming home. Why? But a turtle dove is calling somewhere in the depths of a woodland, and that gives me pause. "Bob white" cries and I think of strange and faroff things to come. A buzzard is poised in the high blue above and I wish I might soar on wings as wide.

Or is it a day with a pet dog? Now they are running

side by side over a stubbly field. Now the dog has wandered away and the boy is calling. Now the boy is sitting in a rocking chair by a window and holding the dog in his lap, studying a gnarled tree in the distance, where sits a hawk all day, meditating no doubt on his midnight crimes. Now the dog is gone forever, shot somewhere for chasing sheep, and the boy, disconsolate, is standing under a tree, calling, calling, calling, until the sadness of his own voice and the futility of his cries moves him nearly to tears.

These and many scenes like these make my rose window of the west.

CHAPTER II

IT was a flash of all this that came to me when in the midst of the blathering and fol de rol of a gay evening Franklin suddenly approached me and said, quite apropos of nothing: "How would you like to go out to Indiana in my car?"

"I'll tell you what, Franklin," I answered, "all my life I've been thinking of making a return trip to Indiana and writing a book about it. I was born in Terre Haute, down in the southwest there below you, and I was brought up in Sullivan and Evansville in the southern part of the state and in Warsaw up north. Agree to take me to all those places after we get there, and I'll go. What's more, you can illustrate the book if you will."

"I'll do that," he said. "Warsaw is only about two hours north of our place. Terre Haute is seventyfive miles away. Evansville is a hundred and fifty. We'll make a oneday trip to the northern part and a three-day trip to the southern. I stipulate but one thing. If we ruin many tires, we split the cost."

To this I agreed.

Franklin's home was really central for all places. It was at Carmel, fifteen miles north of Indianapolis. His plan, once the trip was over, was to camp there in his country studio, and paint during the autumn. Mine was to return direct to New York.

We were to go up the Hudson to Albany and via various perfect state roads to Buffalo. There we were to follow other smooth roads along the shore of Lake Erie to Cleveland and Toledo, and possibly Detroit. There we were to cut southwest to Indianapolis—so close to Carmel. It had not occurred to either of us yet to go direct to Warsaw from Toledo or thereabouts, and thence south to Carmel. That was to come as an after-thought.

But this Hudson-Albany-State-road route irritated me from the very first. Everyone traveling in an automobile seemed inclined to travel that way. I had a vision of thousands of cars which we would have to trail, consuming their dust, or meet and pass, coming toward us. By now the Hudson River was a chestnut. Having traveled by the Pennsylvania and the Central over and over to the west, all this mid-New York and southern Pennsylvania territory was wearisome to think of. Give me the poor, undernourished routes which the dull, imitative rabble shun, and where, because of this very fact, you have some peace and quiet. I traveled all the way up-town the next day to voice my preference in regard to this matter.

"I'd like to make a book out of this," I explained, "if the material is interesting enough, and there isn't a thing that you can say about the Hudson River or the central part of New York State that hasn't been said a thousand times before. Poughkeepsie, Albany, Troy, Syracuse, Rochester—all ghastly manufacturing towns. Why don't we cut due west and see how we make out? This is the nicest, dryest time of the year. Let's go west to the Water Gap, and straight from there through Pennsylvania to some point in Ohio, then on to Indianapolis." A vision of quaint, wild, unexpected regions in Pennsylvania came to me.

"Very good," he replied genially. He was playing with a cheerful, pop-eyed French bull. "Perhaps that would be better. The other would have the best roads, but we're not going for roads exactly. Do you know the country out through there?"

"No," I replied. "But we can find out. I suppose the Automobile Club of America ought to help us. I might go round there and see what I can discover."

"Do that," he applauded, and I was making to depart

when Franklin's brother and his chauffeur entered. The latter he introduced as "Speed."

"Speed," he said, "this is Mr. Dreiser, who is going with us. He wants to ride directly west across Pennsylvania to Ohio and so on to Indianapolis. Do you think you can take us through that way?"

A blond, lithe, gangling youth with an eerie farmer-like look and smile ambled across the room and took my hand. He seemed half mechanic, half street-car conductor, half mentor, guide and friend.

"Sure," he replied, with a kind of childish smile that won instantly—a little girl smile, really. "If there are any roads, I can. We can go anywhere the car'll go."

I liked him thoroughly. All the time I was trying to think where I had seen Speed before. Suddenly it came to me. There had been a car conductor in a recent comedy. This was the stage character to life. Besides he reeked of Indiana—the real Hoosier. If you have ever seen one, you'll know what I mean.

"Very good," I said. "Fine. Are you as swift as your name indicates, Speed?"

"I'm pretty swift," he said, with the same glance that a collie will give you at times—a gay, innocent light of the eyes!

A little while later Franklin was saying to me that he had no real complaint against Speed except this: "If you drive up to the St. Regis and go in for half an hour, when you come out the sidewalk is all covered with tools and the engine dismantled—that is, if the police have not interfered."

"Just the same," put in Fred Booth, "he is one of the chauffeurs who led the procession of cars from New York over the Alleghanies and Rockies to the coast, laying out the Lincoln Highway." (Afterwards I saw testimonials and autographed plates which proved this.) "He can take a car anywhere she'll go."

Then I proceeded to the great automobile club for information.

"Are you a member?" asked the smug attendant, a polite, airy, bufferish character.

"No, only the temporary possessor of a car for a tour."

"Then we can do nothing for you. Only members are provided with information."

On the table by which I was standing lay an automobile monthly. In its pages, which I had been idly thumbing as I waited, were a dozen maps of tours, those deceptive things gotten up by associated roadhouses and hotels in their own interest. One was labeled "The Scenic Route," and showed a broad black line extending from New York via the Water Gap, Stroudsburg, Wilkes-Barré, Scranton, Binghamton, and a place called Watkins Glen, to Buffalo and Niagara Falls. This interested me. These places are in the heart of the Alleghanies and of the anthracite coal region. Visions of green hills, deep valleys, winding rivers, glistering cataracts and the like leaped before my mind.

"The Scenic Route!" I ventured. "Here's a map that seems to cover what I want. What number is this?"

"Take it, take it!" replied the lofty attendant, as if to shoo me out of the place. "You are welcome."

"May I pay you?"

"No, no, you're welcome to it."

I bowed myself humbly away.

"Well, auto club or no auto club, here is something, a real route," I said to myself. "Anyhow it will do to get us as far as Wilkes-Barré or Scranton. After that we'll just cut west if we have to."

On the way home I mooned over such names as Tobyhanna, Meshoppen, Blossburg, and Roaring Branch. What sort of places were they? Oh, to be speeding along in this fine warm August weather! To be looking at the odd places, seeing mountains, going back to Warsaw and Sullivan and Terre Haute and Evansville!

CHAPTER III

ACROSS THE MEADOWS TO THE PASSAIC

I ASSUME that automobiling, even to the extent of a two-thousand-mile trip such as this proved to be, is an old story to most people. Anybody can do it, apparently. The difference is to the man who is making the trip, and for me this one had the added fillip of including that pilgrimage which I was certain of making some time.

There was an unavoidable delay owing to the sudden illness of Speed, and then the next morning, when I was uncertain as to whether the trip had been abandoned or no, the car appeared at my door in Tenth Street, and off we sped. There were some amusing preliminaries. I was introduced to Miss H——, a lady who was to accompany us on the first day of our journey. A photograph was taken, the bags had to be arranged and strapped on the outside, and Speed had to examine his engine most carefully. Finally we were off—up Eighth Avenue and across Fortysecond Street to the West Fortysecond Street Ferry, while we talked of non-skid chains and Silvertown tires and the durability of the machines in general—this one in particular. It proved to be a handsome sixty-horsepower Pathfinder, only recently purchased, very presentable and shiny.

As we crossed the West Fortysecond Street Ferry I stood out on the front deck till we landed, looking at the refreshing scene the river presented. The day was fine, nearly mid-August, with a sky as blue as weak indigo. Flocks of gulls that frequent the North River were dipping and wheeling. A cool, fresh wind was blowing.

As we stood out in front Miss H—— deigned to tell me something of her life. She is one of those self-conscious, carefully dressed, seemingly prosperous maidens of some beauty who frequent the stage and the studios. At present she was Franklin's chief model. Recently she had been in some pantomime, dancing. A little wearied perhaps (for all her looks), she told me her stage and art experiences. She had to do something. She could sing, dance, act a little, and draw, she said. Artists seemed to crave her as a model—so——

She lifted a thin silk veil and dabbed her nose with a mere rumor of a handkerchief. Looking at her so fresh and spick in the morning sunlight, I could not help feeling that Franklin was to be congratulated in the selection of his models.

But in a few minutes we were off again, Speed obviously holding in the machine out of respect for officers who appeared at intervals, even in Weehawken, to wave us on or back. I could not help feeling as I looked at them how rapidly the passion for regulating street traffic had grown in the last few years. Everywhere we seemed to be encountering them—the regulation New York police cap (borrowed from the German army) shading their eyes, their air of majesty beggaring the memories of Rome—and scarcely a wagon to regulate. At Passaic, at Paterson—but I anticipate.

As we hunted for a road across the meadows we got lost in a maze of shabby streets where dirty children were playing in the dust, and, as we gingerly picked our way over rough cobbles, I began to fear that much of this would make a disagreeable trip. But we would soon be out of it, in all likelihood—miles and miles away from the hot, dusty city.

I can think of nothing more suited to my temperament than automobiling. It supplies just that mixture of change in fixity which satisfies me—leaves me mentally poised in inquiry, which is always delightful. Now, for instance, we were coming out on a wide, smooth macadam road, which led, without a break, as someone informed us, into Passaic and then into Paterson. It was the first opportunity that Speed had had to show what the machine could do, and instantly, though various signs read, "Speed limit: 25 miles an hour," I saw the speedometer climb to thirtyfive and then forty and then fortyfive. It was a smooth-running machine which, at its best (or worst), gave vent to a tr-r-r-r-r-r-r-r-r which became after a while somewhat like a croon.

Though it was a blazing hot day (as any momentary pause proved, the leather cushions becoming like an oven), on this smooth road, and at this speed, it was almost too cool. I had decked myself out in a brown linen outing shirt and low visored cap. Now I felt as though I might require my overcoat. There was no dust to speak of, and under the low branches of trees and passing delightful dooryards all the homey flowers of August were blooming in abundance. Now we were following the Hackensack and the Passaic in spots, seeing long, low brick sheds in the former set down in wind rhythmed marsh grass, and on the latter towering stacks and also simple clubs where canoes were to be seen— white, red and green—and a kind of August summer life prevailing for those who could not go further. I was becoming enamored of our American country life once more.

Paterson, to most New Yorkers, and for that matter to most Americans, may be an old story. To me it is one of the most interesting pools of life I know. There is nothing in Paterson, most people will tell you, save silk mills and five-and-ten-cent stores. It is true. Yet to me it is a beautiful city in the creative sense—a place in which to stage a great novel. These mills—have you ever seen them? They line the Passaic river and various smooth canals that branch out from it. It was no doubt the well-known waterfall and rapids of this river that originally drew manufacturers to Paterson, supplied the first mills with water, and gave the city its start. Then along came steam and all the wonders of modern electricity-driven looms. The day we were there they were just completing a power plant or city water supply system. The ground around the falls had been parked, and standing on a new bridge one could look down into a great round, grey-black pit or cup, into which tumbled the water of the sturdy little river above. By the drop of eighty or a hundred feet it was churned into a white spray which bounded back almost to the bridge where we stood. In this gay sunlight a rainbow was ever present—a fine five-striped thing, which paled and then strengthened as the spray thinned or thickened.

Below, over a great flume of rocks, that stretched outward toward the city, the expended current was bubbling away, spinning past the mills and the bridges. From the mills themselves, as one drew near, came the crash of shuttles and the thrum of spindles, where thousands of workers were immured, weaving the silk which probably they might never wear. I could not help thinking, as I stood looking at them, of the great strike that had occurred two years before, in which all sorts of nameless brutalities had occurred, brutalities practised by judges, manufacturers and the police no less than by the eager workers themselves.

In spite of all the evidence I have that human nature is much the same at the bottom as at the top, and that the restless striker of today may be the oppressive manufacturer or boss of tomorrow, I cannot help sympathizing with the working rank and file. Why should the man at the top, I ask myself, want more than a reasonable authority? Why endless houses, and lands, and stocks, and bonds to flaunt a prosperity that he does not need and cannot feel? I am convinced that man *in toto*—the race itself—is nothing more nor less as yet than an embryo in the womb of something which we cannot see. We are to be protected (as a race) and born into something (some state) which we cannot as yet understand or even feel. We, as individual atoms, may never know, any more than the atoms or individual plasm cells which constructed us ever knew. But we race atoms are being driven to do something, construct something—(a race man or woman, let us say)—and like the atoms in the embryo, we are struggling and fetching and carrying. I did not always believe in some one "divine faroff event" for the race. I do not accept the adjective divine even now. But I do believe that these atoms are not toiling for exactly nothing—or at least, that the nothingness is not quite as undeniable as it was. There is something back of man. An avatar, a devil, anything you will, is trying to do something, and man is His medium, His brush, His paint, His idea. Against the illimitable space of things He is attempting to set forth his vision. Is the vision good? Who knows! It may be as bad as that of the lowest vaudeville performer clowning it before a hoodlum audience. But good or bad, here it is, struggling to make itself manifest, and we are of it!

What if it *is* all a mad, aimless farce, my masters? Shan't we clown it all together and make the best of it?

Ha ha! Ho ho! We are all crazy and He is crazy! Ha ha! Ho ho!

Or do I hear someone crying?

CHAPTER IV

BUT in addition to mills and the falls, Paterson offered another subject of conversation. Only recently there had been completed there an evangelical revival by one "Billy" Sunday, who had addressed from eight to twenty thousand people at each meeting in a specially constructed tabernacle, and caused from one to five hundred or a thousand a day to "hit the trail," as he phrased it, or in other words to declare that they were "converted to Christ," and hence *saved*.

America strikes me as an exceedingly intelligent land at times, with its far-flung states, its fine mechanical equipment, its good homes and liberal, rather non-interfering form of government, but when one contemplates such a mountebank spectacle as this, what is one to say? I suppose one had really better go deeper than America and contemplate nature itself. But then what is one to say of nature?

We discussed this while passing various mills and brown wooden streets, so poor that they were discouraging.

"It is curious, but it is just such places as Paterson that seem to be afflicted with unreasoning emotions of this kind," observed Franklin wearily. "Gather together hordes of working people who have little or no skill above machines, and then comes the revivalist and waves of religion. Look at Pittsburg and Philadelphia. See how well Sunday did there. He converted thousands."

He smiled heavily.

" 'Billy' Sunday comes from out near your town," volunteered Speed informatively. "He lives at Winona Lake. That's a part of Warsaw now."

"Yes, and he conducts a summer revival right there occasionally, I believe," added Franklin, a little vindictively, I thought.

"Save me!" I pleaded. "Anyhow, I wasn't born there. I only lived there for a little while."

This revival came directly on the heels of a great strike, during which thousands were compelled to obtain their food at soup houses, or to report weekly to the local officers of the union for some slight dole. The good God was giving them wrathful, condemnatory manufacturers, and clubbing, cynical police. Who was it, then, that "revived" and "hit the trail"? The same who were starved and clubbed and lived in camps, and were railroaded to jail? Or were they the families of the bosses and manufacturers, who had suppressed the strike and were thankful for past favors (for they eventually won, I believe)? Or was it some intermediate element that had nothing to do with manufacturers or workers?

The day we went through, some Sunday school parade was preparing. There were dozens of wagons and autotrucks and automobiles gaily bedecked with flags and bunting and Sunday school banners. Hundreds, I might almost guess thousands, of children in freshly ironed white dresses and gay ribbons, carrying parasols, and chaperoned by various serious looking mothers and elders, were in these conveyances, all celebrating, presumably, the glory and goodness of God!

A spectacle like this, I am free to say, invariably causes me to scoff. I cannot help smiling at a world that cannot devise some really poetical or ethical reason for worshiping or celebrating or what you will, but must indulge in shrines and genuflections and temples to false or impossible ideas or deities. They have made a God of Christ, who was at best a humanitarian poet—but not on the basis on which he offered himself. Never! They had to bind him up with the execrable yah-vah of the Hebrews, and make him now a God of mercy, and now a God of horror. They had to dig themselves a hell, and they still cling to it. They had to secure a church organization and appoint strutting vicars of Christ to misinterpret him, and all that he believed. This wretched mountebank "who came here and converted thousands" —think of him with his yapping about hell, his bar-room and race-track slang, his base-ball vocabulary. And thousands of poor worms who could not possibly offer one reasonable or intelligible thought concerning their faith or history or life, or indeed anything, fall on their knees and "accept Christ." And then they pass the collection plate and build more temples and conduct more revivals.

What does the God of our universe want, anyway? Slaves? Or beings who attempt to think? Is the fable of Prometheus true after all? Is autocracy the true interpretation of all things—or is this an accidental phase, infinitely brief in the long flow of things, and eventually to be done away with? I, for one, hope so.

Beyond Paterson we found a rather good road leading to a place called Boonton, via Little Falls, Singac, and other smaller towns, and still skirting the banks of the Passaic River. In Paterson we had purchased four hardboiled eggs, two pies, four slices of ham and some slices of bread, and four bottles of beer, and it being somewhere near noon we decided to have lunch. The task of finding an ideal spot was difficult, for we were in a holiday mood and content with nothing less than perfection. Although we were constantly passing idyllic scenes— waterfalls, glens, a canal crossing over a stream—none would do exactly. In most places there was no means of bringing the car near enough to watch it. One spot proved of considerable interest, however, for, although we did not stay, in spying about we found an old moss-covered, red granite block three feet square and at least eight feet long, on which was carved a statement to the effect that this canal had been completed in 1829, and that the following gentlemen, as officers and directors, had been responsible. Then followed a long list of names —Adoniram this, and Cornelius that, good and true business men all, whose carved symbols were now stuffed with mud and dust. This same canal was very familiar to me, I having walked every inch of it from New York to the Delaware River during various summer holidays. But somehow I had never before come upon this memorial stone. Here some twenty men, of a period so late as 1829, caused their names to be graven on a great stone which should attest their part in the construction of a great canal—a canal reaching from New York Bay to the Delaware River—and here lies the record under dust and vines! The canal itself is now entirely obsolete. Although the State of New Jersey annually spends some little money to keep it clean, it is rarely if ever used by boats. It was designed originally to bring hard coal from that same region around Wilkes-Barré and Scranton, toward which we were speeding. A powerful railroad corporation crept in, paralleled it, and destroyed it. This same corporation, eager to make its work complete, and thinking that the mere existence of the canal might some day cause it to be revived, and wanting no water competition in the carrying of coal, had a bill introduced into the State legislature of New Jersey, ordering, or at least sanctioning that it should be filled in, in places. Some citizens objected, several newspapers cried out, and so the bill was dropped. But you may walk along a canal costing originally fifty million dollars, and still ornamented at regular intervals with locks and planes, and never encounter anything larger than a canoe. Pretty farm houses face it now; door yards come down to the very water; ducks and swans float on its surface and cattle graze nearby. I have spent as much as two long springtimes idling along its banks. It is beautiful—but it is useless.

We did eventually come to a place that suited us exactly for our picnic. The river we were following widened at this point and skirted so near the road that it was no trouble to have our machine near at hand and still sit under the trees by the waterside. Cottages and tents were sprinkled cheerily along the farther shore, and the river was dotted with canoes and punts of various colors. Under a group of trees we stepped out and spread our feast. It was all so lovely that it seemed a bit out of fairyland or a sketch by Watteau. Franklin being a Christian Scientist, it was his duty, as I explained to him, to "think" any flies or mosquitoes away—to "realize" for us all that they could not be, and so leave us to enjoy our meal in peace. Miss H—— was to be the background of perfection, the color spot, the proof of holiday, like all the ladies in Watteau and Boucher. The machine and Speed, his cap adjusted to a rakish angle, were to prove that we were gentlemen of leisure. On leaving New York I saw that he had a moustache capable of that upward twist so admired of the German Emperor, and so now I began to urge him to make the ends stand up so that he would be the embodiment of the *distingué*. Nothing loath, he complied smilingly, that same collie-like smile in his eyes that I so much enjoy.

It was Franklin who had purchased the eggs. He had gone across the street in Paterson, his belted dust-coat swinging most impressively, and entering a little quick lunch room, had purchased these same eggs. Afterward he admitted that as he was leaving he noticed the black moustached face of a cook and the villainous head of a scullion peering after him from a sort of cook's galley window with what seemed to him "a rumor of a sardonic smile." But suspecting nothing, he went his way. Now, however, I peeled one of these eggs, and touching it with salt, bit into it. Then I slowly turned my head, extracted as much as I could silently with a paper napkin, and deposited it with an air of great peace upon the ground. I did not propose to be the butt of any ribald remarks.

Presently I saw Franklin preparing his. He crushed the shell, and after stripping the glistening surface dipped it in salt. I wondered would it be good. Then he bit into it and paused, took up a napkin with a very graceful and philosophic air, and wiped his mouth. I was not quite sure what had happened.

"Was your egg good?" he said finally, examining me with an odd expression.

"It was not," I replied. "The most villainously bad

egg I have had in years. And here it goes, straight to the fishes."

I threw it.

"Well, they can have mine," observed Miss H——, sniffing gingerly.

"What do you know about that?" exclaimed Speed, who was sitting some distance from the rest of us and consuming his share. "I think the man that sold you those ought to be taken out and slapped gently," and he threw his away. "Say! And four of them all at once too. I'd just like to get a camera and photograph him. He's a bird, he is."

There was something amazingly comic to me in the very sound of Speed's voice. I cannot indicate just what, but his attempt at scorn was so inadequate, so childlike.

"Well, anyhow, the fishes won't mind," I said. "They like nice, fresh Franklin eggs. Franklin is their best friend, aren't you, Franklin? You love fishes, don't you?"

Booth sat there, his esoteric faith in the wellbeing of everything permitting him to smile a gentle, tolerant smile.

"You know, I wondered why those two fellows seemed to smile at me," he finally commented. "They must have done this on purpose."

"Oh no," I replied, "not to a full fledged Christian Scientist! Never! These eggs must be perfect. The error is with us. We have *thought* bad eggs, that's all."

We got up and tossed the empty beer bottles into the stream, trying to sink them with stones. I think I added one hundred stones to the bed of the river without sinking a single bottle. Speed threw in a rock pretending it was a bottle and I even threw at that before discovering my mistake. Finally we climbed into our car and sped onward, new joys always glimmering in the distance.

"Just to think," I said to myself, "there are to be two whole weeks of this in this glorious August weather. What lovely things we shall see!"

CHAPTER V

ACROSS THE DELAWARE

THE afternoon run was even more delightful than that of the morning. Yet one does not really get free of New York—its bustle and thickness of traffic—until one gets west of Paterson, which is twentyfive miles west, and not even then. New York is so all embracing. It is supposed to be chiefly represented by Manhattan Island, but the feel of it really extends to the Delaware Water Gap, one hundred miles west, as it does to the eastern end of Long Island, one hundred miles east, and to Philadelphia, one hundred miles south, or Albany, one hundred miles north. It is all New York.

But west of Paterson and Boonton the surge of traffic was beginning to diminish, and we were beginning to taste the real country. Not so many autotrucks and wagons were encountered here, though automobiles proper were even more numerous, if anything. This was a wealthy residence section we were traversing, with large handsome machines as common as wagons elsewhere, and the occupants looked their material prosperity. The roads, too, as far as Dover, our next large town, thirty miles on, were beautiful—smooth, grey and white macadam, lined mostly with kempt lawns, handsome hedges, charming dwellings, and now and then yellow fields of wheat or oats or rye, with intermediate acres of tall, ripe corn. I never saw better fields of grain, and remembered reading in the papers that this was a banner season for crops. The sky, too, was wholly entrancing, a clear blue, with great, fleecy clouds sailing along in the distance like immense hills or ships. We passed various small hotels and summer cottages, nestling among these low hills, where summer boarders were sitting on verandas, reading books or swinging in hammocks or crocheting, American fashion, in rocking chairs. All my dread of the conventional American family arose as I surveyed them, for somehow, as idyllic as all this might appear on the surface, it smacked the least bit of the doldrums. Youths and maidens playing croquet and tennis, mother (and much more rarely father) seated near, reading and watching. The three regular meals, the regular nine o'clock hour for retiring! Well, I was glad we were making forty miles an hour.

As we passed through Dover it was three o'clock. As we passed Hopatcong, after pausing to sketch a bridge over the canal, it was nearing four. There were pauses constantly which interrupted our speed. Now it was a flock of birds flying over a pool, all their fluttering wings reflected in the water, and Franklin had to get out and make a pencil note of it. Now a lovely view over some distant hills, a small town in a valley, a factory stack by some water side.

"Say, do these people here ever expect to get to Indiana?" remarked Speed in an aside to Miss H——.

We had to stop in Dover—a city of thirty thousand—at the principal drug store, for a glass of ice cream soda. We had to stop at Hopatcong and get a time table in order to learn whether Miss H—— could get a train in from the Water Gap later in the evening. We had to stop and admire a garden of goldenglows and old fashioned August flowers.

Beyond Hopatcong we began to realize that we would no more than make the Water Gap this day. The hills and valleys were becoming more marked, the roads more difficult to ascend. As we passed Stanhope, a small town beyond Hopatcong, we got on the wrong road and had to return, a common subsequent experience. Beyond Stanhope we petitioned one family group—a mother and three children—for some water, and were refused. A half mile further on, seeing a small iron pump on a lawn, we stopped again. A lean, dreamy woman came out and we asked her. "Yes, surely," she replied and re-entered the house, returning with a blue pitcher. Chained to a nearby tree a collie bitch which looked for all the world like a fox jumped and barked for joy.

"Are you going to Hackettstown?" asked our hostess simply.

"We're going through to Indiana," confided Franklin in a neighborly fashion.

A look of childlike wonder at the far off came into the woman's voice and eyes. "To Indiana?" she replied. "That's a long way, isn't it?"

"Oh, about nine hundred miles," volunteered Speed briskly.

As we sped away—vain of our exploit, I fancy—she stood there, pitcher in hand, looking after us. I wished heartily she might ride all the long distances her moods might crave. "Only," I thought, "would it be a fair exchange for all her delightsome wonder?"

This side of Hackettstown we careened along a ridge under beautiful trees surveying someone's splendid country estate, with a great house, a lake and hills of sheep. On the other side of Hackettstown we had a blow out and had to stop and change a tire. A Russian *moujik,* transplanted to America and farming in this region, interested me. A reaper whirring in a splendid field of grain informed me that we were abroad at harvest time—we would see much reaping then. While the wheel was being repaired I picked up a scrap of newspaper lying on the road. It was of recent issue and contained an advertisement of a great farm for sale which read "Winter is no time to look at a farm, for then everything is out of commission and you cannot tell what a farm is worth. Spring is a dangerous time, for then everything is at its best, and you are apt to be deceived by fields and houses which later you would not think of buying. Mid-August is the ideal time. Everything is bearing by then. If a field or a yard or a house or cattle look good at that time you may be sure that they will look as good or better at others. Examine in mid-August. Examine now."

"Ah," I said, "now I shall see this eastern half of the

United States at the best time. If it looks good now I shall know pretty well how good eastern America is."

And so we sped on, passing a little farther on a forlorn, decadent, gloomy hamlet about which I wanted to write a poem or an essay. Edgar Allan Poe might have lived here and written "The Raven." The house of Usher might have been a dwelling in one of these hypochondriacal streets. They were so dim and gloomy and sad. Still farther on as we neared the Delaware we came into a mountain country which seemed almost entirely devoted to cattle and the dairy business. It was not an ultra prosperous land—what mountain country is? You can find it on the map if you choose, lying between Phillipsburg and the river.

Something—perhaps the approach of evening, perhaps the gloom of great hills which make darksome valleys wherein lurk early shadows and cool, damp airs; perhaps the tinkle of cowbells and the lowing of homing herds; perhaps the presence of dooryards where laborers and farmers, newly returned from work, were washing their hands in pans outside of kitchen doors; or the smoke curl of evening fires from chimneys, or the glint of evening lamps through doors and windows—was very touching about all this; anyhow, as we sped along I was greatly moved. Life orchestrates itself at times so perfectly. It sings like a prima donna of humble joys, and happy homes and simple tasks. It creates like a great virtuoso, bow in hand, or fingers upon invisible keys, a supreme illusion. The heart hurts; one's eyes fill with tears. We skirted great hills so close that at times, as one looked up, it seemed as though they might come crashing down on us. We passed thick forests where in this mid-August weather, one could look into deep shadows, feeling the ancient childish terror of the woods and of the dark. I looked up a cliff side—very high up—and saw a railroad station labeled Manunka-Chunk. I looked into a barnyard and saw pigs grunting over corn and swill, and a few chickens trying to flutter up into a low tree. The night was nigh.

Presently, in this sweet gloom we reached a ferry which crosses the river somewhere near the Water Gap and which we were induced to approach because we knew of no bridge. On the opposite side, anchored to a wire which crossed the river, was a low flat punt, which looked for all the world like a shallow saucepan. We called "Yoho!" and back came the answer "All right!" Presently the punt came over and in a silvery twilight Speed maneuvered the car onto the craft. A tall, lank yokel greeted us.

"Goin' to the Water Gap?"

"Yes, how far is it?"

"Seven miles."

"What time is it?"

"Seven o'clock."

That gave us an hour in which to make Miss H——'s train.

"That's Pennsylvania over there, isn't it?"

"Yep, that's Pennsylvania. There ain't nothing in New Jersey 'cept cows and mountains."

He grinned as though he had made a great joke.

Speed, as usual, was examining the engine. Franklin and I were gazing enraptured at the stately hills which sentinel this stream. In the distance was the Water Gap, a great cleft in the hills where in unrecorded days the river is believed to have cut its way through. One could see the vast masonry of some bridge which had been constructed farther up the stream.

We clambered up the bank on the farther side, the car making a great noise. In this sweet twilight with fireflies and spirals of gnats and "pinchin' bugs," as Speed called them, we tore the remainder of the distance, the eyes of the car glowing like great flames. Along this river road we encountered endless groups of strolling summer boarders—girls with their arms about each other, quiescent women and older maids idling in the evening damp.

"A land of summer hotels this, and summer boarding houses," I said.

"Those are all old maids or school teachers," insisted Speed with Indiana assurance, "or I'll eat my hat."

In the midst of our flight Speed would tell stories, tossing them back in the wind and perfumes. Miss H—— was singing "There Was an Old Soldier." In no time at all—though not before it was dark—we were entering a region compact of automobiles, gasoline smoke, and half concealed hotel windows and balconies which seemed to clamber up cliffs and disappear into the skies. Below us, under a cliff, ran a railroad, its freight and passenger trains seeming to thunder ominously near. We were, as I could see, high on some embankment or shelf cut in the hill. Presently we turned into a square or open space which opened out at the foot of the hill, and there appeared a huge caravansary, The Kittatinny, with a fountain and basin in the foreground which imitated the colored waters of the Orient. Lackeys were there to take our bags—only, since Miss H—— had to make her train, we had to go a mile farther on to the station under the hill. To give Franklin and Miss H—— time Speed parked the car somewhere near the station and I went to look for colored picture cards.

I wandered off into a region of lesser hotels and stores —the usual clutter of American mountain resort gayety. It brought back to me Tannersville and Haines Corners in the Catskills, Excelsior Springs and the Hot Springs of Virginia and the Ozarks. American summer mountain life is so naive, so gauche, so early Victorian. Nothing could be duller, safer, more commonplace apparently, and yet with such a lilt running through it, than this scene. Here were windows of restaurants or ball rooms or hotel promenades, all opened to the cool mountain air and all gaily lighted. An orchestra was to be heard crooning here and there. The one street was full of idlers, summer cottagers, hotel guests, the natives—promenading. Many electric lamps cast hard shadows provided by the trees. It was all so delightfully cool and fragrant. All these maidens were so bent on making catches, apparently, so earnest to attract attention. They were decked

out in all the fineries and fripperies of the American summer resort scene. I never saw more diaphanous draperies—more frail pinks, blues, yellows, creams. All the
brows of all the maidens seemed to be be-ribboned. All
the shoulders were flung about with light gauzy shawls.
Noses were powdered, lips faintly rouged, perhaps. The
air was vibrant with a kind of mating note—or search.

"Well, well," I exclaimed, and bought me all the truly
indicative postcards I could find.

CHAPTER VI

I HAVE no quarrel with American summer resorts as such—they are as good as any—but I must confess that scenes like this do not move me as they once did. I can well recall the time—and that not so many years ago—when this one would have set me tingling, left me yearning with a voiceless, indescribable pain. Life does such queer things to one. It takes one's utmost passions of five years ago and puts them out like a spent fire. Standing in this almost operatic street, I did my best to contrast my feelings with those of twenty, fifteen and even ten years before. What had come over the spirit of my dreams? Well, twenty years before I knew nothing about love, actually—ten years before I was not satisfied. Was that it? Not exactly—no—I could not say that it was. But now at least these maidens and this somewhat banal stage setting were not to be accepted by me, at least, at the value which unsophistication and youth place on them. The scene was gay and lovely and innocent really. One could feel the wonder of it. But the stage-craft was a little too obvious.

Fifteen years before (or even ten) these gauche maidens idling along would have seemed most fascinating. Now the brow bands and diaphanous draperies and pink and blue and green slippers were almost like trite stage properties. Fifteen or twenty years before I would have been ready to exclaim with any of the hundred youths I saw bustling about here, yearning with their eyes: "Oh, my goddess! Oh, my Venus! Oh, my perfect divinity! But deign to cast one encouraging glance upon me, your devoted slave, and I will grovel at your feet. Here is my heart and hand and my most sacred vow—and my pocket book. I will work for you, slave for you, die for you. Every night for the next two thousand nights of my life, all my life in fact, I will come home regularly from my small job and place all my earnings and hopes and fears in your hands. I will build a house and I will run a store. I will do anything to make you happy. We will have three, seven, nine children. I will spade a garden each spring, bring home a lawnmower and cut the grass. I will prove thoroughly domesticated and never look at another woman."

That, in my nonage, was the way I used to feel.

And as I looked about me I could see much the same emotions at work here. These young cubs—how enraptured they were; how truly like young puppies with still blinded eyes! The air was redolent of this illusion. That was why the windows and balconies were hung with Japanese lanterns. That was why the orchestras were playing so—divinely! To me now it tanged rather hollowly at moments, like a poor show. I couldn't help seeing that the maidens weren't divinities at all, that most of them were the dullest, most selfish, most shallow and strawy mannikinesses one could expect to find. Poor little half-equipped actors and actresses.

"But even so," I said to myself, "this is the best the master of the show has to offer. *He* is at most a strolling player of limited equipment. Perhaps elsewhere, in some other part of the universe, there may be a showman who can do better, who has a bigger, better company. But these——"

I returned to the hotel and waited for Franklin. We were assigned a comfortable room on the second or third floor, I forget which, down a mile of corridor. Supper in the grill cost us five dollars. The next morning breakfast in the Persian breakfast room cost us three more. But that evening we had the privilege of sitting on a balcony and watching a herd of deer come down to a wire fence and eat grass in the glare of an adjacent arc light. We had the joy of observing the colored fountains (quenched at twelve) and seeing the motoring parties come tearing up or go flying past, wild with a nameless gayety. In the parlors, the music rooms, the miles of promenade balconies, were hosts of rich mammas and daughters—the former nearly all fat, the latter all promising to be, and a little gross. For the life of me I could not help but think of breweries, distilleries, soap factories, furniture factories, stove companies and the like. Where did all these people come from? Where did they all get the money to stay here weeks and weeks at six, eight, and even fifteen and twenty a day a person? Our poor little six dollar rooms! Good Heavens! Some of them had suites with three baths. Think of all the factories, the purpose of which (aside from supplying the world with washtubs, flatirons, sealing wax, etc.) was to supply these elderly and youthful females with plumpness and fine raiment.

While we were in the grill eating our rather late dinner (the Imperial Egyptian dining room was closed), several families strolled in, "pa," in one case, a frail, pale, meditative, speculative little man who seemed about as much at home in his dressy cutaway coat as a sheep would in a lion's skin. He was so very small and fidgety, but had without doubt built up a wholesale grocery or an iron foundry or something of that sort. And "ma" was so short and aggressive, with such a firm chin and such steady eyes. "Ma" had supplied "pa" with much of his fighting courage, you could see that. As I looked at "pa" I wondered how many thousand things he had been driven to do to escape her wrath, even to coming up here in August and wearing a cutaway coat and a stiff white shirt and hard cuffs and collars. He did look as though he would prefer some quiet small town veranda and his daily newspaper.

And then there was "Cerise" or "Muriel" or "Albertina" (I am sure she had some such name), sitting between her parents and obviously speculating as to her fate. Back at Wilson's Corner there may have been some youth at some time or other who thought her divine and implored her to look with favor on his suit, but behold "pa" was getting rich and she was not for such as him.

"Jus' you let him be," I could hear her mother counseling. "Don't you have anything to do with him. We're getting on and next summer we're going up to the Kittatinny. You're sure to meet somebody there."

And so here they were—Cerise dressed in the best that Scranton or Wilkes-Barré or even New York could afford. Such organdies, voiles, swisses, silk crepes—trunks full of them, no doubt! Her plump arms were quite bare, shoulders partly so, her hair done in a novel way, white satin shoes were on her feet—oh dear! oh dear! She looked dull and uninteresting and meaty.

But think of Harvey Anstruther Kupfermacher, son of the celebrated trunk manufacturer of Punxsutawney, who will shortly arrive and wed her! It will be a "love match from the first." The papers of Troy, Schenectady, and Utica will be full of it. There will be a grand church wedding. The happy couple will summer in the Adirondacks or the Blue Ridge. If the trunk factory and the iron foundry continue successful some day they may even venture New York.

"Wilson's Corner? Well I guess not!"

There was another family, the pater familias large and heavy, with big hands, big feet, a bursting pink complexion, and a vociferous grey suit. "Pa" leads his procession. "Ma" is very simple, and daughter is comparatively interesting, and rather sweet. "Pa" is going to show by living at the Kittatinny what it means to work hard and save your money and fight the labor unions and push the little fellow to the wall. "Pa" thinks, actually, that if he gets very rich—richer and richer—somehow he is going to be supremely happy. Money is going to do it. "Yessiree, money can do anything, good old American dollars. Money can build a fine house, money can buy a fine auto, money can give one a splendid office desk, money can hire obsequious factotums, money can make everyone pleasant and agreeable. Here I sit," says Pa, "right in the grill room of the Kittatinny. Outside are colored fountains. My shoes are new. My clothes are of the best. I have an auto. What do I lack?"

"Not a thing, Pa," I wanted to answer, "save certain delicacies of perception, which you will never miss."

" 'Soul, take thine ease; eat, drink and be merry.' "

The next morning we were up bright and early for a long drive. Owing to my bumptiousness in having set aside the regular route of the trip I could see that Franklin was now somewhat depending on me to complete my career as a manager and decide when and where to go. My sole idea was to cut direct through Pennsylvania, but when I consulted a large map which hung on the wall of the baggage room of the Kittatinny I was not so sure. It was about six feet long and two feet high and showed nothing but mountains, mountains, mountains, and no towns, let alone cities of any size. We began to speculate concerning Pennsylvania as a state, but meanwhile I consulted our "Scenic Route" map. This led us but a little way into Pennsylvania before it cut due north to Binghamton, and the socalled "good roads" of New York State. That did not please me at all. At any rate, after consulting with a most discouraging porter who seemed to be sure that there were no good roads in Pennsylvania, I consoled myself with the thought that Wilkes-Barré and Scranton were west of us, and that the "Scenic Route" led through these places. We might go to Wilkes-Barré or Scranton and then consult with the local automobile association, who could give us further information. Quite diplomatically I persuaded Franklin to do that.

The difficulty with this plan was that it left us worrying over roads, for, after all, the best machine, as anyone knows who has traveled much by automobiles, is a delicate organism. Given good roads it can seemingly roll on forever at top speed. Enter on a poor one and all the ills that flesh or machinery is heir to seem at once to manifest themselves. A little mud and water and you are in danger of skidding into kingdom come. A few ruts and you feel momentarily as though you were going to be thrown into high heaven. A bad patch of rocks and holes and you soon discover where all the weak places in your bones and muscles are. Punctures eventuate from nowhere. Blowouts arrive one after another with sickening frequency. The best of engines snort and growl on sharp grades. Going down a steep hill a three-thousand-pound car makes you think always—"My God! what if something should break!" Then a spring may snap, a screw work loose somewhere.

But before we left the Water Gap what joys of observation were not mine! This was such an idle tour and such idle atmosphere. There was really no great need for hurry, as we realized once we got started, and I was desirous of taking our time, as was Franklin, though having no wish to stay long anywhere. We breakfasted leisurely while Speed, somewhere, was doctoring up our tires. Then we strolled out into this summer village, seeing the Water Gappers get abroad thus early. The town looked as kempt by day as it did by night. Our fat visitors of heavy purses were still in bed in the great hotels. Instead you saw the small town American busy about his chores; an ancient dame, for instance, in black bonnet and shawl, driving a lean horse and buggy, the latter containing three milk cans all labeled "Sunset Farm Dairy Co."; a humpnosed, thinbodied, angular grocer, or general store keeper, sweeping off his sidewalk and dusting off his counters; various citizens in "vests" and shirt sleeves crossing the heavily oiled roads at various angles and exchanging the customary American morning greetings:

"Howdy, Jake?"

"Hi, Si, been down t' the barn yet?"

"Did Ed get that wrench he was lookin' for?"

"Think so, yep."

"Well, look at old Skeeter Cheevers comin' along, will yuh"—this last apropos of some hobbling septuagenarian with a willow basket.

I heaved a kind of sigh of relief. I was out of New

York and back home, as it were—even here at the Delaware River—so near does the west come to the east.

Sitting in willow chairs in front of a garage where Speed was looking for a special kind of oil which evidently the more pretentious hotel could not or would not supply, Franklin and I discussed the things we had heard and seen. I think I drew a parallel between this hotel here and similar hotels at Monte Carlo and Nice, where the prices would be no higher, if so high.

It so happened that in the morning, when I had been dressing, there had been a knocking at the door of the next room, and listening I had heard a man's voice calling "Ma! Ma! Have you got an undershirt in there for me?"

I looked out to see a tall, greyheaded man of sixty or more, very intelligent and very forceful looking, a real American business chief.

"Yes," came the answer after a moment. "Wait a minute. I think there's one in Ida's satchel. Is Harry up yet?"

"Yes, he's gone out."

This was at six A. M. Here stood the American in the pretentious hall, his suspenders down, meekly importuning his wife through the closed door.

Imagine this at Nice, or Cannes, or Trouville!

And then the lackadaisical store keeper where I bought my postcards.

"Need any stamps, cap?" was his genial inquiry.

Why the "cap"? An American civility—the equivalent of Mister, Monsieur, Sir,—anything you please.

I had of late been reading much magazine sociology of the kind that is labeled "The Menace of Immigration," etc. I was saying to Franklin that I had been fast coming to believe that America, east, west, north, and south, was being overrun by foreigners who were completely changing the American character, the American facial appearance, the American everything. Do you recall the Hans Christian Andersen story of the child who saw the king naked? I was inclined to be that child. I could not see, from the first hundred miles or so we had traveled, that there was any truth in the assertions of these magazine sociologists. Franklin and I agreed that we could see no change in American character here, or anywhere, though it might be well to look sharply into this matter as we went along. In the cities there were thousands of foreigners, but they were not unamericanizing the cities, and I was not prepared to believe that they are doing any worse by the small towns. Certainly there was no evidence of it here at the Water Gap. All was almost "offensively American," as an Englishman would say. The "caps," "docs," and "howdys" were as common here as in—Indiana, for instance—so Franklin seemed to think —and he lives in Indiana a goodly part of the year. In the Water Gap and Stroudsburg, and various towns hereabout where, because of the various summer hotels and cottages, one might expect a sprinkling of the foreign element, at least in the capacity of servitors, in the streets and stores, yet they were not even noticeably dotted with them. If all that was American is being wiped out the tide had not yet reached northern New Jersey or eastern Pennsylvania. I began to take heart.

CHAPTER VII

THE PENNSYLVANIANS

AND then there was this matter of Pennsylvania and its rumored poor roads to consider, and the smallness and non-celebrity of its population, considering the vastness of its territory—all of which consumed at least an hour of words, once we were started. This matter interested us greatly, for now that we had come to think of it we could not recall anyone in American political history or art or science who had come from Pennsylvania. William Penn (a foreigner) occurred to me, Benjamin Franklin and a certain Civil War governor of the name of Cameron, and there I stuck. Certain financial geniuses, as Franklin was quick to point out, had made money there; a Carnegie, Scotchman; Frick, an American; Widener, an American; Dolan, an Irishman; Elkins, and others; although, as we both agreed, America could not be vastly proud of these. The taint of greed or graft seemed to hang heavy in their wake.

"But where are the poets, writers, painters?" asked Franklin.

I paused. Not a name occurred to me.

"What Pennsylvanian ever did anything?" I asked. "Here is a state one hundred and sixty miles wide, and more than three hundred miles long from east to west, and with five or six fair-sized cities in it, and not a name!" We tried to explain it on the ground that mountainous countries are never prolific of celebrities, but neither of us seemed to know very much about mountainous countries, and so we finally dropped the subject.

But what about Pennsylvania, anyhow? Why hasn't it produced anything in particular? How many millions of men must live and die before a real figure arises? Or do we need figures? Are just men better?

The run from the Water Gap to Factoryville was accomplished under varying conditions. The day promised to be fine, a milky, hazy atmosphere which was still warm and bright like an opal. We were all in the best of spirits, Speed whistling gaily to himself as we raced along. Our way led first through a string of small towns set in great hills or mountains—Stroudsburg, Bartonsville, Tannersville, Swiftwater. We were trying to make up our minds as we rode whether we would cut Wilkes-Barré, since, according to our map, it appeared to be considerably south of a due west course, or whether, because of its repute as a coal center, we would go there. Something, a sense of mountains and picturesque valleys, lured me on. I was for going to Wilkes-Barré if it took us as much as fifty miles out of our course.

But meanwhile our enjoyment in seeing Pennsylvania was such that we did not need to worry very much over its lack of human distinction. Everything appeared to be beautiful to such casual travelers. As we climbed and climbed out of the Water Gap, we felt a distinct change between the life of New Jersey and that of this hilly, almost mountainous land. Great slopes rose on either hand. We came upon long stretches of woodland and barren, rocky fields. The country houses from here to Wilkes-Barré, which we finally reached, were by no means so prosperous. Stroudsburg seemed a stringy, mountain-top town, composed principally of summer hotels, facing the principal street, hotels and boarding houses. Bartonsville and Tannersville, both much smaller, were much the same. The air was much lighter here, almost feathery compared to that of the lowlands farther east. But the barns and houses and stock were so poor. At Swiftwater, another small town or crossroads, we came to a wood so dense, so deep, so black and even purple in its shades that we exclaimed in surprise. The sun was still shining in its opalescent way, but in here was a wonder of rare darks and solitudes which seemed like the depths of some untenanted cathedral at nightfall. And there was a river or stream somewhere nearby, for stopping the car we could hear it tumbling over rough stones. We dismounted, quite spontaneously, and without any "shall we's," and wandered into this bit of forest which was such a splendid natural wonder. Under these heavy cedars and tangled vines all was still, save for the river, and at the foot of trees, in a mulch of rich earth, were growing whole colonies of Indian pipes, those rare fragile, waxylooking orchids. Neither Franklin nor Speed had ever seen any and I aired my knowledge with great gusto. Speed was quite taken aback by the fact that they really looked like pipes with a small fire in their bowls. We sat down—it was too wonderful to leave instantly. I felt that I must come back here some time and camp.

It was about here that our second blowout occurred. Back in Stroudsburg, passing through the principal street, I had spied a horseshoe lying in the road—a new shoe— and jumped out to get it as a sign of good luck. For this I was rewarded by an indulgent glance from Franklin and considerable show of sympathetic interest from Speed. The latter obviously shared my belief in horseshoes as omens of good fortune. He promptly hung it over the speedometer, but alas, within the next three-quarters of an hour this first breakdown occurred. Speed was just saying that now he was sure he would get through safely, and I was smiling comfortably to think that my life was thus charmingly guarded, when "whee!"—have you heard a whistle blowout? It sounds like a spent bullet instead of a revolver shot. Out we climbed to contemplate a large jagged rent in the rim of the tire and the loss of fifteen minutes. This rather dampened my ardor for my omen. Luck signs and omens are rather difficult things at best, for one can really never connect the result with the fact. I have the most disturbing difficulties with my luck signs. A cross-eyed man or boy should mean immediate good luck, but alas, I have seen scores and scores of cross-eyed boys at one time and another and yet my life seemed to go on no better than usual. Cross-eyed women should spell immediate disaster, but to my intense satisfaction I am able to report that this does not seem to be invariably true. Then Franklin and I sat back in the cushions and began to discuss blowouts in general and the mystic power of mind to control such matters—the esoteric or metaphysical knowledge that there is no such thing as evil and that blowouts really cannot occur.

This brings me again to Christian Science, which somehow hung over this whole tour, not so much as a religious irritant as a pleasant safeguard. It wasn't religious or obtrusive at all. Franklin, as I have said, is inclined to believe that there is no evil, though he is perfectly willing to admit that the material appearances seem all against that assumption at times.

"It's a curious thing," he said to me and Speed, "but that makes the fifth blowout to occur in that particular wheel. All the trouble we have had this spring and summer has been in that particular corner of the wagon. I don't understand it quite. It isn't because we have been using poor tires on that wheel or any other. As a matter of fact I put a set of new Silvertown cord tires on the wheels last May. It's just that particular wheel."

He gazed meditatively at the serene hills around us, and I volunteered that it might be "just accident." I could see by Franklin's face that he considered it a lesion in the understanding of truth.

"It may be," he said. "Still you'll admit it's a little curious."

A little later on we ran on to a wonderful tableland, high up in the mountains, where were a lake, a golf course, a perfect macadam road, and interesting inns and cottages—quite like an ideal suburban section of a great city. As we neared a four corners or railway station center I spied there one of those peculiarly constructed wagons intended originally to haul hay, latterly to convey straw-ride parties around the country in mountain resorts—a diversion which seems never to lose its charm for the young. This one, or rather three, for there turned out to be three in a row, was surrounded by a great group of young girls, as I thought, all of them in short skirts and with a sort of gymnasium costume which seemed to indicate that they were going out to indulge in outdoor exercises.

As we drew nearer we discovered, however, to our astonishment, that a fair proportion were women over forty or fifty. It seemed more like a school with many monitors than a mountain outing.

Contemplating this very modern show of arms and legs, I felt that we had come a very long way from the puritanic views of the region in which I had been raised if an inland summer resort permitted this freedom of appearance. In my day the idea of any woman, young or old, save those under fourteen, permitting anything more than their shoe tip and ankles to be seen was not to be thought of. And here were mothers and spinsters of forty and fifty as freely garbed as any bather at a summer resort.

Speed and Franklin and myself were fascinated by the spectacle. There was a general store near at hand and Franklin went to buy some chocolate. Speed sat upright at his wheel and curled his mustachios. I leaned back and endeavored to pick out the most beautiful of the younger ones. It was a difficult task. There were many beauties.

By this spectacle we were led to discuss for a few moments whether sex—the tendency to greater freedom of relationship between men and women—was taking America or the world in an unsatisfactory direction. There had been so much talk on the subject of late in the newspapers and elsewhere that I could not resist sounding Franklin as to his views. "Are we getting better or worse?" I inquired.

"Oh, better," he replied with the air of one who has given the matter a great deal of thought. "I cannot feel that there is any value in repression, or certainly very little. Life as it appeals to me is a flowering out, not a recession. If it is flowering it is becoming richer, fuller, freer. I can see no harm in those girls showing their legs or in peoples' bodies coming into greater and greater evidence. It seems to me it will make for a kind of natural innocence after a while. The mystery will be taken out of sex and only the natural magnetism left. I never see boys bathing naked in the water but what I wish we could all go naked if the climate would only permit." And then he told me about a group of boys in Carmel whom he had once seen on a rainy day racing naked upon the backs of some horses about a field near their swimming hole, their white, rain-washed bodies under lowering clouds making them look like centaurs and fawns. Personally I follow life, or like to, with a hearty enthusiasm wherever it leads.

As we were talking, it began to rain, and we decided to drive on more speedily. A few miles back, after some cogitation at a crossroads, we had decided to take the road to Wilkes-Barré. I shall never feel grateful enough for our decision, though for a time it looked as though we had made a serious mistake. After a time the fine macadam road ended and we took to a poorer and finally a rutty dirt road. The grades became steeper and steeper—more difficult to ascend and descend. In a valley near a bounding stream—Stoddartsville the place was—we had another blowout—or something which caused a flat tire, in the same right rear wheel; and this time in a driving rain. We had to get out and help spread tools in the wet road and hunt leaks in the rubber rim. When this was repaired and the chains put on the wheels we proceeded, up hill and down dale, past miles of apparently tenantless woods and rocky fields—on and on in search of Wilkes-Barré. We had concluded from our maps and some signs that it must be about thirtysix miles farther. As it turned out it was nearly seventy. The roads had a tendency to curve downwards on each side into treacherous hollows, and as I had recently read of an automobile skidding on one of these, overturning and killing three people, I was not very giddy about the prospect. Even with the chains the machine was skidding and our able driver kept his eye fixed on the road. I never saw a man pay more minute attention to his wheel nor work harder to keep his machine evenly balanced. A good chauffeur is a jewel, and Speed was one.

But this ride had other phases than a mere bad road. The clouds were so lowery and the rain so heavy that for a part of the way we had to have the storm curtains on. We could see that it was a wonderful country that we were traversing, deliciously picturesque, but a sopping rain makes one's spirits droop. Franklin sat in his corner and I in mine with scarcely a word. Speed complained at times that we were not making more than four miles an hour. I began to calculate how long it would take to get to Indiana at that rate. Franklin began to wonder if we were not making a mistake trying to cut straight across the poorly equipped state of Pennsylvania.

"Perhaps it would have been better after all if we had gone up the Hudson."

I felt like a criminal trying to wreck a three thousand dollar car.

But beyond a place called Bear Creek things seemed to get better. This was a town in a deep ravine with a railroad and a thundering stream, plunging over a waterfall. The houses were charming. It seemed as if many well-to-do people must live here, for the summer anyhow. But when we asked for food no one seemed to have any. "Better go to Wilkes-Barré," advised the local inn keeper. "It's only fifteen miles." At four miles an hour we would be there in four hours.

Out we started. The rain ceased for a time, though the clouds hung low, and we took up the storm curtains. It was now nearly two o'clock and by three it was plain we were nearing Wilkes-Barré. The roads were better; various railroads running in great cuts came into view. We met miners with bright tin buckets, their faces as black as coal, their caps ornamented with their small lamps. There were troops of foreign women and poorly clad children carrying buckets to or from the mines. Turning a corner of the road we came suddenly upon one of the most entrancing things in the way of a view that I have ever seen. There are city scapes that seem some to mourn and some to sing. This was one that sang. It reminded me of the pen and ink work of Rops or Vierge or Whistler, the paintings of Turner and Moran. Low hanging clouds, yellowish or black, or silvery like a fish, mingled with a splendid filigree of smoke and chimneys and odd sky lines. Beds of goldenglow ornamented and relieved a group of tasteless low red houses or sheds in the immediate foreground, which obviously sheltered the heavy broods of foreign miners and their wives. The lines of red, white, blue and grey wash, the honking flocks of white geese, the flocks of pigeons overhead, the paintless black fences protecting orderly truck gardens, as well as the numerous babies playing about, all attested this. As we stood there a group of heavy-hipped women and girls (the stocky peasant type of the Hungarian-Silesian plains) crossed the foreground with their buckets. Immense mounds of coal and slag with glimpses of distant breakers perfected the suggestion of an individual and characterful working world. Anyhow we paused and applauded while Franklin got his sketching board and I sauntered to find more, if any, attractive angles. In the middle distance a tall white skyscraper stood up, a prelude, or a foretouch to a great yellowish black cloud behind it. A rich, smoky, sketchy atmosphere seemed to hang over everything.

"Isn't Walkes-Barré wonderful?" I said to Franklin. "Aren't you glad now you've come?"

"I am coming down here to paint soon," he said. "This is the most wonderful thing I have seen in a long while."

And so we stood on this hillside overlooking Wilkes-Barré for a considerable period while Franklin sketched, and finally, when he had finished and I had wandered a mile down the road to see more, we entered.

CHAPTER VIII

BEAUTIFUL WILKES-BARRÉ

My own interest in Wilkes-Barré and this entire region indeed dated from the great anthracite coal strike in 1902, in my estimation one of the fiercest and best battles between labor and capital ever seen in America. Who does not know the history of it, and the troubles and ills that preceded it? I recall it so keenly—the complaints of the public against the rising price of coal, the rumors of how the Morgans and the Vanderbilts had secured control of all these coal lands (or the railroads that carried their coal for them), and having this latter weapon or club, proceeded to compel the independent coal operators to do their will. How, for instance, they had detained the cars of the latter, taxed them exorbitant carrying charges, frequently declining to haul their coal at all on the ground that they had no cars; how they charged the independent mine operator three times as much for handling his hard coal (the product of the Eastern region) as they did the soft coal men of the west, and when he complained and fought them, took out the spur that led to his mine on the ground that it was unprofitable.

Those were great days in the capitalistic struggle for control in America. The sword fish were among the blue fish slaying and the sharks were after the sword fish. Tremendous battles were on, with Morgan and Rockefeller and Harriman and Gould after Morse and Heinze and Hill and the lesser fry. We all saw the end in the panic of 1907, when one multimillionaire, the scapegoat of others no less guilty, went to the penitentiary for fifteen years, and another put a revolver to his bowels and died as do the Japanese. Posterity will long remember this time. It cannot help it. A new land was in the throes of construction, a strange race of men with finance for their weapon were fighting as desperately as ever men fought with sword or cannon. Individual liberty among the masses was being proved the thin dream it has always been.

I have found in my book of quotations and labeled for my own comfort "The Great Coal Appeal," a statement written by John Mitchell, then president of the United Mine Workers of America, presenting the miners' side of the case in this great strike of 1902 which was fought out here in Wilkes-Barré, and Scranton and all the country we were now traversing. It was written at the time when the "Coal Barons," as they were called, were riding around in their private cars with curtains drawn to keep out the vulgar gaze and were being wined and dined by governors and presidents, while one hundred and fifty thousand men and boys, all admittedly underpaid, out on strike nearly one hundred and sixty days—a half a year—waited patiently the arbitration of their difficulties. The total duration of the strike was one hundred and sixtythree days. It was a bitter and finally victorious protest against an enlarged and burdensome ton, company houses, company stores, powder at $2.75 a keg which anywhere else could be bought for ninety cents or $1.10.

The quotation from Mitchell reads:

In closing this statement I desire to say that we have entered and are conducting this struggle without malice and without bitterness. We believe that our antagonists are acting upon misrepresentation rather than in bad faith, we regard them not as enemies but as opponents, and we strike in patience until they shall accede to our demands or submit to impartial arbitration the difference between us. We are striking not to show our strength but the justice of our cause, and we desire only the privilege of presenting our case to a fair tribunal. We ask not for favors but for justice and we appeal our case to the solemn judgment of the American people.

Here followed a detailed statement of some of the ills

they were compelled to hear and which I have in part enumerated above. And then:

> Involved in this fight are questions weightier than any question of dollars and cents. The present miner has had his day. He has been oppressed and ground down; but there is another generation coming up, a generation of little children prematurely doomed to the whirl of the mill and the noise and blackness of the breaker. It is for these children that we are fighting. We have not underestimated the strength of our opponents; we have not overestimated our own power of resistance. Accustomed always to live upon a little, a little less is no unendurable hardship. It was with a quaking of hearts that we called for a strike. It was with a quaking of hearts that we asked for our last pay envelopes. But in the grimy, bruised hand of the miner was the little white hand of the child, a child like the children of the rich, and in the heart of the miner was the soul rooted determination to starve to the last crust of bread and fight out the long dreary battle to the end, in order to win a life for the child and secure for it a place in the world in keeping with advancing civilization.

Messieurs, I know the strong must rule the weak, the big brain the little one, but why not some small approximation towards equilibrium, just a slightly less heavily loaded table for Dives and a few more crumbs for Lazarus? I beg you—a few more crumbs! You will appear so much more pleasing because of your generosity.

Wilkes-Barré proved a city of charm—a city so instinct with a certain constructive verve that merely to enter it was to feel revivified. After our long, dreary drive in the rain the sun was now shining through sultry clouds and it was pleasant to see the welter of thriving foundries and shops, smoky and black, which seemed to sing of prosperity; the long, smooth red brick pavement of the street by which we entered, so very kempt and sanitary; the gay public square, one of the most pleasing small parks I have ever seen, crowded with long distance trolley cars and motors—the former bearing the names of towns as much as a hundred and a hundred and fifty miles away. The stores were bright, the throngs interesting and cheerful. We actually, spontaneously and unanimously exclaimed for joy.

Most people seem to have concluded that America is a most uninteresting land to travel in—not nearly so interesting as Europe, or Asia or Africa—and from the point of view of patina, ancient memories, and the presence of great and desolate monuments, they are right. But there is another phase of life which is equally interesting to me and that is the youth of a great country. America, for all its hundreds and some odd years of life, is a mere child as yet, or an uncouth stripling at best— gaunt, illogical, elate.   It has so much to do before it can call itself a well organized or historic land, and yet humanly and even architecturally contrasted with Europe, I am not so sure that it has far to go.   Contrasted with our mechanical equipment Europe is a child.   Show me a country abroad in which you can ride by trolley the distance that New York is from Chicago, or a state as large as Ohio or Indiana—let alone both together—gridironed by comfortable lines, in such a way that you can travel anywhere at almost any time of the night or day.   Where but in America can you at random step into a comfortable telephone booth and telephone to any city, even one so far as three thousand miles away; or board a train in almost any direction at any time, which will take you a thousand miles or more without change; or travel, as we did, two hundred miles through a fruitful, prosperous land with wonderful farms and farming machinery and a general air of sound prosperity—even lush richness? For this country in so far as we had traversed it seemed wonderfully prosperous to me, full of airy, comfortable homes, of spirited, genial and even witty people—a really happy people.   I take that to be worth something—and a sight to see.

In Europe the country life did not always strike me as prosperous, or the people as intelligent, or really free in their souls.   In England, for instance, the peasantry were heavy, sad, dull.

But Wilkes-Barré gave evidences of a real charm. All the streets about this central heart were thriving marts of trade.   The buildings were new, substantial and with a number of skyscrapers—these inevitable evidences of America's local mercantile ambitions, quite like the cathedrals religionists of the twelfth and thirteenth centuries loved to build. 'As the Florentines, Venetians and European high mightinesses of the middle ages generally went in for castles, palaces, and "hotels de Ville," so Americans of money today "go in" for high buildings. We love them. We seem to think they are typical of our strength and power. As the Florentines, Venetians, Pisans and Genoese looked on their leaning towers and campaniles, so we on these. When America is old, and its present vigor and life hunger has gone and an alien or degenerate race tramp where once we lived and builded so vigorously, perhaps some visitors from a foreign country will walk here among these ruins and sigh: "Ah, yes. The Americans were a great people. Their cities were so wonderful. These mouldy crumbling skyscrapers, and fallen libraries and post offices and city halls and state capitals!"

In Wilkes-Barré it was easy to find a very pretentious restaurant of the "grill" and "rathskeller" type, so familiar and so dear, apparently, to the American heart—a partly underground affair, with the usual heavy Flemish paneling, a colored frieze of knights and goose girls and an immense yellow bill of fare. And here from our waiter, who turned out to be one of those dreadful creatures one sees tearing along country roads in khaki, army boots and goggles—a motor cyclist—we learned there were not good roads west of Wilkes-Barré. He had motorcycled to all places within a hundred or so miles east of here—Philadelphia, Dover, the Water Gap; but he knew of no good roads west. They were all dirt or rubble and full of ruts.

Later advice from a man who owned a drug and stationery store, where we laid in a stock of picture postcards, was to the same effect. There were no large towns and no good roads west. He owned a Ford. We should take the road to Binghamton, via Scranton (our original "Scenic Route"), and from there on by various routes to Buffalo. We would save time going the long way round. It seemed the only thing to do. Our motorcycling waiter had said as much.

By now it was nearly five o'clock. I was so enamored of this town with its brisk world of shoppers and motorists and its sprinkling of black faced miners that I would have been perfectly willing to make a night of it here—but the evening was turning out to be so fine that I could think of nothing better than motoring on and on. That feel of a cool breeze blowing against one, of seeing towns and hills and open fields and humble farm yards go scudding by! Of hearing the tr-r-r-r-r-r of this sound machine! The sun was coming out or at least great patches of blue were appearing in the heavy clouds and we had nineteen miles of splendid road, we understood, straight along the banks of the Susquehanna into Scranton and thence beyond, if we wished. As much as I had come to fancy Wilkes-Barré (I promised myself that I would certainly return some day), I was perfectly willing to go.

Right here began the most delightful portion of this trip—indeed one of the most delightful rides I have ever had anywhere. Hitherto the Susquehanna had never been anything much more than a name to me. I now learned that it takes its rise from Otsego Lake in Otsego County, New York, flows west to Binghamton and Owego and thence southeast via Scranton, Wilkes-Barré and Harrisburg to the Chesapeake Bay at Havre de Grace. Going west over the Pennsylvania I had occasionally seen a small portion of it gemmed with rocky islands and tumbling along, thinly bright it seemed to me, over a wide area of stones and boulders. Here at Wilkes-Barré, bordered for a part of the way by a public park, alongside of which our road lay, it was quite sizable, smooth and greenish grey. Perhaps it was due to the recent heavy rains that it was so presentable.

At any rate, sentineled by great hills, it seemed to come with gentle windings hither and yon, direct from the north. And the valley through which it moved—how beautiful it really was! Here and there, on every hand between Wilkes-Barré and Scranton were to be seen immense breakers with their attendant hills of coal or slag marking the mouths of mines. As we rode out tonight, finding it easy to make five to thirty miles an hour, even through the various mining towns we encountered on the way, we were constantly passing groups of miners, some on foot, some in trolleys, some in that new invention, the jitney bus, which seemed to be employed even on these stretches of road where one would have imagined the street car service was ample. How many long lines of miners' cottages and yellowish frame tenements we passed! I wonder why it is that a certain form of such poverty and work seems to be inseparably identified with yellow or drab paints? So many of these cheap wooden tenements were thus enameled, and then darkened or smudged by grey soot.

Many of the dwellers in these hives were to be seen camped upon their thresholds. We ran through one long dreary street—all these towns followed the shores of the river—and had the interest of seeing a runaway horse, drawing a small load of fence posts, dashing toward us and finally swerving and crashing into a tree. Again a group of boys, seeing the New York license tag on our car, hailed us with a disconcerting, "Eh, look at the New York bums!" Still farther on, finding some difficulty with the lamps, Speed drew up by the roadside to attend to them while Franklin made a rough sketch of a heavenly scene that was just below us—great hills, a wide valley, some immense breakers in the foreground, a few clouds tinted pink by the last expiring rays of the day. This was such a sky and such a scene as might prelude a voice from heaven.

CHAPTER IX

DARKNESS had fallen when we reached Scranton. We approached from the south along a ridge road which skirted the city and could see it lying below to the east and ablaze with arc lights. There is something so appealing about a city in a valley at dark. Although we had no reason for going in—our road lay really straight on—I wanted to go down, because of my old weakness, curiosity. Nothing is more interesting to me than the general spectacle of life itself in these thriving towns of our new land—though they are devoid of anything historic or in the main artistic (no memories even of any great import). I cannot help speculating as to what their future will be. What writers, what statesmen, what arts, what wars may not take their rise in some such place as this?

And there are the indefinable and yet sweet ways of just life. We dwellers in big cities are inclined to overlook or forget entirely the half or quarter cities in which thousands upon thousands spend all their lives. For my part, I am never tired of looking at just mills and factories and those long lines of simple streets where just common people, without a touch perhaps of anything that we think of as great or beautiful or dramatic, dwell. I was not particularly pleased with Scranton after I saw it—a sprawling world of perhaps a hundred and fifty or two hundred thousand people without the verve or snap of a half hundred places half its size,—but still here were all these people. It was a warm night and as we descended into commonplace streets we could look through the open windows of homes or "apartments" or "flats" and see the usual humdrum type of furniture and hangings, the inevitable lace curtains, the centre tables, the huge, junky lamps, the upright pianos or vic-trolas. Whenever I see long, artless streets like these in the hot, breathless summer time, I feel a wave of com-miseration sweep over me, and yet I am drawn to them by something which makes me want to live among these people.

Oh, to escape endless cogitation! To feel that a new centre table or a new lamp or a new pair of shoes in the autumn might add something to my happiness! To believe that mere eating and drinking, the cooking of meals, the prospect of promotion in some small job might take away the misery of life, and so to escape chemistry and physics and the horror of ultimate brutal law! "In the streets of Ur," says an old Chaldean chronicle, "the women were weeping for that Bel was dead." Bel was their Christ and they were weeping as some people weep on Good Friday to this day. Such women one might find here in Scranton, no doubt; believers in old tales of old things. After five or six thousand years there is still weeping in simple streets over myths as vain!

Once down in the heart of Scranton, I did not care for it at all. It was so customary—an American city like Utica or Syracuse or Rochester or Buffalo—and Ameri-can cities of the hundred thousand class are so much alike. They all have the long principal street—possibly a mile long. They all have the one or two skyscrapers and the principal dry goods store and the hotel and the new post office building and the new Carnegie library and sometimes the new court house (if it's a county seat), or the new city hall. Sometimes these structures are very charming in themselves—tastefully done and all that—but most American cities of this class have no more imagination than an owl. They never think of doing an original thing.

Do you think they would allow the natural configura-tion of their land or any river front, or lake, or water of any kind to do anything for them? Not at all. It's the rarest exception when, as at Wilkes-Barré for instance, a city will take the slightest æsthetic advantage of any natural configuration of land or water.

What! put a park or esplanade or a wall along a handsome river bank in the heart of the town! Impossible. Put it far out in the residence section where it truly belongs and let the river go hang. Isn't the centre of a city for business? What right has a park there?

Or perhaps it is a great lake front as at Buffalo or Cleveland, which could or should be made into something splendid—the municipal centre, for instance, or the site of a great park. No. Instead the city will bend all its energies to growing away from it and leave it to shabby factories and warehouses and tumble-down houses, while it constructs immense parks in some region where a park could never possibly have as much charm as on the water front.

Take the City of St. Louis as a case in point. Here is a metropolis which has a naturally fascinating water front along the Mississippi. Here is a stream that is quite wonderful to look at—broad and deep. Years ago, when St. Louis was small and river traffic was important, all the stores were facing this river. Later railroads came and the town built west. Today blocks and blocks of the most interesting property in the city is devoted to dead-alive stores, warehouses and tenements. It would be an easy matter and a profitable one for the city to condemn sufficient property to make a splendid drive along this river and give the city a real air. It would transform it instantly into a kind of wonder world which thousands would travel a long way to see. It would provide sites for splendid hotels and restaurants and give the city a suitable front door or façade.

But do you think this would ever be seriously contemplated? It would cost money. One had better build a park away from the river where there are no old houses. The mere thought of trading the old houses for a wonderful scene which would add beauty and life to the city is too much of a stretch of the imagination for St. Louisians to accomplish. It can't be done. American cities are not given to imagination outside the walks of trade.

Scranton was no worse than many another American city of the same size and class that I have seen—or indeed than many of the newer European cities. It was well paved, well lighted and dull. There were the usual traffic policemen (like New York, b'gosh!), but with no traffic to guide, the one hotel designed to impress, the civic square surrounded by rows of thickly placed five-lamp standards. It was presentable, and, because Speed wanted to get oil and gasoline and we wanted to see what the town was like, we ran the machine into a garage and wandered forth, looking into shoe and bookstore windows and studying the people.

Here again I could see no evidence of that transformation of the American by the foreigner into something different from what he has ever been—the peril which has been so much discussed by our college going sociologists. On the contrary, America seemed to me to be making over the foreigner into its own image and likeness. I learned here that there were thousands of Poles, Czechs, Croatians, Silesians, Hungarians, etc., working here in the coal mines and at Wilkes-Barré, but the young men on the streets and in the stores were Americans. Here were the American electric signs in great profusion, the American bookstores and newsstands crowded with all that mushy adventure fiction of which our lady critics are so fond. Five hundred magazines and weekly publications blazed the faces of alleged pretty girls. "The automat," the "dairy kitchen," the "Boston," "Milwaukee" or "Chicago" lunch, and all the smart haberdasheries so beloved of the ambitious American youth, were in full bloom. I saw at least a half dozen moving-picture theatres in as many blocks—and business and correspondence schools in ample array.

What becomes of all the young Poles, Czechs, Croatians, Serbians, etc., who are going to destroy us? I'll tell you. They gather on the street corners when their parents will permit them, arrayed in yellow or red ties, yellow shoes, dinky fedoras or beribboned straw hats and "style-plus" clothes, and talk about "when I was out to Dreamland the other night," or make some such observation as "Say, you should have seen the beaut that cut across here just now. Oh, mamma, some baby!" That's all the menace there is to the foreign invasion. Whatever their original intentions may be, they can't resist the American yellow shoe, the American moving picture, "Stein-Koop" clothes, "Dreamland," the popular song, the automobile, the jitney. They are completely undone by our perfections. Instead of throwing bombs or lowering our social level, all bogies of the sociologist, they would rather stand on our street corners, go to the nearest moving pictures, smoke cigarettes, wear high white collars and braided yellow vests and yearn over the girls who know exactly how to handle them, or work to some day own an automobile and break the speed laws. They are really not so bad as we seem to want them to be. They are simple, gauche, de jeune, "the limit." In other words, they are fast becoming Americans.

·   ·   ·   ·   ·   ·   ·

I think it was during this evening at Scranton that it first dawned on me what an agency for the transmission of information and a certain kind of railway station gossip the modern garage has become. In the old days, when railroads were new or the post road was still in force, the depot or the inn was always the centre for a kind of gay travelers' atmosphere or way station exchange for gossip, where strangers alighted, refreshed themselves and did a little talking to pass the time. To-day the garage has become a third and even more notable agency for this sort of exchange, automobile travelers being for the most part a genial company and constantly reaching out for information. Anyone who knows anything about the roads of his native town and country is always in demand, for he can fall into long conversation with chauffeurs or tourists in general, who will occasionally close the conversation with an offer of a drink or a cigar, or, if he is going in their direction, take him for a part of the way at least as a guide.

Having found Scranton so dull that we could not make up our minds to remain overnight, we returned to the garage we were patronizing and found it crowded to the doors with cars of all descriptions and constantly being invaded by some others in search of something. Here were a group of those typical American hangers-on or loafers or city gossips or chair warmers—one scarcely knows what to call them—who, like the Roman frequenters of the Forum or the Greek "sitters at the place of customs," gather to pass the time by watching the activity and the enthusiasm of others. Personally my heart rather yearns over that peculiar temperament, common enough to all the abodes of men, which for lack of spirit or strength or opportunity in itself to get up and do, is still so moved by the spectacle of life that it longs to be where others are doing. Here they were, seven or eight of them, leaning against handsome machines, talking, gesticulating and proffering information to all and sundry who would have it. Owing to the assertion of the proprietor's helper (who was eager, naturally enough, to have the car housed here for the night, as he would get a dollar for it) that the roads were bad between here and Binghamton, a distance of sixtynine miles, we were a little uncertain whether to go on or no. But this charge of a dollar was an irritation, for in most garages, as Speed informed us, the night charge was only fifty cents. Besides, the same youth was foolish enough to confess, after Speed questioned him, that the regular charge to local patrons was only fifty cents.

Something in the youth's description of the difficulties of the road between here and Binghamton caused me to feel that he was certainly laying it on a little thick. According to him, there had been terrible rains in the last few weeks. The road in spots was all but impassable. There were great hills, impossible ravines, and deadly railroad crossings. I am not so much of an enthusiast for night riding as to want to go in the face of difficulties—indeed I would much rather ride by day, when the beauties of the landscape can be seen,—still this attempt to frighten us irritated me.

And then the hangers-on joined in. Obviously they were friends of the owner and, like a Greek chorus, were brought on at critical moments to emphasize the tragedy or the terror or the joy, as the case might be. Instantly we were assailed with new exaggerations—there were dreadful, unguarded railway crossings, a number of robberies had been committed recently, one bridge somewhere was weak.

This finished me.

"They are just talking to get that dollar," I whispered to Franklin.

"Sure," he replied; "it's as plain as anything. I think we might as well go on."

"By all means," I urged. "We've climbed higher hills and traversed worse or as bad roads today as we will anywhere else. I don't like Scranton very well anyhow."

My opposition was complete. Speed looked a little tired and I think would have preferred to stay. But my feeling was that at least we could run on to some small inn or country town hotel where the air would be fresher and the noises less offensive. After a long year spent in the heart of New York, I was sick of the city— any city.

So we climbed in and were off again.

It was not so long after dark. The road lay north, through summery crowded streets for a time and then out under the stars. A cool wind was blowing. One old working man whom we had met and of whom we had asked the way had given us something to jest over.

"Which way to Dalton?" we called. This was the next town on our road.

"Over the viderdock," he replied, with a wave of his arm, and thereafter all viaducts became "viderdocks" for us. We sank into the deep leather cushions and, encountering no bad roads, went comfortably on. The trees in places hung low and seemed to make arched green arbors through which we were speeding, so powerful were our lamps. At one place we came upon a brilliantly lighted amusement resort and there we could not resist stopping. There was music and dancing and all the young clerks and beaus for miles around were here with their girls. I was so entranced that I wanted to stay on, hoping that some young girl might talk to me, but not one gave me even so much as a smile. Then we came to a country inn—an enticing looking thing among great trees—but we were awake now, enjoying the ride, and Speed was smoking a cigarette—why quit now? So on and on, up hills and down dale, and now and then we seemed to be skirting the Susquehanna. At other times we seemed to be off in side hills where there were no towns of any size. A railroad train came into view and disappeared; a trolley track joined us and disappeared; a toll road made us pay fifteen cents— and disappeared. At last as it neared unto midnight I began to get sleepy and then I argued that, whatever town came next, we should pause there for the night.

"All right," said Franklin genially, and then more aisles and more streams and more stores—and then in the distance some manufactories came into view, brightly lighted windows reflected in some water.

"Here we are," I sighed sleepily, but we weren't, not quite. This was a crossroad somewhere—a dividing of the ways—but the readable signs to say which way were not visible. We got out and struck matches to make the words more intelligible. They had been obliterated by rust. I saw a light in a house and went there. A tall, spare man of fifty came out on the porch and directed us. This was Factoryville or near it, he said— another mile on we would find an inn. We were something like twentyfive miles from Scranton. If you stop and look at electric parks and watch the dancers, you can't expect to make very good time. In Factoryville, as dark and silent as a small sleeping town may be, we found one light—or Franklin did—and behind it the village barber reading a novel. In the shadow of his doorway Franklin entered into a long and intimate discussion with him—about heaven only knows what. I had already noted of Franklin that he could take up more time securing seeming information than any human being I had ever known. It was astounding how he could stand and gossip, coming back finally with such a simple statement as, "He says turn to the right," or "We go north." But why a week to discover this, I used to think. Finally, almost arm in arm with the barber, they disappeared around a corner. A weary string of moments rolled past before Franklin strolled back to say there was no real inn—no hotel that had a license—but there was a man who kept a "kind of a hotel" and he had a barn or shed, which would do as a garage.

"Better stay, eh?" he suggested.

"Well, rather," I answered.

When we had unslung our bags and coats, Speed took the car to the barn in the rear and up we went into a typical American papier mâché room. The least step, the least movement, and wooden floors and partitions seemed to shout. But there were two large rooms with three beds and, what was more, a porch with a wooden swing. There was a large porcelain bath in a room at the rear and pictures of all the proprietor's relatives done in crayon.

How we slept! There were plenty of windows, with a fresh breeze blowing and no noises, except some katydids sawing lustily. I caught the perfume of country woods and fields and, afar off, as I stretched on an easy bed, I could hear a train whistling and rumbling faintly—that far off Ooh!—ooh!—oo!—oo!

I lay there thinking what a fine thing it was to motor in this haphazard fashion—how pleasant it was not to know where you were going or where you would be tomorrow, exactly. Franklin's car was so good, Speed so careful. Then I seemed to be borne somewhere on great wings, until the dawn coming in at the window awakened me. The birds were singing.

"Oh, yes, Factoryville," I sighed. "That's where we are. We're motoring to Indiana."

And I turned over and slept another hour.

CHAPTER X

FACTORYVILLE, as we found this morning, was one of these very small places which, to one weary of metropolitan life, occasionally prove entertaining through an extreme simplicity and a sense of rest and peace. It was, as I saw sitting in my dressing gown in our convenient wooden swing, a mere collection of white cottages with large lawns or country yard spaces and flowers in profusion and a few stores. Dr. A. B. Fitch, Druggist (I could see this sign on the window before which he stood), was over the way sweeping off the sidewalk in front of his store. I knew it was Dr. A. B. Fitch by his solemn proprietary air, his alpaca coat, his serious growth of thick grey whiskers. He was hatless and serene. I could almost hear him saying: "Now, Annie, you tell your mother that this medicine is to be taken one teaspoonful every three hours, do you hear?"

Farther down the street H. B. Wendel, hardware dealer, was setting out a small red and green lawnmower and some zinc cans capable of holding anything from rain water to garbage. This was his inducement to people to come and buy. Although it was still very early, citizens were making their way down the street, a working man or two, going to some distant factory not in Factoryville, a woman in a gingham poke bonnet standing at a corner of her small white home examining her flowers, a small barefooted boy kicking the damp dust of the road with his toes. It reminded me of the time when, as a youth in a similar town, I used to get up early and see my mother browsing over early, dew-laden blossoms. I was for staying in Factoryville for some time.

But Franklin, energetic soul, would have none of it. He had lived in a small town or on a farm for the greater part of his life and, unlike me, had never really deserted the country. Inside the room, on the balcony of which I was already swinging and idly musing, he was industriously shaving—a task I was reserving for some city barber. Presently he came out and sat down.

"Isn't it wonderful—the country!" I said. "This town! See old Dr. Fitch over there, and that grocery man putting out his goods."

"Yes!" replied Franklin. "Carmel is very much like this. There's no particular life there. A little small-town trading. Of course, Indianapolis has come so near now that they can all go down there by trolley, and that makes a difference."

Forthwith he launched into amusing tales of Carmelite character—bits too idle or too profane to be narrated here. One only I remember—that of some yokels who were compelled to find a new hangout because the old building they frequented was torn down. When Franklin encountered them in the new place he said quite innocently: "This place hasn't as much atmosphere as the old one." "Oh, yes, it has," rejoined the rural. "When you open the back windows."

Speed was shaving too by now, inside, and, hearing me sing the delights of rural life (windows and doors were open), he put in:

"Yes, that's all well enough, but after you'd lived here awhile you mightn't like it so much. Gee! people in the country aren't any different from people anywhere else."

Speed had a peculiarly pained and even frightened look on his face at times, like a cloud passing over a landscape or something that made me want to put my hand on his shoulder and say, "There, there." I wondered sometimes whether he had often been hungry or thrown out of a job or put upon in some unkind way. He could seem momentarily so pathetic.

"I know, I know," I said gaily, "but there are the

cows and the trees and the little flower gardens and the farmers mowing hay and——"

"Huh!" was all he deigned to reply, as he shaved. Franklin, in his large tolerance of vagaries and mush, did not condescend to comment. I did not even win a smile. He was looking at the drugstore and the hardware store and an old man in a shapeless, baggy suit hobbling along on a cane.

"I like the country myself," he said finally, "except I wouldn't want to have to farm for a living."

I could not help thinking of all the days we (I am referring to a part of our family) had lived in these small towns and how as a boy I used to wish and wish for so many things. The long trains going through! The people who went to Chicago, or Evansville, or Terre Haute, or Indianapolis! A place like Brazil, Indiana, a mere shabby coal town of three or four thousand population, seemed something wonderful. All the world was outside and I, sitting on our porch—front or back— or on the grass or under a tree, all alone, used to wonder and wonder. When would I go out into the world? Where would I go? What would I do? What see? And then sometimes the thought of my father and mother not being near any more—my mother being dead, perhaps—and my sisters and brothers scattered far and wide, and—I confess a little sadly even now—a lump would swell in my throat and I would be ready to cry.

A sentimentalist?

Indeed!

In a little while we were called to breakfast in a lovely, homely diningroom such as country hotels sometimes boast—a diningroom of an indescribable artlessness and crudity. It was so haphazard, so slung together of old yellow factory made furniture, chromos, lithographs, flychasers, five jar castors, ironstone "china," and heaven only knows what else, that it was delightful. It was clean, yes; and sweet withal—very—just like so many of our honest, frank, kindly psalm singing Methodists and Baptists are. The father and mother were eating their breakfast here, at one table. The little fair haired hired girl—with no more qualification as a waitress than a Thibetan Llama—was waiting on table. The traveling men, one or two of them at every breakfast no doubt, were eating their fried ham and eggs or their fried steak, and their fried potatoes, and drinking unbelievable coffee or tea.

Dear, crude, asinine, illusioned Americans! How I love them! And the great fields from the Atlantic to the Pacific holding them all, and their dreams! How they rise, how they hurry, how they run under the sun! Here they are building a viaduct, there a great road, yonder plowing fields or sowing grain, their faces lit with eternal, futile hope of happiness. You can see them religiously tending store, religiously running a small-town country hotel, religiously mowing the grass, religiously driving shrewd bargains or thinking that much praying will carry them to heaven—the dear things!—and then among them are the bad men, the loafers, the people who chew tobacco and swear and go to the cities Saturday nights and "cut up" and don't save their money!

Dear, dear, darling Yankee land—"my country tis"—when I think of you and all your ills and all your dreams and all your courage and your faith—I could cry over you, wringing my hands.

But you, you great men of brains—you plotters of treason, of taxes which are not honest, of burdens too heavy to be borne, beware! These be simple souls, my countrymen singing simple songs in childish ignorance and peace, dreaming sweet dreams of life and love and hope. Don't awake them! Let them not once suspect, let them not faintly glimpse the great tricks and subterfuges by which they are led and harlequined and cheated; let them not know that their faith is nothing, their hope nothing, their love nothing—or you may see the bonfires of wrath alight—in the "evening dews and damp," the camps of the hungry—the lifting aloft of the fatal stripes—red for blood and white for spirit and blue for dreams of man; the white drawn faces of earnest seeking souls carrying the symbols of their desire, the guns and mortars and shells of their dreams!

Remember Valley Forge! Remember Germantown; remember the Wilderness; remember Lookout Mountain! These will not be disappointed. Their faith is too deep—their hope too high. They will burn and slay, but the fires of their dreams will bring other dreams to make this old illusion seem true.

.   .   .   .

It can hardly be said that America has developed a culinary art, because so many phases of our cooking are not, as yet, common to all parts of the country. In the southeast south you have fried chicken and gravy, cornpone, corn pudding, biscuit, and Virginia ham, southern style; in the southwest south you have broilers, chicken tamales, chile con carne, and all the nuances acquired from a proximity to Mexico. In New England one encounters the baked bean, the *cold* biscuit, pie for breakfast, and codfish cakes. In the great hotels and best restaurants of the large cities, especially in the east, the French cuisine dominates. In the smaller cities of the east and west, where no French chef would deign to waste his days, German, Italian and Greek—to say nothing of Jewish—and purely American restaurants (the dairy kitchen, for example) now contest with each other for patronage. We have never developed a single, dominating system of our own. The American "grill" or its companion in dullness, the American "rathskeller," boast a mixture of everything and are not really anything. In all cities large and small may be found these horrible concoctions which in their superficial treatment are supposed to be Flemish or Elizabethan or old German combined with the worse imaginings of the socalled mission school of furniture. Here German pancakes, knackwurst and cheesecake come cheek by jowl with American biscuit, English muffins, French rolls, Hungarian goulash, chicken à la Maryland, steaks, chops, and ham and eggs. It's serviceable, and yet it's offensive.

The atmosphere is deadly—the idea atrocious. By comparison with a French inn or a German family restaurant such as one finds in Frankfort or Berlin, or even an English chophouse, it is unbelievably bad. Yet it seems to suit the present day spirit of America.

All restaurant forms are being tried out—French, Greek, Italian, Turkish, English, Spanish, German—to say nothing of teahouses of all lands. In the long run, possibly some one school will become dominant or a compromise among them all. By that time American cooking will have become a complex of all the others. I sincerely trust that in the internecine struggle fried chicken, gravy, fresh hot biscuit, blackberry pie and fried mush do not wholly disappear. I am fond of French cooking and have a profound respect for the German art—but there! Supposing that never anywhere, any more, was there to be any fried mush or blackberry pie!!!

CHAPTER XI

THE MAGIC OF THE ROAD AND SOME TALES

OUR particular breakfast consisted of a choice of several "flake" breakfast foods, a hard fried chop, an egg or two, fried, some German fried potatoes, and all done as an American small town hotelkeeper used to dealing with farmers and storekeepers and "hands" would imagine they ought to be done. Where did the average American first get the idea that meals of nearly all kinds need to be fried *hard?* Or that tea has to be made so strong that it looks black and tastes like weeds? Or that German fried potatoes ought to be soggy and that *all* people prefer German fried potatoes? If you should ask for French fried potatoes or potatoes *au gratin* or potatoes O'Brien in a small country town hotel you would be greeted with a look of uncertainty if not of resentment. French fried potatoes, pray—or meat medium or broiled? Impossible! And as for weak, clear, tasteful tea—shades of Buffalo Bill and Davy Crockett! "Whoever heard of weak, clear tea? The man has gone mad. He is some 'city fellow,' bent on showing off. It is up to us to teach him not to get smart. We must frown and delay and show that we do not approve of him at all."

While we were eating, I was thinking where our car would take us this day, and the anticipation of new fields and strange scenes was enough to make a mere poor breakfast a very trivial matter indeed. Clouds and high hills, and spinning along the bank of some winding stream, were an ample exchange for any temporary inconvenience. After breakfast and while Franklin and I once more tightened up our belongings, Speed brought about the machine and in the presence of a few residents—a young girl of fifteen for one, who looked at us with wide, wishful eyes—we strapped on the bags and took our seats. I could not help feeling as I looked at some of them who observed us that they were wishing they were in our places. The car was good to look at. It was quite obvious from the various bags and wraps that we were en route somewhere. Someone was always asking us where we were from and where we were going—questions which the magic name of New York, particularly this distance away, seemed to make all the more significant. The night before in the garage at Scranton a youth, hearing us say that we were from there, had observed with an air: "How is old New York anyway?" And then, with a flourish: "I'll have to be going over there pretty soon now. I haven't been over in some time."

Leaving Factoryville, we ran through country so beautiful that before long I regretted sincerely that we had done any traveling after dark the night before. We were making our way up a wide valley as I could see, the same green Susquehanna Valley, between high hills and through a region given over entirely to dairy farming. The hills looked as though they were bedded knee deep in rich, succulent grass. Groups of black and white Holstein cattle were everywhere to be seen. Some of the hills were laid out in checkerboard fashion by fields of grain or hay or buckwheat or great thick groves of trees. Before many a farm dooryard was a platform on which stood a milk can, or two or three: now and then a neighborhood creamery would come into view, where the local milk was churned wholesale and butter prepared and shipped. The towns for the most part were rarely factory towns, looking more as if they harbored summer boarders or were but now starting on a manufacturing career. Girls or women were reading or sewing on porches. The region of the mines was far behind.

And what a day! The everchanging panorama—how wonderful it was! Tr-r-r-r-r and we were descending a steep hill, at the bottom of which lay a railroad track (one of those against which we had been warned, no doubt), and in the distance more great hills, sentineling this wide valley; the road showing like a white thread, miles and miles away.

Tr-r-r-r-r-r, and now we were passing a prosperous farmyard, aglow with strident flowers, one woman sewing at a window, others talking with a neighbor at the door. Tr-r-r-r-r-r, here we were swinging around a sharp curve, over an iron bridge, noisy and shaky and beneath which ran a turbulent stream, and in the immediate foreground was an old mill or a barnyard alive with cattle and poultry. I had just time to think, "What if we should crash through this bridge into the stream below," when T-r-r-r-r-r-r, and now came a small factory or foundry section with tall smokestacks, and beyond it a fair-sized town, clean, healthy, industrious. No tradition, you see, anywhere. No monuments or cathedrals or great hotels or any historic scene anywhere to look forward to: but Tr-r-r-r-r and here we are at the farther outskirts of this same small town with more green fields in the distance, the scuff and scar of manufacturing gone and only the blue sky and endless green fields and some birds flying and a farmer cutting his grain with a great reaper. Tr-r-r-r-r-r—how the miles do fly past, to be sure!

And T-r-r-r-r-r-r (these motors are surely tireless things), here is a lake now, just showing through the tall, straight trunks of trees, a silvery flash with a grey icehouse in the distance; and then, Tr-r-r-r-r-r, a thick green wall of woods, so rich and dark, from which pour the sweetest, richest, most invigorating odors and into the depth of which the glance sinks only to find cooler and darker shadows and even ultimate shadow or a green blackness; and then—Tr-r-r-r-r—a line of small white cottages facing a stream and a boy scuffing his toes in the warm, golden dust—oh, happy boyland!—and then, Tr-r-r-r-r—but why go on? It was all beautiful. It was all so refreshing. It was all like a song—only—Tr-r-r-r-r

—and here comes another great wide spreading view, which Franklin wishes to sketch. He has a large pad of some peculiarly white porous paper, on which he works and from which he tears the sketches when they are done and deposits them in a convenient portfolio. By now Speed has become resigned to *not* getting to Indiana as fast as he would like.

"Shucks!" I heard him say once, as he was oiling up his engine, "if we didn't have to stop this way every few minutes, we'd soon get into Indiana. Give me half way decent roads and this little old motor will eat up the miles as good as anyone. . . ." But when you have two loons aboard who are forever calling "Whoa!" and jumping up or out or both and exclaiming, "Well now, what do you think of that?—isn't it beautiful?"—what are you going to do? No real chauffeur can get anywhere that way—you know that.

Here we were now backing the machine in the shade of a barn while Franklin fixed himself on the edge of a grey, lichen covered wall and I strolled off down a steep hill to get a better view of a railroad which here ran through a granite gorge. Perhaps Franklin worked as many as thirty or forty minutes. Perhaps I investigated even longer. There was a field on this slope with a fine spring on it. I had to speculate on what a fine pool could be made here. In the distance some horizon clouds made a procession like ships. I had to look at those. The spear pines here at the edge of this field were very beautiful and reminded me of the cypresses of Italy. I had to speculate as to the difference. Then Tr-r-r-r-r-r, and we were on again at about thirtyfive miles an hour.

While we were riding across this country in the bright morning sunshine, Speed fell into a reminiscent or taletelling mood. Countrymen born have this trait at times and Speed was country bred. He began, as I had already found was his way, without any particular announcement, or a "Didjah ever hear of the old fellow," etc., and then he would be off on a series of yarns the exact flavor and charm of which I cannot hope to transcribe, but some of which I nevertheless feel I must paraphrase as best I may.

Thus one of his stories concerned a wedding somewhere in the country. All the neighbors had been invited and the preacher and the justice of the peace. The women were all in the house picking wool for a pastime. The men were all out at the edge of the woods around a log heap they had built, telling stories. The bride-to-be was all washed and starched and her hair done up for once, and she was picking wool, too. When the fatal moment came the preacher and the prospective husband came in, followed by all the men, and the two stood in the proper position for a wedding before the fireplace; but the girl never moved. She just called, "Go on; it'll be all right." So the preacher read or spoke the ceremony, and when it came to the place where he asked her, "Do you take this man to be your lawful wedded husband, etc.," she stopped, took a chew of tobacco out of her mouth, threw it in the fire, expectorated in the same direction, and said, "I reckon." Then she went on working again.

Another of these yarns concerned the resurveying of the county line between Brown and Monroe counties in Indiana which a little while before had been moved west about two hundred and fifty yards. That put the house of an old Brown County farmer about ten yards over the Monroe County line. A part of Monroe County in this region was swampy and famous for chills and fever— or infamous. When the old farmer came home that night his wife met him at the gate and said: "Now we just got tuh move, paw; that's all there is to it. I'm not goin' to live over there in Monroe with all these here swamps. We'll all die with chills and yuh know it."

. . . .

Fishing was great sport in some county in Indiana—I forget which. They organized fishing parties, sometimes thirty or forty in a drove, and went fishing, camping out for two or three days at a time, only they weren't so strong for hooks and lines, except for the mere sport of it. To be sure of having enough fish to go 'round, they always took a few sticks of dynamite and toward evening or noon someone would light a fuse and attach it to a stick of dynamite and, just as it was getting near the danger line, throw it in the water.

Well, once upon a time there was just such a fishing party and they had a stick of dynamite, or two or three. There was also an old fat hotel man who had come along and he had a very fine big dog with him— a retriever—that he thought a great deal of. Whenever anyone would shoot a duck or throw a stick into the water, the dog would go and get it. On this occasion toward evening someone threw a stick of dynamite in the water with the fuse lit. Only instead of falling in the water it fell on some brush floating there and the darn fool dog seeing it jumped in and began to swim out toward it. They all commenced to holler at the dog to come back, but in vain. He swam to the dynamite stick, got it in his mouth, and started for shore— the fuse burning all the while. Then they all ran for their lives—all but the old fat hotel man, who couldn't run very well, though he did his best, and it was his dog. He lit out, though, through the green briars and brush, hollering, "Go home, Tige! Go home, Tige!" at every jump. But old Tige was just a-bounding on along behind him and a-wagging his tail and a-shaking the water off him. What saved the old man was that at one place the dog stopped to shake the water off and that gave him a fair start, but he only missed him by about forty feet at that. The dog was just that near when, bang! and say, there wasn't a thing left but just about a half inch of his tail, which somebody found and which the old man used to wear as a watch-charm and for good luck. He always said it was mighty good luck for him that the dog didn't get any nearer.

.   .   .   .

And once more upon a time there was a very stingy old man who owned a field opposite the railway station of a small town. A shed was there which made a rather good billboard and itinerant showmen and medicine men occasionally posted bills on it—not without getting the permission of the owner, however, who invariably extracted tickets or something—medicine even.

One day, however, the station agent, who was idling in front of his office, saw a man pasting showbills. He fancied Zeke Peters' (the owner's) permission had not been obtained, but he wasn't sure. It must be remembered that he was in no way related to Peters. Walking over to the man, he inquired:

"Does paw know you're putting up them bills here?"

"Why, no, I didn't think there'd be any trouble. They're only small bills, as you see."

The agent pulled a long face.

"I know," he replied, "but I don't think paw'd like this."

The showman handed him a ticket for the circus—one ticket.

"Well, I don't know about this," said the station agent heavily. "If you didn't ask paw, I don't know whether you'd better do this or not."

The billposter handed him another ticket.

"Won't that fix it?" he asked.

"Well," replied the agent, seemingly somewhat mollified, "paw's awful particular, but I guess I can fix it. I'll try anyhow"—and he walked solemnly back to the station.

Old Peters didn't chance to see the bills until a day or two before the circus. He was very angry, but at this time there were no circus men around to complain to. When the show came to town he looked up the box-office and found he had been done. Then he hurried to the agent.

"Where's them tickets?" he demanded.

"What tickets?" replied the agent.

"That you got from that billposter."

"Well, I'm usin' 'em. He gave 'em to me."

"What fer, I'd like to know? It's my billboard, ain't it?"

"Well, it was my idea, wasn't it?"

There Speed stopped.

"Well, did he get the tickets?" I asked.

"Course not. Nobody liked him, so he couldn't do nothing."

I liked the ending philosophy of this the best of all.

. . . .

And once upon a time in some backwoods county in Indiana there was an election for president. There weren't but sixtynine voters in the district and they kept straggling in from six A. M., when the polls opened, to six P. M., when they closed. Then they all hung around to see how the vote stood. And guess how it stood?

"Well?"

"It was this-a-way. W. J. Bryan, 15; Andrew Jackson, 12; Jeff Davis, 9; Abraham Lincoln, 8; Thomas Jefferson, 8; Moses, 6; Abraham, 15; John the Baptist, 3; Daniel Boone, 2; William McKinley, 1."

"What about George Washington, Speed?"

"Well, I guess they musta fergot him."

. . . .

And, once more now, not every family in Indiana or elsewhere is strong for education, and especially in the country. So once upon a time there was a family— father and mother, that is—that got into a row over this very thing. An old couple had married after each had been married before and each had had children. Only, now, each of 'em only had one son apiece left, that is, home with 'em. The old man believed in education and wanted his boy educated, whereas the woman didn't. "No, siree," she said, "I don't want any of my children to ever git any of that book learnin'. None o' the others had any and I 'low as Luke can git along just as well as they did."

But the old man he didn't feel quite right about it and somehow his boy liked books. So, since he was really the stronger of the two, he sent the two boys off and made 'em go. The old woman grieved and grieved. She felt as though her boy was being spoiled, and she said so.

"Shucks!" said the old man, "he'll git along all right. What's the matter with you, anyhow? If my boy don't go to school he'll feel bad, and if I send him to school and keep yours at home to work the neighbors will talk— now I just can't manage it, that's all."

So the two boys kept on going for awhile longer. Only the old woman kept feelin' worse and worse about it. All at once one day she got to feelin' so terrible bad that she just gathered up her boy's clothes and took him over to his grandfather's to live, and gee! the old grandfather was sore about it. Say!

"Send that boy to school!" he says. "Never! Why, he ain't the same boy any more at all already. I'll be hanged if he ain't even fergot how to cuss," and he wouldn't even let the boy's fosterfather come near him. Not a bit of it, no siree.

.   .   .   .

And once upon a time, in the extreme southern part of Indiana where the ice doesn't get very thick—not over three inches—there was a backwoods preacher who made a trip to Evansville and saw an ice machine making ice a foot thick, and he came back and told his congregation about it.

"Whaddy think of that!" one of the old members exclaimed. "The Lord can't make it more'n three inches around here, and he says men in Evansville can make it a foot thick!"

So they turned the old preacher out for lying, b'gosh!

.   .   .   .

Once upon a time there was an old Irishman got on the train at Carmel, Indiana, and walked in the car, but the seats were all taken. One was occupied by an Indiana farmer and his dog. The Irishman knew, if he tried to make the dog get down and give him the seat, he would have the farmer and the dog to fight.

"That's a very fine darg ye have."

"Yes, stranger; he's the finest dog in the county."

"And he has the marks of a good coon darg."

"That's right. He can come as near findin' coons where there ain't any as the next one."

"What brade of darg is he?"

"Well, he's a cross between an Irishman and a skunk."

"Bejasus, then he must be related to the both of us!"

.   .   .   .

Somewhere in the country in Indiana they once built a railroad where there never had been one and it created great excitement. One old farmer who had lived on his farm a great many years and had never even seen a train or a track and had raised a large family, mostly girls, was so interested that he put his whole family in the wagon and drove up close to the track so they could get a good view of the cars the first time they came through. But before the train came he got uneasy. He was afraid the old grey mare would get scared and run away. So he got out, unhitched the old horse and tied it to a tree, gave it some hay and got back into the wagon. Pretty soon he saw the train coming very fast, and as the old wagon was quite close to the track he thought the train might jump the track and kill them all, so he leaped out, got between the shafts and started to pull the wagon a little farther down the hill. Just then the train neared the station and he got so excited that he lost all control of himself and away he went down the hill, lickety split. He ran upon a stump, upset the wagon and threw the old woman and all the children out, and hurt them worse than ever the old mare would have. The old woman was furious. She didn't have any bridle on him and while he was running she missed seeing the train.

"Gol darn you," she hollered, "if I didn't have a sprained ankle now, I'd fix you—runnin' away like the crazy old fool that you are!"

"That's all right, Maria," he called back meekly. "I was a leetle excited, I'll admit; but next week when the train goes through again you and the children kin come down and I'll stay to home. I just can't stand these newfangled things, I reckon."

. . . .

And once upon a time (and this is the last one for the present) there was a real wildcat fight somewhere—a most wonderful wildcat fight. An old farmer was sitting on a fence hoeing corn—that's the way they hoe corn in some places—and all at once he saw two Thomas wildcats approaching each other from different directions and swiftly. He was about to jump down and run when suddenly the cats came together. It was all so swift that he scarcely had time to move. They came along on their hind feet and when they got together each one began to claw and climb up the other. In fifteen minutes they were out of sight in the air, each one climbing rapidly up the other; but he could hear them squalling for two hours after they were out of sight, and froth and hair fell for two days!

CHAPTER XII

RAILROADS AND A NEW WONDER OF THE WORLD

It wouldn't surprise me in the least if the automobile, as it is being perfected now, would make over the whole world's railway systems into something very different from what they are today. Already the railways are complaining that the automobile is seriously injuring business, and this is not difficult to understand. It ought to be so. At best the railways have become huge, clumsy, unwieldy affairs little suited to the temperamental needs and moods of the average human being. They are mass carriers, freight handlers, great hurry conveniences for overburdened commercial minds, but little more. After all, travel, however much it may be a matter of necessity, is in most instances, or should be, a matter of pleasure. If not, why go forth to roam the world so wide? Are not trees, flowers, attractive scenes, great mountains, interesting cities, and streets and terminals the objective? If not, why not? Should the discomforts become too great, as in the case of the majority of railroads, and any reasonable substitute offer itself, as the automobile, the old form of conveyance will assuredly have to give way.

Think what you have to endure on the ordinary railroad—and what other kind is there—smoke, dust, cinders, noise, the hurrying of masses of people, the ringing of bells, the tooting of whistles, the brashness and discourtesy of employes, cattle trains, coal trains, fruit trains, milk trains in endless procession—and then they tell you that these are necessary in order to give you the service you get. Actually our huge railways are becoming so freight logged and trainyard and train terminal infested, and four tracked and cinder blown, that they are a nuisance.

Contrast travel by railroad with the charm of such a trip as we were now making. Before the automobile, this trip, if it had been made at all, would have had to be made by train—in part at least. I would not have ridden a horse or in any carriage to Indiana—whatever I might have done after I reached there. Instead of green fields and pleasant ways, with the pleasure of stopping anywhere and proceeding at our leisure, substitute the necessity of riding over a fixed route, which once or twice seen, or ten times, as in my case, had already become an old story. For this is one of the drawbacks to modern railroading, in addition to all its other defects—it is so fixed; it has no latitude, no elasticity. Who wants to see the same old scenes over and over and over? One can go up the Hudson or over the Alleghanies or through the Grand Canyon of the Arizona once or twice, but if you have to go that way always, if you go at all—— But the prospect of new and varied roads, and of that intimate contact with woodland silences, grassy slopes, sudden and sheer vistas at sharp turns, streams not followed by endless lines of cars—of being able to change your mind and go by this route or that according to your mood—what a difference! These constitute a measureless superiority. And the cost per mile is not so vastly much more by automobile. Today it is actually making travel cheaper and quicker. Whether for a long tour or a short one, it appears to make man independent and give him a choice of life, which he must naturally prefer. Only the dull can love sameness.

North of Factoryville a little way—perhaps a score of miles—we encountered one of these amazing works of man which, if they become numerous enough, eventually make a country a great memory. They are the bones or articulatory ligaments of the body politic which, like the roads and viaducts and baths of ancient Rome, testify to the prime of its physical strength and after its death lie like whitening bones about the fields of the world which once it occupied.

We were coming around a curve near Nicholsen, Pennsylvania, approaching a stream which traversed this great valley, when across it from ridge's edge to ridge's edge suddenly appeared a great white stone or concrete viaduct or bridge—we could not tell at once which—a thing so colossal and impressive that we instantly had Speed stop the car so that we might remain and gaze at it. Ten huge arches—each say two hundred feet wide and two hundred feet high—were topped by eleven other arches say fifteen feet wide and forty feet high, and this whole surmounted by a great roadbed carrying several railway tracks, we assumed. The builders were still at work on it. As before the great Cathedral at Rouen or Amiens or Canterbury, or those giant baths in Rome which so gratify the imagination, so here, at Nicholsen, in a valley celebrated for nothing in particular and at the edge of a town of no size, we stood before this vast structure, gazing in a kind of awe. These arches! How really beautiful they were, how wide, how high, how noble, how symmetrically planned! And the smaller arches above, for all the actually huge size, how delicate and lightsomely graceful! How could they carry a heavy train so high in the air? But there they were, nearly two hundred and forty feet above us from the stream's surface, as we discovered afterwards, and the whole structure nearly twentyfour hundred feet long. We learned that it was the work of a great railroad corporation—a part of a scheme for straightening and shortening its line about three miles!—which incidentally was leaving a monument to the American of this day which would be stared at in centuries to come as evidencing the courage, the resourcefulness, the taste, the wealth, the commerce and the force of the time in which we are living—now.

It is rather odd to stand in the presence of so great a thing in the making and realize that you are looking at one of the true wonders of the world. As I did so I could not help thinking of all the great wonders America has already produced—capitals, halls, universities, bridges, monuments, water flumes, sea walls, dams, towering structures—yet the thought came to me how little of all that will yet *be* accomplished have *we* seen. What towers, what bridges, what palaces, what roads will not yet come! Numerous as these great things already are—a statue of Lincoln in Chicago, a building by Woolworth in New York, a sea wall at Galveston, an Ashokan dam in the Catskills, this bridge at Nicholsen —yet in times to come there will be thousands of these wonders—possibly hundreds of thousands where now there are hundreds. A great free people is hard at work day after day building, building, building—and for what? Sometimes I think, like the forces and processes which produce embryonic life here or the coral islands in the Pacific, vast intelligences and personalities are at work, producing worlds and nations. As a child is builded in the womb, so is a star. We socalled individuals are probably no more than mere cell forms constructing something in whose subsequent movements, passions, powers we shall have no share whatsoever. Does the momentary cell life in the womb show in the subsequent powers of the man? Will we show in the subsequent life of the nation that we have helped build? When one thinks of how little of all that is or will be one has any part in—are we not such stuff as dreams are made of, and can we feel anything but a slave's resignation?

.   .   .   .

While we were sightseeing, Speed was conducting a social conference of his own in the shade of some trees in one of the quiet streets of Nicholsen. I think I have never seen anyone with a greater innate attraction for boys. Speed was only twentyfive himself. Boys seemed to understand Speed and to be hail-fellow-well-met with him, wherever he was. In Dover, at the Water Gap, in Wilkes-Barré, Scranton—wherever we chanced to stop, there was a boy or boys. He or they drew near and a general conversation ensued. In so far as I could see, the mystery consisted of nothing more than a natural ability on Speed's part to take them at their own value and on their own terms. He was just like any other boy among them, questioning and answering quite as if he and they were all grownups and very serious. Here in Nicholsen, as we came back, no less than five youngsters were explaining to him all the facts and wonders of the great bridge.

"Yes, and one man fell from the top of them there little arches way up there last winter down to the back of the big arch and he almost died."

"Those little arches are forty feet above the big ones," another went on.

"Yes, but he didn't die," put in another informatively. "He just, now, broke his back. But he almost died, though. He can't do any more work."

"That's too bad," I said, "and how does he manage to live now?"

"Well, his wife supports him, I believe," put in one quietly.

"He's goin' to get a pension, though," said another.

"There's a law now or something," volunteered a fourth. "They have to give him money."

"Oh, I see," I said. "That's fine. Can any of you tell me how wide those arches are—those big arches?"

"One hundred and eighty feet wide and two hundred feet high," volunteered one boy.

"And the little arches are sixteen feet and three inches wide and forty feet high," put in another.

"And how long is it?"

"Two thousand, three hundred and ninetyfive feet from ridge to ridge," came with schoolboy promtpness from three at once.

I was flabbergasted.

"How do you know all this?" I inquired.

"We learned it at school," said two. "Our teacher knows."

I was so entertained by the general spirit of this group that I wanted to stay awhile and listen to them. American boys—I know nothing of foreign ones—are so frank, free and generally intelligent. There was not the slightest air of sycophancy about this group. They were not seeking anything save temporary entertainment. Some of them wanted to ride a little way,—perhaps to the nearest store—but only a little way and then only when invited. They all looked so bright, and yet in this group you could easily detect the varying characteristics which, other things being equal, would make some successes materially and others failures, possibly. Here was the comparatively dull boy, the bashful boy, the shrewd boy, the easy going, pleasure loving boy. You could see it in their eyes. One of them, a tallish, leanish youth, had instantly on the appearance of Franklin and myself crowded the others back and stood closest, his shrewd, examining eyes taking in all our characteristics. By looking into his eyes I could see how shrewd, independent, and selfprotective he was. He was not in the least overawed like some of the others, but rather superior, like one who would have driven a clever bargain with us, if he might have, and worsted us at it.

Except for this bridge and these children, Nicholsen held nothing, at least nothing obvious. It was just a small town with retail stores, at one of which, a druggist's, we stopped for picture cards. One would have supposed, with so vast a thing as this bridge, there would have been excellent photographs of it; but no, there was none that was really good. The main street, some country roads, a wheat field which some rural poet had snapped—that was all. This country druggist's store was very flyspecked. I wished for Nicholsen's sake, as well as for my own, that something worthy had been prepared, which the sightseeing public might take away as a memento.

CHAPTER XIII

A COUNTRY HOTEL

BEYOND Nicholsen, somewhere in this same wondrous valley and in a winelike atmosphere, came New Milford and with it our noonday meal. We were rolling along aimlessly, uncertain where next we would pause. The sight of an old fashioned white hotel at a street corner with several rurals standing about and a row of beautiful elms over the way gave us our cue. "This looks rather inviting," said Franklin; and then, to the figure of a heavy nondescript in brown jeans who was sitting on a chair outside in the shade:

"Can't we get something to eat here?"

"You can," replied the countryman succinctly; "they'll be putting dinner on the table in a few minutes."

We went into the bar, Franklin's invariable opening for these meals being a cocktail, when he could get one. It was a cleanly room, but with such a field hand atmosphere about those present that I was a little disappointed, and yet interested. I always feel about most American country saloons that they are patronized by ditchers and men who do the rough underpaid work of villages, while in England and France I had a very different feeling.

I was much interested here by the proprietor, or, as he turned out afterward, one of two brothers who owned the hotel. He was an elderly man, stout and serious, who in another place perhaps and with a slightly different start in life might, I am sure, have been banker, railroad offcer, or director. He was so circumspect, polite, regardful. He came to inquire in a serious way if we were going to take dinner? We were.

"You can come right in whenever you are ready," he commented.

Something in his tone and presence touched me pleasantly.

Beause of the great heat—it was blazing outside—I had left my coat in the car and was arrayed in a brown khaki shirt and grey woolen trousers, with a belt. Because of the heat it did not occur to me that my appearance would not pass muster. But, no. Life's little rules of conduct are not so easily set aside, even in a country hotel. As I neared the diningroom door and was passing the coatrack, mine host appeared and, with a grace and tact which I have nowhere seen surpassed, and in a voice which instantly obviated all possibility of a disagreeable retort, he presented me a coat which he had taken from a hook and, holding it ready, said: "Would you mind slipping into this?"

"Pardon me," I said, "I have a coat in the car; I will get that."

"Don't trouble," he said gently; "you can wear this if you like. It will do."

I had to smile, but in an entirely friendly way. Something about the man's manner made me ashamed of myself—not that it would have been such a dreadful thing to have gone into the diningroom looking as I was, for I was entirely presentable, but that I had not taken greater thought to respect his conventions more. He was a gentleman running a country hotel—a real gentleman. I was the brash, smart asininity from the city seeking to have my own way in the country because the city looks down on the country. It hurt me a little and yet I felt repaid by having encountered a man who could fence so skilfully with the little and yet irritable and no doubt difficult problems of his daily life. I wanted to make friends with him, for I could see so plainly that he was really above the thing he was doing and yet content in some philosophical way to make the best of it. How this man came to be running a country hotel, with a bar attached, I should like to know.

After luncheon, I fell into a conversation with him, brief but interesting. He had lived here many years.

The place over the way with the beautiful trees belonged to a former congressman. (I could see the forgotten dignitary making the best of his former laurels in this out-of-the-way place.) New Milford, a very old place, had been hurt by the growth of other towns. But now the automobile was beginning to do something for it. Last Sunday six hundred machines had passed through here. Only last week the town had voted to pave the principal street, in order to attract further travel. One could see by mine host's manner that his hotel business was picking up. I venture to say he offered to contribute liberally to the expense, so far as his ability would permit.

I could not help thinking of this man as we rode away, and I have been thinking of him from time to time ever since. He was so simple, so sincere, so honorably dull or conventional. I wish that I could believe there are thousands of such men in the world. His hotel was tasteless; so are the vast majority of other hotels, and homes too, in America. The dining room was execrable from one point of view; naïve, and pleasingly so, from another. One could feel the desire to "set a good table" and give a decent meal. The general ingredients were good as far as they went, but, alas! the average American does not make a good servant—for the public. The girl who waited on us was a poor slip, well intentioned enough, I am sure, but without the first idea of what to do. I could see her being selected by mine host because she was a good girl, or because her mother was poor and needed the money—never because she had been trained to do the things she was expected to do. Americans live in a world of sentiment in spite of all their business acumen, and somehow expect God to reward good intentions with perfect results. I adore the spirit, but I grieve for its inutility. No doubt this girl was dreaming (all the time she was waiting on us) of some four-corners merry-go-round where her beau would be waiting. Dear, naïve America! When will it be different from a dreaming child, and, if ever that time arrives, shall we ever like it as much again?

. . . .

And then came Halstead and Binghamton, for we were getting on. I never saw a finer day nor ever enjoyed one more. Imagine smooth roads, a blue sky, white and black cattle on the hills, lovely farms, the rich green woods and yellow grainfields of a fecund August. Life was going by in a Monticelli-esque mood. Dooryards and houses seemed to be a compound of blowing curtains, cool deep shadows, women in summery dresses reading, and then an arabesque of bright flowers, golden-glow, canna, flowering sage, sweet elyssum, geraniums and sunflowers. At Halstead we passed an hotel facing the Susquehanna River, which seemed to me the ideal of what a summer hotel should be—gay with yellow and white awnings and airy balconies and painted with flowers. Before it was this blue river, a lovely thing, with canoes and trees and a sense of summer life.

Beyond, on a smooth white road, we met a man who was selling some kind of soap—a soap especially good for motorists. He came to us out of Binghamton, driving an old ramshackle vehicle, and hailed us as we were pausing to examine something. He was a tall, lean, shabby American, clothed in an ancient frock coat and soft rumpled felt hat, and looked like some small-town carpenter or bricklayer or maker of cement walks. By his side sat a youngish man, who looked nothing and said nothing, taking no part in what followed. He had a dreamy, speculative and yet harassed look, made all the more emphatic by a long pointed nose and narrow pointed chin.

"I've got something here I'd like to show you, gentlemen," he called, drawing rein and looking hopefully at Franklin and Speed.

"Well, we're always willing to look at something once," replied Franklin cheerfully and in a bantering tone.

"Very well, gentlemen," said the stranger, "you're just

the people I'm looking for, and you'll be glad you've met me." Even as he spoke he had been reaching under the seat and produced a small can of something which he now held dramatically aloft. "It's the finest thing in the way of a hand or machine soap that has ever been invented, no akali (he did not seem to know there were two ls in the word), good for man or woman. Won't soil the most delicate fabric or injure the daintiest hands. I know, now, for I've been working on this for the last three years. It's my personal, private invention. The basis of it is cornmeal and healing, soothing oils. You rub it on your hands before you put them in water and it takes off all these spots and stains that come from machine oil and that ordinary turpentine won't take out. It softens them right up. Have you got any oil stains?" he continued, seizing one of Speed's genial hands. "Very good. This will take it right out. You haven't any water in there, have you, or a pan? Never mind. I'm sure this lady up here in this house will let me have some," and off he hustled with the air of a proselytizing religionist.

I was interested. So much enthusiasm for so humble a thing as a soap aroused me. Besides he was curious to look at—a long, lean, shambling zealot. He was so zealous, so earnest, so amusing, if you please, or hopeless. "Here really," I said, "is the basis of all zealotry, of all hopeless invention, of struggle and dreams never to be fulfilled." He looked exactly like the average inventor who is destined to invent and invent and invent and never succeed in anything.

"Well, there is character there, anyhow," said Franklin. "That long nose, that thin dusty coat, that watery blue, inventive eye—all mountebanks and charlatans and street corner fakers have something of this man in them —and yet——"

He came hustling back.

"Here you are now!" he exclaimed, as he put down a small washpan full of water. "Now you just take this and rub it in good. Don't be afraid; it won't hurt the finest fabric or skin. I know what all the ingredients are. I worked on it three years before I discovered it. Everybody in Binghamton knows me. If it don't work, just write me at any time and you can get your money back."

In his eager routine presentation of his material he seemed to forget that we were present, here and now, and could demand our money back before he left. In a fitting spirit of camaraderie Speed rubbed the soap on his hands and spots which had for several days defied ordinary soap-cleansing processes immediately disappeared. Similarly, Franklin, who had acquired a few stains, salved his hands. He washed them in the pan of water standing on the engine box, and declared the soap a success. From my lofty perch in the car I now said to Mr. Vallaurs (the name on the label of the bottle), "Well, now you've made fifteen cents."

"Not quite," he corrected, with the eye of a holy disputant. "There are eight ingredients in that besides the cornmeal and the bottle alone costs me four and one-half cents."

"Is that so?" I continued—unable to take him seriously and yet sympathizing with him, he seemed so futile and so prodigal of his energy. "Then I really suppose you don't make much of anything?"

"Oh, yes, I do," he replied, seemingly unconscious of my jesting mood, and trying to be exact in the interpretation of his profit. "I make a little, of course. I'm only introducing it now, and it takes about all I make to get it around. I've got it in all the stores of Binghamton. I've been in the chemical business for years now. I got up some perfumes here a few years ago, but some fellows in the wholesale business did me out of them."

"I see," I said, trying to tease him and so bring forth any latent animosity which he might be concealing against fate or life. He looked to me to be a man who had been kicked about from pillar to post. "Well, when you get this well started and it looks as though it would be a real success, some big soap or chemical manufacturer will come along and take it away from you. You won't make anything out of it."

"Won't I?" he rejoined defiantly, taking me with entire seriousness and developing a flash of opposition in his eyes. "No, he won't, either. I've had that done to me before, but it won't happen this time. I know the tricks of them sharps. I've got all this patented. The last time I only had my application in. That's why I'm out here on this road today interducin' this myself. I lost the other company I was interested in. But I'm going to take better care of this one. I want to see that it gets a good start."

He seemed a little like an animated scarecrow in his mood.

"Oh, I know," I continued dolefully, but purely in a jesting way, "but they'll get you, anyhow. They'll swallow you whole. You're only a beginner; you're all right now, so long as your business is small, but just wait until it looks good enough to fight for and they'll come and take it away from you. They'll steal or imitate it, and if you say anything they'll look up your past and have you arrested for something you did twenty or thirty years ago in Oshkosh or Oskaloosa. Then they'll have your first wife show up and charge you with bigamy or they'll prove that you stole a horse or something. Sure —they'll get it away from you," I concluded.

"No, they won't either," he insisted, a faint suspicion that I was joking with him beginning to dawn on him. "I ain't never had but one wife and I never stole any horses. I've got this patented now and I'll make some money out of it, I think. It's the best soap"—(and here as he thought of his invention once more his brow cleared and his enthusiasm rose)—"the most all-round useful article that has ever been put on the market. You gentlemen ought really to take a thirty-cent bottle"— he went back and produced a large one—"it will last you a lifetime. I guarantee it not to soil, mar or injure the finest fabric or skin. Cornmeal is the chief ingredient and eight other chemicals, no akali. I wish you'd take a few of my cards"—he produced a handful of these—"and if you find anyone along the road who stands in need of a thing of this kind I wish you'd just be good enough to give 'em one so's they'll know where to write. I'm right here in Binghamton. I've been here now for twenty years or more. Every druggist knows me."

He looked at us with an unconsciously speculative eye —as though he were wondering what service we would be to him.

Franklin took the cards and gave him fifteen cents. Speed was still washing his hands, some new recalcitrant spots having been discovered. I watched the man as he proceeded to his rattletrap vehicle.

"Well, gentlemen, I'll be saying good day to you. Will you be so kind as to return that pan to that lady up there, when you're through with it? She was very accommodating about it."

"Certainly, certainly," replied Franklin, "we'll attend to it."

Once he had gone there ensued a long discussion of inventors and their fates. Here was this one, fifty years of age, if he was a day, and out on the public road, advertising a small soap which could not possibly bring him the reward he desired soon.

"You see, he's going the wrong way about it," Franklin said. "He's putting the emphasis on what he can do personally, when he ought to be seeing about what others can do for him; he should be directing as a manager, instead of working as a salesman. And another thing, he places too much emphasis upon local standards ever to become broadly successful. He said over and over that all the druggists and automobile supply houses in Binghamton handle his soap. That's nothing to us. We are, as it were, overland citizens and the judgments of Binghamton do not convince us of anything any more than the judgments of other towns and crossroad communities along our route. Every little community has its standards and its locally successful ones. The thing that will determine actual success is a man's ability or inability to see outside and put upon himself the test of a standard peculiar to no one community but common to all. This man was not only apparently somewhat mystified when we asked him what scheme he had to reach the broader market with his soap; he appeared never to have approached in his own mind that possibility at all. So he could never become more than partially successful or rich."

"Very true," I assented, "but a really capable man wouldn't work for him. He'd consider him too futile and try to take his treasure away from him and then the poor creature would be just where he was before, compelled to invent something else. Any man who would work for him wouldn't actually be worth having. It would be a case of the blind leading the blind."

There was much more of this—a long discussion. We agreed that any man who does anything must have so much more than the mere idea—must have vision, the ability to control and to organize men, a magnetism for those who are successful—in short, that mysterious something which we call personality. This man did not have it. He was a poor scrub, blown hither and yon by all the winds of circumstance, dreaming of some far-off supremacy which he never could enjoy or understand, once he had it.

CHAPTER XIV

BINGHAMTON—"Bimington," as Franklin confusedly called it in trying to ask the way of someone—now dawned swiftly upon us. I wouldn't devote a line to those amazingly commercial towns and cities of America which are so numerous if the very commercial life of the average American weren't so interesting to me. If anyone should ask me "What's in Binghamton?" I should confess to a sense of confusion, as if he were expecting me to refer to something artistic or connected in any way with the world of high thought. But then, what's in Leeds or Sheffield or Nottingham, or in Stettin or Hamburg or Bremen? Nothing save people, and people are always interesting, when you get enough of them.

When we arrived in Binghamton there was a parade, and a gala holiday atmosphere seemed everywhere prevailing. Flags were out, banners were strung across the roadway; in every street were rumbling, large flag-bedecked autotrucks and vehicles of various descriptions loaded with girls and boys in white (principally girls) and frequently labeled "Boost Johnson City."

"What in the world is Johnson City, do you suppose?" I asked of Franklin. "Are they going to change the name of Binghamton to Johnson City?"

Speed was interested in the crowds. "Gee, this is a swell town for girls," he commented; but after we had alighted and walked about among them for a time, they did not seem so attractive to me. But the place had a real if somewhat staccato air of gayety.

"Where is Johnson City?" I asked of a drug clerk of whom we were buying a sundae.

"Oh, it's a town out here—a suburb that used to be called Leicestershire. They're renaming it after a man out there—R. G. Johnson."

"Why?"

"Oh, well, he's made a big success of a shoe business out there that employs two thousand people and he's given money for different things."

"So they're naming the town after him?"

"Yes. He's a pretty good fellow, I guess. They say he is."

Not knowing anything of Mr. Johnson, good, bad, or indifferent, I agreed with myself to suspend judgment. A man who can build up a shoe manufacturing business that will employ two thousand people and get the residents of a fair-sized city or town to rename it after him is doing pretty well, I think. He couldn't be a Dick Turpin or a Jesse James; not openly, at least. People don't rename towns after Dick Turpins.

But Binghamton soon interested me from another point of view, for stepping out of this store I saw a great red, eight or nine story structure labeled the Kilmer Building, and then I realized I was looking at the home of "Swamp Root," one of those amazing cure-all remedies which arise, shine, make a fortune for some clever compounder and advertiser, and then after a period disappear. Think of Hood's Sarsaparilla, Ayer's Sarsaparilla, Peruna, Omega Oil, Lydia E. Pinkham's Vegetable Compound! American inventions, each and all, purchased by millions. Why don't the historians tell us of the cure-alls of Greece and Rome and Egypt and Babylon? There must have been some.

Looking at Dr. Kilmer's Swamp Root Building reminded me of a winter spent in a mountain town in West Virginia. It had a large and prosperous drug store, where one night I happened to be loafing for a little while, to take shelter from the snow that was falling heavily. Presently there entered an old, decrepit negro woman who hobbled up to the counter, and fumbling under her black shawl, produced a crumpled dollar bill.

"I want a bottle of Swamp Root," she said.

"I'll tell you how it is, mammy," said the clerk, a dapper country beau, with a most oily and ingratiating manner. "If you want to take six bottles it's only five dollars. Six bottles make a complete cure. If you take the whole six now, you've got 'em. Then you've got the complete cure."

The old woman hesitated. She was evidently as near the grave with any remedy as without one.

"All right," she said, after a moment's pause.

So the clerk wrapped six bottles into a large, heavy parcel, took the extra bills which she produced and rang them up in his cash register. And meanwhile she gathered her cure under her shawl, and hobbled forth, smiling serenely. It depressed me at the time, but it was none of my business.

Now as I looked at this large building, I wondered how many other hobbling mammies had contributed to its bricks and plate glass—and why.

There was another large building, occupied by a concern called the Ansco Company, which seemed to arouse the liveliest interest in Franklin. He had at some previous time been greatly interested in cameras and happened to know that a very large camera company, situated somewhere in America, had once stolen from this selfsame Ansco Company some secret process relating to the manufacture of a flexible film and had proceeded therewith to make so many millions that the user of the stolen process eventually became one of the richest men in America, one of our captains of great industries.

But the owners of the Ansco Company were dissatisfied. Like the citizens in the ancient tale who are robbed and cry "Stop thief!" they sued and sued and sued in the courts. First they sued in a circuit court, then in a state court of appeals, then in a federal court and then before the United States Supreme Court. There were countless lawyers and bags and bags of evidence; reversals, new trials, stays, and errors in judgment, until finally, by some curious turn of events, the United States Supreme Court decided that the process invented by the Ansco Company really did belong to said Ansco Company and that all other users of the process were interlopers and would have to repay to said Ansco Company all they had ever stolen and more—a royalty on every single camera they had ever sold.   So the Ansco Company, like the virtuous but persecuted youth or girl in the fairy tale, was able to collect the millions of which it had been defrauded and live happily ever afterwards.

Leaving Binghamton, we went out along the beautiful Susquehanna, which here in the heart of the city had been parked for a little way, and saw all the fine houses of all the very wealthy people of Binghamton.   Then we drove along a street crowded with more and more beautiful homes, all fresh and airy with flowers and lawns and awnings, and at last we came to Johnson City, or Leicestershire as it once was.   Here were the remains of a most tremendous American celebration—flags and buntings and signs and a merry-go-round.   In front of a new and very handsome Catholic Church which was just building hung a large banner reading "The noblest Roman of them all—R. G. Johnson"—a flare of enthusiasm which I take it must have had some very solid substance behind it.   Down in a hollow, was a very, very, very large red factory with its countless windows and great towering stacks and a holiday atmosphere about it, and all around it were houses and houses and houses, all new and all very much alike.   You could see that Mr. Johnson and his factory and his protégés had grown exceedingly fast.   And in the streets still were wagons with bunting on them and people in them, and we could see that there had just been a procession, with soldiers and boy scouts and girls—but alas, we had missed it.

"Well," I said to Franklin, "now you see how it is. Here is the reward of virtue.   A man builds a great business and treats his employés fairly and everybody loves him.   Isn't that so?"

Franklin merely looked at me. He has a way of just contemplating you, at times—noncommittally.

It was soon after leaving Binghamton that we encountered the first of a series of socalled "detours," occurring at intervals all through the states of New York, Ohio and Indiana, and which we later came to conclude were the invention of the devil himself. Apparently traffic on the roads of the states has increased so much of late that it has necessitated the repairing of former "made" roads and the conversion of old routes of clay into macadam or vitrified brick. Here in western New York (for we left Pennsylvania at Halstead for awhile) they were all macadam, and in many places the state roads socalled (roads paid for by the money of the state and not of the county) were invariably supposed to be the best. All strolling villagers and rurals would tell you so. As a matter of fact, as we soon found for ourselves, they were nearly always the worst, for they hummed with a dusty, whitey traffic, which soon succeeded in wearing holes in them of a size anywhere from that of a dollar to that of a washtub or vat. Traveling at a rate of much more than ten miles an hour over these hollows and depressions was almost unendurable. Sometimes local motorists and farmers in a spirit of despair had cut out a new road in the common clay, while a few feet higher up lay the supposedly model "state road," entirely unused. At any rate, wherever was the best and shortest road, there were repairs most likely to be taking place, and this meant a wide circle of anywhere from two or three to nine miles. A wretched series of turns and twists calculated to try your spirit and temper to the breaking point.

"Detours! Detours! Detours!" I suddenly exclaimed at one place in western Ohio. "I wish to heaven we could find some part of this state which wasn't full of detours." And Speed would remark: "Another damn detour! Well, what do you think of that? I'd like to have a picture of this one—I would!"

This, however, being the first we encountered, did not

seem so bad. We jounced and bounced around it and eventually regained the main road, spinning on to Owego, some fifteen or twenty miles away.

Day was beginning to draw to a close. The wane of our afternoons was invariably indicated these August days by a little stir of cool air coming from somewhere —perhaps hollows and groves—and seeming to have a touch of dew and damp in it. Spirals of gnats appeared spinning in the air, following us a little way and then being left behind or overtaken and held flat against our coats and caps. I was always brushing off gnats at this hour. We were still in that same Susquehanna Valley I have been describing, rolling on between hills anywhere from eight hundred to a thousand feet high and seeing the long shadows of them stretch out and cover the valley. Wherever the sun struck the river it was now golden—a bright, lustreful gold—and the hills seemed dotted with cattle, some with bells that tinkled. Always at this time evening smokes began to curl up from chimneys and the labor of the day seemed to be ending in a pastoral of delight.

"Oh, Franklin," I once exclaimed, "this is the ideal hour. Can you draw me this?"

At one point he was prompted to make a sketch. At another I wanted to stop and contemplate a beautiful bend in the river. Soon Owego appeared, a town say of about five thousand, nestling down by the waterside amid a great growth of elms, and showing every element of wealth and placid comfort. A group of homes along the Susquehanna, their backs perched out over it, reminded us of the houses at Florence on the Arno and Franklin had to make a sketch of these. Then we entered the town over a long, shaky iron bridge and rejoiced to see one of the prettiest cities we had yet found.

Curiously, I was most definitely moved by Owego. There is something about the old fashioned, comfortable American town at its best—the town where moderate wealth and religion and a certain social tradition hold— which is at once pleasing and yet comfortable—a gratifying and yet almost disturbingly exclusive state of affairs. At least as far as I am concerned, such places and people are antipodal to anything that I could ever again think, believe or feel. From contemplating most of the small towns with which I have come in contact and the little streets of the cities as contrasted with the great, I have come to dread the conventional point of view. The small mind of the townsmen is antipolar to that of the larger, more sophisticated wisdom of the city. It may be that the still pools and backwaters of communal life as represented by these places is necessary to the preservation of the state and society. I do not know. Certainly the larger visioned must have something to direct and the small towns and little cities seem to provide them. They are in the main fecundating centres—regions where men and women are grown for more labor of the same kind. The churches and moral theorists and the principle of self preservation, which in the lowly and dull works out into the rule of "live and let live," provide the rules of their existence. They do not gain a real insight into the fact that they never practise what they believe or that merely living, as man is compelled to live, he cannot interpret his life in the terms of the religionist or the moral enthusiast. Men are animals with dreams of something superior to animality, but the small town soul—or the little soul anywhere—never gets this straight. These are the places in which the churches flourish. Here is where your theologically schooled numskull thrives, like the weed that he is. Here is where the ordinary family with a little tradition puts an inordinate value on that tradition. All the million and one notions that have been generated to explain the universe here float about in a nebulous mist and create a dream world of error, a miasmatic swamp mist above which these people never rise. I never was in such a place for any period of time without feeling cabined, cribbed, confined, intellectually if not emotionally.

Speed went around the corner to look for a garage and Franklin departed in another direction for a bag of popcorn. Left alone, I contemplated a saloon which stood next door and on the window of which was pasted in gold glass letters "B. B. Delano." Thirsting for a glass of beer, I entered, and inside I found the customary small town saloon atmosphere, only this room was very large and clean and rather vacant. There was a smell of whiskey in the cask, a good smell, and a number of citizens drinking beer. A solemn looking bartender, who was exceptionally bald, was waiting on them. Some bits of cheese showed dolefully under a screen. I ordered a beer and gazed ruefully about. I was really not here, but back in Warsaw, Indiana, in 1886.

And in here was Mr. B. B. Delano himself, a small, dapper, rusty, red faced man, who, though only moderately intelligent, was pompous to the verge of bursting, as befits a small man who has made a moderate success in life. Yet Mr. B. B. Delano, as I was soon to discover, had his private fox gnawing at his vitals. There was a worm in the bud. Only recently there had been a great anti-liquor agitation and a fair proportion of the saloons all over the state had been closed. Three months before in this very town, at the spring election, "no license" had been voted. All the saloons here, to the number of four, would have to be closed, including Mr. Delano's, in the heart of the town. That meant that Mr. Delano would have to get another business of some kind or quit. I saw him looking at me curiously, almost mournfully.

"Touring the state?" he asked.

"We're riding out to Indiana," I explained. "I come from there."

"Oh, I see. Indiana! That's a nice little trip, isn't it? Well, I see lots of machines going through here these days, many more than I ever expected to see. It's made a difference in my business. Only"—and here followed a long account of his troubles. He owned houses and lands, a farm of three hundred acres not far out, on which he lived, and other properties, but this saloon obviously was his pet. "I'm thinking of making an eating place of it next fall," he added. " 'No license' may not last —forever." His eye had a shrewd, calculating expression.

"That's true," I said.

"It keeps me worried, though," he added doubtfully. "I don't like to leave now. Besides, I'm getting along. I'm nearly sixty," he straightened himself up as though he meant to prove that he was only forty, "and I like my farm. It really wouldn't kill me if I never could open this place any more." But I could see that he was talking just to hear himself talk, boasting. He was desperately fond of his saloon and all that it represented; not ashamed, by any means.

"But there's Newark and New York," I said. "I should think you'd like to go down there."

"I might," he agreed; "perhaps I will. It's a long way for me, though. Won't you have another drink— you and your friends?" By now Franklin and Speed were returning and Mr. Delano waved a ceremonious, inclusive hand, as if to extend all the courtesies of the establishment.

The bartender was most alert—a cautious, apprehensive person. I could see that Mr. Delano was inclined to be something of a martinet. For some reason he had conceived of us as personages—richer than himself, no doubt—and was anxious to live up to our ideas of things and what he thought we might expect.

"Well, now," he said, as we were leaving, "if you ever come through here again you might stop and see if I'm still here."

As Speed threw on the ignition spark and the machine began to rumble and shake, Mr. Delano proceeded up the handsome small town street with quite a stride. I could see that he felt himself very much of a personage— one of the leading figures of Owego.

CHAPTER XV

IT was a glorious night—quite wonderful. There are certain summer evenings when nature produces a poetic, emotionalizing mood. Life seems to talk to you in soft whispers of wonderful things it is doing. Marshes and pools, if you encounter any, exhale a mystic breath. You can look into the profiles of trees and define strange gorgon-like countenances—all the crones and spectres of a thousand years. (What images of horror have I not seen in the profiles of trees!) Every cottage seems to contain a lamp of wonder and to sing. Every garden suggests a tryst of lovers. A river, if you follow one, glimmers and whimpers. The stars glow and sing. They bend down like lambent eyes. All nature improvises a harmony—a splendid harmony—one of her rarest symphonies indeed.

And tonight as we sped out of Owego and I rested in the deep cushions of the car it seemed as if some such perfect symphony was being interpreted. Somewhere out of the great mystery of the unknowable was coming this rare and lovely something. What is God, I asked, that he should build such scenes as this? His forces of chemistry! His powers of physics! We complain and complain, but scenes like these compensate for many things. They weave and sing. But what are they? Here now are treetoads cheep-cheeping. What do they know of life—or do their small bodies contain a world of wonder, all dark to my five dull senses? And these sweet shadows—rich and fragrant—now mellowing, now poignant! I looked over my right shoulder quite by accident and there was a new moon hanging low in the west, a mere feather, its faintness reflected in the bosom of a still stream. We were careening along a cliff overhanging this river and as we did so along came a brightly lighted train following the stream bed and rushing somewhere, probably to New York. I thought of all the people on it and what they were doing, what dreaming, where going; what trysts, what plots, what hopes nurturing. I looked into a cottage door and there a group of people were singing and strumming—their voices followed us down the wind in music and laughter.

Somewhere along this road at some wayside garage we had to stop for oil and gas, as Speed referred to gasoline—always one quart of oil, I noticed, and about seven gallons of gasoline, the price being anywhere from $1.25 to $1.75, according to where we chanced to be. I was drowsing and dreaming, thinking how wonderful it all was and how pleasant our route would surely be, when a man came up on a motorcycle, a strained and wiry looking individual, who said he had just come through western New York and northern Ohio—one of those fierce souls who cover a thousand miles a day on a motorcycle. They terrify me.

Franklin, with an honest interest in the wellbeing of his car, was for gathering information as to roads. There was no mystery about our immediate course, for we were in a region of populous towns—Waverley, Elmira, Corning, Hornell—which on our map were marked as easy of access. The roads were supposed to be ideal. The great proposition before us, however, was whether once having reached Elmira we would go due north to Canandaigua and Rochester, thereby striking, as someone told us, a wonderful state road to Buffalo— *the* road—or whether we would do as I had been wishing and suggesting, cut due west, following the northern Pennsylvania border, and thereby save perhaps as much as a hundred and fifty miles in useless riding north and south.

Franklin was for the region that offered the best roads. I was for adventure, regardless of machines or roads. We had half compromised on the thought that it might be well to visit Warsaw, New York, which lay about half way between the two opposing routes with which we were opposing each other, and this solely because the name of one of my home towns in Indiana was Warsaw and this Warsaw, as my pamphlet showed, was about the same size. It was a sort of moonshiny, nonsensical argument all around; and this man who had just come through Warsaw from Buffalo had no particular good word to say for the roads. It was a hilly country, he said. "You climb one hill to get into Warsaw and five others to get out, and they're terrors." I could see a look of uncertainty pass over Franklin's face. Farewell to Warsaw, I thought.

But another bystander was not so sure. All the roads from here on leading toward Buffalo were very good. Many machines came through Warsaw. My spirits rose. We decided to postpone further discussion until we reached Elmira and could consult with an automobile club, perhaps. We knew we would not get farther than Elmira tonight; for we had chaffered away another hour, and it was already dusk.

We never experienced a more delightful evening on the whole trip. It was all so moving—the warm air, the new silvery moon, the trees on the hills forming dark shadows, the hills themselves gradually growing dim and fading into black, the twinkling lights here and there, fireflies, the river, this highroad always high, high above the stream. There were gnats but no mosquitoes—at least none when we were in motion—and our friend Speed, guiding the car with a splendid technique, was still able between twists and turns and high speeds and low speeds to toss back tale after tale of a daring and yet childlike character, which kept me laughing all the while. Speed was so naïve. He had such innocently gross and yet comfortable human things to relate of horses, cows, dogs, farm girls, farm boys, the studfarm business, with which he was once connected, and so on.

"Put on a slip and come down," he called to her.

"So she slipped on the stairs and came down."

(Do you remember that one? They were all like that.)

Once out of Owego, we were soon in Waverley, a town say of ten or fifteen thousand population, which we mistook at first for Elmira. Its streets were so wide and clean, its houses so large and comfortable, we saw on entering. I called Franklin's attention to the typical American atmosphere of this town too—the America of a slightly older day. There was a time not long ago when Americans felt that the beginning and end of all things was the home. Not anything great in construction or tragically magnificent, but just a comfortable home in which to grow and vegetate. Everything had to be sacrificed to it. It came to have a sacrosanct character: all the art, the joy, the hope which a youthful and ingenuous people were feeling and believing, expressed, or attempted to express themselves, in the home. It was a place of great trees, numerous flowerbeds, a spacious lawn, French windows, a square cupola, verandas, birdhouses. All the romance of a youthful spirit crept into these things and still lingers. You can feel as you look at them how virtuous the owners felt themselves to be, and how perfect their children, what marvels of men and women these latter were to become—pure and above reproach.

Alas for a dusty world that would not permit it—that will never permit any perfect thing to be. These houses, a little faded now, a little puffy with damp, a little heavier for paint, a little grey or brown or greenish black, suggest by their atmosphere that they have yielded up crops of children. We have seen several generations go by since they were built. Have they been any better than their sires, if as good? It seems to me as if I myself have witnessed a great revolt against all the binding perfection which these lovely homes represented. In my youthful day it was taken for granted that we were to be good and beautiful and true, and God was to reward us in heaven. We were to die and go straight before the throne of grace. Each of us was to take one wife or one husband to our heart and hearth. We were never to swindle or steal or lie or do anything wrong whatsoever. America was to make the sermon on the mount come true—and look at us. Have we done it?

I call attention to Pittsburg, Chicago, and New York, to go no further: to the orgies of trust building, stock gambling, stock watering, get rich quick-ing; to the scandals of politics and finance; to the endless divorces and remarriages and all the license of the stage and the hungry streets of harlots and kept women. Have we made the ten commandments work? Do not these small towns with their faded ideal homes stand almost as Karnak and Memphis—in their frail way pointing the vanity of religious and moral ideals in this world? We have striven for some things but not the ideals of the sermon on the mount. Our girls have not been virtuous beyond those of any other nation—our boys more honest than those of any other land. We have simply been human, and a little more human for being told that we were not or ought not to be so.

In Waverley, despite the fact that we had determined to reach Elmira before stopping for dinner, we became suddenly hungry and while "cruising," as Speed put it, down the principal street, about three quarters of a mile long, with various stores and movies in full swing, we discovered an irresistible "lunch car" crowded in between two buildings. Inside was the usual "hash slinger," at his pots and pans. He was a swarthy skinned black-haired youth, this impresario with a penchant for doing his work gallantly, like an acrobat. He had nothing to offer save pork and beans, ham and eggs, various sandwiches, and one kind of pie. All the remainder of his stock had been disposed of. I ordered ham and eggs— somehow in small towns I always feel safest in so doing. It was amusing to watch him "flip" an egg with a turn of the wrist and at the same time hold bantering converse with a frowsy headed youth whose face was pressed to a small porthole giving out onto the sidewalk. Every now and then, as we were eating, some familiar of the town would tap on the window to give evidence of his passing, and soon the place was invaded by five evening roysterers, smart boys of the town, who made all sorts of quips and jests as to the limited bill of fare.

"How about a whole egg? Have you got one?"

"Do you ever keep any salt and pepper here, Jake?"

"Somebody said you'd have a new pie, tomorrow. Is that right?"

"What's the matter with the old one?" inquired someone.

"Why, a feller bit into it by mistake. They're goin' to sell it to the shootin' gallery for a target."

"Why don't you fellers get up a new line o' dope?" interjected the host at one place. "My pies ain't in it with what you're springin'."

This drew a laugh and more chatter.

As I sat on a stool looking out and munching my "ham-and" I could not help thinking of the high spirits of all these towns we were passing. In Europe, in places of four or five times the size of this—Rotterdam, Amsterdam, The Hague, Dover, Amiens, Florence, Perugia, even Venice, I might say, I found no such flare nor any such zest for just living. What is it about Americans that gives all their small towns such an air? Somebody had already introduced the five-light lamp standard here, in one or two places. The stores were all brightly lighted and you could see boys and girls going up and down in the hope of those chance encounters with adventure which youths and maidens of all strata so crave. Noting all this, I said to myself that in Europe somehow, in towns of this size and much larger, things always seemed duller. Here in America there are always these boys and girls of no particular social caste, I take it, whose homes are not very attractive, whose minds and bodies are craving a touch of vitality—gay contact with someone of the other sex—and who find their social life in this way, on the streets. No doubt at this point someone will rise to say that they need more supervision. I am not so sure. As life expresses itself, so it should be, I fancy. All my sympathies go out to such young people, for I recall with what earnestness as a boy I used to do this same thing—how I wished and longed and how my body tingled at the thoughts of love and the promise of life to come.

Once on the road again, I hummed and meditated until suddenly I found myself dreaming. I wasn't on the high road between Binghamton and Elmira at all but in some happy land that hadn't anything to do with motoring— a land of youth and affection. Suddenly I sat up, wondering whether I had keeled over toward Franklin, and he had discovered that I had been asleep.

"We don't have to spend the night in Elmira, do we?" I ventured cautiously.

"Oh, no," said Franklin, amiably.

"Since it's so late, the next hotel we come to, we'd better tie up, don't you think,—I'm getting sleepy."

"All right for me," agreed Franklin. I couldn't tell whether he was sleepy or not.

Presently a great square old house came into view with trees and flowers and a light burning before it. It was so still now we seemed to have the night all to ourselves. No automobiles were in sight. We debated whether we would stay here.

"Oh, let's risk it," said Franklin. "It's only for one night, anyhow."

We were greeted by a tall, angular country boy with the air of one who is half asleep and a habit of running his hand through his hair. He had been serving three men in the rear with drinks. He led us up warm, stuffy, carpeted halls, lighted by oil lamps, into a small, musty chamber with a large, yellow, creaky bed. This and another similar apartment for Speed were all he could offer us.

It was hot. A few mosquitoes were buzzing. Still the prospect of a deep black sky and stars through the open window was soothing. I made a few joyless comments, which Franklin received in silence; and then we slept.

CHAPTER XVI

CHEMUNG

NEXT morning I was aroused at dawn, it seemed to me, by a pounding on a nearby door.

"Get up, you drunken hound!" called a voice which was unmistakably that of the young man who had rented us the room. "That's right, snore, after you stay up all night," he added; and he beat the door vehemently again.

I wanted to get up and protest against his inconsiderateness of the slumber of others and would have, I think, only I was interested to discover who the "drunken hound" might be and why this youth should be so abrupt with him. After all, I reflected, we were in a very poor hotel, the boy doing the knocking was a mere farm hand translated to the country hotel business, and anyhow we should soon be out of here. It was all life and color and if I didn't like it I needn't have stayed here the night before. Franklin would have gone on. But who was the "drunken hound"? The sound had ceased almost as abruptly as it had begun. The boy had gone downstairs. After awhile the light grew stronger and Franklin seemed to stir. I rose and pulled the shutters to, but could not sleep any more. The world outside looked so inviting. There were trees and great fields of grass and a few white houses scattered here and there and a heavy dew. I at once thought how delightful it would be to get up and ride on again.

"This is a typical middle west country hotel, even if it is in New York," said Franklin, sitting up and running his hand through his tousled hair. "That fellow he's calling a 'drunken hound' must be his father. I heard him tell Speed last night that his father slept in there."

Presently we threw open the shutters and made what use we could of the bowl and pitcher and the two small towels provided.

"How did you ever come to be an artist, Franklin?" I inquired idly, as I watched him stare out at the surrounding fields, while he sat putting on his shoes. "You told me once that you were a farm hand until you were nearly twentyfive."

"Nearly twentysix," he corrected. "Oh, I always wanted to draw and did, a little, only I didn't know anything about it. Finally I took a course in a correspondence school."

"Get out," I replied incredulously.

"Yes, I did," he went on. "They sent me instructions how to lay in with pen and ink various sorts of line technique on sheets of paper that were ruled off in squares—long lines, short lines, stipple, 'crosspatch' and that sort of thing. They made some other suggestions that had some value: what kind of ink and pens and paper to buy. I used to try to draw with ordinary writing ink and pens."

"But a correspondence school——" I protested.

"I know," he said. "It seems ridiculous. It's true, just the same. I didn't know where else to go and besides I didn't have the money. There was a school in Indianapolis but they wanted too much—I tried it awhile but the instructor knew very little. The correspondence school wanted only six dollars for fifteen lessons, and they took it in part payments."

He smiled reminiscently.

"Well, how did you come to get started, finally?"

"Oh, I worked most of my method out for myself. Art is a matter of feeling, anyhow. The drawing in squares gave me an idea which made me abandon the squares. I used to write poetry too, of sorts—or tried to—and one day I wrote a poem and decided to illustrate it and take it down to one of the Indianapolis newspapers, because I had seen others in there somewhat like it—I mean illustrated in pen and ink. It was a poem about

October, or something. My father thought I was wasting my time. He wanted me to tend the farm. But I took the poem down and they bought it right away—gave me six dollars for it."

"And then what?" I asked, deeply interested.

"Well, that rather astonished my father—as much, if not more, than it did me. He never imagined there was any money in that sort of thing—and unless you were going to make money——" He waved his hand deprecatively.

"I know," I agreed. "And then what?"

"Well, they bought another and my father began to think there was something in it—in art, you know, if you want to call it that, in Indiana, at that time!"—he paused. "Still I can't tell you how much feeling I put in those things, either,—the trees, the birds flying, the shocked corn. I used to stop when I was plowing or reaping and stand and look at the sky and the trees and the clouds and wish I could paint them or do something. The big cities seemed so far off. But it's Indiana that seems wonderful to me now."

"And to me," I said. "Like a mother. Because we were brought up there, I suppose."

Sitting on the edge of this wretched hotel bed, Franklin smiled vaguely, his fine hand moving through his glistening white hair.

"And then?"

"Well, one day the editor in Indianapolis said I ought to send some of my drawing down to New York, or go down—that I would get along. He thought I ought to study art."

"Yes?"

"Well, I saved enough drawing for the *Indianapolis News* and writing poetry and pitching hay and plowing wheat to go that autumn to Chicago; I spent three months in the Art Institute. Being in those days a good Sunday School boy, a publisher of religious literature, socalled, bought some work of me and at Christmas time I sold a half page to the old Chicago *Record*. The following fall I went to New York. I found a little room and sold sketches, and then I got on a paper—the *News*. You remember."

"Certainly. Was that your first place?"

"The very first."

"And I thought you had been in New York years and years."

I can see Franklin even yet, standing before his drawingboard in the newspaper office, making horrible Sunday "layouts." He was so gentle, good looking and altogether attractive.

"Yes, and then what?"

"Well, after my year's contract which started with the *News* had expired, I tried freelancing. This didn't go very well; so I determined not to spend all my savings visiting art editors. I boarded a boat one day and went to Europe. Four months later, I returned to New York and rented a studio. After I had paid my first month's rent I was broke. At the magazines I would say that I had just returned from abroad, so that I got plenty of work, but I owned neither easel nor chair. After a few days the janitor, if you please, came to me and said that he and his wife had been talking about me and thought perhaps I needed some money and that they had eighty dollars upstairs which I could have right away if I wanted to use it. It sounds wild, but it's true. They said I could take it and pay it back whenever I got ready, in six months or a year or two years."

My estimate of poor old human nature was rapidly rising.

"Did you take it?"

"Yes, a part of it. I had to, in a way; but I paid it back in a little while. I often think of those people."

We stopped talking about his career then and went down to look in the diningroom and after our car. The place was so unsatisfactory and it was still so early we decided not to remain for breakfast.

As I was sitting on the porch, Franklin having gone off to rout out Speed, an automobile approached containing a man and three women and bearing a plumcolored pennant labeled "Lansing, Michigan." Pennants seem to be a habit with cars coming from the west. These tourists halted, and I was morally certain that they did so because of my presence here. They thought others were breakfasting. With much fluttering of their motoring regalia, the women stepped out and shook themselves while their escort departed to make inquiries. Presently he returned and with him our young host, who in the clear morning light seemed much more a farmer than ever —a plow hand. Something about his crude, untutored strength and energy appealed to me. I thought of his drunken father and how he might be trying to make the best of this place, against lack of experience and with a ne'er do well parent on his hands. Now he fixed me with a steady eye.

"You people goin' to have breakfast?" he asked.

"No," I replied, pleasantly.

"You ain't?"

"No."

"Well," he went on, turning to the newcomers, "then *you* people can have breakfast."

So, I thought, these people will have to eat the very poor breakfast that is being prepared for us. It will serve them right—the vulgar, showy creatures. As we were departing, however, Franklin explained that there was an extra charge which he had not troubled to dispute, for something which we had apparently not had. I explained that it was for the meal we had not eaten.

Once more, then, we drove off along more of those delightful country roads which in the early morning sun, with the fields glistening with dew, and laborers making their way to work, and morning birds on the wing, were too lovely. The air, after our stuffy room, was so refreshing, *I* began to sing. Little white houses hugged distant green hillsides, their windows shining like burnished gold. Green branches hung over and almost brushed our faces. The sky, the shade, the dew was heavenly. I thought of Franklin and his father and of him in his father's fields at dawn, looking at the trees—those fog wrapped trees of dawn—and wishing he was an artist.

Meanwhile, my mind was busy with the sharp contrast this whole progress was presenting to my tour of Europe, even the poorest and most deserted regions I visited. In England, France, Germany, Italy, Holland, Belgium, Switzerland, there was so much to see—so much that was memorable or quaint or strange or artistic —but here; well, here there were just towns like this one and Binghamton and Scranton and Wilkes-Barré, places the best for which you could say was that they were brisk and vivid and building something which in the future will no doubt seem very beautiful,—I'm sure of it.

And yet I kept saying to myself that notwithstanding all this, all I could sum up against America even, it was actually better than Europe. And why? Well, because of a certain indefinable something—either of hope or courage or youth or vigor or illusion, what you will; but the average American, or the average European transplanted to America, is a better or at least a more dynamic person than the average European at home, even the Frenchman. He has more grit, verve, humor, or a lackadaisical slapdash method which is at once efficient, self-sustaining, comforting. His soul, in spite of all the chains wherewith the ruling giants are seeking to fetter him, is free. As yet, regardless of what is or may be, he does not appear to realize that he is not free or that he is in any way oppressed. There are no ruling classes, to him. He sings, whistles, jests, laughs boisterously; matches everybody for cigars, beers, meals; chews tobacco, spits freely, smokes, swears, rolls to and fro, cocks his hat on one side of his head, and altogether by and large is a regular "hell of a feller." He doesn't know anything about history, or very little, and doesn't give a damn. He doesn't know anything about art,—but, my God, who with the eternal hills and all nature for a background cannot live without representative art? His food isn't extraordinarily good, though plentiful, his

clothes are made by Stein-Bloch, or Hart, Schaffner &
Marx, and altogether he is a noisy, blatant, contented
mess—but oh, the gay, selfsufficient soul of him! no
moans! no tears! Into the teeth of destiny he marches,
whistling "Yankee Doodle" or "Turkey in the Straw."
In the parlance of his own streets, "Can you beat him?"

Nevertheless my sympathies kept reverting to the
young innkeeper and I finally got out a map to see if
I could discover the name of the very small town or
crossroads where this hotel was situated. It proved to
be Chemung.

Instantly I recalled the story of a gubernatorial aspir-
ant of twenty years before who had come from this very
place or county in New York. Previously a district at-
torney or lieutenant governor, he had one day been nominated for the governorship, on the reigning ticket. His
chances were splendid. There was scarcely a cloud in
the sky. He was believed to be brilliant, promising, a
presidential possibility of the future. An important
meeting was called in New York, I believe, at Madison
Square Garden very likely, to ratify and celebrate his
nomination. All the élite politically who customarily
grace such events were present. The Garden was filled.
But, alas, at the sound of the applause called forth by
his opening burst of oratory, he paused and took off his
coat—quite as he would at an upstate rally, here in
Chemung. The audience gasped. The sophisticated
leaders of the city groaned. What! Take off your coat
at a political address in Madison Square Garden? A
candidate for governorship of the state of New York?
It completely destroyed him. He was never heard of
more. I, a mere stripling at the time, brooded long over
this sudden turn of fortune as exemplifying a need to
discriminate between audiences and classes. It put a
cool, jesuitical thought in my mind that I did not soon
forget. "Never remove your coat in the wrong place,"
was a maxim that dwelt with me for some time. And
here we were in Chemung, the place to which this man
subsequently retired, to meditate, no doubt, over the

costly follies and errors we sometimes commit without the ability or the knowledge to guard against them.

An hour and a half later we were having breakfast at Elmira, a place much like Binghamton, in the customary "Rathskeller-Grill-Café de Berlin." This one was all embossed with gold paper and Teutonic hunting scenes, and contained the usual heavy mission tables, to say nothing of a leftover smell of cigarettes burned the night before. There were negro waiters too, and another group of motorists having a most elaborate breakfast and much talk of routes and cars and distant cities. Here it was necessary for us to decide the course of our future progress, so we shortly set off in search of the local automobile club.

CHAPTER XVII

WE found an official of the Elmira Automobile Club, a small, stoop-shouldered, bald, eye-sockety person who greeted us with a genial rub of his hands and a hearty smirk as though we were just *the* persons, among all others, whom he was most pleased to see.

"Come right in, gentlemen," he called, as Franklin and I appeared in the doorway. "What can I do for you? Looking for maps or a route or something?"

"Tell me," I inquired, anxious to make my point at once, "are there any good roads due west of here which would take us straight into Ohio, without going north to Buffalo?"

He scratched his head.

"No, I don't think there are," he replied; "most of the good roads are north of here, around Rochester, where the main line of traffic is. Now there is a good road—or a part of one"—and then he commenced a long rambling account of some road that was about to be built—but as yet—etc., etc. I saw my idea of a somewhat different trip going glimmering.

"But here," he went on, picking up one of those maps which various hotels and towns combine to get up to attract automobile trade, "what's the matter with the Onondaga trail from here on? That takes you up through Corning, Bath, Avoca, Dansville, Geneseo, and Avon, and up there you strike the main road through Batavia right into Buffalo. That's a fine road, good hard macadam nearly all the way, and when you get to Avon you strike one of the best hotels anywhere. When you get up there you just roll your car right into the grounds —walk into the restaurant and ask 'em to give you some of their chicken and waffles. You'll just be about ready for it when you get there and you'll thank me for telling you."

I fancied I could see the cloven hoof of the Avon hotel keeper mystically present in that speech. However, far to the left on another branch of the same trail I saw my beloved Warsaw, New York.

"What's the matter with the road up through here?" I asked, putting my finger on it.

"Well, I'll tell you," he said, "there it is mostly dirt and there are no good dirt roads as you know, if you've autoed much. A man called up here this morning and wanted to know if there were any good dirt roads out of here to Utica and I said to him, 'My dear sir, there aren't any good dirt roads anywhere. There ain't any such thing.' "

I seemed to see the Avon hotel keeper smiling and beckoning once more—a chicken in one hand, a plate of waffles in the other—but he didn't appeal to me at all. These hotel routes and these Americans who are so quick to capitalize everything—motor routes, scenery, water falls, everything! "Curses, curses, curses," I said to myself softly, "why must everything be turned into business?" Besides, many portions of the roads over which we had come in New Jersey and Pennsylvania were dirt and they were excellent. I smiled serenely, determined to make the best of whatever happened and however much I might want to go to Warsaw, New York.

But our friend seemed determined to send us via Avon and Batavia. He went on telling us how anxious he had been to convince the man who had telephoned that there were no good dirt roads, but I was happy to note that apparently he had not been successful. The man probably knew something about state and dirt roads, as we had found them, and refused to take his direction. I was pleased to think that whatever Franklin might be concluding, because of his advice, we still had some distance yet to travel before we would have to decide not to go to Warsaw—all of seventyfive or a hundred miles anyhow. For, extending that distance our proposed route was directly toward Warsaw, and that cheered me a bit.

And now beyond Elmira for a distance of one hundred and twenty miles or more, all the way into Warsaw, we had one of the most delightful days of any—a perfectly heavenly day, the weather so fine, the sky so blue, and not a tinge of anything save harvesting weather anywhere. As we rolled along the sound of the reaper was heard in the land—great mechanical combinations of engines and threshers and grain separators and straw stack builders—a great flume or trough reaching high in the air and carrying out the grainless straw and chaff, blowing it on a single mound. It was really wonderful to see America's daily bread being garnered mile after mile, and mile after mile.

And the marvelous herds of cattle, mostly Holstein, which yield the milk supply for the trains that pour nightly and daily towards that vast plexus of cities called New York, with its eight million people.

In this Pennsylvania-New York valley alone, which seemed to stretch unbroken from Wilkes-Barré to western New York, from the Chesapeake really to the falls of the Geneseo, there were indeed cattle on a thousand hills.

There was too much traffic along the first portion of the road out of Elmira and by now I was beginning to get an idea of the magnitude of the revolution which the automobile had effected. Thirty years ago these roads would have been traveled as elsewhere, if at all, by wagons and buggies, but now on this Saturday morning the ways were crowded with farmers coming to town in automobiles, or as Speed always put it, "in autos and Fords." Why this useful little machine should be sniffed at is a puzzle to me, for it seemed to look nearly as well and to travel quite as fast as any of the others. The farmers were using it as a family carryall—taking in sacks of wheat or other products to town and bringing home groceries and other needfuls.

In Corning, a town of about ten or twelve thousand population, some twenty miles west of Elmira, we found a city as prosperous as most of the others apparently, and as naïve. It being Saturday, the natives from the surrounding country were beginning to come in, but I did not notice any of that rural flavor which had seemed to characterize them in my youth. On leaving every town where we had loitered too long we made a solemn pact that we would not waste so much time in unimportant towns that were nearly all alike; but whenever one rose into view and we dashed into a principal street lined with stores and crowded with people, it was beyond human nature not to get out and look around a little. There was always the excuse of picture cards for a record of our trip, or meals or a drink of some kind or even popcorn (Franklin's favorite), or peanuts or candy. Think of it—three grown men getting out to buy candy!

Here in Corning it was that I first noticed that Franklin had a peculiarly sharp nose and eye for ferreting out ideal rural types. Those who have read Hamlin Garland's "Main Traveled Roads" will understand instantly what I mean—not the crude, obvious, one might almost say burlesque types, but those more difficult and pathetic characters who do their best not to seem to be of the country and yet who are always so obviously of it. I tried my best, as Franklin nudged my arm at different times, to formulate to myself what it is about these interesting individuals—the boy or woman or young man from the country—dressed in those peculiarly new and store-y store clothes that makes them so appealing and so pathetic to me. In "Main Traveled Roads" one gets a sense of it all. Times have changed a little since then and yet here were the same types—the red-cheeked, wide-eyed boy in the new brown suit and twentyfive cent hat looking at people as if all the world and its every gesture were a surprise, and the women walking about streets impossible, one must say, from a social and intellectual point of view, trying to look as if they had something to do and some place to go. I always suspect them of

eating their meals in some wagon back of some store—
a cold snack brought along for the occasion or asking the
privilege of adding a few things out of a basket to the
repast provided, say, by a glass of ice-cream soda.

Oh, the lovely roads by which they came, the sylvan
nooks where their homes are, the small schoolhouses,
the wide spacious fields with crows and blackbirds and
bluejays for company, the grey snowy fields in winter,
these black filigree trees for a border—and the great
cities which haunt the dreams of these boys and girls
and finally lure so many of them away.

Beyond Corning came more delightful small towns,
"Painted Post," with a church so singularly plain, a small
spire so thin and tall that it was truly beautiful; Camp-
bell, with one of these typical rural streets of homes
which make you wish that you might stay for days, visiting country relatives; Savona, a hot country store street
where Speed stopped for oil and gas. Anent Savona,
which hadn't a tree to bless itself with, where Franklin
and I sat and baked while Speed replenished his stores,
Franklin told me the story of why the principal street of
Carmel, his home town, was treeless. Once there had
been trees there, beautiful ones, but with the arrival of
the metropolitan spirit and a desire to catch passing
automobile trade it was decided to widen the street somewhat and make it more commercial and therefore more
attractive. The idea which first popped into the minds
of all who desired metropolitan improvement was that
the trees should come down.

"Why?" asked some lover of the trees as things of
beauty.

"Well, you don't see any trees in Main Street, Indianapolis, do you?" replied another triumphantly.

The battle was lost and won right there—Main Street,
Indianapolis, was the criterion. "Are we going to be
like Indianapolis—or Chicago or New York—or are
we not?" I can hear some sturdy rural asking. "If
not, let the trees stand."

What rural would save any tree as against being like

New York, I'd like to know. That is why, I suspect, we baked for fifteen minutes in Savona.

And then came "the toon o' Bath," as we forever after called it, for a reason which will appear,—a dear, lovely, summery town, with a square so delightful that on sight of it we instantly got out and loitered in the shade for over an hour, in spite of our resolution.

Here in the east, for some reason, this idea of a plain green open square, without any execrable reproduction of an American Civil War soldier perched high aloft on a tall shaft, has remained untainted. Wilkes-Barré, New Milford, Owego and now Bath had one, and in New England and New Jersey I have seen scores. The county offices are as a rule put around it, but not in it, as is the rule farther west.

In the west—everywhere west of Pennsylvania and sometimes east of it—a public square is not complete without a courthouse or at least a soldiers' or sailors' monument—or both—planted in the centre of it, and these almost an exact reproduction of every other courthouse or monument for one thousand miles about. The idea of doing anything original is severely frowned upon. Whatever else you may be in America or elsewhere, apparently you must not be different. Hold fast to the type, and do as your ancestors did! Build all courthouses and monuments as courthouses and monuments should be built—that is, true to tradition. If you don't believe this, visit any countyseat between New York and Seattle.

But this square, in Bath, like some others in New England and that in Owego, was especially pleasing because it had no courthouse and no monuments, merely a bandstand and a great spread of benches placed under wide-armed and sturdy trees. Under their high branches, which spread as a canopy over the walks and benches below, were festooned, on wires, a number of lights for the illumination of the place at night. About it, on the different sides, were residences, churches, a public school, some county offices, and to the east stores, all with a peaceful, rural flavor. Several farmer families were eating their meals from baskets as they sat in wagons, their horses unhitched and fastened behind. On the benches were seated a number of old soldiers idling in the shade. Why old soldiers should be so numerous at this day and date was more than I could understand, and I said so. It was now fiftyfour years since the war began, and here they were, scores of them apparently, all fairly hale and looking scarcely sixtyfive. They must have been at least seventy years each to have been of any service in the great war of the rebellion.

Near here, we discovered, there was an old soldiers' home—a state home—and this being Saturday afternoon, the streets were full of them. They looked to be a crotchety, cantankerous crew. Later on we saw many of them in the road leading out to their institution—drunk. In order to strike up a conversation with some of the old soldiers, we asked three of them sitting on a bench about a drunken woman who was pirouetting before them in a frowzy, grimy gaiety.

"That," said one, a little, thin-shouldered, clawy type of man with a high, cracked voice, a clownish expression, and a laugh as artificial and mechanical as any laugh could be, a sort of standard, everyday habit laugh, "Oh, that's the Pete and Duck." (I give it as it sounded.)

"The Pete and Duck!" I exclaimed.

"Yes, sir, the Pete and Duck"—and then came the high, cackling, staccato laugh. "That's what they call her round here, the Pete and Duck. I dunno howsoever they come to call her that, but that's what they call her, the Pete and Duck, and a drunken old —— she is, too, —just an old drunken girl"—and then he went off into a gale of pointless laughter, slapping his knees and opening his mouth very wide.

"That's all I've ever hearn her called. Ain't that so, Eddie—he, he! ho, ho! ha, ha! Yes—that's what they allus call 'er—the Pete and Duck. She's nothin' but just a poor old drunken fool like many another in this here toon o' Bath—he, he! ho, ho! ha, ha!

"But then she ain't the only funny thing in Bath neither. There's a buildin' they're puttin' up over there," he continued, "that has front and back but no sides— the only buildin' in the toon o' Bath that ain't got no sides but just front and back. He, he! ha, ha! ho, ho!"

We looked in the direction of this building, but it was nothing more than an ordinary store building, being erected between two others by the party wall process. It was a bank, apparently, and the front was being put together out of white marble.

"Yes, sir, the only buildin' in the toon o' Bath that ain't got no sides, but just front and back," and he lapsed again into his vacant, idle laughter. Evidently he had been given over to the task of making sport, or trying to, out of the merest trifles for so many years that he had lost all sense of proportion and value. The least thing, where there was so little to be gay over, took on exaggerated lines of the comic. He was full of unconsicous burlesque. Suddenly he added with a touch of seriousness, "and they say that the front is goin' to cost seventeen thousand dollars. Jee-hosaphat!" He hung onto the "Jee" with breathless persistence. It was really evident in this case that seventeen thousand dollars represented an immense sum to his mind.

It was pathetic to see him sitting there in his faded, almost ragged clothes, and all these other old lonely soldiers about. I began to feel the undertow of this clanking farce called life. What a boneyard old age seems, anyhow!

There was another old soldier, tall, heavy, oleaginous, with some kind of hip trouble, who explained that he lived in Brooklyn up to the year previous, and had been with Grant before Richmond and in the battle in the Wilderness. These endless, ancient tales seemed a little pale just now beside the heavy storms of battle raging in Europe. And I could not help thinking how utterly indifferent life is to the individual. How trivial, and useless and pointless we become in age! What's the good of all the clatter and pathos and fuss about war to these ancients? How does patriotism and newspaper bluster and the fighting of other men's battles avail them, now they are old? Here they were, stranded, wrecked, forgotten. Who cares, really, what becomes of them? Fifty years ago they were fawned upon for the moment as the saviors of their country. And now they hobble about such squares as this, condemned by the smug gentry of small towns, despised for indulging in the one salve to disillusioned minds and meditating on things that are no more. I wanted to leave, and we soon did leave, anxious to feel the soothing waves of change.

Although in Bath the sun seemed suddenly overcast by these reflections in regard to the remorseless tread of time, outside, in the open fields, it was as inspiriting as ever. A few miles out and we came to the banks of a small river which flowed for a number of miles through this region, tumbling thinly over rough boulders, or forming itself into deep, grey-green pools. Gone were the ancient soldiers in blue, the miseries of a hag like "the Pete and Duck." Just here the hills seemed to recede, and the land was very flat, like a Dutch landscape. We came to a section of the stream where it was sheltered by groves of trees which came to its very edge, and by small thickets of scrub willow. Just below a little way, some girls, one of them in a red jacket, were fishing. A little farther a few Holstein cows were standing in the water, knee deep. It looked so inviting that I began to urge that we all take a swim. A lovely bank coming into view, and an iron bridge above, which was a poem among trees, Franklin was inspired. "That looks rather inviting," he said.

As usual, Speed had something to do—heaven only knows what—polishing some bolts, probably. But Franklin and I struck out through waving patterns of ox-eye daisies and goldenrod to the drab and pea green willow groves, where, amid rank growths of weeds and whitish pebbles and stones, we presently reached the water's edge and a little hillock of grass at the foot of a tree. Here on bushes and twigs we hung our clothes and went out into the bright, tumbling waters. The current was very swift, though very shallow—no deeper than just above the knees. By clearing away the stones and lying down on the pebbles and sand underneath, you could have the water race over you at breakneck speed, and feel as though you were being fingered by mystic hands. It was about all we could do, lying thus, to brace ourselves so that the stream would not keep moving us on.

The sky, between the walls of green wood, was especially blue. The great stones about us were all slippery with a thin, green moss, and yet so clean and pretty, and the water gurgled and sipped. Lying on my back I could see robins and bluejays and catbirds in the trees about. I amused myself kicking my feet in the air and throwing stones at the farther bank and watching Franklin's antics. He had a strong, lean white body, which showed that it had been shaped in hayfields in his youth. His white hair and straight nose made him look somewhat like an ancient Etruscan, stalking about in the waters. We were undisturbed by any sound, and I could have spent the rest of the day lying in this babbling current—it was so warm—listening to the birds, watching the wind shake the leaves, and contemplating the blue sky. It was so warm that when one sat up the wind and sun soon dried the flesh. I was loath to leave.

THE OLD ESSEX AND MORRIS CANAL

WILKES-BARRE

A rich, smoky, sketchy atmosphere

A COAL BREAKER NEAR SCRANTON

FRANKLIN STUDIES AN OBLITERATED SIGN

FACTORYVILLE BIDS US FAREWELL

THE GREAT BRIDGE AT NICHOLSEN

FLORENCE AND THE ARNO, AT OWEGO

BEYOND ELMIRA
Early morning

FRANKLIN DREAMS OVER A RIVER BEYOND SAVONA

THE "TOON O' BATH"

EGYPT AT BUFFALO
A Grain Elevator

PLEASURE BEFORE BUSINESS
The Tackawanna Steel Works

CONNEAUT, OHIO

Trading Coal for Iron

THE BRIDGE THAT IS TO MAKE FRANKLIN FAMOUS

WHERE I LEARN THAT I AM NOT TO LIVE EIGHTY YEARS

CEDAR POINT, LAKE ERIE
A Norse Sky

CHAPTER XVIII

AVOCA, just beyond here, was a pleasant little town, with a white church steeple drowsing in the afternoon sun. We tried to get something to eat and couldn't— or rather could only obtain sandwiches, curse them!— and ham sandwiches at that. My God, how I do hate ham sandwiches when I am hungry enough to want a decent meal! And a place called Arkport was not better, though we did get some bananas there—eight—and I believe I ate them all. I forget, but I think I did. Franklin confined himself almost exclusively to popcorn and candy!

At Avoca we learned of two things which altered our course considerably.

First, in leisurely dressing after our bath, Franklin began browsing over a map to see where we were and what the name of this stream was, when suddenly his eye lighted on the magic name of East Aurora. (Imagine a town named *East* Aurora!) Here had lived until recently (when the *Lusitania* went down he and his wife were drowned) a certain Elbert Hubbard, author, publisher, lecturer, editor, manufacturer of "art" furniture and articles of virtu, whose personal characteristics and views seemed to have aroused more feverish interest in the minds of a certain type of American than almost any other man's, unless, perchance, it might have been William Jennings Bryan's, or Billy Sunday's.

In my youth, when he was first writing his interesting "Little Journeys to the Homes of Good Men and Great" (think of that for a title!), I thought him wonderful too. I never heard of his stirring those hard, sophisticated, unregerenate sanctums and halls of the great cities where lurk the shrewd, the sharp and evil, to say nothing of the dullest of the dull; but when it came to the rural places, there he shone. In the realms of the vast and far flung Chautauqua, with its halls and shrines of homage, he was *au fait,* a real prophet. Here he was looked up to, admired, adored. These people bought his furniture and read his books, and in the entertainment halls of public schools, clubs, societies, circles for the promotion of this, that, or the other, they quoted his thoughts. Personally, I early outgrew Mr. Hubbard. He appealed to me for about four months, in my twenty-fourth or twentyfifth year, and then he was gone again. Later on his Roycroft furniture, book bindings, lamps and the like came to have a savage distaste to me. They seemed impossible, the height of the inane; but he went on opening salesrooms in New York, Chicago and elsewhere, and increasing his fame. He came to be little more than a shabby charlatan, like so many of those other itinerant evangelists that infest America.

This great man had established himself years before, in this place called East Aurora, near Buffalo, and there had erected what I always imagined were extensive factories or studios, or mere rooms for the manufacture and storage and sale of all the many products of art on which he put the stamp of his approval. Here were printed all those rare and wonderful books in limp leather and handstitched silk linings and a host of artistic blank flyleaves, which always sickened me a little when I looked at them. Here were sawed and planed and hand polished, no doubt, all the perfect woods that went into his Roycroft furniture. Here were hammered and polished and carefully shaped the various metals that went into his objects of art. I always felt that really it must be a remarkable institution, though I cared no whit for the books or furniture or objects of art. They were too fixy.

In all his writings he was the preacher of the severe, the simple, the durable—that stern beauty that has its birth in necessity, its continuance in use. With all such products, as he himself was forever indicating, art was a by-product,—a natural outcome of the perfection impulse of the life principle. Somewhere in all nature was something which wanted and sought beauty, the clear, strong, natural beauty of strength and necessity. Who shaped the tiger? Who gave perfection to the lion? Behold the tree. See the hill. Were they not beautiful, and did they not conform to the laws of necessity and conditional use? Verily, verily.

Whenever I looked at any of his books or objects of art or furniture, while they had that massiveness or durability or solidity which should be in anything built for wear and severe use, they had something else which did not seem to suggest these needs at all. There was a luxuriousness of polish and ornamentation and inutile excrescence about them which irritated me greatly. "Here is a struggle," I said to myself, "to mix together two things which can never mix—oil and water,—luxury and extreme, rugged durability." It was as if one took Abraham Lincoln and dressed him in the drawingroom clothes of a fop, curling his hair, perfuming his beard, encasing his feet in patent leather shoes, and then said, "Gentlemen, behold the perfect man."

Well, behold him!

And so it was with this furniture and these art objects. They were log cabin necessities decked out in all the gimcrackery of the Petit Trianon. They weren't log-cabin necessities any more, and they certainly bore no close relationship to the perfection of a Heppelwhite or a Sheraton, or the convincing charms of the great periods. They were just a combination of country and city, as their inventor understood them, without having the real merit of either, and to me they seemed to groan of their unhappy union. It was as if a man had taken all the worst and best in American life and fastened them together without really fusing them. It was a false idea. The author of them was an artistic clown.

But when it came to the possibility of seeing his place I was interested enough. Only a few weeks before the country had been ringing with the news of his death and the tragedy of it. Long, appreciative editorials had appeared in all our American papers (on what subjects will not the American papers write long, appreciative editorials!). So I was interested, as was Franklin. He suggested going to East Eurora, and I was pleased to note that if we went there we would have to go through Warsaw, New York. That settled it. I agreed at once.

Another thing that we discussed at Avoca was that if we took the best road from there and followed it to Portageville, we would be in the immediate vicinity of the Falls of the Geneseo, "and they're as fine as anything I ever see in America," was the way one countryman put it. "I've seen Niagara and them falls down there on the Big Kanawha in West Virginia, but I never expect to see anything finer than these." It was the village blacksmith and garage owner of Avoca who was talking. And Portageville was right on the road to Warsaw and East Aurora.

We were off in a trice—ham sandwiches in hand.

It was while we were speeding out of Arkport and on our way to Canaseraga and the Falls of the Geneseo that I had my first taste of what might be called an automobile flirtation. It was just after leaving Arkport and while we were headed for a town called Canaseraga that we caught up with and passed three maids in a machine somewhat larger than our own, who were being piloted at a very swift pace by a young chauffeur. It is a rule of the road and a state law in most states that unless a machine wishes to keep the lead by driving at the permitted speed it must turn to the right to permit any machine approaching from the rear and signaling to pass.

Most chauffeurs and all passengers I am sure resent doing this. It is a cruel thing to have to admit that any machine can go faster than yours or that you are in the mood to take the dust of anyone. Still if a machine is trailing you and making a great row for you to give way, what can you do, unless you seek open conflict and possibly disaster—a wreck—for chauffeurs and owners are occasionally choleric souls and like to pay out stubborn, greedy "road hogs," even if in paying them out you come to grief yourself. Franklin had just finished a legal argument of this kind some few weeks before, he told us, in which some man who would not give the road and had been "sideswiped" by his car (Franklin being absent and his chauffeur who was out riding choleric) had been threatening to bring suit for physical as well as material injury. It was this threat to sue for physical injuries which brought about a compromise in Franklin's favor, for it is against the law to threaten anyone, particularly by mail, as in this instance; and so Franklin, by threatening in return, was able to escape.

Be that as it may, these three maids, or their chauffeur, when we first came up refused to give the road, although they did increase their speed in an effort to keep it. One of them, a gay creature in a pink hat, looked back and half smiled at our discomfiture. I took no more interest in her than did any of the others apparently, at the time, for in a situation of this kind how is one to tell which is the favored one?

As an able chauffeur, the master of a good machine, and the ex-leader of the Lincoln Highway procession for a certain distance, how was a man like Speed to take a rebuff like this? Why, as all good and true chauffeurs should, by increasing his own speed and trailing them so close and making such a row that they would have to give way. This he did and so for a distance of three or four miles we were traveling in a cloud of dirt and emitting a perfect uproar of squawks. In consequence we finally were permitted to pass, not without certain unkind and even contemptuous looks flung in our direction, as who should say: "You think yourselves very smart, don't you?"—although in the case of the maiden in the pink hat it did not seem to me that her rage was very great. She was too amused and cheerful. I sat serene and calm, viewing the surrounding landscape, only I could not help noting that the young ladies were quite attractive and that the one in the pink hat was interested in someone in our car—Speed or Franklin, I decided—preferably Franklin, since he looked so very smart in his carefully cut clothes. I did not think it could be myself. As for Speed, mustachios up and a cigarette between his teeth, he looked far too handsome to condescend to flirt with a mere country —heiress, say. These chauffeurs—you know! But a little later, as we were careening along, having attained a good lead as we thought and taking our ease, what should come trailing up behind us but this same car, making a great clatter, and because of a peculiar wide width of road and our loitering mood, passing us before we could say "Jack Robinson." Again the maid in the pink hat smiled—it seemed to me—but at whom? And again Speed bustled to the task of overtaking them. I began to sit up and take notice.

What a chase! There was a big, frail iron bridge over a rocky, shallow stream somewhere, which carried a sign reading: "Bridge weak, walk your horses. Speed limit four miles an hour." I think we crossed it in one bound. There was a hollow where the road turned sharply under a picturesque cliff and a house in a green field seemed to possess especial beauty because of a grove of pines. At another time I would have liked to linger here. A sign read: "Danger ahead. Sharp Curve. Go Slow." We went about it as if we were being pursued by the devil himself. Then came a rough place of stone somewhere, where ordinarily Speed would have slowed down and announced that he would "like to have a picture of this road." Do you think we slowed down this time? Not much. We went over it as if it were as smooth as glass. I was nearly jounced out of the car.

Still we did not catch up, quite. The ladies or the chauffeur or all were agreed apparently to best us, but we trailed them close and they kept looking back and laughing at us. The pink-hatted one was all dimples.

"There you are, Mr. Dreiser," called Speed. "She's decided which one she wants. She doesn't seem to see any of the rest of us."

Speed could be horribly flattering at times.

"No," I said, "without a mustache or a cigarette or a long Napoleonic lock over my brow, never. It's Franklin here."

Franklin smiled—as Julius Cæsar might have smiled.

"Which one is it you're talking about?" he inquired innocently.

"Which one?—you sharp!" I scoffed. "Don't come the innocent, guileless soul on me. You know whom she's looking at. The rest of us haven't a chance."

Inwardly I was wondering whether by any chance freak of fancy she could have taken a tentative interest in me. While there is life—you know!

Alas, they beat us and for awhile actually disappeared because of a too rough stretch at one point and then, as I had given up all hope of seeing them any more, there they were, just a little ahead of us, in the midst of a most beatific landscape; and they were loitering—yes, they were!—people can loiter, even in motors.

My mind was full of all the possibilities of a gay, cheerful flirtation. Whose wouldn't be, on a summery evening like this, with a car full of girls and one bolder and prettier than the others, smiling back at you. The whole atmosphere was one of romance. It was after four now, with that rather restful holiday feeling that comes into the air of a Saturday afternoon when every laborer and rich man is deciding to knock off for the day and "call it a day," as they express it, and you are wondering why there is any need to hurry over anything. The sky was so blue, the sun so warm. If you had been there you would have voted to sit on the grass of one of these lovely slopes and talk things over. I am sure you would.

Alas, for some distance now we had been encountering signs indicating that a place called Hornell was near and not on our route. It was off to the left or south and we were headed north, Canaseraga-ward. If our car turned north at the critical juncture of the dividing roads, would they miss us if we did not follow them and turn back, or was it not our duty to get the lead and show them which way we were going, or failing that, follow them into Hornell for a bit of food or something? I began to puzzle.

"How about Hornell, for dinner?" I suggested mildly. "I see that these signs indicate a place of about ten thousand."

"What's got into you?" exclaimed my host. "Didn't you just eat eight bananas?"

"Oh, I know; but bananas, in this air——"

"But it isn't any more than four thirty. It would only be five by the time we got there. I thought you wanted to see the falls yet tonight—and Warsaw?"

"I did—only—you know how beautiful falls are likely to be in the morning——"

"Oh, of course, I see—only—but, seriously, do you think we'd better? It might turn out all right, but again, there are three of them, and two of them are not very good looking and we're only two actually."

"Right! Right!" I sighed. "Well, if it must be——"
I sank heavily against the cushion.

And then they did let us pass them, not far from the fatal juncture. Just as we neared it they decided to pass us and turned off toward Hornell.

"Oh, heaven! heaven! Oh, woe! woe!" I sighed. "And she's looking back. How can such things be?"

Speed saw the point as quickly as anyone. Our better judgment would naturally have asserted itself anyhow, I presume.

"We turn to the right here, don't we?" he called chipperly, as we neared the signpost.

"Of course, of course," I called gaily. "Don't we, Franklin?"

"Yes, that's the way," he smiled, and off we went, northwest, while they were going southwest.

I began to wonder then whether they would have sense enough to turn back and follow us, but they didn't.

"And it is such a lovely afternoon," I said to myself. "I'd like to see Hornell."

"That was a good little car they had," called back Speed consolingly. "That girl in the pink hat certainly had a fancy for someone here."

"Not me," said Franklin. "I know that."

"Not me," I replied. "She never looked at me."

"Well, I know damn well she never looked at me," added Speed. "She must have liked the car."

We both laughed.

I wonder what sort of place Hornell is, anyhow?

CHAPTER XIX

THE REV. J. CADDEN McMICKENS

THE last twelve miles of the run into Portageville had seemed if anything the most perfect of all. Before we reached Canaseraga we traversed a number of miles of dirt road—"one of the finest dirt roads anywhere," a local enthusiast described it,—and it was excellent, very much above the average. After Canaseraga it continued for twelve miles, right into Portageville and the Falls, and even on to Warsaw and East Aurora, some forty miles farther, as we found out later. Following it we skirted a hillside with a fine valley below it, and few, if any, houses to evidence the thriving farm life which the fields seemed to suggest. Evening gnats were whirling everywhere. Breaths of cool air were beginning to emanate from the grove of woods which we occasionally passed. The long rays of the sun slanted so heavily that they came under my visor and found my eyes. A fine vigorous type of farm boy swinging along with an axe over his shoulder, and beads of perspiration on his brow, informed us that we were on the right road. I envied him his pink cheeks and his lithe body and his clear blue eyes.

But the Falls, when we found them, were not quite all that I expected. Three Falls—an upper, a lower and a middle—were all included in a park called "Letchworth," but it did not seem to me that much parking had been accomplished. A great house near them at the spot where a railroad crosses on a high trestle, deceived us into thinking that we had found a delightful hotel for the night; but no, it was an institution of some kind. Deep down in a valley below the Falls we found Portageville, a small, crossroads place that looked for all the world like one of those cowboy towns one sees so persistently displayed in the moving pictures. There were two or three frame hotels of drab or green shades, facing a large open square, and a collection of small white frame houses, with a host of rather primitive looking Americans sitting outside the hotels in rocking or arm chairs, the men in their shirt sleeves. Franklin, who is precise in his apparel, was rather irritated, I think. He was not expecting anything quite so crude. We inquired as to rooms and meals and found that we could have both, only the evening meal should be eaten very soon, if we wanted any. The hour for it was from six to seven, with no à la carte service.

The individual who volunteered this information was a little, short, stout man in belted trousers and shirt sleeves who stood beside the car as it lay alongside the hotel platform, picking his teeth with a toothpick. He was so blandly unconscious of the fact that the process might be a little annoying that he was amusing. I got the feeling that things would not be so comfortable here as they might be, and so I was glad when Franklin suggested that we seek a more perfect view of the Falls, which someone had said was to be obtained from below the Falls. It would take only ten or fifteen minutes, so the proprietor suggested,—straight up the road we were on —so we went on seeking it. We did not return.

In the first place, we could not find the view indicated, and in the second place, we encountered a man who wanted to ride and who told such a queer story of being robbed of his bicycle while assisting another man to repair his machine, that we began to suspect he was a little crazy or that he had some scheme in mind of robbing us,—just which we could not determine. But in parleying with him and baffling him by suggesting we were going back into the village instead of the way he thought we were going, we lost so much time that it was night, and we did not think we would get a decent meal if we did return. So we questioned another stranger as to the route to Warsaw, found that it was only twenty miles, and struck out for it.

Over a road that was singularly smooth for a dirt one, and through land as flat as Illinois, a tableland on the top of a ridge,—which proved the last we were to see—we raced Warsaw-ward. It was strangely like my school days home, or I romanticised myself into the belief that it was. It was the same size as Warsaw, Indiana, when I left it—thirtyfive hundred—and its principal east and west street, as I discovered the next morning, was named Buffalo, as at home. It differed in one respect greatly, and that was that it had no courthouse square, and no lakes immediately adjoining it; but otherwise its general atmosphere was quite the same. It had a river, or small stream about the size of the Tippecanoe. The similarity is not so startling when one considers how many towns of thirtyfive hundred are county seats in the middle west, and how limited their opportunities for difference are. Assemble four or five hundred frame and brick houses of slightly varying size and architecture and roominess, surround them with trees and pleasing grass plots, provide the town a main street and one cross street of stores, place one or two red brick school houses at varying points in them, add one white sandstone courthouse in a public square, and a railroad station, and four or five or six red brick churches, and there you have them all. Give one town a lake, another a stream, another a mill pond—it makes little difference.

And actually, as we dashed along toward Warsaw under a starry sky, with a warm, summery wind blowing, a wind so warm that it felt suspiciously like rain, I allowed myself to sink into the most commemorative state. When you forget the now and go back a number of years and change yourself into a boy and view old scenes and see old faces, what an unbelievably strange and inexplicable thing life becomes! We attempt solutions of this thing, but to me it is the most vacuous of all employments. I rather prefer to take it as a strange, unbelievable, impossible orchestral blending of sounds and scenes and moods and odors and sensations, which have no real meaning and yet which, tinkling and kaleidoscopic as they are, are important for that reason. I never ride this way at night, or when I am tired by day or night, but that life becomes this uncanny blur of nothingness.

Why should something want to produce two billion people all alike,—ears, eyes, noses, hands, unless for mere sensory purposes,—to sensitize fully and voluptuously something that is delicious? Why billions of trees, flowers, insects, animals, all seeking to feel, unless feeling without socalled reason is the point? Why reason, anyway? And to what end? Supposing, for instance, that one could reason through to the socalled solution, actually found it, and then had to live with that bit of exact knowledge and no more forever and ever and ever! Give me, instead, sound and fury, signifying nothing. Give me the song sung by an idiot, dancing down the wind. Give me this gay, sad, mad seeking and never finding about which we are all so feverishly employed. It is so perfect, this inexplicable mystery.

And it was with some such thoughts as these that I was employed, sitting back in the car and spinning along over these roads this night. I was only half awake and half in a dreamland of my own creating. The houses that we passed with open doors, lamp on table, people reading, girls playing at pianos, people sitting in doorsteps, were in the world of twentyfive or thirty years before, and I was entering the Warsaw of my school days. There was no real difference. "What ideas have we today that we did not have then?" I was dreamily asking myself. "How do people differ? Are the houses any better, or the clothes? Or the people in their bodies and minds? Or are their emotions any richer or keener or sweeter?" Euripides wrote the Medea in 440 B. C. Shakespeare wrote "Macbeth" in 1605 A. D. "The Song of Songs"—how old is that? Or the Iliad? The general feeling is that we are getting on, but I should like to know what we can get on to, actually. And beyond the delight of sensory response, what is there to get on to? Mechanicalizing the world does not, *cannot,* it seems to me, add to the individual's capacity for sensory response. Life has always been vastly varied. How, by inventing things, can we make it more so? As a matter of fact, life, not man, is supplying its own inventions and changes, adding some, discarding others. To what end? Today we have the automobile. Three thousand years ago we had the chariot. Today we fight with forty-centimeter guns and destructive gases. Three thousand years ago we fought with catapults and burning pitch and oil. Man uses all the forces he can conceive, and he seems to be able to conceive of greater and greater forces, but he does not understand them, and his individual share in the race's sensory response to them is apparently no greater than ever. We are capable of feeling so much and no more. Has any writer, for instance, felt more poignantly or more sweetly than those whose moods and woes are now the Iliad? And when Medea speaks, can anyone say it is ancient and therefore less than we can feel today? We know that this is not true.

I may seem to grow dim in my researches, but I can conceive of no least suggestion of real change in the sensory capacity of life. As it was in the beginning, so it appears that it is now—and shall I say, ever shall be? I will not venture that. I am not all-wise and I do not know.

When we entered Warsaw I had just such thoughts in my mind, and a feeling that I would like very much to have something to eat. Since it was early Saturday evening, the streets were crowded with country vehicles, many automobiles, and a larger percentage of tumble-down buggies and wagons than I had so far seen elsewhere. Why? The oldest, poorest, most ratty and rickety looking auto I had seen in I don't know when was labeled "For Hire."

"Gee whiz!" exclaimed Speed when he caught sight of it. And I added, "Who would want to ride in that, anyhow?"

Yet, since it was there, it would seem as if somebody might want to do so.

However, at the north end of the principal street, and close to a small park, we discovered one of the most comfortable little hotels imaginable. All the rooms were done in bright, cheerful colors, and seemed to be properly cared for. There were baths and an abundance of hot water and towels, and electric lights and electric call bells,—rather novel features for a country hotel of this size. The lobby was as smart and brisk as most hotels of a much more expensive character. We "spruced up" considerably at the sight of it. Franklin proceeded with his toilet in a most ambitious manner, whereupon I changed to a better suit. I felt quite as though I were dressing for an adventure of some kind, though I did not think there was the slightest likelihood of our finding one in a town of this size, nor was I eager for the prospect. A half dozen years before—perhaps earlier—I would have been most anxious to get into conversation with some girl and play the gallant as best I could, or roam the dark in search of adventure, but tonight I was interested in no such thing, even if I might have.

Surely I must be getting along in years, I said to myself, to be thus indifferent to these early enthusiasms. Twenty years before, if anyone had told me that I could go forth into a brisk Saturday evening crowd such as was filling this one street, and, seeing the young girls and boys and women and men going about, feel no least thrill of possible encounters, I would have said that life, under such circumstances, would not be worth living. Yet here I was, and here we were, and this was exactly what I was doing and life seemed fairly attractive.

Out in the buzzing country street we did nothing but stroll about, buy picture postcards, write on and address them, buy some camera films, get our shoes shined, and finally go for our dinner to a commonplace country restaurant. I was interested in the zealous, cadaverous, overambitious young man who was the proprietor, and a young, plump blonde girl acting as waitress, who might have been his wife or only a hired girl. Her eyes looked swollen and as though she had been crying recently. And he was in a crotchety, non-palliative mood, taking our orders in a superior, contemptuous manner, and making us feel as though we were of small import.

"What ails mine host, do you suppose?" I asked of Franklin.

"Oh, he thinks that we think we're something, I suppose, and he's going to prove to us that we're not. You know how country people are."

I watched him thereafter, and I actually think Franklin's interpretation was correct.

As we ambled about afterwards, Speed told us the harrowing story of the descent of the Rev. J. Cadden McMickens on the fair city of Kokomo, Indiana, some few years before, when he was working there as a test man for one of the great automobile companies. After a reasonable period of religious excitement and exhortation, in which the Rev. J. Cadden conducted a series of meetings in a public hall hired for the occasion and urged people to reform and repent of their sins, he suddenly announced that on a given day the end of the world would certainly take place and that all those not reformed or "saved" by that date would be damned. On the night before the fatal morning on which the earth was to be consumed by fire or water, or both, Speed suddenly awoke to the fact that he was not "saved" and that he could not get a train out of Kokomo to Carmel, Indiana, where his mother lived. To him at that time the world was surely coming to an end. Fire, brimstone, water, smoke, were already in the air. As he related this story to us I got the impression that his knees knocked under him. In consequence of the thought of never being able to see his dear mother any more, or his sister or brothers, he nearly succumbed of heart failure. Afterwards, finding that the earth was not destroyed and that he was as safe and sound as ever, he was seized by a great rage against the aforesaid Rev. J. Cadden McMickens, and went to seek him out in order that he might give him "a damned good licking," as he expressed it, but the Rev. J. Cadden, having seen his immense prophecy come to nothing, had already fled.

"But, Speed," I protested, "how comes it that you, a sensible young fellow, capable of being a test man for a great automobile factory like that of the H—— Company, could be taken in by such fol de rol? Didn't you know that the earth was not likely to be consumed all of a sudden by fire or water? Didn't you ever study geology or astronomy or anything like that?"

"No, I never," he replied, with the only true and perfect Hoosier response to such a query. "I never had a chance to go to school much. I had to go to work when I was twelve."

"Yes, I know, Speed," I replied sympathetically, "but you read the newspapers right along, don't you? They rather show that such things are not likely to happen—in a general way they do."

"Yes, I know," he replied, "but I was just a kid then. That doggone skunk! I'd just like to have a picture of him, I would, frightening me like that."

"But, Speed," I said, "surely you didn't believe that the earth was going to be swallowed by fire that next morning after you were so frightened?"

"Yes, I did, too," he replied. "He was just agettin' out papers and handbills with great big type, and hollerin' there on the corner. It was enough to scare anybody. Why wouldn't I? Just the same, I wasn't the only one. There were hundreds—mostly everybody in Kokomo. I went over to see an old lady I knew, and she said she didn't know if it would happen or not—she wasn't sure."

"You poor kid," I mumbled.

"Well, what did you do, Speed, when you found you couldn't get out of town?" inquired Franklin. "Why didn't you walk out?"

"Yes, walk out," replied Speed resentfully. "I have a picture of myself walking out, and Carmel forty miles away or more. I wanted to be with my mother when the earth burned up."

"And you couldn't make it by morning," I commented.

"No, I couldn't," he replied.

"Well, then, what did you do?" persisted Franklin.

"Well, I went to see this old lady where I boarded once, and I just stayed with her. We sat and waited together."

At this point I was troubled between a desire to laugh and to weep. This poor youth! And the wild-eyed J. Cadden McMickens! And Kokomo! And the hundreds who believed! Can't you see Speed and the old lady—the young boy and the woman who didn't know and couldn't be sure, and Kokomo, and the Rev. J. Cadden McMic——

I feel as if I would like to get hold of the Rev. J. Cadden even at this late date and shake him up a bit. I won't say kick him, but——

CHAPTER XX

NEXT morning it was raining, and to pass the time before breakfast I examined a large packet of photographs which Speed had left with me the night before—mementoes of that celebrated pioneer venture which had for its object the laying out of the new Lincoln Highway from New York to San Francisco. We had already en route heard so much of this trip that by now we were fairly familiar with it. It had been organized by a very wealthy manufacturer, and he and his very good looking young wife had been inclined to make a friend of Speed, so that he saw much that would not ordinarily have fallen under his vision. I was never tired of hearing of this particular female, whom I would like to have met. Speed described her as small, plump, rosy and very determined,—an iron-willed, spiteful, jealous little creature—in other words, a real woman, who had inherited more money than her husband had ever made. Whenever anything displeased her greatly she would sit in the car and weep, or even yell. She refused to stay at any hotel which did not just suit her and had once in a Chicago hotel diningroom slapped the face of her spouse because he dared to contradict her, and another time in some famous Kansas City hostelry she had thrown the bread at him. Both were always anxious to meet only the best people, only Mr. Manufacturer would insist upon including prize-fighters and auto-speed record men, greatly to her displeasure.

I wish you might have seen these pictures selected by Speed to illustrate his trip. Crossing a great country like America, from coast to coast, visiting new towns each day and going by a route hitherto not much followed, one might gather much interesting information and many pictures (if no more than postcards) of beautiful and striking things.

Do you imagine there were any in this collection which Speed left with me? Not one! The views, if you will believe me, were all of mired cars and rutty roads and great valleys which might have been attractive or impressive if they had been properly photographed. The car was always in the foreground, spoiling everything. He had selected dull scenes of cars in procession—the same cars always in the same procession, only in different order, and never before any radically different scene.

As a matter of fact, as I looked at these photographs I could tell exactly how Speed's mind worked, and it was about the way the average mind would work under such circumstances. Here was a great automobile tour, including say forty or fifty cars or more. The cars contained important men and women, or were supposed to, because the owners had money. Ergo, the cars and their occupants were the great things about this trip, and wherever the cars were, there was the interest—never elsewhere. Hence, whenever the cars rolled into a town or along a great valley or near a great mountain, let the town be never so interesting, or the mountain, or the valley, the great thing to photograph was the cars in the procession. It never seemed to occur to the various photographers to do anything different. Cars, cars, cars, —here they were, and always in a row and always the same. I finally put the whole bunch aside wearily and gave them back to him, letting him think that they were very, very remarkable—which they were.

Setting off after breakfast we encountered not the striking mountain effects of the region about Delaware Water Gap and Stroudsburg, nor yet the fine valley views along the Susquehanna, but a spent hill country—the last receding heaves and waves of all that mountainous country east of us. As we climbed up and up out of Warsaw onto a ridge which seemed to command all the country about for miles, I thought of the words of that motorcyclist at Owego who said he had come through Warsaw and that you climbed five hills to get in, but only one to get out, going east. It was true. In our westward course the hills we were to climb were before us. You could see two or three of them—the road ascending straight like a ribbon, ending suddenly at the top of each one and jumping as a thin whitish line to the next hill crest beyond.

The rain in which we began our day was already ceasing, so that only a few miles out we could put down the top. Presently the sun began to break through fleecy, whitish clouds, giving the whole world an opalescent tinge, and then later, as we neared East Aurora, it became as brilliant as any sun lover could wish.

A Sabbath stillness was in the air. One could actually feel the early morning preparations for church. As we passed various farmyards, the crowing of roosters and the barking of dogs seemed especially loud. Seeing a hen cross the road and only escape being struck by the car by a hair's breath, Franklin announced that he had solved the mystery of why hens invariably cross the road, or seem to, in front of any swift moving vehicle.

"You don't mean to tell me that it's because they want to get to the other side, do you?" I inquired, thereby frustrating the possibility of the regulation Joe Miller.

"Actually, yes, but I'm not trying to put that old one over on you. It's because they always have the instinct, when any dangerous object approaches, to run toward their home—their coop, which is often just opposite where they are eating. Now you watch these chickens from now on. They'll be picking peacefully on the side of the road opposite the farmyard. Our car will come along, and instead of moving a few feet farther away from their home, and so escaping altogether, they will wait until the car is near and then suddenly decide to run for home—the longest way out of danger. Lots of times they'll start, as this last one did, and then find, when they're nearly half way over, that they can't make it. Then they start to run ahead of the car and of course nearly always they're overtaken and killed."

"Well, that's an ingenious explanation, anyhow," I said.

"They lose their heads and then they lose their heads," he added.

"Franklin!" I exclaimed reproachfully and then turning to Speed added: "Don't let that make you nervous, Speed. Be calm. We must get him to East Aurora, even though he will do these trying things. Show that you are above such difficulties, Speed. Never let a mere attempt at humor, a beggarly jest, cause you to lose control of the car."

Speed never even smiled.

Just here we stopped for gas and oil. We were unexpectedly entertained by a store clerk who seemed particularly anxious to air his beliefs and his art knowedge. He was an interesting young man, very, with keen blue eyes, light hair, a sharp nose and chin—and decidedly intelligent and shrewd.

"How far is it to East Aurora from here?" inquired Franklin.

"Oh, about fifteen miles," answered the youth. "You're not from around here, eh?"

"No," said Franklin, without volunteering anything further.

"Not bound for Elbert Hubbard's place, are you?"

"We thought we'd take dinner there," replied Franklin.

"I ask because usually a number of people go through here of a Sunday looking for his place, particularly now that he's dead. He's got quite an institution over there, I understand—or did have. They say his hotel is very good."

"Haven't you ever been there?" I inquired, interested.

"No, but I've heard a good deal about it. It's a sort of new art place, as I understand it, heavy furniture and big beams and copper and brass things. He had quite a trade, too. He got into a bad way with some people over there on account of his divorcing his first wife and taking up with this second woman for awhile without being married to her. He was a pretty shrewd business man, I guess, even if he wore his hair long. I saw him once. He lectured around here—and everywhere else, I suppose. I think he was a little too radical for most people out this way."

He looked as though he had vindicated his right to a seat among the intellectuals.

I stared at him curiously. America is so brisk and well informed. Here was a small, out of the way place, with no railroad and only two or three stores, but this youth was plainly well informed on all the current topics. The few other youths and maids whom we saw here seemed equally brisk. I was surprised to note the Broadway styles in suits and dresses—those little nuances of the ready made clothes manufacturers which make one feel as if there were no longer any country nor any city, but just smart, almost impudent life, everywhere. It was quite diverting.

Looking at this fine country, dotted with red barns and silos and ripe with grain, in which already the reapers were standing in various places ready for the morrow's work, I could see how the mountains of the east were puffing out. This was a spent mountain country. All the real vigor of the hills was farther east. These were too rolling—too easy of ascent and descent—long and trying and difficult as some of them were. It seemed as if we just climbed and climbed and climbed only to descend, descend, descend, and then climb, climb, climb again. Speed put on the chains,—his favorite employment in hilly regions.

But presently, after a few more hills, which finally gave way to a level country, we entered East Aurora.

It is curious how any fame, even meretricious or vulgar, is likely to put one on the *qui vive*. I had never been greatly impressed with the intellect or the taste of Elbert Hubbard. He seemed too much the quack savior and patent nostrum vender strayed into the realm of art.

His face as photographed suggested the strolling Thespian of country "opera house" fame. I could never look upon his pictures without involuntarily smiling.

Just the same, once here, I was anxious to see what he had achieved. Many people have I known who, after visiting East Aurora and the Roycroft (that name!) Shops, had commended its sacred precincts to my attention. I have known poets who lived there and writers to whom he allotted cottages within the classic precincts of his farm because of their transcendent merits in literature. *Sic transit gloria mundi!* I cannot even recall their names!

But here we were, rolling up the tree shaded streets of a handsome and obviously prosperous town of about twentyfive hundred which is now one of the residential suburbs of Buffalo. Our eyes were alert for any evidence of the whereabouts of the Roycroft Inn. Finally in the extreme western end of the city we found a Roycroft "sign" in front of a campus like yard containing a building which looked like a small college "addition" of some kind—one of those small halls specially devoted to chemistry or physics or literature. The whole place had the semi-academic socio-religious atmosphere which is associated by many with aspiration and intellectual supremacy and sweetness and light. Here on the sidewalk we encountered a youth who seemed to typify the happy acolyte or fanner of the sacred flame. His hair was a little long, his face and skin pale, quite waxen, and he wore a loose shirt with a blowy tie, his sleeves being rolled up and his negligee trousers belted at the waist. He had an open and amiable countenance and looked as though life had fortunately, but with rare discrimination, revealed much to him.

"What is this?" I inquired, waving my hand at the nearest building.

"Oh, one of the shops," he replied pleasantly.

"Is it open?"

"Not on Sunday—not to the general public, no."

He looked as though he thought we might gain special

permission possibly, if we sought it.   But instead we inquired the location of the Inn and he accompanied us
thither on the running board of our machine.   It turned
out to be a low, almost rectangular affair done in pea
green, with a fine line of veranda displaying swings,
rockers, wicker chairs and deep benches where a number
of passing visitors were already seated.   It was a brisk,
summery and rather conventional hotel scene.

Within, just off the large lobby was a great music or
reception hall, finished as I had anticipated in the Al-
bertian vein of taste—a cross between a farm home and
the Petit Trianon.   The furniture was of a solid, log-
cabin foundation but hopelessly bastardized with oil,
glaze, varnish and little metal gimcracks in imitation of
wooden pegs.   A parqueted floor as slippery as glass,
great timbers to support the ceiling which was as meticu-
lously finished as a lorgnette, and a six-panel frieze of
Athens, Rome, Paris, London and New York—done in
a semi-impressionistic vein, and without real distinction,
somehow—completed the effect.   There were a choice
array of those peculiar bindings for which the Roycroft
shop is noted—limp leather, silk linings and wrought-
bronze corners and clasps, and a number of odd lamps,
bookracks, candelabra and the like, which were far from
suggesting that rude durability which is the fine art of
poverty.   One cannot take a leaf out of St. Francis of
Assisi, another out of the Grand Louis and a third out
of Davy Crockett and combine them into a new art.   The
thing was bizarre, overloaded, soufflé, a kind of tawdry
botch.   Through it all were tramping various American
citizens of that hybrid, commercial-intellectual variety
which always irritates me to the swearing stage.   In the
lobby, the library, and various halls was more of the same
gimcrackery—Andrew Jackson attempting to masquerade
as Lord Chesterfield, and not succeeding, of course.
Franklin, a very tolerant and considerate person when it
comes to human idiosyncrasies, was at first inclined to
bestow a few mild words of praise.   "After all, it did

help some people, you know. It was an advance in its way."

After a time, though, I noticed that his interest began to flag. We were scheduled to stay for dinner, which was still three quarters of an hour away, and had registered ourselves to that effect at the desk. In the meantime the place was filling up with new arrivals who suggested that last word of social investiture which the ownership of a factory may somehow imply. They would not qualify exactly as "high brow," but they did make an ordinary working artist seem a little *de trop*. As I watched them I kept thinking that here at last I had a very clear illustration in the flesh of a type that has always been excessively offensive to me. It is the type which everywhere having attained money by processes which at times are too contemptible or too dull to mention, are, by reason of the same astonishing dullness of mind or impulse, attempting to do the thing which they think they ought to do. Think of how many you personally know. They have some hazy idea of a social standard to which they are trying to attain or "up to" which they are trying to live. Visit for example those ghastly gaucheries, the Hotels Astor or Knickerbocker in New York or those profitable Bohemian places in Greenwich village (how speedily any decent rendezvous is spoiled once the rumor of it gets abroad!) or any other presumably smart or different place and you will see for yourself. A hotel like the Astor or the Knickerbocker may be trying to be conventionally smart as the mob understands that sort of thing, the Bohemian places just the reverse. In either place or case these visitors will be found trying to live up to something which they do not understand and do not really approve of but which, nevertheless, they feel that they must do.

In this East Aurora restaurant the dinner hour was one o'clock. That is the worst of these places outside the very large cities. They have a fixed time and a fixed way for nearly everything. I never could understand here or anywhere else why a crowd should be made to

wait and eat all at once. Where does that silly old mass
rule come from anyhow? Why not let them enter and
serve them as they come? The material is there as a rule
to serve and waiting. But, no. They have a fixed dinner
hour and neither love nor money will induce them to
change it or open the doors one moment before the hour
strikes. Then there is a rush, a pell-mell struggle! Think
of the dullness, the reducing shame of it, really. The
mere thought of it sickened me. I tried to talk to Franklin about it. He, too, was irritated by it. He said something about the average person loving a little authority
and rejoicing in rules and following a custom and being
unable to get an old idea or old ideas out their heads. It
was abominable.

There was the female here with the golden-rimmed eye-
glasses and the stern, accusing eye behind it. "Are you
or are you not of the best, artistically and socially?
Answer yes or avaunt." There were tall, uncomfortable-
looking gentlemen in cutaway coats, and the stiffest of
stiff collars, led at chains' ends by stout, executive wives
who glared and stared and pawed things over. The
chains were not visible to the naked eye, but they
were there. Then there were nervous, fussy, somewhat
undersized gentlemen with white side whiskers and an air
of delicate and uncertain inquiry, going timidly to and
fro. There were old and young maids of a severe literary and artistic turn. I never saw better materials nor
poorer taste than in their clothes. I remarked to Franklin that there was not one easy, natural, beautiful woman
in the whole group, and after scrutinizing them all he
agreed with me.

"Now, Franklin," I said, "this shows you what the best
circles of art and literature should really be like. Once
you're truly successful and have established a colony of
your own—East Franklinia, let us say, or Booth-a-rootha
—they will come and visit you in this fashion."

"Not if I know it, they won't," he replied.

The crowd increased. Those who in some institutions
might be known as waiters and waitresses, but who here

were art directors and directoresses at the very least, were bustling to and fro, armed with all authority and not at all overawed by the standing throng which had now gathered outside the diningroom door. I never saw a more glistening array of fancy glass, plates, cups, knives, forks, spoons, flowers. The small black mission tables—Elbert Hubbardized, of course—were stuffed with this sort of thing to the breaking point. The room fairly sparkled as though the landlord had said, "I'll give these people their money's worth if it takes all the plate in the place. They love show and must have it." I began to feel a little sick and nervous. It was all so grand, and the people about us so plainly avid for it, that I said, "Oh, God, just for a simple, plain board, with an humble yellow plate in the middle. What should I be doing here, anyhow?"

"Well, Franklin," I said, as gaily as I could, "this is going to be a very sumptuous affair—a very, very sumptuous affair."

He looked at me wisely, at the crowd, at the long curio case diningroom, and hesitated, but something seemed to be stirring within him.

"What do you say to leaving?" he finally observed. "It seems to me"—then he stopped. His essential good nature and charity would not permit him to criticize. I heaved a sigh of relief, hungry as I was.

We hustled out. I was so happy I forgot all about dinner. There was dear old Speed, as human as anything, sitting comfortably in the front seat, no coat on, his feet amid the machinery for starting things, a cigarette in his mouth, the comic supplement of some Sunday paper spread out before him, as complacent and serene as anyone could be.

He swung the car around in a trice, and was off. Before us lay a long street, overhung with branches through which the sunlight was falling in lovely mottled effects. Overhead was the blue sky. Outward, to right and left, were open fields—the great, enduring, open fields.

"It was a bit too much, wasn't it?" said Franklin.

CHAPTER XXI

WE had traveled now between six and seven hundred miles, and but for a short half mile between Nicholsen and New Milford, Pennsylvania, we could scarcely say that we had seen any bad roads—seriously impeding ones. To be sure, we had sought only the best ones in most cases, not always, and there were those patches of state road, cut up by heavy hauling, which we had to skirt; but all things considered, the roads so far had been wonderful. From East Aurora into Buffalo there was a solid, smooth, red brick boulevard, thirty feet wide and twelve miles long, over which we raced as though it were a bowling alley. The bricks were all vitrified and entirely new. I know nothing about the durability of such a road, and this one gave no evidence of its wearing qualities, but if many such roads are to be built, and they stand the wear, America will have a road system unrivaled.

As we were spinning along, the factories and high buildings and chimneys of Buffalo, coming into view across a flat space of land, somehow reminded me of those older hill cities of Europe which one sees across a space of land from a train, but which are dead, dead. "Here is life," I said to myself, "only here nothing has happened as yet, historically; whereas there, men have fought to and fro over every inch of the ground." How would it be if one could say of Buffalo that in 2316 A. D. —four hundred years after the writing of this—there was a great labor leader who having endured many injuries was tired of the exactions of the money barons and securing a large following of the working people seized the city and administered it cooperatively, until he had been routed by some capitalistic force and hanged from the highest building, his followers also being put to death? Or suppose a great rebellion had originated in New Mexico, and it had reached Buffalo and Pittsburg in its onsweep, and that here an enormous battle had been fought—an Austerlitz or a Waterloo? How we should stare at the towers as we came across this plain! How great names would rise up and flash across the sky! We would hear old war songs in our ears and dream old war dreams. Or suppose there were a great cathedral or a great museum crowded with the almost forgotten art of the twentieth, twentyfirst and twentysecond centuries!

I dream. Yet such are the things which somehow make a great city. But lacking in historic charm as Buffalo might be, the city had a peculiar interest for me, a very special one indeed, egoist that I am. For here, one springtime, twenty years before this, I entered Buffalo looking for work. Fear not, I am not going to begin a romantic and sentimental account of my youth and early struggles. It was still late March and very chilly. There was snow on the ground, but a touch of Spring in the air. I had come on from Cleveland, where I had failed to find anything to do, and was destined to go on to Pittsburg from here, for I could not make a permanent connection with any Buffalo paper. I was a lonely, lank, impossible newspaper type as I see myself now, and so sentimental and wistful that I must have seemed a fool to practical men. They never troubled to pay me a decent salary, I know that. But instead of looking briskly and earnestly for work, as you might think a boy with only a few dollars in his pocket and no friends anywhere within hundreds of miles would do, I spent my time mooning over what seemed then great streets and over the harbor waters near at hand, with their great grain elevators and ships and coal pockets. Ah, those small rivers with their boats and tugs and their romantic suggestion of the sea,—how I yearned over them!

At that time I traveled by trolley to Niagara, nearly forty miles away, and looked at that tumbling flood, which was then not chained or drained by turbine water power sluices. I was impressed, but somehow not quite so much as I thought I would be. Standing out on a rock near the greatest volume of water, under a grey sky, I got dizzy and felt as though I were being carried along, whether I wanted to or not. Farther up stream I stared at the water as it gathered force and speed, and wondered how I should feel if I were in a small canoe and were fighting it for my life. Below the falls I gazed up at the splendid spray and wanted to shout, so vigorously did the water fall and smash the rocks below. When I returned to Buffalo and my room, I congratulated myself that if I had got nothing else, so far, out of Buffalo, at least I had gained this.

Beyond having traveled from Warsaw to Chicago and thence to St. Louis and from St. Louis to this same city, via Toledo, and Cleveland, I had never really been anywhere, and life was all wonderful. No songs of Shelley, nor those strange wild lines of Euripides could outsing my mood at this time. I dreamed and dreamed here in this crude manufacturing town, roaming about these chilly streets, and now as I look back upon it, knowing that never again can I feel as I then felt, I seem to know that actually it was as wonderful as I had thought it was.

The spirit of America at that time was so remarkable. It was just entering on that vast, splendid, most lawless and most savage period in which the great financiers, now nearly all dead, were plotting and conniving the enslavement of the people and belaboring each other for power. Those crude and parvenu dynasties which now sit enthroned in our democracy, threatening its very life with their pretensions and assumptions, were just in the beginning. John D. Rockefeller was still in Cleveland. Flagler, William Rockefeller, H. H. Rogers, were still comparatively young and secret agents. Carnegie was still in Pittsburg—an iron master—and of all his brood of powerful children only Frick had appeared. William H. Vanderbilt and Jay Gould had only recently died.

Cleveland was president and Mark Hanna was an unknown business man in Cleveland. The great struggles of the railroads, the coal companies, the gas companies, the oil companies, were still in abeyance, or just beginning. The multimillionaire had arrived, it is true, but not the billionaire. Giants were plotting, fighting, dreaming on every hand, and in this city, as in every other American city I then visited, there was a singing, illusioned spirit. Actually, the average American then believed that the possession of money would certainly solve all his earthly ills. You could see it in the faces of the people, in their step and manner. Power, power, power, —everyone was seeking power in the land of the free and the home of the brave. There was almost an angry dissatisfaction with inefficiency, or slowness, or age, or anything which did not tend directly to the accumulation of riches. The American world of that day wanted you to eat, sleep and dream money and power.

And I, to whom my future was still a mystery (would that it were so still!), was dreaming of love and power, too, but with no theory of realizing them and with no understanding, indeed, of any way in which I could achieve the happiness and pleasures which I desired. Knowing this, I was unhappy. All day, after a fifteen cent breakfast in some cheap restaurant, or some twenty-five cent dinner in another, I would wander about, staring at these streets and their crowds, the high buildings, the great hotels, uncertain whether to go on to Pittsburg or to hang on here a little while longer in the hope of getting a suitable position as a reporter. Ah, I thought, if I could just be a great newspaper man, like McCullagh of St. Louis, or Dana of New York! In my pocket was a letter from the proprietor of the St. Louis *Republic,* telling all and sundry what a remarkable youth he had found me to be, but somehow I never felt courageous enough to present it. It seemed so vainglorious! Instead, I hung over the rails of bridges and the walls of water fronts, watching the gulls, or stopped before the windows of shops and stores, and outside great factories, and stared. At night I would return to my gloomy room and sit and read, or having eaten somewhere, walk the streets. I haunted the newspaper offices at the proper hours, but finding nothing, finally departed. Buffalo seemed a great but hard and cold city. Spinning into it this day, over long viaducts and through regions of seemingly endless factories and cars, it still seemed quite as vigorous, only not so hard, because my circumstances were different. Alas, I said to myself, I am no longer young, no longer really poor in the sense of being uncertain and inefficient, no longer so dreamy or moony over a future the details of which I may not know. Then all was uncertain, gay with hope or dark with fear. It might bring me anything or nothing. But now, now—what can it bring as wonderful as what I thought it might bring? What youth, I said to myself, is now walking about lonely, wistful, dreaming great dreams, and wishing, wishing, wishing? I would be that one if I could. Yes, I would go back for the dreams' sake,—the illusion of life. I would take hold of life as it was, and sigh and yearn and dream.

Or would I go back if I could?

We did not stay so long in Buffalo this day, but longer than we would have if we could have discovered at once that Canada had placed a heavy license tax on all cars entering Canada, and that, because of the European War, I presume, we would have to submit to a more thorough and tedious examination of our luggage than ordinarily. Naturally there was much excitement, and on all sides were evidences of preparations being made to send armaments and men to the Mother Country. We had looked forward with the greatest pleasure to a trip into Canada, but the conditions were so unfavorable that we hesitated to chance it. We didn't go. In spite of our plans to cross into Canada here and come out at Detroit at the west end of Lake Erie, we listened to words of wisdom and refrained. The automobile expert of the Statler assured us that

we would have a great deal of trouble. There would
be an extra tax, delays, explanations, and examination of
our luggage. A very handsome cigar clerk in this same
hotel—what an expensive youth he was, in a very high
collar, a braided suit, and most roseate necktie!—told
us with an air of condescension that made me feel like
a mere beginner in this automobiling world: "It's nothing to do now. What car have you?"

We told him.

"Ah, no, you need a big racer like the ———— (naming a car which neither Franklin nor I had ever heard
of). Then you can make it in a day. There's nothing
to see. You don't wanta stop."

He patronized us so thoroughly from the vantage
point of his youth (say eighteen years), and his knowledge of all the makes of machines and the roads about
Buffalo, that I began to feel that perhaps as a boy I
had not lived at all. Such shoes, such a tie, such rings
and pins! Everything about him seemed to speak of
girls and barbers and florists and garages and tailors.
The Buffalo white light district rose up before me, and
all the giddy-gaudy whirl of local rathskellers and the
like.

"What a rowdy-dow boy it is, to be sure," I observed
to Franklin.

"Yes, there you have it," he replied. "Youth and inexperience triumphing over any possible weight of knowledge. What's the Encyclopedia Britannica compared to
that?"

Our lunch at one of the big (I use the word advisedly)
restaurants, was another experience in the same way.
Speed had gone off somewhere with the car to some
smaller place and Franklin and I ambled into the large
place. It was as bad as the Roycroft Inn from the point
of view of pretentiousness and assumed perfection, but
from another it was even worse. When we try to be
luxurious in America, how luxurious we can really be!
The heaviness of our panelings and decorations! the
thickness of our carpets! the air of solidity and vigor and

cost without very much tast . It is Teutonic without that bizarre individuality which so often accompanies Teutonic architecture and decoration. We are so fine, and yet we are not—a sort of raw uncouthness showing like shabby woodwork from behind curtains of velvet and cloth of gold.

Sometimes, you know, I remember that we are a mongrel race and think we may never achieve anything of great import, so great is my dissatisfaction with the shows and vulgar gaucheries to be seen on all sides. At other times, viewing the upstanding middle class American with his vivid suit, yellow shoes, flaring tie and conspicuous money roll, I want to compose an ode in praise of the final enfranchisement of the common soul. How much better these millions, I ask you, with their derby and fedora hats, their ready made suits, their flaring jewelry, automobiles and a general sense of well being, and even perfection, if you will, than a race of slaves or serfs, dominated by grand dukes, barons, beperfumed and beribboned counts, daimios and lords and ladies, however cultivated and artistic these may appear! True, the latter would eat more gracefully, but would they be any the more desirable for that, actually? I hear a thousand patrician minded souls exclaiming, "Yes, of course," and I hear a million lovers of democracy insisting "No." Personally, I would take a few giants in every field, well curbed, and then a great and comfortable mass such as I see about me in these restaurants, for instance, well curbed also. Then I would let them mix and mingle.

But, oh, these restaurants!

And how long will it be before we will have just a few good ones in our cities?

CHAPTER XXII

IF anyone doubts that this is fast becoming one of the most interesting lands in the world, let him motor from Buffalo to Detroit along the shore of Lake Erie, mile after mile, over a solid, vitrified brick road fifteen feet wide at the least, and approximately three hundred miles long. As a matter of fact, the vitrified brick road of this description appears to be seizing the imagination of the middle west, and the onslaught of the motor and its owner is making every town and hamlet desirous of sharing the wonders of a new life. Truly, I have never seen a finer road than this, parts of which we traversed between Buffalo and Cleveland and between Cleveland and Sandusky. There were great gaps in it everywhere, where the newest portions were in process of completion, and the horrific "detour" sign was constantly in evidence, but traveling over the finished sections of it was something like riding in paradise. Think of a long, smooth red brick road stretching out before you mile after mile, the blue waters of Lake Erie to your right, with its waves, ships and gulls; a flat, Holland-like farming land to your left, with occasional small white towns, factory centers, and then field upon field of hay, corn, cabbages, wheat, potatoes—mile after mile and mile after mile.

Ohio is too flat. It hasn't the rural innocence and unsophistication which Indiana seems still to retain, nor yet the characteristics of a thoroughgoing manufacturing world. There are too many factories and too many trolley lines, and a somewhat unsettled and uncertain feeling in the air, as if the state were undecided whether it would be all city and manufacturing or not. I hate that midstate, uncertain feeling, which comes with a changing condition anywhere. It is something like that restless simmering into which water bursts before it boils. One wishes that it would either boil or stop simmering. This, as nearly as I can suggest it, is the way the northern portion of Ohio that we saw impressed me.

And, unlike my feeling of fifteen or twenty years ago, I think I am just a little weary of manufacturing and manufacturing towns, however well I recognize and applaud their necessity. Some show a sense of harmony and joy in labor and enthusiasm for getting on and being happy; but others, such as Buffalo and Cleveland, seem to have fallen into that secondary or tertiary state in which all the enthusiasm of the original workers and seekers has passed, money and power and privileges having fallen into the hands of the few. There is nothing for the many save a kind of spiritless drudgery which no one appreciates and which gives a city a hard, unlovely and workaday air. I felt this to be so, keenly, in the cases of Buffalo and Cleveland, as of Manchester, Leeds and Liverpool.

Years ago these American cities were increasing at the rate of from ten to fifty thousand a year. Then there was more of hope and enthusiasm about them than there is now, more of happy anticipation. It is true that they are still growing and that there is enthusiasm, but neither the growth nor the enthusiasm is of the same quality. As a nation, although we are only twentyfive to thirty years older in point of time, we are centuries older in viewpoint. We have experienced so much in these past few years. We have endured so much. That brood of giants that rose and wrought and fell between 1870 and 1910 —children of the dragon's teeth, all of them—wrought shackles in the night and bound us hand and foot. They have seized nearly all our national privileges, they have bedeviled the law and the courts and the national and state seats of legislation, they have laid a heavy hand upon our highways and all our means of communication, poisoned our food and suborned our colleges and newspapers; yet in spite of them, so young and strong are we, we have been going on, limping a little, but still advancing. Giants who spring from dragon's teeth are our expensive luxury. In the high councils of nature there must be some need for them, else they never would have appeared. But I am convinced that these western cities have no longer that younger, singing mood they once had. We are soberer as a nation. Not every man can hope to be president, as we once fancied,—nor a millionaire. We are nearer the European standard of quiet, disillusioned effort, without so many great dreams to stir us.

Departing from Buffalo, not stopping to revisit the Falls or those immense turbine generators or indeed any other thing thereabout, we encountered some men who knew Speed and who were starting a new automobile factory. They wanted him to come and work for them, so well known was he as a test man and expert driver. Then we came to a grimy section of factories on a canal or pond, so black and rancidly stale that it interested us. Factory sections have this in common with other purely individual and utilitarian things,—they can be interesting beyond any intention of those who plan them. This canal or pond was so slimy or oily, or both, that it constantly emitted bubbles of gas which gave the neighborhood an acrid odor. The chimneys and roofs of these warehouses rose in such an unusual way and composed so well that Franklin decided he should like to sketch them. So here we sat, he on the walking beam of a great shovel derrick lowered to near the ground, behind two tug boats anchored on the shore, while I made myself comfortable on a pile of white gravel, some of which I threw into the water. I spent my time speculating as to what sort of people occupied the small drab houses which faced this picturesque prospect. I imagined a poet as great as Walt Whitman being able to live and take an interest in this grimy beauty, with thieves and pickpockets and prostitutes of a low order for neighbors.

A few blocks farther on there came into view an enormous grain elevator, standing up like a huge Egyptian temple in a flat plain. This elevator was composed of a bundle of concrete tubes or stand pipes, capable of being separately filled or emptied, thus facilitating the loading and unloading of cars and allowing the separate storage of different lots of grain. Before it, as before the great bridge at Nicholsen, we paused, awestruck by its size and design, something colossal and ancient suggested by its lines.

Then we sped out among small yellow or drab workingmen's cottages, their yards treeless for the most part, their walls smoky.

Lone women were hanging over gates and workingmen plodding heavily about with pipes in their mouths, and squeaky shoes and clothes too loose covering their bodies. Every now and then a church appeared—one of those noble institutions which represent to these poor clowns heaven, pearly gates and jasper streets. Great iron bridges came into view, or some small river or inlet crowded with great ships. Then came the lake shore, lit by a sinking and glorious afternoon sun, and a long stretch of that wonderful brick road, with enormous steel plants on either hand, thousands of automobiles, and lines of foreign looking workingmen going in and out of cottages straggling in conventional order across distant fields. Out over the water was an occasional white sail or a gull, or many gulls. Oh, gulls, gulls, I thought, take me into your free, wild world when I die!

Just outside Buffalo, on a spit of land between this wonderful brick road and the lake, we came to the Tackawanna Steel Company, its scores of tall, black stacks belching clouds of smoke and its immense steel pillar supported sheds showing the fires of the forges below. The great war had evidently brought prosperity to this concern, as to others. Thousands of men were evidently working here, Sunday though it was, for the several gates were crowded by foreign types of women carrying baskets and buckets, and the road and the one trolley line which ran along here for a distance were crowded with grimy workers, mostly of fine physical build. I naturally thought of all the shells and machine guns and cannon they might be making, and somehow it brought the great war a little nearer. Personally, I felt at the time that the war was likely to eventuate in favor of the Germans because they were better prepared.

Be that as it may, my mood was not belligerent and not pro-moral or pro-anything. I am too doubtful of life and its tendencies to enthuse over theories. With nations, as with individuals, the strongest or most desired win, and in the crisis which was then the Germans seemed to me the strongest. I merely hoped that America might keep out of it, in order that she might attain sufficient strength and judgment to battle for her own ideals in the future. For battle she must, never doubt it, and that from city to city and state to state. If she survives the ultimate maelstrom, with her romantic ideals of faith and love and truth, it will be a miracle.

This matter of manufacture and enormous industries is always a fascinating thing to me, and careening along this lake shore at breakneck speed, I could not help marveling at it. It seems to point so clearly to a lordship in life, a hierarchy of powers, against which the common man is always struggling, but which he never quite overcomes, anywhere. The world is always palavering about the brotherhood of man and the freedom and independence of the individual; yet when you go through a city like Buffalo or Cleveland and see all its energy practically devoted to great factories and corporations and their interests, and when you see the common man, of whom there is so much talk as to his interests and superiority, living in cottages or long streets of flats without a vestige of charm or beauty, his labor fixed in price and his ideas circumscribed in part (else he would never be content with so meager and grimy a world), you can scarcely believe in the equality or even the brotherhood of man, however much you may believe in the sympathy or good intentions of some people.

These regions around Buffalo were most suggestive of the great division that has arisen between the common man and the man of executive ability and ideas here in America,—a division as old and as deep as life itself. I have no least complaint against the common man toiling for anybody with ideas and superior brains—who could have?—if it were not for the fact that the superior man inevitably seeks to arrange a dynasty of his blood, that his children and his children's children need never to turn a hand, whereas it is he only who is deserving, and not his children. Wealth tends to aristocracy, and your strong man comes almost inevitably to the conclusion that not only he but all that relates to him is of superior fiber. This may be and sometimes is true, no doubt, but not always, and it is the exception which causes all the trouble. The ordinary mortal should not be compelled to moil and delve for a fool. I refuse to think that it is either necessary or inevitable that I, or any other man, should work for a few dollars a day, skimping and longing, while another, a dunce, who never did anything but come into the world as the heir of a strong man, should take the heavy profits of my work and stuff them into his pockets. It has always been so, I'll admit, and it seems that there is an actual tendency in nature to continue it; but I would just as lief contend with nature on this subject, if possible, as any other. We are not sure that nature inevitably wills it at that. Kings have been slain and parasitic dynasties trampled into the earth.

Why not here and now?

CHAPTER XXIII

THE APPROACH TO ERIE

BEYOND the Tackawanna Steel Works there was a lake beach with thousands of people bathing and sausage and lemonade venders hawking their wares (I couldn't resist buying one "hot dog") ; and after that a long line, miles it seemed to me, of sumptuous country places facing the lake, their roofs and gables showing through the trees; then the lake proper with not much interruption of view for a while; and then a detour, and then a flat, open country road, oiled until it was black, and then a white macadam road. Now that we were out of the hill and mountain country, I was missing those splendid rises and falls of earth which had so diverted me for days; but one cannot have hill country everywhere, and so as we sped along we endeavored to make the best of what was to be seen. These small white and grey wooden towns, with their white wooden churches and Sabbath ambling citizens, began to interest me. What a life, I said to myself, and what beliefs these people entertain! One could discern their creeds by the number of wooden and brick churches and the sense of a Sabbath stillness and propriety investing everything. At dusk, tiny church bells began to ring, church doors, revealing lighted interiors, stood open, and the people began to come forth from their homes and enter. I have no deadly opposition to religion. The weak and troubled mind must have something on which to rest. It is only when in the form of priestcraft and ministerial conniving it becomes puffed up and arrogant and decides that all the world must think as it thinks, and do as it does, and that if one does not one is a heretic and an outcast, that I resent it.

The effrontery of these theorists anyhow, with their

sacraments and their catechisms! Think of that mad dog Torquemada bestriding Spain like a Colossus, driving out eight hundred thousand innocent Jews, burning at the stake two thousand innocent doubters, stirring up all the ignorant animal prejudice of the masses, and leaving Spain the bleak and hungry land it is today! Think of it!—a priest, a theorist, a damned speculator in monastic abstrusities, being able to do anything like that! And then the Inquisition as a whole, the burning of poor John Huss, the sale of indulgences and the driving out of Luther. Beware of the enthusiastic religionist and his priestly servitors and leaders! Let not the theorist become too secure! Think of those who, in the name of a mystic unproven God, would seize on all your liberties and privileges, and put them in leash to a wild-eyed exorcist romancer of the type of Peter the Hermit, for instance. Do not Asia and Africa show almost daily the insane uprising of some crack-brained Messiah? Beware! Look with suspicion upon all Billy Sundays and their ilk generally. Let not the uplifter and the reformer become too bold. They inflame the ignorant passions of the mob, who never think and never will. Already America is being too freely tramped over by liquor reformers, magazine and book and picture censors, dreamers and cranks and lunatics who think that mob judgment is better than individual judgment, that the welfare of the ignorant mass should guide and regulate the spiritual inspiration of the individual. Think of one million, or one billion, factory hands, led by priests and preachers, able to dictate to a Spencer whether or not he should compile a synthetic philosophy—or to a Synge, whether he should write a "Play Boy of the Western World," or to a Voltaire, whether he should publish a "Candide."

Out on them for a swinish mass! Shut up the churches, knock down the steeples! Harry them until they know the true place of religion,—a weak man's shield! Let us have no more balderdash concerning the duty of man to respect any theory. He can if he chooses. That is his business. But when he seeks to dictate to his neighbor what he shall think, then it is a different matter.

As I rode through this region this evening, I could not help feeling and seeing still operating here all the conditions which years ago I put safely behind me. Here were the people who still believed that God gave the Ten Commandments to Moses on Sinai and that Joshua made the sun to stand still in Avalon. They would hound you out of their midst for lack of faith in beliefs which otherwhere are silly children's tales,—or their leaders would.

About seven o'clock, or a little later, we reached the town of Fredonia, still in New York State but near its extreme western boundary. We came very near attending church here, Franklin and I, because a church door on the square stood open and the congregation were singing. Instead, after strolling about for a time, we compromised on a washup in a charming oldfashioned white, square, colonnaded hotel facing the park. We went to the only restaurant, the hotel diningroom being closed, and after that, while Speed took on a supply of gas and oil, we jested with an old Scotchman who had struck up a friendship with Speed and was telling him the history of his youth in Edinburgh, and how and why he wanted America to keep out of the war. He, too, had a mechanical laugh, like that odd creature in the square at Bath, a kind of wild jackalesque grimace, which was kindly and cheerfully meant, however. Finally he grew so gay, having someone to talk to, that he executed a Jack-knife-ish automaton dance which amused me greatly. When Speed was ready we were off again, passing hamlet after hamlet and town after town, and entering Pennsylvania again a few miles west (that small bit which cuts northward between Ohio and New York at Erie and interferes with the natural continuation of New York).

The night was so fine and the wind so refreshing that I went off into dreamland again, not into actual sleeping dreams, but into something that was neither sleeping nor waking. These states that I achieved in this way were so peculiar that I found myself dwelling on them afterward. They were like the effects of a drug. In the trees that we passed I could see strange forms, all the more weird for the moonlight, which was very weak as yet,—grotesque hags and demons whose hair and beards were leaves and whose bony structures were branches. They quite moved me, as in childhood. And on the road we saw strolling lovers occasionally, arm in arm, sometimes clasped in each other's arms, kissing, couples whom the flare of our headlights illumined with a cruel realism.

A town called Brocton was passed, a fire arch over its principal street corner bidding all and sundry to stop and consider the joys of Brocton. A town called Pomfret, sweet as trees and snug little houses could make it, had an hotel facing a principal corner, which caused us to pause and debate whether we would go on, it was so homelike. But having set our hearts, or our duty, on Erie, we felt it to be a weakness thus to pause and debate.

On and on, through Westfield, Ripley, Northeast, Harbor Creek. It was growing late. At one of these towns we saw a most charming small hotel, snuggled in trees, with rocking chairs on a veranda in front and a light in the office which suggested a kind of expectancy of the stranger. It was after midnight now and I was so sleepy that the thought of a bed was like that of heaven to a good Christian. The most colorful, the most soothing sensations were playing over my body and in my brain. I was in that halcyon state where these things were either real or not, just as you chose—so intoxicating or soothing is fresh air. Sometimes I was here, sometimes in Warsaw or Sullivan or Evansville, Indiana, thirty years before, sometimes back in New York. Occasionally a jolt had brought me to, but I was soon back again in this twilight land where all was so lovely and where I wanted to remain.

"Why should we go on into Erie?" I sighed, once we were aroused. "It'll be hot and stuffy."

Franklin got down and rang a bell, but no one answered. It was nearing one o'clock. Finally he came back and said, "Well, I can't seem to rout anybody out over there. Do you want to try?"

Warm and sleepy, I climbed down.

On the porch outside were a number of comfortable chairs. In the small, clean office was a light and more chairs. It looked like an ideal abiding place.

I rang and rang and rang. The fact that I had been so drowsy made me irritable, and the fact that I could hear the bell tinkling and sputtering, but no voice replying and no step, irritated me all the more. Then I kicked for a while and then I tried beating.

Not a sound in response.

"This is one swell hotel," I groaned irritably, and Speed, lighting a cigarette, added,

"Well, I'd like to have a picture of that hotel keeper. He must be a sight, his nose up, his mouth open."

Still no answer. Finally, in despair, I went out in the middle of the road and surveyed the hotel. It was most attractive in the moonlight, but absolutely dead to the world.

"The blank, blank, blank, blank, blank, blank, blank," I called, resuscitating all my best and fiercest oaths. "To think that a blank, blank, blank, blank, blank could sleep that way anyhow. Here we are, trying to bring him a little business, and off he goes to bed, or she. Blank, blank, blank, the blank, blank, blanked old place anyhow," and back I went and got into the car.

"Say," called Speed, derisively, "ain't he a bird? Whaddy y'know. He's a great hotel keeper."

"Oh, well," I said hopelessly, and Franklin added, "We're sure to get a good bed in Erie."

So on we went, tearing along the road, eager to get anywhere, it was so late.

But if we had known what was in store for us we would have returned to that small hotel, I think, and broken in its door, for a few miles farther on, an arrow, pointing northward, read, "Erie Main Road Closed." Then we recalled that there had been a great storm a few days or weeks before and that houses had been washed out by a freshet and a number of people had been killed. The road grew very bad. It was a dirt road, a kind of marshy, oily, mucky looking thing, cut into deep ruts. After a short distance under darksome trees, it turned into a wide, marshy looking area, with a number of railroad tracks crossing it from east to west and numerous freight trains and switch engines jangling to and fro in the dark. A considerable distance off to the north, over a seeming waste of marshy land, was an immense fire sign which read, "Edison General Electric Company, Erie." Overhead, in a fine midnight translucence, hung the stars, innumerable and clear, and I was content to lie back for a while, jolting as we were, and look at them.

"Well, there's Erie, anyhow," I commented. "We can't lose that fire sign."

"Yes, but look what's ahead of us," sighed Speed.

As it developed, that fire sign had nothing to do with Erie proper but was stuck off on some windy beach or marsh, no doubt, miles from the city. To the west of it, a considerable distance, was a faint glow in the sky, a light that looked like anything save the reflection of a city, but so it was. And this road grew worse and worse. The car lurched so at times that I thought we might be thrown out. Speed was constantly stopping it and examining the nature of certain ruts and pools farther on. He would stop and climb down and walk say four or five hundred feet and then come back, and bump on a little further. Finally, having gone a considerable distance on this course, we seemed to be mired. We would dash into a muddy slough and there the wheels would just spin without making any progress. The way out of this was to trample earth behind the wheels and then back up. I began to think we were good for a night in the open. Franklin and I walked back blocks and blocks to see whether by chance we hadn't gotten on the wrong road. Having decided that we were doing as well as could be expected under the circumstances, we returned and sat in the car. After much time wasted we struck a better portion of the road, coming to where it turned at right angles over the maze of unguarded tracks which we had been paralleling all this while. It was a treacherous place, with neither gates nor watchmen, but just a great welter of dark tracks with freight cars standing here and there, signal lights glimmering in the distance, and engines and trains switching up and down.

"Shall we risk it?" asked Speed cautiously.

"Sure, we'll have to," replied Franklin. "It's dangerous but it's the only way."

We raced over it at breakneck speed and into more unfriendly marshy country beyond. We reached a street, a far-out one, but nevertheless a street, without a house on it and only a few gas lamps flickering in the warm night air. In a region of small wooden cottages, so small as to be pathetic, we suddenly encountered one of those mounted police for which Pennsylvania is famous, sitting by the curbing of a street corner, his gun in his hand and a saddle horse standing near.

"Which way into Erie?" we called.

"Straight on."

"Is this where the storm was?" we asked.

"Where the washout was," he replied.

We could see where houses had been torn down or broken into or flung askew by some turbulent element much superior to these little shells in which people dwelt.

Through brightly lighted but apparently deserted streets we sped on, and finally found a public square with which Speed was familiar. He had been here before. We hurried up to an hotel, which was largely darkened for the night. Out of the door, just as we arrived, were coming two girls in frills and flounces, so conspicuously arrayed that they looked as though they must have been attending an affair of some kind. An hotel attendant was showing them to a taxi. Franklin went in to arrange for three adjoining rooms if possible, and as I followed I heard one attendant say to another,—they had both been showing the girls out—"Can you beat it? Say, they make theirs easy."

I wondered. The hotel was quite dark inside.

In a few minutes we had adjusted our accommodations and were in our rooms, I in one with a tall window looking out into a spacious court. The bed was large and soft. I fairly fell out of my clothes and sank into it, just having sense enough to turn out the light. In a minute I fancy I was sound asleep, for the next thing I was conscious of was three maids gossiping outside my door.

"Blank, blank, blank," I began. "Am I not going to be allowed to get any sleep tonight?"

To my astonishment, I discovered the window behind the curtains was blazing with light.

I looked at my watch. It was nine o'clock. And we had turned in at three thirty.

CHAPTER XXIV

THE WRECKAGE OF A STORM

THE next day was another of travel in a hot sun over a country that in part lacked charm, in other parts was idyllically beautiful. We should have reached Sandusky and even the Indiana line by night, if we had been traveling as we expected. But to begin with, we made a late start, did not get out of Erie until noon, and that for various reasons,—a late rising, a very good breakfast and therefore a long one, a shave, a search for picture cards and what not. Our examination of the wreck made by the great storm and flood was extended, and having been up late the night before we were in a lazy mood anyhow.

Erie proved exceedingly interesting to me because of two things. One of these was this: that the effects of the reported storm or flood were much more startling than I had supposed. The night before we had entered by some streets which apparently skirted the afflicted district, but today we saw it in all its casual naturalness, and it struck me as something well worth seeing. Blocks upon blocks of houses washed away, upset, piled in heaps, the debris including machinery, lumber, household goods, wagons and carts. Through one wall front torn away I saw a mass of sewing machines dumped in a heap. It had been an agency. In another there was a mass of wool in bags stacked up, all muddied by the water but otherwise intact. Grocery stores, butcher shops, a candy store, a drug store, factories and homes of all kinds had been broken into by the water or knocked down by the cataclysmic onslaught of water and nearly shaken to pieces. Ceilings were down, plaster stripped from the walls, bricks stacked in great heaps,—a sorry sight. We learned that thirtyfive people had been killed and many others injured.

Another was that, aside from this Greek-like tragedy, it looked like the native town of Jennie Gerhardt, my pet heroine, though I wrote that she was born in Columbus, a place I have never visited in my life.

[That reminds me that a Columbus book reviewer once remarked that it was easy to identify the various places mentioned in Columbus, that the study was so accurate!] But never having seen Columbus, and having another small city in mind, it chanced now that Erie answered the description exactly. These long, narrow, small housed, tree-shaded streets (in many instances saplings) dominated at intervals by large churches or factories,—this indubitably was the world in which Jennie originally moved, breathed, and had her being. I was fascinated when I arose in the morning, to find that this hotel was one such as the pretentious Senator Brander might have chosen to live in, and the polished brasses of whose handrails and stairsteps a woman of Mrs. Gerhardt's limited capabilities would have been employed to polish or scrub. Even the great plate-glass windows lined within and without by comfortable chairs commanding, as they did, the principal public square or park and all the fascinating forces of so vigorous and young a town, were such as would naturally be occupied by the bloods and sports of the village, the traveling salesmen, and the idling bigwigs of political and other realms. It was an excellent hotel, none better; as clean, comfortable and tasteful as one would wish in this workaday world; and past its windows when I first came down looking for a morning paper, were tripping a few shop girls and belated workers carrying lunch boxes.

"Jennie's world to the life," I thought. "Poor little girl."

But the seventyfive thousand people here—how did they manage to pass their lives without the manifold opportunities and diversions which fill, or can, at least, the minds of the citizens of Paris, Rome, London, Chicago, New York? Here were all these thousands, working and dreaming perhaps, but how did they fill their lives? I pictured them as dressing at breakfast time, going to work each morning, and then after a day at machines or in stores, with lunches on counter or workbench, returning at night, a fair proportion of them at any rate, to the very little houses we had seen coming in; and after reading those impossible, helter-skelter, higgledy-piggledy, hodge-podges of rumor, false witness, romance, malice, evil glamour and what not—the evening newspapers—retiring to their virtuous couches, socalled, to rise again the next day.

I am under no illusions as to these towns, and I hold no highflown notions as to our splendid citizenry, and yet I am intensely sympathetic with them. I have had too much evidence in my time of how they do and feel. I always wonder how it is that people who entertain such highflown ideas of how people are and what they think and say—in writing, theorizing, editorializing—manage to hold such practical and even fierce relations with life itself. Every one of those simple American towns through which we had been passing had its red light district. Every one had its quota of saloons and dives, as well as churches and honorable homes. Who keeps the vulgar, shabby, gross, immoral, inartistic end of things going, if we are all so splendid and worthy as so many current, top-lofty theorizers would have us believe? Here in this little city of Erie, as in every other peaceful American hamlet, you would find the more animal and vigorous among them turning to those same red streets and dives we have been speaking of, while the paler, more storm-beaten, less animal or vigorous, more life-harried, take to the darksome doors of the church. Necessity drives the vast majority of them along paths which they fain would not travel, and the factories and stores in which they work eat up a vitality which otherwise might show itself in wild and unpleasant ways.

Here, as I have said, in these plain, uninteresting streets was more evidence of that stern destiny and inconsiderateness of the gods which the Greeks so well understood and with such majesty noted, and which always causes me to wonder how religion manages to survive in any form.   For here, several weeks before, was this simple, virtuous town (if we are to believe the moralistic tosh which runs through all our American papers), sitting down after its dinner and a hard day's work to read the evening paper.   It was deserving not only of the encomiums of men, but of gods, presumably.   And then, the gods presiding over and regulating all things in the interest of man, a rainstorm comes up and swells a small creek or rivulet running through the heart of the town and under small bridges, culverts and even houses— so small is it—into a kind of foaming torrent.   All is going well so far.   The culverts and bridges and stream beds are large enough to permit the water to be carried away. Only a few roofs are blown off, a few churches struck by lightning, one or two people killed in an ordinary, electric storm way.

Enters then the element of human error.   This is always the great point with all moralists.   Once the crimes or mistakes or indifferences of the ruling powers could be frankly and squarely placed on the shoulders of the devil.   No one could explain how a devil who could commit so much error came to live and reign in the same universe with an omnipotent God, but even so.   The devil, however, having become a mythical and threadbare scapegoat, it finally became necessary to invent some new palliative of omnipotent action, and so human error came into being as a whipping dummy—man's troubles are due to his own mistaken tendencies, though there is a God who creates and can guide him and who does punish him for doing the things which he ought to know better than to do.

Selah!   So be it.   But here in Erie is this honest or reprehensible community, as you will, and here is the extra severe thunder and rain storm,—a cloudburst, no less.   The small brook or rivulet swells and swells.   People notice it, perhaps, looking out of their doors and windows, but it seems to be doing well enough.   Then, unknown to the great majority of them, a barn a number of blocks out, a poor, humanly erroneous barn, is washed away against a fair-sized culvert, blocking it completely.

The gully beyond the culvert, upstream, is very large and it fills and fills with water. Because of its somewhat widening character a small lake forms,—a heavy body of water pressing every moment more and more heavily against the culvert. When the former has swollen to a great size this latter gives way. There is a downward rush of water—a small mountain of water, no less. Bridges, culverts, houses built over the brook, houses for two blocks on either hand, are suddenly pressed against or even partially filled by water. Citizens reading their evening newspapers, or playing the accordeon or the victrola or cards or checkers or what you will, feel their houses begin to move. Chimneys and plaster fall. Houses collapse completely. In one house eight are instantly killed,—a judgment of God, no doubt, on their particular kind of wickedness. In another house three, in another house four; death being apportioned, no doubt, according to the quality of their crimes. Altogether, thirtyfive die, many are injured, and scores upon scores of houses, covering an area of twentysix blocks in length, are moved, upset, floated blocks from their normal position, or shaken to pieces or consumed by fire.

The fire department is called out and the Pennsylvania mounted police. The moving picture camera men come and turn an honest penny. Picture postcard dealers who make money out of cards at a cent apiece photograph all the horrors. The newspapers get out extras, thereby profiting a few dollars, and all Erie, and even all America is interested, entertained, emotionalized. Even we, coming several weeks later and seeing only carpenters, masons, and plumbers at work, where houses are lying about in ruins, are intensely concerned. We ride about examining all the debris and getting a fine wonder out of it, until we are ordered back, at one place, by a thick-witted mounted policeman whose horse has taken fright at our machine; a thing which a mounted policeman's horse should never do, and which makes a sort of fool of him and so irritates him greatly.

"Get out of here!" he shouted angrily at one street corner, glaring at us, "sticking your damn noses into everything!"

"What the hell ails you anyhow?" I replied, equally irritable, for we had just been directed by another mounted policeman whose horse had not been frightened by us, to come down in here and see some real tragedy—"The policeman at the last corner told us to come in here."

"Well, you can't come in. Get out!" and he flicked his boot with his hand in a contemptuous way.

"Ah, go to hell," I replied angrily, but we had to move just the same. The law in boots and a wide rimmed hat, à la Silver City, was before us.

We got out, cursing the mounted policeman, for who wants to argue with a long, lean, thin-faced, sallow Pennsylvanian armed with a great sixteen shot revolver? God has never been just to me. He has never made me a mounted policeman. As we cruised about in Franklin's car, looking at all the debris and ruin, I speculated on this problem in ethics and morals or theism or what you will: Why didn't God stop this flood if he loved these people? Or is there no God or force or intelligence to think about them at all? Why are we here, anyhow? Were there any *unjust*, or only *just* among them? Why select Erie when He might have assailed Pittsburg or Broadway and Fortysecond Street, New York, or Philadelphia? Think of what a splendid evidence of judgment that last would have been, or Brooklyn! Oh, God, why not Brooklyn? Why eight people in one house and only one in another and none in many others? Do I seem much too ribald, dear reader? Were the people themselves responsible for not building good barns or culverts or anticipating freshets? Will it come about after a while that every single man will think of the welfare of all other men before he does anything, and so build and so do that no other man will be injured by any action of his? And will every man have the brains (given by God) so to do—or will God prevent freshets and washouts and barns being swept against weak culverts?

I am an honest inquirer. I was asking myself these very questions, wondering over the justice or injustice of life. Do you think there is any such thing as justice, or will you agree with Euripides, as I invariably feel that I must?

> "Great treasure halls hath Zeus in heaven,
> From whence to man strange dooms are given
> Past hope or fear.
> And the end looked for cometh not,
> And a path is there where no man thought.
> So hath it fallen here."

CHAPTER XXV

CONNEAUT

MORE splendid lake road beyond Erie, though we were constantly running into detours which took us through sections dreadful to contemplate. The next place of any importance was the city of Conneaut, Ohio, which revealed one form of mechanical advance I had never dreamed existed. Conneaut being "contagious," as Philosopher Dooley used to say, to the coal fields of Pennsylvania—hard and soft—and incidentally (by water) to the iron and copper mines "up Superior way" in northern Michigan, a kind of transshipping business has sprung up, the coal from these mines being brought here and loaded onto boats for all points on the Great Lakes. Similarly copper and iron coming down from upper Michigan and Wisconsin on boats are here taken out and loaded into cars. I never knew before that iron ore was powdered for shipment—it looks just like a dull red earth—or that they stored it in great hills pending a day of use,—hills which looked to me as though a thousand ships might not lower them in a year. John D. Rockefeller, I am told, was the guiding spirit in all this development here, having first seen the profit and convenience of bringing ore from the mines in northern Michigan south by water to the mills of Pennsylvania and incidentally returning in the same carriers coal to all parts of the Great Lakes and elsewhere. A canny man, that. Won't some American Homer kindly sing of him as one of the great wonders of the world?

Optically and for a material thrill, the machinery for transshipping these enormous supplies was most interesting to me.

Suppose you were able to take an iron car weighing

say thirty or forty thousand pounds, load it with coal weighing thirty or forty thousand pounds more, and turn it up, quite as you would a coal scuttle, and empty the contents into a waiting ship. . . . Then suppose you looked in the car and saw three or four pieces of coal still lying in it and said to yourself, "Oh, well, I might as well dump these in, too," and then you lifted up the car and dumped the remaining two or three pieces out— wouldn't you feel rather strong?

Well, that is what is being done at Conneaut, Ohio, morning, noon and night, and often all night, as all day. The boats bringing these immense loads of iron ore are waiting to take back coal, and so this enormous process of loading and unloading goes on continually. Franklin and I were standing on a high bank commanding all this and a wonderful view of Lake Erie, never dreaming that the little box-like things we saw in the distance being elevated and turned over were steel coal cars, when he suddenly exclaimed, "I do believe those things over there are cars, Dreiser,—steel coal cars."

"Get out!" I replied incredulously.

"That's what they are," he insisted. "We'll have Speed run the machine over onto that other hill, and then we can be sure."

From this second vantage point it was all very clear— great cars being run upon a platform, elevated quickly to a given position over a runway or coal chute leading down into the hold of a waiting steamer, and then quickly and completely upset; the last few coals being shaken out as though each grain were precious.

"How long do you think it takes them to fill a ship like that?" I queried.

"Oh, I don't know," replied Franklin meditatively.

"Let's see how long it takes to empty a car."

We timed them—one car every three minutes.

"That means twenty cars an hour," I figured, "or one hundred cars in five hours. That ought to fill any steamer."

A little farther along this same shore, reaching out

toward the lake, where eventually was a small, white lighthouse, were those same hills of red powdered iron I have been telling you about—great long hills that it must have taken ships and ships and ships of iron to build. I thought of the ownership of all those things, the iron and copper mines in northern Michigan, the vast coal beds in Pennsylvania and elsewhere, and how they were acquired. Did you ever read a true history of them? I'll wager you haven't. Well, there is one, not so detached as it might be, a little propagandistic in tone in spots, but for all that a true and effective work. It is entitled "A History of the Great American Fortunes," by one Gustavus Myers, a curious soul, and ill repaid, as I have reason to know, for his untiring energy. It is really a most important work, and can be had in three compact volumes for about six dollars. It is almost too good to be true, a thorough going, forthright statement of the whole process. Some of his expositions make clear the almost hopeless nature of democracy,—and that is a very important thing to discover.

As I have said, this northern portion of Ohio is a mixture of half city and half country, and this little city of Conneaut was an interesting illustration of the rural American grappling with the metropolitan idea. In one imposing drug or candy store (the two are almost synonymous these days) to which Franklin and I went for a drink of soda, we met a striking example of the rural fixity of idea, or perhaps better, religiosity of mind or prejudice, in regard to certain normal human appetites or vices. In most of these small towns and cities in Ohio these days, total abstinence from all intoxicating liquors is enforced by local option. In Conneaut local option had decided that no intoxicating liquor of any kind should be sold there. But since human nature is as it is and must have some small outlet for its human naturalness, apparently they now get what are sometimes called near-drinks, which are sold under such enticing names as "Sparkade" (which is nothing more than a carbonated cider or apple juice), "Gayola," "Cheercoala," and a score of other,—all dosed, no doubt, with a trace of some temporarily bracing drug, like caffeine or kolanut. The one which I tried on this occasion was "Sparkade," a feeble, watery thing, which was advertised to have all the invigorating qualities of champagne and to taste the same.

"Has this any real champagne in it?" I asked the conventional but rosy cheeked girl who waited on me, jestingly.

"No, sir. I don't think so, sir. I've never tried it, though."

"What?" I said, "Never tried this wonderful drink? Have you ever tasted champagne?"

"Indeed, not!" she replied, with a concerned and self-preservative air.

"What, never? Well, then, there's your chance. I'm going to drink a bottle of Sparkade and you can taste mine."

I poured out the bubbling stuff and offered it to her.

"No, thank you," she replied haughtily, and as I still held it toward her, *"No, thank you!* I never touch anything of that kind."

"But you say it is a nonintoxicant?"

"Well, I think it is, but I'm not sure. And anyhow, I don't think I'd care for it."

"Don't you belong to some society that is opposed to intoxicants of all kinds?" I queried teasingly.

"Yes, sir. Our church is opposed to liquor in any form."

"Even Sparkade?" I persisted.

She made a contemptuous mouth.

"There you have it, Franklin," I said to him. "You see—the Church rules here—a moral opinion. That's the way to bring up the rising generation—above corruption."

But outside Conneaut was so delightful. There was such a downpour of sunlight upon great, wide armed trees and mottling the sidewalks and roadways. In the local garage where we stopped for oil and some tools all was so orderly and clean—a veritable cosmos of mechanical intricacies which set me to meditating on the vast array of specialties into which the human mind may delve and make a living. Citizens were drifting about in an easy, summery way it seemed to me,—not with that hard pressure which seems to afflict the members of many larger cities. I felt so comfortable here, so much like idling. And Franklin and Speed seemed in the same mood.

Query. Was it the noon hour? or the gay, delicious sunlight seen through trees? or some inherent, spiritual quality in Conneaut itself? Query.

Beyond Conneaut we scuttled over more of that wonderful road, always in sight of the lake and so fine that when completed it will be the peer of any scenic route in the world, I fancy. Though as yet but earth, it was fast being made into brick. And positively I may assure you that you need never believe people you meet on the road and of whom you seek information as to shortest routes, places to eat, condition of road or the best roads. No traveling motorist seems to know, and no local resident or wiseacre anywhere is to be trusted. People tell you all sorts of things and without the slightest positive information. Franklin told me that out in his home town, Carmel, he had discovered that the wise loafers who hang about the post office and public stores, and had lived in Hamilton County all their lives, had been for years uniformly misdirecting passing automobilists as to the best or shortest route between Carmel and Nobelsville, Indiana. In some cases it might be done, he thought, in a spirit of deviltry, in others prejudice as to routes was responsible, in still others nothing more than blank ignorance as to what constitutes good roads!

Here in Conneaut, as we were entering the city by "the largest viaduct in the world," we asked an old toll keeper, who collected thirty cents from us as a token of his esteem, which was the shortest and best road to Ashtabula and whether there wasn't a good shore road.

"Well, now, I'll tell you," he began, striking a position

and beginning to smooth his abundant whiskers. "There is a shore road that runs along the lake, but it hain't no good. If you're a-goin' fer business you'll take the Ridge Road, but if you're just out joy ridin' and don't care where you go, you can go by the lake. The Ridge Road's the business man's road. There hain't no good road along the lake at this time o' year, with all the rain we've been havin.' "

Franklin, I am sure, was inclined to heed his advice at first, whereas I, having listened to similar bits of misinformation all the way out from New York, was inclined to be skeptical and even angry, and besides the car wasn't mine. These wretched old fixtures, I said to myself, who had never been in an automobile more than a half dozen times in their lives, were the most convinced, apparently, as to the soundness of their information. They infuriated me at times, particularly when their advice tended to drive us out of the course I was interested in, and the shore road was the road I wanted to follow. I persuaded Franklin to pay no attention to this old fussbutton.

"What does he know?" I inquired. "There he sits at that bridge day in and day out and takes toll. Farmers with heavy loads may report all sorts of things, but we've seen how fine the dirt roads have been everywhere we've followed them."

Speed agreed with me.

So we struck out along the shore road and nothing could have been better. It was not exactly smooth, but it was soft with a light dust and so close to the lake that you could see the tumbling waves and throw a stone into them if you chose; and at certain points where a cove gave a wider view, there were people bathing and tents tacked down along the shore against the wind. It was wonderful. Every now and then we would encounter young men and women bathers ambling along the road in their water costumes, and in one instance the girl was so very shapely and so young and attractive that we exclaimed with pleasure. When she saw us looking at her she merely laughed and waved her hands. At another point two young girls standing beside a fence called, "Don't you wish you could take us along?" They were attractive enough to make anybody wish it.

CHAPTER XXVI

THE GAY LIFE OF THE LAKE SHORE

THEN came Ashtabula with another such scene as that at Conneaut, only somewhat more picturesque, since the road lay on high ground and we had a most striking view of the lake, with a world of coal cars waiting to be unloaded into ships, and ships and cranes and great moving derricks which formed a kind of filigree of iron in the distance with all the delicacy of an etching.

These coal and iron towns of Ohio were as like in their way as the larger manufacturing centers of the East in theirs. Coming into this place we passed through a small slum section at the end of the bridge by which we were entering, and because there was a water scene here which suggested the Chicago River in its palmiest days before it was renovated and practically deserted, I suggested that we stop and look at it. Three bums of the "Chimmie" Fadden-"Chuck" Connors type were standing in a doorway adjoining a saloon. No sooner did they see us pause than they nudged each other and whispered. Franklin and I passed them to look at the scene. Coming back we climbed in the car, and as we did so the huskiest of the three stepped up and, with a look of humility assumed for the occasion, whimpered: "Say, boss, could you help a poor down-and-out to a mouthful of food?"

I looked at him wearily, because the bluff was too much.

Franklin, however, reached in his pocket and gave him fifteen cents.

"Why fifteen cents, Franklin?" I enquired.

"Oh, well," he replied, "it's an easy way to get rid of them. I don't like the looks of this place."

I turned to look at the recipient back among his friends. His mouth was pulled down at one corner as he related, with a leer of contempt, how easy it was to bleed these suckers. He even smiled at me as much as to say, "You mark!" I leered back with the greatest contempt I could assemble on such short notice—a great deal—but it did not cheer me any. He had the fifteen cents. He was of the same order of brain that today can be hired to kill a man for fifty dollars, or will undertake to rob or burn a house.

And after Ashtabula, which was as charming as any of these little cities to look at, with wide shady streets of homes and children playing gaily on lawns and in open lots everywhere, came Geneva-on-the-Lake, or Geneva Beach, as it seemed to be called—one of those new-sprung summer resorts of the middle west, which always amuse me by their endless gaucheries and the things they have not and never seem to miss. One thing they do have is the charm of newness and hope and possibility, which excels almost anything of the kind you can find elsewhere.

America can be the rawest, most awkward and inept land at times. You look at some of its scenes and people on occasions, and you wonder why the calves don't eat them. They are so verdant. And yet right in the midst of a thought like this you will be touched by a sense of youth and beauty and freedom and strength and happiness in a vigorous, garish way which will disarm you completely and make you want to become a part of it all, for a time anyhow.

Here lay this particular beach, high up above the lake, for all along this northern portion of Ohio the land comes close to the water, retaining an altitude of sixty or seventy feet and then suddenly dropping, giving room for a sandy beach say sixty or seventy feet wide, where a few tents may sometimes be found. And on this higher land, facing the water, are strung out all the cottages and small hotels or summer boarding places, with occasionally some stores and merry-go-rounds and restaurants, though not as a rule the gaudy rumble-jumble of a beach like Coney Island.

And the costumes! Heaven bless and preserve us! The patrons of this beach, as I learned by inquiry, come mostly from Pittsburg and points south in Ohio—Columbus, Dayton, Youngstown. They bring their rattan bags and small trunks stuffed to bursting with all the contraptions of assumed high life, and here for a period of anywhere from two days to three months, according to their means, associations, social position, they may be seen disporting themselves in the most colorful and bizarre ways. There was a gay welter of yellow coats with sky-blue, or white, or black-and-white skirts—and of blue, green, red or brown coats, mostly knit of silk or near-silk—with dresses or skirts of as sharply contrasting shades. Hats were a minus quantity, and ribbons for the hair ranged all the way from thin blue or red threads to great flaring bands of ribbon done into enormous bows and fastened over one ear or the other. Green, blue, red and white striped stick candy is nothing by comparison.

There were youths in tan, blue and white suits, but mostly white with sailor shirts open at the neck, white tennis shoes and little round white navy caps, which gave the majority of them a jocular, inconsequential air.

And the lawns of these places! In England, and most other countries abroad, I noticed the inhabitants seek a kind of privacy even in their summer gaieties—an air of reserve and exclusiveness even at Monte Carlo—but here!! The lawns, doors and windows of the cottages and boarding houses were open to the eyes of all the world. There were no fences. Croquet, tennis, basketball were being played at intervals by the most vivid groups. There were swings, hammocks, rockers and camp chairs scattered about on lawns and porches. All the immediate vicinity seemed to be a-summering, and it wanted everyone to know it.

As we sped into this region and stopped in front of a restaurant with a general store attachment at one side, two youths of that summering texture I have indicated, and both in white, drew near. They were of a shallow, vacant character. The sight of a dusty car, carrying a license tag not of their own state, and with bags and other paraphernalia strapped onto it, seemed to interest them.

"From New York, eh?" inquired the taller, a cool, somewhat shrewd and calculating type, but with that shallowness of soul which I have indicated—quite vacant indeed. "Did you come all the way from New York City?"

"Yes," said Franklin. "Is there a good restaurant anywhere hereabout?"

"Well, this is about the best, outside the boarding houses and inns around here. You might find it nicer if you stayed at one of the inns, though."

"Why?" asked Franklin. "Is the food better?"

"Well, not so much better—no. But you'd meet nicer people. They're more sociable."

"Yes, now our inn," put in the smaller one of the two, a veritable quip in his ultra-summer appearance. "Why don't you come over to our place? It's very nice there—lots of nice people."

I began to look at them curiously. This sudden burst of friendship or genial companionship—taking up with the stranger so swiftly—interested me. Why should they be so quick to invite one to that intimacy which in most places is attained only after a period—and yet, when you come to think of it, I suddenly asked myself why not. Is chemistry such a slow thing that it can only detect its affinities through long, slow formal movements? I knew this was not true, but also I knew that there was no affinity here, of any kind—merely a shallow, butterfly contact. These two seemed so very lightminded that I had to smile.

"They're nice genial people, are they?" I put in. "Do you suppose we could introduce ourselves and be friendly?"

"Oh, we'd introduce you—that's all right," put in this latest Sancho. "We can say you're friends of ours."

"Shades of the Hall Room Boys!" I exclaimed to myself. "What kind of world is this anyway—what sort of people? Here we ride up to a casino door in the heart of a summering community, and two soufflé youths in white offer to introduce us to their friends as friends of theirs. Is it my looks, or Franklin's, or the car, or what?"

A spirit of adventure began to well up in me. I thought of a few days spent here and what they might be made to mean. Thus introduced, we might soon find interesting companionship.

But I looked at Franklin and my enthusiasm cooled slightly. For an adventure of any kind one needs an absolutely unified enthusiasm for the same thing, and I was by no means sure that it existed here. Franklin is so solemn at times—such a moral and social mainstay. I argued that it was best, perhaps, not to say all that was in my mind, but I looked about me hopefully. Here were all those costumes I have indicated.

"This seems to be quite a place," I said to this camp follower. "Where do they all come from?"

"Oh, Pittsburg principally, and Cleveland. Most of the people right around here are from Pittsburg."

"Is there very good bathing here?"

"Wonderful. As good as anywhere."

I wondered what he knew about bathing anywhere but here.

"And what else is there?"

"Oh, tennis, golf, riding, boating." He fairly bristled with the social importance of the things he was suggesting.

"They seem to have bright colors here," I went on.

"You bet they do," he continued. "There are a lot of swell dressers here, aren't there, Ed?"

"That's right," replied his summery friend. "Some beauts here. George! You ought to see 'em some days."

"They're very glorious, are they?"

"That's what."

The conversation now turned back to us. Where were we going? What were we going for? Were we enjoying the trip? Were the roads good?

We told them of Indiana, and rose immediately in their estimation. We finally declined the invitation to be introduced into their circle. Instead we went into this restaurant, where the reception room was also a salesroom of sorts, and here we idled, while awaiting dinner.

I was still examining picture postcards when a young man, quite young, with a pink face and yellowish hair— a Scandinavian, I took it—came up beside me and stood looking at the pictures—almost over my shoulder I thought, though there was plenty of room in either direction. After a few moments I turned, somewhat irritated by his familiarity, and glanced at his shoes and suit, which were not of the best by any means, and at his hands, which were strong and well formed but rough.

"Nice pictures of things about here," he observed, in a voice which seemed to have a trace of the Scandinavian in it.

"Yes, very," I replied, wondering a little, uncertain whether it was merely another genial American seeking anyone to talk to or someone desirous of aid. You never can tell.

"Yes," he went on a little nervously, with a touch of strain in his voice, "it is nice to come to these places if you have the money. We all like to come to them when we can. Now I would like to come to a place like this, but I haven't any money. I just walked in and I thought maybe I might get something to do here. It's a nice brisk place with lots of people working."

"Now, what's his game?" I asked myself, turning toward him and then away, for his manner smacked a little of that unctuous type of religious and charitable emotion which one encounters in side-street missions—a most despicable type of sanctimonious religiosity and duty worship.

"Yes, it seems to be quite brisk," I replied, a little coldly.

"But I have to get something yet tonight, that is sure, if I am to have a place to sleep and something to eat."

He paused, and I looked at him, quite annoyed I am sure. "A beggar," I thought. "Beggars, tramps, and ne'er-do-wells and beginners are always selecting me. Well, I'll not give him anything. I'm tired of it. I did not come in here to be annoyed, and I won't be. Why should I always be annoyed? Why didn't he pick on Franklin?" I felt myself dreadfully aggrieved, I know.

"You'll find the manager back there somewhere, I presume," I said, aloud. "I'm only a stranger here myself." Then I turned away, but only to turn back as he started off. Something about him touched me—his youth, his strength, his ambitions, the interesting way he had addressed me. My rage wilted. I began to think of times when I was seeking work. "Wait a minute," I said; "here's the price of a meal, at least," and I handed him a bit of change. His face, which had remained rather tense and expressionless up to this time—the face that one always puts on in the presence of menacing degradation—softened.

"Thank you, thank you," he said feverishly. "I haven't eaten today yet. Really I haven't. But I may get something to do here." He smiled gratefully.

I turned away and he approached the small dark American who was running this place, but I'm not sure that he got anything. The latter was a very irritable, waspish person, with no doubt many troubles of his own. Franklin approached and I turned to him, and when I looked again my beggar was gone.

I often wish that I had more means and a kindlier demeanor wherewith to serve difficult, struggling youth.

.   .   .   .

I could not help noticing that the whole region, as well as this restaurant, seemed new and crudely assembled. The very management of this restaurant, the best in the place, was in all likelihood not the same which had obtained in the previous year. A thing like that is so characteristic of these mid-western resort atmospheres. The help (you could by no means call them waiters, for they were untrained in that branch of service) were girls, and mostly healthy, attractive ones—here, no doubt, in order to catch a beau or to be in a summer resort atmosphere. As I have previously indicated, anybody, according to the lay mind west of the Atlantic, can run a restaurant. If you have been a cook on a farm for some hay workers or reapers, so much the better. You are thereby entitled to cook and to be hailed as a restaurateur. Any domestic can "wait on table." All you have to do is to bring in the dishes and take them out again. All you need to do to steak or fish or fowl is to fry it. The art of selection, arrangement, combination are still mysteries of the decadent East. The West is above these things—the new West— God bless it! And if you ask for black coffee in a small cup, or potatoes prepared in any other way than fried, or should you desire a fish that carried with it its own peculiar sauce, they would stare at *you* as peculiar, or, better yet, with uncomprehending eyes.

But these girls, outside and in—what a contrast in American social relationships they presented! During our dinner the two youths had departed and got two maids from somewhere—maids of the mildest, most summery aspect—and were now hanging about, pending our return, in order to have more words and to indicate to us the true extent of their skill as beaux and summer gentlemen in waiting. As I looked through the windows at those outside and contrasted them with those within and now waiting on us, I was struck with the difference, class for class, between the girl who chooses to work and the girl of the same station practically who would rather do something else. The girls outside were of the gum-chewing, typewriter brand of summer siren, decked in white and blue dresses of the most feathery, flouncy character, and sport coats or jackets in broad, heavy stripes, one black and white, another orange and blue, and the usual ribbon in their hair. They seemed to me to be obsessed by the idea of being summery and nonchalant and sporty and preternaturally gay—indeed, all the things which the Sunday newspaper summer girl should be—a most amazing concoction at best, and purely a reflection or imitation of the vagrant thoughts of others —copies, marsh fire. Incidentally it struck me that in the very value of things they were destined to be nothing more than the toys and playthings of men—such men as they might be able to attract—not very important, perhaps, but as vigorous and inconsequential as themselves. On the other hand, those on the inside were so much more attractive because they lacked the cunning or silly sophistication of these others and because, by the very chemistry of their being, apparently, they were drawn to routine motherhood, legitimate or otherwise.

Personally I am by no means a conventionalist. I have never been able to decide which earthly state is best. All life is good, all life, to the individual who is enjoying himself and to the Creator of all things. The sting of existence is the great thing—the sensory sting, not its vocal theories—but that shuts out the religionist and the moralist and they will damn me forever. But still I so believe. Those girls outside, and for all their fineness and fripperies, were dull; whereas, those inside (some of them anyhow) had a dreamy, placid attractiveness which needed no particular smartness of speech or clothing to set them off. One of them, the one who waited on us, was a veritable Tess, large, placid, sensuous, unconsciously seductive. Many of the others seemed of a life they could not master but only gaze after. Where are the sensible males to *see* them, I thought. How is it that they escape while those others flaunt their dizzy gauds? But I soon consoled myself with the thought that they would not escape—for long. The strong male knows the real woman. Over and above ornament is the chemic attraction which laughs at ornament. I could see how the waitresses might fare better in love than the others.

But outside were the two youths and their maids waiting for us and we were intensely interested and as genial and companionable as might be. One of these girls was dark, svelte, languorous, rouged—a veritable siren of the modern moving picture school—or rather a copy of a siren. The other was younger, blonde, less made-up-ish, but so shallow. Dear, kind heaven, how shallow some people really are! And their clothes!

The conversation going on between them, for our benefit largely, was a thing to rejoice in or weep over, as you will. It was a hodge-podge of shallow humor and innuendo, the innuendo that conceals references to sex and brings smiles of understanding to the lips of the initiated.

"Lelah here is some girl, I'd have you know." This from the taller of the two summer men, who was feeling of her arm familiarly.

"How do *you* know?" This from Lelah, with a quizzical, evasive smile.

"Don't I?"

"Do you?"

"Well, you ought to know."

"I notice that you have to ask."

Or this other gem from the two men:

"Ella has nice shoes on today."

"That isn't all Ella has on, is it?"

"Well, not quite. She has a pretty smile."

I gathered from the many things thus said, and the way the girls were parading up and down in all directions in their very pronounced costumes, that if sex were not freely indulged in here, the beholding of it with the eyes and the formulation of it in thought and appearance were great factors in the daily life and charm of the place. There are ways and ways for the natural tendency of the world to show itself. The flaunting of desire, in its various aspects, is an old process. It was so being flaunted here.

CHAPTER XXVII

SHORTLY after leaving Ashtabula we ran into a storm
—one of those fine, windy, dusty, tree-groaning rains
that come up simply and magnificently and make you feel
that you are going to be blown into kingdom come and
struck by lightning en route. As we sped through great
aisles of trees and through little towns all bare to our
view through their open doors, as though they had not
a thing to conceal or a marauder to fear, the wind began to rise and the trees to swish and whistle, and by the
glare of our own powerful headlight we saw clouds of
dust rolling toward us. A few heavy drops of water hit
my head and face and someone, I suppose Franklin (let
me put all the blame I can on him in this story—what
else are hosts for?), suggested that we put up the top.

Now I, for one, vote automobile tops a nuisance.
They are a crime, really. Here was a fine electric storm,
with the heavens torn with great poles of light and the
woods and the fields and distant little cottages revealed
every few seconds with startling definiteness—and we
had to put up the top. Why? Well, there were bags
and coats and a camera and I know not what else, and
these things had to be protected. My own glasses began
to drip and my chin and my hair were very wet. So
up went the top.

But, worse than that, the sides had to go up, for now
the wind was driving the rain sidewise and we were all
getting soaked anyhow—so up went the sides. Then,
thus protected and with all the real beauty of the night
shut out, we rattled along, I pressing my nose to the
isinglass windows and wishing that I might see it all. I

cursed God and man and close, stuffy automobiles. I snuggled down in my corner and began to dream again when presently, say one hour later, or two or three (it must have been two or three, now that I think of it), another enormous bridge such as that we had seen at Nicholsen, Pennsylvania, hove into view, down a curve which our lamps illuminated with amazing clearness.

"Whoa!" I called to Speed, as though he were a horse.

"You're right," commented Franklin, without further observation on my part. "That is interesting, isn't it?" Though it was still raining, we opened those storm curtains and clambered out, walking on ahead of the car to stand and look at it. As we did a train came from somewhere—a long, brightly lighted passenger train—and sped over it as noiselessly as if it had been on solid ground. A large arch rose before us, an enormous thing, with another following in the distance and bridging a stream.

"Think I'd better sketch that?" queried Franklin.

"Indeed I do," I replied, "if it interests you. It's wonderful to me."

We wandered on down the curve and under it, through a great arch. A second bridge came into view—this time of iron—the one over which our road ran, and beyond that a third, of iron or steel also, much higher than either of the others. This last was a trolley bridge, and as we stood here a trolley car approached and sped over it. At the same time another train glided over the great stone arch.

"What is this—Bridge Centre?" I inquired.

"Transportationsburg," replied Franklin. "Can't you see?"

We fell to discussing lights and shadows and the best angle at which to make the drawing.

But there was no umbrella between us—useless things, umbrellas—and so I had to lay my mackintosh on Franklin's head and hold it out in front of him like an awning, while he peered under it and sketched and I played porch posts. Sketching so, we talked of the great walls of Europe—Spain and Italy—old Roman walls—and how these new things being built here in this fashion must endure—long after we were gone—and leave traces of what a wonderful nation we were, we Americans (German-Americans, Austro-Americans, Greek-Americans, Italian-Americans, French-Americans, English-Americans, Hindu-Americans).

"Just think, Franklin," I chortled, "you and I may be remembered for thousands and thousands of years as having stood here tonight and sketched this very bridge."

"Uh, huh," he commented.

"It may be written that 'In A. D. 1915, Theodore Dreiser, accompanied by one Franklin Booth, an artist, visited the site of this bridge, which was then in perfect condition, and made a sketch of it, preserved now in that famous volume entitled "A Hoosier Holiday," by Theodore Dreiser.' "

"You know how to advertise your own wares, don't you?" he said. "Who made the sketch?"

"Why, Franklin Booth, of course."

"But you didn't say so."

"Why didn't I?"

"Because you didn't."

"Oh, well. We'll correct all little errors like that in the proof. You'll be safe enough."

"Will I?"

"Surely you will."

"Well, in that case I'll finish the sketch. For a moment I thought I wouldn't. But now that I'm sure to be preserved for posterity——"

He went scratching on.

.   .   .   .

The lights we saw ahead of us were those of Painesville, Ohio, another manufacturing and trans-shipping city like Conneaut and Ashtabula, and this was the Grand River we were crossing, a rather modest stream, it seemed to me, for so large a name. (I learned its title from a picture postcard later in the city.)

One should be impressed with the development of this

picture postcard business in American towns. What is there to photograph, you might ask, of any of these places, large or small? Well, waterworks and soldiers' monuments and the residences of principal citizens, and so on and so forth. When I was a boy in Warsaw and earlier in Evansville and Sullivan, there wasn't a single picture postcard of this kind—only those highly colored "panoramas" or group views of the principal cities, like New York and Chicago, which sold for a quarter or at least fifteen cents. Of the smaller towns there was nothing, literally nothing. No small American town of that date would have presumed to suppose that it had anything of interest to photograph, yet on this trip there was scarcely a village that did not contain a rack somewhere of local views, if no more than of clouds and rills and cattle standing in water near an old bridge. By hunting out the leading drug store first, we could almost invariably discover all there was to know about a town in a scenic way, or nearly all. It was most gratifying.

This change in the number and character of our national facilities as they affect the very small towns had been impressing me all the way. When I was from eight to sixteen years of age, there was not a telephone or a trolley car or an ice cream soda fountain (in the modern sense of that treasure) or a roller-skating rink or a roller skate or a bicycle, or an automobile or phonograph, or a moving picture theatre, or indeed anything like the number of interesting and new things we have now—flying machines and submarines, for instance. It is true that just about that time—1880-1886—when I left Warsaw for the world outside, I was beginning to encounter the first or some solitary examples of these things. Thus the first picture postcards I ever found were in Chicago in 1896 or thereabouts, several years after I had visited the principal eastern cities, and I would have seen them if there had been any. The first electric light I ever saw was in Evansville, Indiana, in 1882, where to my youthful delight and amazement they were erecting tall, thin skeleton towers of steel, not less than one hundred and twentyfive feet high, and only about four feet in diameter—(you may still see them in Fort Wayne, Indiana)—and carrying four arc lights each at the top. Fifty such towers were supposed to light the whole city of Evansville, a place of between forty and fifty thousand, and they did, in a dim, mooney way. I remember as a boy of twelve standing in wonder, watching them being put up. Evansville seemed such a great city to me then. These towers were more interesting as a spectacle than useful as a lighting system, however, and were subsequently taken down.

The first telephone I ever saw was one being installed in the Central Fire Station at Vincennes, Indiana, in 1880 or thereabouts. At the time my mother was paying the enforced visit, later to be mentioned, to the wife of the captain of this particular institution, a girl who had worked for her as a seamstress years before. I was no more than eight at the time, and full of a natural curiosity, and I remember distinctly staring at the peculiar instrument which was being hung on a post in the centre of the fire station, and how the various firemen and citizens stood about and gaped. There was much excitement among the men because of the peculiar powers of the strange novelty. I think, from the way they stared at it, while Frank Bellett, the Captain, first talked through it to some other office in the little city, they felt there must be something spooky about it—some legerdemain by which the person talking at the other end made himself small and came along the wire, or that there was some sprite with a voice inside the box which as an intermediary did all the talking for both parties. I know I felt that there must be some such supernatural arrangement about it, and for this reason I too looked with awe and wonder. As days passed, however, and considerable talking was done through it, and my own mother, putting the receiver to her ear, listened while her friend, the wife, called from somewhere outside, my awe, if not the wonder, wore off. For years, though, perhaps because I never used one until nearly ten years later, the mystic character of the thing stuck in my mind.

It was much the same thing with the trolley car and the roller skate and the bicycle. I never saw a trolley car until I was seventeen or eighteen years of age, and then only an experimental one conducted on a mile of track laid on North Avenue, Chicago, by the late Charles T. Yerkes, at that time the principal traction magnate of Chicago. He was endeavoring to find out whether the underground trolley was a feasible thing for use in Chicago or not and had laid a short experimental section, or had had it laid for him. I was greatly astonished, when I first saw it, to think it would go without any visible means of propulsion—and that in spite of the fact that I had already seen the second cable road built in America running in State Street, Chicago, as early as 1884. At that time, our family having come to Chicago for the summer, I ran an errand for a West Madison Street confectioner which took me to a candy manufacturer's basement in State Street. There, through a window in the front of the store, underground, I saw great engines going, and a cable on wheels spinning by. Every now and then the grip of a car would appear and disappear past an opening under the track, which was here. It was most astonishing, and gave me a sense of vast inexplicable mystery which is just as lively today as it ever was, and as warranted.

In regard to the bicycle, the first one I ever saw was in Warsaw in 1884—a high-wheeled one, not a safety!—and the first pair of roller skates I ever saw was in the same place in 1885, when some adventurous amusement provider came there and opened a roller-skating parlor. It was a great craze for a while, and my brother Ed became an expert, though I never learned. There were various storms in our family over the fact that he was so eager for it, staying out late and running away, and because my mother, sympathetic soul, aided and abetted him, so keen was her sympathy with childhood and play, whereas my father, stern disciplinarian that he was, objected. Often have I seen Ed hanging about my mother's skirts, and she, distressed and puzzled, finally giving him a quarter out of her hard earned store to enjoy himself. He ought certainly to have the most tender memories of her.

The first ice cream soda fountain I ever saw, or the first ice cream soda I ever tasted, was served to me in Warsaw, Indiana, at the corner book store, opposite the courthouse, subsequently destroyed. That was in 1885. It was called to my attention by a boy named Judson Morris, whose father owned the store, and it served as an introduction and a basis for future friendship, our family having newly moved to Warsaw. It had just succeeded a drink known as the milk shake, which had attained great popularity everywhere the preceding year. But ice cream soda! By my troth, how pale and watery milk shake seemed in comparison! I fell, a giddy victim, and have never since recovered myself or become as enthusiastic over any other beverage.

And so I could continue—leaving Franklin and Speed waiting patiently in Painesville, Ohio, in the rain, but I won't. We hastened in after Franklin made his sketch, and, owing to some extraordinary rush of business which had filled the principal hotel, were compelled to take refuge in a rickety barn of a house known as "The Annex"—an annex to this other and much better one.

CHAPTER XXVIII

THE next morning we set off under grey, lowery clouds, over the shore road to Cleveland, which proved better than that between Erie and Painesville, having no breaks and being as smooth as a table. At one place we had to stop in an oatfield where the grain had been newly cut and shocked, to see if we could still jump over the shocks as in days of yore, this being a true test, according to Speed, as to whether one was in a fit condition to live eighty years, and also whether one had ever been a true farmer. Franklin and Speed leaped over the shocks with ease, Franklin's coat skirts flying out behind in a most bird-like manner, and Speed's legs and arms taking most peculiar angles. When it came my turn to do it, I funked miserably. Actually, I failed so badly that I felt very much distressed, being haunted for miles by the thought of increasing age and impending death, for once I was fairly athletic and could run three miles at a steady jog and not feel it. But now—well now, whenever I reached the jumping point I couldn't make it. My feet refused to leave the ground. I felt heavy.

Alas! Alas!

And then we had to pause and look at the lake, which because of the storm the night before and the stiff northwest wind blowing this morning, offered a fine tumbling spectacle. As to dignity and impressiveness I could see no difference between this lake shore and most of the best sea beaches which I have seen elsewhere. The waves were long and dark and foamy, rolling in, from a long distance out, with a thump and a roar which was as fierce as that of any sea. The beach was of smooth, grey sand, with occasional piles of driftwood scattered along its length, and twisted and tortured trees hanging over the banks of the highland above. In the distance we could see the faint outlines of the city of Cleveland, a penciled blur, and over it a cloud of dark smoke, the customary banner of our manufacturing world. I decided that here would be a delightful place to set up a writing shack or a studio, transferring all my effects from my various other dream homes, and spending my latter days. I should have been a carpenter and builder, I think. It would save me money constructing houses for myself.

In the suburbs of Cleveland were being built the many comfortable homes of those who could afford this handsome land facing the lake. Hundreds of cottages we passed were done in the newer moods of our American architects, and some of them were quite free of the horrible banalities to which the American country architect seems addicted. There were homes of real taste, with gardens arranged with a sense of their architectural value and trees and shrubs which enhanced their beauty. Here, as I could tell by my nerves, all the ethical and social conventions of the middle class American and the middle West were being practised, or at least preached. Right was as plain as the nose on your face; truth as definite a thing as the box hedges and macadam roads which surrounded them; virtue a chill and even frozen maid. If I had had the implements I would have tacked up a sign reading "Non-conformists beware! Detour south through factory regions."

As we drew nearer Cleveland, this same atmosphere continued, only becoming more dense. Houses, instead of being five hundred feet apart and set in impressive and exclusive spaces, were one hundred feet apart or less. They were smartly suburban and ultra-respectable and refined. The most imposing of churches began to appear—I never saw finer—and schools and heavily tree-shaded streets. Presently we ran into Euclid Avenue, an amazingly long and wide street, once Cleveland's pride and the centre of all her wealthy and fashionable life, but now threaded by a new double tracked trolley line and fallen on lesser, if not absolutely evil, days. This street was once the home, and still may be for all I know (his immortal residence was pointed out to us by a policeman), of the sacrosanct John D. Rockefeller. Yes, in his earlier and poorer years, when he was worth only from seventy to eighty millions, he lived here, and the house seemed to me, as I looked at it this morning, actually to reflect all the stodgy conservatism with which he is credited. It was not smart—what rich American's house of forty or fifty years ago ever is?—but it was solid and impressive and cold. Yes, cold is the word,—a large, roomy, silent thing of grey stone, with a wide smooth lawn at least a hundred feet wide spreading before it, and houses of its same character flanking it on either hand. Here lived John D. and plotted, no doubt, and from here he issued to those local religious meetings and church socials for which he is so famous. And no doubt some one or more of the heavy chambers of this house consumed in their spaciousness the soft, smooth words which meant wealth or poverty to many an oil man or competitor or railroad manipulator whose rates were subsequently undermined. For John D. knew how to outplot the best of them. As an American I forgive him for outplotting the rest of the world. As an individual, well, if he weren't intellectually and artistically so dull I could forgive him everything.

"What is this?" I queried of Franklin. "Surely Euclid Avenue isn't being given over to trade, is it? See that drug store there, built in front of an old home—and that garage tacked on to that mansion—impossible!"

But so it was. These great old mansions set back in their tremendous spaces of lawn were seeing the very last of their former glory. The business heart of the city was apparently overtaking them, and these car tracks were so new I was uncertain whether they were being put down or taken up.

I hailed a policeman.

"Are these tracks being removed or put in?"

"Put in," he replied. "They've just finished a long fight here. The rich people didn't want it, but the people won. Tom Johnson began fighting for this years ago."

Tom Johnson! What an odd sense of the passing of all things the name gave me. Between 1895 and 1910 his name was on nearly everyone's tongue. How he was hated by the growing rich! In the face of the upspringing horde of financial buccaneers of that time—Hanna, Rockefeller, Morgan, Harriman, Ryan—he stood out as a kind of tribune of the people. He had made money in business, and by much the same methods as every other man, taking and keeping, but now he declared himself desirous of seeing something done for the people—of doing something—and so he fought for three cent fares in Cleveland, to be extended, afterwards, everywhere, I suppose.

Don't smile, dear reader. I know it sounds like a joke. In the face of the steady settling of all powers and privileges in America in the hands of a powerful oligarchy, the richest and most glittering the world has ever seen, the feeble dreamings of an idealist, and a but slightly equipped one at that, are foolish; but then, there is something poetic about it, just the same, quite as there is about all the other poets and dreamers the world has ever known. We always want to help the mass, we idealists, *at first*. We look about and see human beings like ourselves, struggling, complaining, dying, pinching along with little or nothing, and our first thought is that some one human being or some group of beings is responsible, that nature has designed all to have plenty, and that all we have to do is to clear away the greed of a few individuals who stand between man and nature, and presto, all is well again. I used to feel that way and do yet, at times. I should hate to think it was all over with America and its lovely morning dreams.

And it's fine poetry, whether it will work or not. It fits in with the ideas of all prophets and reformers since the world began. Think of Henry George, that lovely soul, dying in New York in a cheap hotel, fighting the battle of a labor party—he, the dreamer of "Progress and Poverty." And Doctor (The Reverend Father) McGlynn, declaring that some day we would have an American Pope strolling down Broadway under a silk hat and being thoroughly social and helpful and democratic; and then being excommunicated from the church for it or silenced—which was it? And W. J. Bryan, with his long hair and his perfect voice (that moving, bell-like voice), wishing to solve all the ills of man by sixteen to one—the double standard of gold and silver; and John P. Altgeld, high, clear, dreamy soul, with his blue eyes and his sympathy for the betrayed anarchists and the poor; and "Potato" Pingree, as they used to call him, once governor of Michigan, who wanted all idle land in Detroit and elsewhere turned over to the deserving poor in order that they might grow potatoes or something else on it. And Henry Ford with his "peace ship" and his minimum of five dollars a day for every man, and Hart, Schaffner and Marx with their minimum of two dollars for every little seamstress and poorest floor washer. What does it all mean?

I'll tell you.

It means a sense of equilibrium, or the disturbance of it. Contrasts remain forever,—vast differences in brain, in heart, in opportunity, in everything; but now and then when the contrasts become too sharp or are too closely juxtaposed, up rises some tender spirit—Isaiah, or Jeremiah, or Christ, or St. Francis, or John Huss, or Savanarola, or Robert Owen, or John Brown, or Abraham Lincoln, or William Lloyd Garrison, or Walt Whitman, or Lloyd George, or Henry Ford, or John P. Altgeld, or W. J. Bryan—and begins to cry "Ho! Assyrian" or its equivalent. It is wonderful. It is positively beautiful and thrilling, this love of balance and "fair play" in nature. These men are not always thinking of themselves, you may depend on it. It is inherent in the scheme of things, just as are high mountains and deep valleys, but oh, those who have the sense of it—those dreamers and poets and seekers after the ideal!

"They can kill my body but not what I stand for."—*John Brown*.

"Blessed are the merciful, for they shall obtain mercy."—*Christ*.

"Though I speak with the tongues of men and of angels and have not charity, I am become as sounding brass or a tinkling cymbal."—*St. Paul*.

"Oh, poorest Jesus, the grace I beg of Thee is to bestow on me the grace of the highest poverty."—*St. Francis*.

"I with my barbaric yawp, yawping over the roofs of the world." —*Walt Whitman*.

Are things to be made right by law? I will admit that some wide and sweeping differences can be eliminated. Tyrants can occasionally be pulled down and humanitarians elevated for the time being. Yes, yes. A rough equation can be struck always, and it is something of that of which these men were dreaming. But even so, in the face of all the physical, temperamental, spiritual, intellectual, to say nothing of climatic and planetary differences, what matter? Will law save an idiot or undo a Shelley or a Caesar? Will law pull down the sun and set the moon in its place? My masters, we can only sympathize at times where we cannot possibly act,—and we can act and aid where we cannot cure. But of a universal panacea there is only a dream—or so I feel. Yet it is because we can and do dream—and must, at times— and because of our dreams and the fact that they must so often be shattered, that we have art and the joy of this thing called Life. Without contrast there is no life. And without dreams there might not be any alteration in these too sharp contrasts. But where would our dreams be, I ask you—or the need of them—if all of that of which we are compelled to dream and seek in an agony of sweat and despair were present and we did not need to dream? Then what?

But let us away with abstrusities. Let us sing over Life as it is. These tall, poetic souls—are they not beautiful? And would you not have it so that they may appear?

. . . .

In riding up this same street I was on familiar ground,

for here, twentytwo years before, in that same raw spring which took me to Buffalo, I stopped, looking for work—and found some, of sorts. I connected myself for a very little while (a week or two) with the Sunday issue of the *Plain Dealer* and did a few specials, trying to prove to the incumbent of the high office of Sunday editor that I was a remarkable man. He did not see it—or me. He commented once that my work was too lofty in tone, that I loved to rhapsodize too much. I know he was right. Nevertheless, the second city afterwards (Pittsburg), like the others from which I had just come (Toledo, St. Louis, and Chicago), liked me passing well. But my ambition did not run to a permanent position in Cleveland anyhow.

Just the same, and what was of interest to me this morning as I rode into Cleveland, was that here, after a most wonderful ramble east from St. Louis, I had arrived, quite as in Buffalo, spiritually very hungry and lorn. As I look back on it now I know that I must have been a very peculiar youth, for nothing I could find or do contented me for so much as an hour. I had achieved a considerable newspaper success in St. Louis, but had dropped it as being meaningless; and because of a silly dream about running a country newspaper (which I shall narrate later) in a town called Grand Rapids, Ohio, I had a chance to take over said country paper, but when I looked it over and pictured to myself what the local life would be, I fled in horror. In Toledo I encountered a poet and an enthusiast, a youth destined to prove one of the most helpful influences in my whole career, with whom I enjoyed a period of intense mental cerebration, yet him I left also, partly because I lacked money and an interesting future there, but more because I felt restless and wanted to see more of the world.

One of my principal trials at this time was that I was in love and had left the object of my adoration behind me, and was not sure that I would ever earn enough money to go and fetch her,—so uncertain were my talents and my opportunities in my own eyes.

And like Buffalo, which came after Cleveland in my experience, this city seemed dirty and raw and black, but forceful. America was in the furnace stage of its existence. Everything was in the making,—fortunes, art, its social and commercial life, everything. The most astonishing thing in it was its rich men, their houses, factories, institutions of commerce and pleasure. Nothing else had occurred. There was nothing to see but business and a few hotels,—one, really—and theatres. I remember looking at a great soldiers' monument (it is still here in the principal square) and wondering why so large a monument. I do not recall that any man of Cleveland particularly distinguished himself in the Civil War.

But the one thing that struck me as of greatest import in those days was Euclid Avenue with its large houses and lawns which are now so close to the business heart, and its rich men, John D. Rockefeller and Mark Hanna and Henry M. Flagler and Tom Johnson. Rockefeller had just given millions and millions to revivify the almost defunct University of Chicago, then a small Baptist College, to say nothing of being hailed (newly then) as the richest man in America. All of these people were living here in Euclid Avenue, and I looked up their houses and all the other places of interest, envying the rich and wishing that I was famous or a member of a wealthy family, and that I might meet some one of the beautiful girls I imagined I saw here and have her fall in love with me.

Tra, la! Tra, la! There's nothing like being a passionate, romantic dunce if you want to taste this wine of wizardry which is life. I was and I did. . . .

CHAPTER XXIX

THE FLAT LANDS OF OHIO

But now Cleveland by no means moved me as it once had. Not that there was anything wrong with Cleveland. The change was in me, no doubt—a septicæmia which makes things look different in middle life. We breakfasted at a rather attractive looking restaurant which graced a very lively outlying corner, where a most stately and perfect featured young woman cashier claimed our almost undivided attention. (Hail, Eros!) And then we sped on to the Hollenden, an hotel which I recalled as being the best in my day, to consult the Cleveland Automobile Club as to the condition of the roads west.

Sitting before this hotel in our car, under a grey sky and with the wind whipping about rather chilly for an August morning, I was reminded of other days spent in this same hotel, not as a guest but as a youthful chair warmer between such hours as I was not working on the Cleveland *Plain Dealer* or walking the streets of the city, or sleeping in the very dull room I had engaged in a very dingy and smoky looking old house. Why didn't I get a better place? Well, my uncertainty as to whether I should long remain in Cleveland was very great. This house was convenient to the business heart, the rooms were clean, and from the several windows on the second floor I could see a wide sweep of the lake, with its white caps and gulls and ships, and closer at hand the imposing buildings of the city. It was a great spectacle, and I was somewhat of a recluse and fonder of spectacles than I was of people.

But the Hollenden, which was then the principal hotel of the city and centre of all the extravagant transient life of the time, appealed to me as a convenient method of obtaining comfort of sorts without any expense. Newspaper men have a habit of making themselves at home almost anywhere. Their kaleidoscopic contact with the rough facts of life, and their commercial compulsion to go, do, see, under all circumstances and at all hours, soon robs them of that nervous fear or awe which possesses less sophisticated souls. When you are sent in the morning to attend a wedding or a fire, at noon to interview a celebrity or describe a trial, and at night to report an explosion, a political meeting or a murder, you soon lose all that sense of unwelcomed intrusion which restrains the average citizen. Celebrities become mere people. Gorgeous functions melt into commonplace affairs, no better than any other function that has been or will be again; an hotel like this is little more than a mere lounging place to the itinerant scribe, to the comforts of which as a representative of the press he is entitled.

If not awe or mystery, then certainly nervous anticipation attaches to the movements and personality of nearly all reporters. At least it does in my case. To this day, though I have been one in my time, I stand in fear of them. I never know what to expect, what scarifying question they are going to hurtle at me, or what cold, examining eyes are going to strip me to the bone—eyes that represent brains so shrewd and merciless that one wonders why they do not startle the world long before they usually do.

In those days this hotel was the most luxurious in Cleveland, and here, between hours, because it was cold and I was lonely, I came to sit and stare out at all the passing throng, vigorous and active enough to entertain anyone. It was a brisk life that Cleveland presented, and young. The great question with me always was, how did people come to be, in the first place? What were the underlying laws of our being? How did it come that human beings could separate themselves from cosmic solidarity and navigate alone? Why did we all have much the same tastes, appetites, desires? Why should two billion people on earth have two feet, two eyes, two hands? The fact that Darwin had already set forward his facts as to evolution did not clear things up for me at all. I wanted to know who started the thing evolving, and why. And so I loved to sit about in places like this where I could see people and think about it.

Incidentally I wanted to think about government and the growth of cities and the value and charm of different professions, and whether my own somewhat enforced profession (since I had no cunning, apparently, for anything else) was to be of any value to me. I was just at the age when the enjoyment of my life and strength seemed the most important thing in the world. I wanted to live, to have money, to be somebody, to meet and enjoy the companionship of interesting and well placed people, to seem to be better than I was. While I by no means condemned those above or beneath, nor ignored the claims of any individual or element to fair and courteous treatment, still, materialist that I was, I wanted to share on equal terms with the best, in all the more and most exclusive doings and beings. The fact that the world (in part) was busy about feasts and pleasures, that there were drawingrooms lighted for receptions, dining-rooms for dinner, ballrooms for dancing, and that I was nowhere included, was an aching thorn. I used to stroll about where theatres were just receiving their influx of evening patrons or where some function of note was being held, and stare with avid eyes at the preparations. I felt lone and lorn. A rather weak and profitless tendency, say you? Quite so; I admit it. It interests me now quite as much as it possibly could you. I am now writing of myself not as I am, but as I was.

.   .   .   .

We gained the information that the best road to Fort Wayne was not via the lake shore, as we wished, but through a town called Elyria and Vermilion, and so on through various Ohio towns to the Indiana line. I did not favor that at all. I argued that we should go by the lake anyhow, but somehow we started for Elyria —or "Delirious," as we called it.

In leaving Cleveland I urged Franklin to visit the region where originally stood the house in which I had stopped, and to my surprise I found the place entirely done over—cleared of all the old tracks, houses and docks which, from the formal point of view, once marred the waterfront.   In their stead were several stately municipal buildings facing the wide bosom of the lake and surrounded by great spaces of smooth grass.   It was very imposing.   So the spot I had chosen as most interesting to me had become the civic centre of the city!   This flattered me not a little.

But Elyria and Vermilion—what about them?

Nothing.   Just Ohio towns.

At Elyria we found a stream which had been diverted and made to run a turbine engine in order that the town might have light; but it was discovered afterward that there wasn't enough water power after all to supply the town, and so extra light had to be bought and paid for. The works were very picturesque—a deep, craggy cave, at the bottom of which was the turbine engine room, cut out of the solid rock apparently, the water pouring down through it.   I thought what a delightful place it was for the town boys to play!

But this inland country was really too dreary.   All the uncomfortable experiences of my early youth began to come back as I viewed these small cottages set in endless spaces of flat land, with nothing but scrubby trees, wire fences and occasionally desolately small and bare white churches to vary the landscape.   "What a life!" I kept saying to myself.   "What a life!"   And I still say it, "What a life!"   It would require endless friends to make such a landscape endurable.

Before reaching the lake again, we traversed about twenty miles of a region that seemed to me must be devoted to the chicken raising business, we saw so many of them.   In one place we encountered a huge natural amphitheatre or depression which could easily have been turned into a large lake—the same hollowed out by a stream known as the Vermilion River.   In another we came to a fine threshing scene with all the implements for the work in full motion—a scene so attractive that we stopped and loafed a while, inquiring as to the rewards of farming in this region. In still another place we passed a small river pleasure ground, a boating and bathing place which was probably patronized by the villagers hereabout. It suggested all sorts of sweet, simple summer romances.

Then Vermilion came into view with a Chautauqua meeting announced as "coming soon," and a cove with a lighthouse and pretty launches and sailboats at anchor. Speed announced that if we were going to idle here, as usual, he would stop at the first garage and get oil and effect certain repairs, and there we left him, happy at his task, his body under the machine, while we walked on into the heart of the village. It being noontime, the hope of finding a restaurant lured us, as well as that possibility of seeing something different and interesting which the sight of every new town held out, at least to me. Here we had lunch then, and quite a good one too, with a piece of cherry pie thrown in for good measure, if you please, and then because the restaurant was conducted by a Japanese by the name of B. Kagi, and because the girl who waited on us looked like an Americanized product of the Flowery Kingdom, I asked her if she was Japanese.

I never got a blacker look in my life. For a moment her dark eyes seemed to shoot sparks. Her whole demeanor, which hitherto had been pleasant and helpful, changed to one of deadly opposition. "Certainly not," she replied with a sting in her voice, and I saw clearly that I had made a most painful *faux pas*. I felt called upon to explain or apologize to Franklin, who heard and saw it all. He was most helpful.

"I suppose," he commented, "in these small middle West towns it is *declassé* to be Japanese. They don't discriminate much between Japanese and Chinese. To suggest anything like that probably hurts her feelings dreadfully. If people here discover it, it lowers her in their eyes, or that is what she thinks."

"But she looks Japanese to you, doesn't she?" I queried, humbly.

"Not very, no."

I looked again and it semed very obvious. Back in the kitchen was occasionally visible B. Kagi, and it seemed to me even then that the girl looked like him. However, the air was so frigid from then on that I scarcely enjoyed my meal. And to confound me, as it were, several towns-people came in and my supposedly purely Japanese maid talked in the normal middle West fashion, even to a kind of a nasal intonation which we all have. Obviously she was American born and raised in this region. "But why the likeness?" I kept saying to myself in my worst and most suspicious manner. And then I began to build up a kind of fictional background for her, with this B. Kagi as her real, but for reasons of policy, concealed father, and so on and so forth, until I had quite a short story in mind. But I don't suppose I'll ever come to the pleasure of writing it.

CHAPTER XXX

AT Vermilion the sun suddenly burst forth once more, clear and warm from a blanket of grey, and the whole world looked different and much more alluring. Speed arrived with the car just when we had finished luncheon, and we had the pleasure of sitting outside and feeling thoroughly warm and gay while he ate. Betimes Franklin commented on the probable character of the life in a community like this. He was of the conviction that it never rose above a certain dead level of mediocrity—however charming and grateful the same might be as life—and that all the ideas of all concerned ran to simple duties and in grooves of amusing, if not deadly prejudice; which was entirely satisfactory, so long as they did not interfere with or destroy *your* life. He was convinced that there was this narrow, solemn prejudice which made all life a sham, or a kind of rural show piece, in which all played a prescribed part, some thinking one thing, perhaps, and secretly conforming to it as much as possible, while publicly professing another and conforming to that, publicly, or, as is the case with the majority, actually believing in and conforming to life as they found it here. I know there were many such in the home communities in which I was brought up. Franklin was not one to charge general and widespread hypocrisy, as do some, but rather to sympathize with and appreciate the simple beliefs, tastes, and appetites of all concerned.

"Now take those four town loafers sitting over there on that bin in front of that store," he commented, apropos of four old cronies who had come out to sun themselves. "They haven't a single thing in their minds above petty little humors which do not seriously affect anyone but themselves. They sit and comment and jest and talk about people in the town who are doing things, quite as four ducks might quack. They haven't a single thing to do, not an important ambition. Crime of any kind is nearly beyond them."

Just then a boy came by crying a Cleveland afternoon paper. He was calling, "All about the lynching of Leo Frank." This was a young Jew who had been arrested in Atlanta, Georgia, some months before, charged with the very disturbing crime of attempted rape and subsequent murder, the victim being a pretty working girl in a factory of which the murderer, socalled, was foreman or superintendent. The trick by which the crime was supposed to have been accomplished, as it was charged, was that of causing the girl to stay after work and then, when alone, attempting to seduce or force her. In this instance a struggle seems to have ensued. The girl may have fallen and crushed her head against a table, or she may have been struck on the head. The man arrested denied vigorously that he had anything to do with it. He attempted, I believe, to throw the blame on a negro janitor, or, if not that, he did nothing to aid in clearing him of suspicion. And there is the bare possibility that the negro did commit the crime, though personally I doubted it. When, upon trial, Frank's conviction of murder in the first degree followed, a great uproar ensued, Jews and other citizens in all parts of the country protested and contributed money for a new trial. The case was appealed to the supreme court, but without result. Local or state sentiment was too strong. It was charged by the friends of the condemned man that the trial had been grossly unfair, and that Southern opposition to all manner of sex offenses was so abnormal and peculiar, having a curious relationship to the inversion of the psychoanalyst, that no fair trial could be expected in that section. Personally, I had felt that the man should have been tried elsewhere because of this very sectional characteristic, which I had noticed myself.

It had been charged that a southern mob overawed the jury in the very court room in which the case had been conducted, that the act of rape had never really been proved, that the death had really been accidental as described, that the very suspicious circumstance of the body being found in the cellar was due to fear on the part of the murderer, whoever he was, of being found out, and that the girl had not been brutally slain at all. Nevertheless, when the reigning governor, whose term was about to expire, commuted the sentence from death to life imprisonment, he had to leave the state under armed protection, and a few weeks later the criminal, if he was one, was set upon by a fellow convict in the penitentiary at Atlanta and his throat cut. It was assumed that the convict was employed by the element inimical to Frank at the trial. A little later, while he was still in the hospital, practically dying from this wound, Frank was taken out by a lynching party, taken to the small home town of the girl, Marietta, Georgia, and there lynched. It was this latest development which was being hawked about by the small newsboy at Vermilion.

Personally, as I say, I had the feeling that Frank had been unjustly dealt with. This seemed another exhibition of that blood lust of the South which produces feuds, duels, lynchings and burning at the stake even to this day and which I invariably relate to the enforced suppression of very natural desires in another direction. Southerners are usually so avid of women and so loud in their assertions that they are not. I have no opposition to Southerners as such. In many respects they are an interesting and charming people, courteous, hospitable, a little inclined to over-emphasis of gallantry and chivalry and their alleged moral purity, but otherwise interesting. But this sort of thing always strikes me as a definite indictment of the real native sense of the people. Have they brains, poise, judgment? Why, then, indulge in the antics and furies of children and savages?

I raged at the South for its narrowness and inefficiency and ignorance. Franklin, stung by the crime, no doubt, agreed with me. He told me of being in a quick lunch room in New York one day when a young Southerner entered and found a negro in the place, eating. Now as everyone knows, this is a commonplace. I, often, have sat next to a negro and eaten in peace and comfort. But according to Franklin, the first impulse of this Southerner was to make a scene and stir up as much prejudice as possible, beginning, as usual, with "What the hell is a damned negro doing in here, anyhow?"

"He looked about for sympathy," said Franklin, "but no one paid the slightest attention to him. Then he began pushing his chair about irritably and swaggering, but still no one heeded him. Finally, reducing his voice to a grumble, he went quietly and secured his sandwich, his coffee and his pie, like any other downtrodden American."

"But what a blow it must have been to him to find himself swamped by a sea of indifference!" I said—"not a soul to share his views!"

"It is that sort of thing that makes the South a jest to me," continued Franklin. "I can't stand it."

His face was quite sour, much more so than I had seen it on any other occasion on this tour.

"Oh, well," I said, "those things adjust themselves in the long run. Frank is dead, but who knows, lynching may be killed by this act. The whole North and West is grieved by this. They will take it out of the South in contempt and money. Brutality must pay for itself like a stone flung in the water, if no more than by rings of water. The South cannot go on forever doing this sort of thing."

After we had raged sufficiently we rode on, for by now Speed had finished his lunch. Here, following that lake road I have mentioned, we were in an ideal realm for a time again, free of all the dreary monotony of the land farther south. The sun shone, the wind blew, and we forgot all about Frank and careened along the shore looking at the tumbling waves. Once we climbed down a steep bank and stood on the shore, expatiating on how fine it all was. Another time we got off to pick a few apples ready to our hand. There were many detours and we passed a fair sized town called Huron, basking in a blaze of afternoon light, but for once not stopping because it lay a little to the right of our road to Sandusky. In another hour we were entering the latter place, a clean, smooth paved city of brick and frame cottages, with women reading or sewing on doorsteps and porches, and a sense of American solidarity and belief in all the virtues hovering over it all.

I never knew until I reached there and beheld it with my own eyes that Sandusky has near it one of the finest fresh water beaches in the world—and I have seen beaches and beaches and beaches, from those at Monte Carlo, Nice and Mentone to those that lie between Portland, Maine, and New Brunswick, Georgia. It is called Cedar Point, and is not much more than twenty minutes from the pier at the foot of Columbus Avenue, in the heart of the city—if you go by boat. They have not been enterprising enough as yet to provide a ferry for automobiles. Once you get there by a very roundabout trip of twelve miles, you can ride for seven miles along a cement road which parallels exactly the white sand of the beach and allows you to enjoy the cool lake winds and even the spray of the waves when the wind is high. It is backed by marsh land, some of which has been drained and is now offered as an ideal and exclusive residence park.

But the trip was worth the long twelve miles—splendidly worth it—once we had made up our minds to return there,—for coming we had passed it without knowing it. What induced us to go was a number of picture cards we saw in the principal department store here, showing Cedar Point Beach in a storm, Cedar Point Beach crowded with thousands of bathers, Cedar Point Beach Pier accommodating three or four steamers at once, and so forth, all very gay and summery and all seeming to indicate a world of Monte Carloesque proportions.

As a matter of fact, it was nothing like Monte Carlo or any other beach, except for its physical beauty as a sea beach, for how could a watering place on a lake in Ohio have any of the features of a cosmopolitan ocean resort? In spite of the fact that it boasted two very large hotels, a literally enormous casino and bathing pavilion, and various forms of amusement pavilions, it was without the privilege of selling a drop of intoxicants, and its patrons, to the number of thousands, were anything but smart—just plain, Middle West family people.

What'll we do with the Middle West and the South? Are they gradually and unconsciously sinking into the demnition doldrums? Suppose our largest soap factories, our largest reaper works, and our largest chewing gum emporiums are out there—what of it? It doesn't help much to amass large fortunes making routine things that merely increase the multitude who then sit back and do dull, routine things. Life was intended for the spectacular, I take it. It was intended to sting and hurt so that songs and dreams might come forth. When it becomes mere plethora and fixity, it is nothing—a stultifying world. When a great crisis comes—as come it surely will at some time or other—if people have just eaten and played and not dreamed vastly and beautifully, they are as chaff blown by the wind or burned in the oven. They do not even make a good spectacle. They are just pushed aside, destroyed, forgotten.

But this resort was so splendid in its natural aspects I could not help contrasting its material use by these middle westerners with what would have been the case if it were situate say in the South of France, or on the shores of Holland or Belgium. Anyone who has visited Scheveningen or Ostend, or Nice or Cannes, need scarcely be told there is a certain smartness not even suggested by the best of our American resorts. Contrasted even with these latter, this island place was lower in the scale. (I presume the Christian Middle West would say it was higher.) We motored out there positively thrilled by a halcyon evening in which a blood red sun, aided by tattered, wind whipped clouds, combined to give the day's close a fabled, almost Norse aspect. The long beach was so beautiful that it evoked exclamations of surprise and delight. Think of being able to tear along for seven miles and more, the open water to your right, a weird, grass grown marsh world dotted with tall, gaunt trees to your left, this splendid cloud world above, turgid with red and pink, and a perfect road to ride on! We tore. But when we reached the extreme point of land known as Cedar Point, and devoted, as I have said, to the more definite entertainment of the stranger, things were very different. The exterior of all that I saw was quite charming, but imagine an immense casino devoted to tables for people who bring their own lunch or dinner and merely want to buy coffee or milk or soda!!—No beer sold here, if you please. A perfectly legitimate and laudable atmosphere, say you? Quite so, only——

And then the large hotels! We looked at them. The prices of the best one ranged from two to four dollars a day; the other from one to two!!! Shades of Atlantic City and Long Beach!—And remember that these were well built, well equipped hotels. The beach pavilions were attractive, but the crowd was of a simple, inexperienced character. I am not sniffing. Did I not praise Geneva Beach? I did. And before I left here I was fond of this place and would not have changed it in any least detail. I would not have even these mid-westerners different, in spite of anything I may have said. They seem to know that Sunday School meetings are important and that one must succeed in business in some very small way; but even so, they are a vivacious, hopeful crew, and as such deserving of all praise.

Franklin and I walked about talking about them and contrasting them with the East. Our conclusion was that the East is more schooled in vice and sensuality, and show and luxury, perhaps, and that these people were sweet and amusing and all right—here. We found a girl tending a cigar counter in the principal casino—a very angular, not too attractive creature, but not homely either, and decidedly vivacious. I could not help contrasting her with the maidens who wait on you at telephone booths and stands generally in New York, and who fix you with an icy stare and, at telephone booths, inquire, "Numbah, please?" She was quite set up, in a pleasantly human way, by the fact that she was in charge of a cigar stand in so vivacious a world, and communicated her thoughts to us with the greatest pleasure and fluency.

"Do you have many people here every day?" I asked, thinking that because I had seen three excursion steamers lying at anchor at the foot of the principal street in Sandusky it might merely be overrun by holiday crowds occasionally.

"Indeed, yes," she replied briskly. "The two big hotels here are always full, and on the coldest days we have four or five hundred in bathing. Haven't you been here in the day time yet? Well, ya just ought to be here when it's very hot and the sun is bright. Crowds! Course, I haven't been to Atlantic City or any of them swell eastern places, but people that have tell me that this is one of the finest beaches anywhere. Style! You just oughta see. And the crowds! The bathing pavilions are packed, and the board walk. There are thousands of people here."

"I suppose, then, this casino fills up completely?" I said, looking round and seeing a few empty tables here and there.

It had evidently been raining the day before, and even early this morning, for it was pleasantly cool tonight and this seemed to have kept away some people.

"Well, you just oughta see it on a real hot night, if you don't think we have crowds here. Full! Why people stand around and wait. It's wonderful!"

"Indeed? And is there much money spent here?"

"Well, I suppose as much as anywhere. I don't know about them big resorts in the East, but there's enough money spent here. Goodness! People come and take whole soots of rooms at these big hotels. You see some mighty rich people here."

Franklin and I availed ourselves of the cafeteria system of this place to serve ourselves and be in the life. We walked along the beach looking at the lights come out on the hotel verandas and in the pavilions and under the trees. We walked under these same trees and watched the lovers courting, and noted the old urge of youth and blood on every hand. There was dancing in one place, and at a long pier reaching out into the bay on the landward side, a large ferry steamer was unloading hundreds more. Finally at ten o'clock we returned Sanduskyward, listening to the splash of the waves on the shore, and observing the curious cloud formations which hung overhead, interspersed with stars. In them once I saw a Russian *moujik's* head with the fur cap pulled low over the ears—that immemorial cap worn by the Assyrians and Chaldeans. Again I saw an old hag pursuing a wisp of cloud that looked like a fleeing hare, and then two horsemen riding side by side in the sky. Again I saw a whale and a stag, and finally a great hand, its fingers outspread—a hand that seemed to be reaching up helplessly and as if for aid.

The night was so fine that I would have counseled riding onward toward Fort Wayne, but when we reached Sandusky again and saw its pleasant streets and a clean-looking hotel, we concluded that we would stay by the ills we knew rather than to fly toward others that we knew not of.

CHAPTER XXXI

It is Anatole France, I think, who says somewhere that "robbery is to be condoned; the result of robbery respected." Even so, listen to this story. We came into this hotel at eleven P. M. or thereabouts. Franklin, who is good at bargaining, or thinks he is, sallied up to the desk and asked for two rooms with bath, and an arrangement whereby our chauffeur could be entertained for less—the custom. There was a convention of some kind in town—traveling salesmen in certain lines, I believe—and all but one room in this hotel, according to the clerk, was taken. However, it was a large room—very, he said, with three beds and a good bath. Would we take that? If so, we could have it, without breakfast, of course, for three dollars.

"Done," said Franklin, putting all three names on the registry.

It was a good room, large and clean, with porcelain bath of good size. We arose fairly early and breakfasted on the usual hotel breakfast. I made the painful mistake of being betrayed by the legend "pan fish and fried mush" from taking ham and eggs.

After our breakfast we came downstairs prepared to pay and depart, when, in a polite voice—oh, very suave—the day clerk, a different one from him of the night—announced to Franklin, who was at the window, "Seven-fifty, please."

"How do you make that out?" inquired Franklin, taken aback.

"Three people in one room at three dollars a day each (two dollars each for the night)—six dollars. Breakfast, fifty cents each, extra—one-fifty. Total, seven-fifty."

"But I thought you said this room was three for the night for three?"

"Oh, no—three dollars each per day. Two dollars each for the night. We always let it that way."

"Oh, I see," said Franklin, curiously. "You know what the night clerk said to me, do you?"

"I know the regular rate we charge for this room."

For the fraction of a moment Franklin hesitated, then laid down a ten dollar bill.

"Why do you do that, Franklin?" I protested. "It isn't fair. I wouldn't. Let's see the manager."

"Oh, well," he half whispered in weariness. "What can you do about it? They have you at their mercy."

In the meantime, the clerk had slipped the bill in the drawer and handed back two-fifty in change.

"But, Franklin," I exclaimed, "this is an outrage. This man doesn't know anything about it, or if he does, he's swindling. Why doesn't he get the manager here if he's on the level?"

This gentle clerk merely smiled at me. He had a comfortable, even cynical, grin on his face, which enraged me all the more.

"You know what you are?" I asked him asudden. "You're a damned, third rate fakir and swindler! You know you're lying when you say that room rents for three per person when three occupy it. That's nine dollars a day for a room in an hotel that gets two or three dollars at the outside."

He smiled, unperturbed, and then turned to wait on other people.

I raged and swore. I called him a few more names, but it never disturbed him the least. I demanded to see the mythical manager—but he remained mythical. Franklin, shocked, went off to get a cigar, and then helped Speed carry out the bags, porters being scarce. Meanwhile, I hung around hoping that glaring and offering to fight would produce some result. Not at all. Do you think I got back our three dollars, or that I ever saw the manager? Never. The car was ready. Franklin was waiting. He looked at me as much as to say, "Well, you *do* love to fight, don't you?" Finally I submitted to the inevitable, and, considerably crestfallen, clambered into the car, while Franklin uttered various soothing comments about the futility of attempting to cope with scoundrels en route. What was a dollar or two, more or less? But as we rode out of Sandusky I saw myself (1) beating the hotel clerk to death, (2) tearing the hotel down and throwing it into the lake, (3) killing the manager and all the clerks and help, (4) marching a triumphant army against the city at some future time, and razing it to the last stone.

"I would show them, by George! I would fix them!"

"Aren't the clouds fine this morning?" observed Franklin, looking up at the sky, as we rolled out of the city. "See that fine patch of woods over there. Now that we're getting near the Indiana line the scenery is beginning to improve a little, don't you think?"

We were in a more fertile land, I thought—smoother, more prosperous. The houses looked a little better, more rural and homey.

"Yes, I think so," I grumbled.

"And that's the lake off there. Isn't the wind fresh and fine?"

It was.

In a little while he was telling me of some Quakers who inhabited a Quaker community just north of his home town, and how one of them said to another once, in a fit of anger:

"Wilbur, thee knows I can lick thee, the best day thee ever lived."

The idea of two Quakers fighting cheered me. I felt much better.

But now tell me—don't you think I ought to destroy Sandusky anyhow, as a warning?

.   .   .   .   .   .

After we left Sandusky I began to feel at home again, for somehow this territory southwest was more like Indiana than any we had seen—smooth and placid and

fertile—it was a homelike land. We scudded through a
place called Clyde, hung madly with hundreds of little
blue and white triangular banners announcing that a Chautauqua was to be held here within a few days—one of
those simple, country life Chautauquas which do so much,
apparently, to enliven this mid-western world. And then
we came to a place called Fremont, which had once had
the honor of being the home and death place (if not birthplace) of the Hon. Rutherford B. Hayes, once President
of the United States by accident—the man who stole the
office from Samuel J. Tilden, who was elected. A queer
honor—but dishonor is as good as honor any day for
ensuring one a place in the memory of posterity.

And after that we drove through places called Woodside and Pemberton and Portage—you know the size—
only in these towns, by now, I was seeing exact dupli-
cates of men I had known in my earliest days. Thus
at Woodside where we asked our way to Pemberton and
Bowling Green, Ohio, the man who leaned against our
car was an exact duplicate of a man I had known in
Sullivan, over thirty years before, who used to drive a
delivery wagon, and the gentleman he was driving (a
local merchant of some import, I took it) was exactly
like old Leonard B. Welles, who used to run one of the
four or five successful grocery stores in Warsaw. He
had a short, pointed, and yet full beard, with steely blue
eyes and a straight, thin-lipped mouth—but not an un-
kindly expression about them. I began to think of the
days when I used to wait for old Mr. Welles to serve me.

Later we came to a river called Portage, yellow and
placid and flowing between winding banks that separated fields of hay from fields of grain; and then we
began to draw near to a territory with which I had been
exceedingly familiar twenty years before—so much so
that it remains as fresh as though it had been yesterday.

You must know, because I propose to tell you, that in
the fair city of St. Louis, at the age of twentytwo, I was
fairly prosperous as a working newspaper man's prosperity goes, and in a position to get or make or even keep

a place not only for myself but for various others—such friends, for instance, as I chose to aid. I do not record this boastfully. I was a harum scarum youth, who was fairly well liked by his elders, but with no least faculty, apparently, of taking care of his own interests. From Chicago one of those fine days blew a young newspaper man whom I had known and liked up there. He was not a very good newspaper man, humdrum and good natured, but a veritable satellite of mine. He wanted me to get him a place and I did. Then he wanted counsel as to whether he should get married, and I aided and abetted him in that. Then he lost his job through his inability to imagine something properly one night, and I had to get him another one. Then he began to dream of running a country paper with me as a fellow aspirer to rural honors and emoluments, and if you will believe me, so rackbrained was I, and so restless and uncertain as to my proper future, that I listened to him with willing ears. Yes, I had some vague, impossible idea of being first State Assemblyman Dreiser of some rural region, and then, perchance, State Senator Dreiser, and then Congressman Dreiser, or Governor Dreiser, if you please, and all at once, owing to my amazing facility and *savoir faire,* and my clear understanding of the rights, privileges, duties and emoluments of private citizens, and of public officers, and because of my deep and abiding interest in the welfare of the nation—President Dreiser— the distinguished son of the state of Indiana, or Ohio, or Michigan, or wherever I happened to bestow myself.

I had only one hundred and fifty dollars all told in the world at the time—but somehow money didn't seem so very important. Perhaps that was why I listened to him. Anyhow, he hailed from this northern section of Ohio. His father lived just outside of the village of Grand Rapids (Ohio, not Michigan), and between there and a town called Bowling Green, which we were now approaching, lay the region which we were to improve with our efforts and presence.

Looking at the country now, and remembering it as it

was then, I could see little, if any, change. Oh, yes—
one. At that time it was dotted on every hand with tall
skeleton derricks for driving oil wells. The farming
world was crazy about oil wells, believing them to be the
open sesame to a world of luxury and every blessed thing
which they happened to desire. And every man who
owned so much as a foot of land was sinking an oil well
on it. The spectacle which I beheld when I first ventured
into this region was one to stir the soul of avarice, if
not of oil. As far as the eye could see, the still wintry
fields were dotted with these gaunt structures standing
up naked and cold—a more or less unsatisfactory sight.
I remember asking myself rather ruefully why it was
that I couldn't own an oil well and be happy. Now when
I entered this region again all these derricks had disappeared, giving place to small dummy engines, or some
automatic arrangement lying close to the ground, and
controlled from afar, by which the oil pumping was done.
These engines were very dirty, but fortunately incon-
spicuous. And apparently nearly all the wells which I
had seen being dug in 1893 had proved successful. In
every field was at least one of these pumping devices, and
sometimes two and three, all in active working order.
They looked odd in fields of corn and wheat. But where
were the palaces of great beauty which the farmers of
1893 expected if they struck oil? I saw none; merely
many fairly comfortable, and I trust happy, homes.

But to return to my venture into this region. The most
disturbing thing about it, as I look back on it now, is that
it shows me how nebulous and impractical I was at that
time. Clearly I had had a sharp desire to be rich and
famous, without any understanding of how to achieve
these terms of comfort. On the other hand, I had the
true spirit of adventure, else I would never have dropped
so comfortable a berth as I had, where I was well liked,
to come up here where I knew nothing of what the future
held in store. Great dreams invariably shoot past the
possibilities of life.

Those cold, snowy, silent streets, those small bleak

homes, shut in from the February or March cold, with all the force of their country life centered around the parlor stove! H——, my fellow adventurer, had preceded me, occupying with his wife a comfortable portion of his father's home, and it was he who met me at the train. He could live here comfortably and indefinitely, and think nothing of it. He was home. After a single day's investigation, I now saw that there was nothing to his proposition as far as I or Grand Rapids was concerned—not a thing. The paper which he had outlined to me as having a working circulation of sixteen hundred and advertising to the value of a thousand or more had really nothing at all. The county, which had only perhaps 10,000 population, had already more papers than it could support. The last editor had decamped, leaving a novice who worked for the leading druggist, owner of the printing press and other materials of construction, to potter about, endeavoring to explain what was useless to explain. And I had thrown up a good position to pursue a chimera.

But in spite of this, H—— wished to see all the leading citizens to discover what encouragement they would offer to two aspiring souls like ourselves! I can see them yet—one a tall, bony man of a ministerial cast of countenance. He was the druggist, and by the same token one of several doctors living here. There was a short, fat, fussy man, who ran the principal feed and livery stable. He had advertised occasionally in other days. Then there were the local banker and four or five others, all of them meager, unimportant intellects.

They looked us over as if we were adventurers from Mars. They weren't sure whether they needed a newspaper here or not. I agree now that they did not. They talked about small advertisements which they might or might not run, but which they were certain had never paid when they did—advertisements which they had placed as a favor to the former editor or editors. In addition, they wanted assurances as to how the paper would be run and whether we were good, moral boys and whether we would work hard for the interests of the town and against certain unsatisfactory elements. It was amazing. Oh, yes, the paper had to be Republican in politics.

"No, no, no," I finally said to H——, in a spirit of dissatisfaction and at the end of a long, cold, windy day. We had walked out the country road toward his house and I had stopped to stare at an array of crows occupying a bleak woodpatch, and at the red sun, smiling over a floor of white. "There's nothing in this. It would set me crazy. It's a wild goose chase. Is there anything else around here, or shall I skip out tonight?"

He wanted me to stay and visit Bowling Green, a town near at hand. (This was the one we were now approaching.) There was another newspaper there for sale on easy terms. I agreed after some coaxing, and, having lingered three days to secure suitable roads—the distance was twentyfive miles—we drove over. That was the time I saw the gas wells. It was a better place than Grand Rapids, but the price of the paper, when we reached there, was much more than we could pay. I think we figured, between us, that we could put down two hundred dollars and the owners wanted five hundred, with the balance on mortgage and a total selling price of eight thousand. So that dream went glimmering. In the meanwhile, I browsed about studying country life, admiring the Maumee River at Grand Rapids (H——'s home faced it from a beautiful rise). Then one fine spring day the sun rose on fields from which the snow had suddenly melted, and I felt that I must be off. I went, as I have said, to Toledo first. Here I encountered the youth to whom I have frequently referred and with whom I was destined to lead a curious career.

But now that I am upon the subject, perhaps I might as well include the story of my journey into Toledo, where was a principal paper called the *Blade* with which I wished to connect myself, if possible. The place only had a hundred thousand at the time, and I did not think it worth the remaining years of my life, but I thought it might be good for a little while—say six months. Although I was considered (I am merely quoting others) an exceptional newspaper man, I did not know what I wanted to be. Already the newspaper profession was boring me. It seemed a hopeless, unremunerative, more or less degrading form of work, and yet I could think of nothing else to do. Apparently I had no other talent.

I shall never forget the first morning I went into Toledo. The train followed the bank of a canal and ran between that canal and the Maumee River. The snow which had troubled us so much a day or two before had gone off, and it was as bright and encouraging as one might wish. I was particularly elated by the natural aspects of this region, for the Maumee River, beginning at Fort Wayne, Indiana, and flowing northeastward, makes a peculiarly attractive scenic diversion. It is a beautiful stream, with gently sloping banks on either hand, and in places rapids and even slight falls. At Grand Rapids and farther along it broadened out into something essentially romantic to look upon, and Toledo itself, when I reached it, was so clean and new and industrious—without all the depressing areas of factory and tenement life which lowers the charm of some cities. It seemed to me as I looked at it this Spring morning as if life must be better here than in cities older, or at least greater—cities like St. Louis and Chicago, where so much of the oppressive struggle for existence had already manifested itself. And yet I knew I liked those cities better. Be that as it may, it was a happy prospect which I contemplated, and I sought out the office of the *Blade* with the air of one who is certain of his powers and not likely to be daunted by mere outward circumstances.

I have always felt of life that it is more fortuitous than anything else. People strive so mightily to do things—to arrange life according to some scheme of their own—but little, if anything, comes of it in most cases. Children are taught by their parents that they must be this, that, or the other to get along—economical, industrious, sober, truthful and the like—and what comes of it? Unless they are peculiarly talented and able to use

life in a direct and forceful way—unless they have qualities or charms which draw life to them, or compel life to
come, willy-nilly, they are used and then discarded. A
profound schooling in manners, morals and every other
virtue and pleasantry will not make up for lack of looks
in a girl. Honesty, sobriety, industry, and even other
solemn virtues, will not raise a lad to a seat of dignity.
Life is above these petty rules, however essential they
may be to the strong in ruling the weak, or to a state
or nation in the task of keeping itself in order. We succeed or fail not by the socalled virtues or their absence,
but by something more or less than these things. All
good things are gifts—beauty, strength, grace, magnetism, swiftness and subtlety of mind, the urge or compulsion to do. Taking thought will not bring them to
anyone. Effort never avails save by grace or luck or
something else. The illusion of the self made is one of
the greatest of all.

Here in Toledo I came upon one of the happiest illustrations of this. In the office of the *Blade* in the city edi-
torial room, sat a young man as city editor who was
destined to take a definite and inspiriting part in my life.
He was small, very much smaller than myself, plump,
rosy cheeked, with a complexion of milk and cream, soft
light brown hair, a clear, observing blue eye. Without
effort you could detect the speculative thinker and
dreamer. In the rôle of city editor of a western manufacturing town paper, one must have the air, if not the
substance, of commercial understanding and ability (executive control and all that), and so in this instance, my
young city editor seemed to breathe a determination to
be very executive and forceful.

"You're a St. Louis newspaper man, eh?" he said,
estimating me casually and in a glance. "Never worked
in a town of this size though? Well, the conditions are
very different. We pay much more attention to small
items—make a good deal out of nothing," he smiled.
"But there isn't a thing that I can see anyhow. Nothing
much beyond a three or four day job, which you wouldn't

want, I'm sure. As a matter of fact, there's a street car strike on—you may have noticed it—and I could use a man who would have nerve enough to ride round on the cars which the company is attempting to run and report how things are. But I'll tell you frankly, it's dangerous. You may be shot or hit with a brick."

"Yes," I said, smiling and thinking of my need of experience and cash. "Just how many days' work would you guarantee me, if any?"

"Well, four. I could guarantee you that many."

He looked at me in a mock serious and yet approving way. I could see that he was attracted to me—fate only knows why. Something about me (as he told me later) affected him vigorously. He could not, he admitted, get me out of his mind. He was slightly ashamed of offering me so wretched a task, and yet urged by the necessity of making a showing in the face of crisis. He, too, was comparatively new to his task.

I will not go into this story further than to say that it resulted in an enduring and yet stormy and disillusioning friendship. If he had been a girl he would have married me, of course. It would have been inevitable, even though he was already married, as he was. That other marriage would have been broken up. We were intellectual affinities, as it were. Our dreams were practically identical, approaching them though we were, at different angles. He was more the sentimentalist in thought, though the realist in action; I the realist in thought, and sentimentalist in action. He kept looking at me and that same morning, when having ridden about over all the short lines unharmed and made up a dramatic story, and when, in addition, for a "Romance Column" which the paper ran, I had written one or two brief descriptions of farm life about Toledo, he came over to tell me that he was impressed. My descriptions were beautiful, he said.

We went out to lunch, and stayed nearly three hours. He took me out to dinner. Though he was newly married and his delightful young wife was awaiting him in their home a few miles out of the city, duty compelled him to stay in town. Damon had met Pythias—Gawayne, Ivaine. We talked and talked and talked. He had worked in Chicago; so had I. He had known various newspaper geniuses there—so had I. He had dreams of becoming a poet and novelist—I of becoming a playwright. Before the second day had gone, a book of fairytales and some poems he had completed and was publishing locally had been shown me. Under the action of our joint chemistries I was magically impressed. I became enamoured of him—the victim of a delightful illusion—one of the most perfect I have ever entertained.

Because he was so fond of me, so strikingly adoring, he wanted me to stay on. There was no immediate place, and he could not make one for me at once, but would I not wait until an opening might come? Or better yet— would I not wander on toward Cleveland and Buffalo, working at what I chose, and then, if a place opened, come back? He would telegraph me (as he subsequently did at Pittsburg). Meanwhile we reveled in that wonderful possession—intellectual affection—a passionate intellectual rapprochement, in youth. I thought he was beautiful, great, perfect. He thought—well, I have heard him tell in after years what he thought. Even now, at times, he fixes me with hungry, welcoming eyes.

Alas, alas, for the dreams and the perfections which never stay!

CHAPTER XXXII

To me, therefore, this region was holy Ganges—Mecca, Medina—the blessed isles of the West. In approaching Bowling Green, Ohio, I was saying to myself how strange it will be to see H—— again, should he chance to be there! What an interesting talk I will have with him! And after Bowling Green how interesting to pass through Grand Rapids, even though there was not a soul whom I would wish to greet again! Toledo was too far north to bother about.

When we entered Bowling Green, however, by a smooth macadam road under a blazing sun, it was really not interesting at all; indeed it was most disappointing. The houses were small and low and everything was still, and after one sees town after town for eight hundred or a thousand miles, all more or less alike, one town must be different and possessed of some intrinsic merit not previously encountered to attract attention.

I persuaded Franklin to stop at the office of the principal newspaper, in order that I might make inquiry as to the present whereabouts of H——. He had written me, about four years before, to say that he was connected with a paper here. He wanted me to teach him how to write short stories! It was a dull room or store, facing the principal street, like a bank. In it were a young, reporterish looking boy, very trig and brisk and curious as to his glance, and a middle aged man, bald, red faced, roundly constructed like a pigeon, and about as active.

"Do you happen to recall a man by the name of H—— who used to work here in Bowling Green?" I inquired of the elder, not willing to believe that he had controlled a paper, though I had understood from someone that he had.

"B——— H———?" he replied, looking me over.

"Yes, that's the man."

"He did work here on the other paper for a while," he replied with what seemed to me a faint look of contempt, though it may not have been. "He hasn't been here for four or five years at the least. He's up in Michigan now, I believe—Battle Creek, or Sheboygan, or some such place as that. They might tell you over at the other office." He waved his hand toward some outside institution—the other paper.

"You didn't happen to know him personally, I presume?"

"No, I saw him a few times. He was their general utility man, I believe."

I went out, uncertain whether to bother any more or not. Twentythree years is a long time. I had not seen him in all of that. I started to walk toward the other newspaper office, but the sight of the bare street, with a buggy or two and an automobile, and the low, quiet store buildings, deterred me.

"What's the use?" I asked myself. "This is a stale, impossible atmosphere. There isn't an idea above hay and feed in the whole place."

I climbed back in the car and we fled.

It was not much better for some distance beyond here until we began to draw near Napoleon, Ohio. The country for at least twenty miles was dreadfully flat and uninteresting—houses with low fences and prominent chicken coops, orchards laden with apples of a still greenish yellow color, fields of yellowing wheat or green corn —oh, so very flat. Not a spire of an interesting church anywhere, not a respectable piece of architecture, nothing. Outside of one town, where we stopped for a glass of water, we did encounter a brick and plaster mausoleum—the adjunct, I believe, of a crematory—set down at the junction of two macadam crossroads, and enclosed by a most offensive wooden fence. Although there were some wide fields and some patches of woods, which might have been utilized to give an institution of this kind a little grace—it had none, not the faintest trace. The ground was grassless, or only patched in spots with it. The stained glass windows which ornamented its four sides were botches—done by some wholesale stained-glass window company, very likely of Peoria, Illinois.

"Kind heaven," I exclaimed, on sight of it, "what is the matter with a country where such things can be? What's the trouble with their minds anyhow? What a deadly yearning for the commonplace and crude and offensive possesses them!"

"Yes, and they slave to do it," replied Franklin. "You haven't any idea how people will toil for years under a hot sun or in cold or snow to be able to build a thing like that"—and he pointed to a new yellow house of the most repulsive design.

"You're right! You're right!" I replied.

"This country isn't so bad, perhaps, but the intellectual or temperamental condition of the people spoils it—their point of view. I feel a kind of chicken raising mind to be dominant here. If another kind of creature lived on this soil it would be lovely, I'm sure of it."

We sank into a deep silence. The car raced on. Once Franklin, seeing some fine apples on a tree, stopped the car, climbed a fence, and helped himself to a dozen. They were better to look at than to eat.

It was only when we reached the region of the Maumee that things began to brighten up again. We were entering a much fairer land—a region extending from the Maumee here at Grand Rapids, Ohio, to Fort Wayne, Warsaw and North Manchester, Indiana, and indeed, nearly all the rest of our journey. We were leaving the manufacturing section of Ohio and the East, and entering the grain growing, rural life loving middle West. The Maumee, when we reached it again, revivified all my earliest and best impressions of it. It was a beautiful stream, dimpling smoothly between raised banks of dark earth and fringed for the most of the way by lines of poplar, willow, and sycamore. Great patches of the parasite gold thread flourished here—more gold thread than I ever saw in my life before—looking like flames of light on a grey day, and covering whole small islands and steep banks for distances of thirty or forty feet or more at a stretch. We might have ridden into and through Grand Rapids, but I thought it scarcely worth while. What would I see anyhow? Another town like Bowling Green, only smaller, and the farm of H——'s parents, perhaps, if I could find it. All this would take time, and would it be worth while? I decided not. The Maumee, once we began to skirt its banks, was so poetic that I knew it could not be better nor more reminiscent of those older days, even though I followed it into Toledo.

But truly, this section, now that we were out of the cruder, coarser manufacturing and farming region which lay to the east of it, appealed to me mightily. I was beginning to feel as if I were in good company again—better company than we had been in for some time. Perhaps the people were not so pushing, so manufacturing,— for which heaven be praised. We encountered three towns, Napoleon, Defiance and Hicksville, before nightfall, which revived all the happiest days and ideals of my youth. Indeed, Napoleon was Warsaw over again, with its stone and red brick courthouse,—surmounted by a statute of Napoleon Bonaparte (gosh!)—and its O. N. G. Armory, and its pretty red brick Methodist and brown stone Presbyterian Churches and its iron bridges over the Maumee. The river here was as wide and shallow a thing as had been the Tippecanoe at home, at its best, with a few small boat houses at one place, and lawns or gardens which came down to the water's edge at others. The principal street was crowded with ramshackle buggies and very good automobiles (exceedingly fancy ones, in many instances) and farmers and idlers in patched brown coats and baggy, shapeless trousers—delightful pictures, every one of them. We eventually agreed to stop, and got out and hung about, while Speed went back to a garage which we had seen and treated himself to oil and gas.

Truly, if I were a poet, I would now attempt a "Rubaiyat of a Middle West Town," or I would compose "The Ballad of Napoleon, Ohio," or "Verses on Hicksville," or "Rondels of Warsaw." You have no idea what a charm these places have—what a song they sing—to one who has ever been of them and then gone out into the world and changed and cannot see life any more through the medium—the stained glass medium, if you will—of the time and the mood which we call our youth.

Here, as at Warsaw, the railroad station of an older day was hidden away in a side street, where possibly six trains a day may have stopped. At Warsaw we had the village bus, which took passengers to the one hotel. Here they had a Ford, by heck!

"None o' your cheap busses for us any more!"

And in the plain red brick business street was this motley and yet charming collection of people. I have indicated farmers and farmers' wives in (the equivalent of) homespun and linen. Behold, now, your town dandy, bustling into the bank or bookstore at two P. M. of this fine afternoon, a veritable village Beau Brummell, very conscious of his charms. He is between twentyone and twentythree, and very likely papar owns the book or the clothing store and is proud of his son's appearance. In my day son would have had a smart runabout, with red or yellow wheels, in which he would have arrived, picking up a very pretty girl by the way. Now he has an automobile—even if it is only a Buick—and he feels himself to be the most perfect of youths.

And here come three girls, arm in arm, village belles, so pretty in their bright, summery washdresses. Do you think New York can teach them anything—or Paris? Tush! Not so fast. Look at our skirts, scarcely below the knees, with pointed ruffles, and flaring flounces, and our bright grey kid slippers, and the delicate frills about our necks, and the soft bloomy gaiety of our "sport" hats. New York teach us anything? We teach New

York, rather! We are down for mail, or stationery, or an ice cream soda, and to see and be seen. Perhaps Beau Brummell will drive us home in his car, or we may refuse and just laugh at him.

And, if you please, here is one of the town's young scarlet women. No companionship for her. She is dressed like the others, only more so, but to emphasize the difference she is rouged as to cheeks and lips. Those eager, seeking eyes! No woman will openly look at her, nor any girl. But the men—these farmers and lawyers and town politicians! Which one of them will seek her out first tonight, do you suppose—the lawyer, the doctor, or the storekeeper?

How good it all tasted after New York! And what a spell it cast. I can scarcely make you understand, I fear. Indiana is a world all unto itself, and this extreme western portion of Ohio is a part of it, not by official, but rather by natural arrangement. The air felt different— the sky and trees and streets here were sweeter. They really were. The intervening years frizzled away and once more I saw myself quite clearly in this region, with the ideas and moods of my youth still dominant. I was a "kid" again, and these streets and stores were as familiar to me as though I had lived in them all my life.

Franklin and I were looking in at the window of the one combined music and piano store, to see what they sold. All the popular songs were there—"I Didn't Raise My Boy To Be a Soldier," "It's a Long, Long Way to Tipperary," "He's a Devil in His Own Home Town," and others such as "Goodbye, Goodbye" and "Though We Should Never Meet Again." As I looked at these things, so redolent of small town love affairs and of calling Wednesdays and Saturdays, my mind went back to all the similar matters I had known (not my own—I never had any) and the condition of the attractive girl and the average young men in a town like this. How careful is their upbringing—supposedly. How earnestly is the Sunday School and the precept and the maxim invoked, and how persistently so many of them go their

own way. They do not know what it is all about, all
this talk about religion and morality and duty. In their
blood is a certain something which responds to the light
of the sun and the blue of the sky.

Did you ever read "The Ballad of the Nun," by John
Davidson? See if this doesn't suggest what I'm talking
about:

> "The adventurous sun took heaven by storm,
>   Clouds scattered largesses of rain,
> The sounding cities, rich and warm,
>   Smouldered and glittered in the plain.
>
> "Sometimes it was a wandering wind,
>   Sometimes the fragrance of the pine,
> Sometimes the thought how others sinned,
>   That turned her sweet blood into wine.
>
> "Sometimes she heard a serenade,
>   Complaining, sweetly, far away.
> She said, 'A young man woos a maid';
>   And dreamt of love till break of day.
>
> "For still night's starry scroll unfurled,
>   And still the day came like a flood:
> It was the greatness of the world
>   That made her long to use her blood."

Somehow this region suggested this poem.

But, oh, these youngsters, the object of so much attention and solicitation, once they break away from these
sheltering confines and precepts and enter the great world
outside—then what? Do they fulfil any or all of the
ideals here dreamed for them? I often think of them in
the springtime going forth to the towns and the cities,
their eyes lit with the sheen of new life. Ninetynine per
cent. of them, as you and I know, end in the most humdrum fashion—not desperately or dramatically—just
humdrum and nothing at all. Death, disease, the doldrums, small jobs, smaller ideas claim the majority of
them. They grow up thinking that to be a drug clerk or
a dentist or a shoe dealer is a great thing. Well, maybe
it is—I don't know. Spinoza was a watch repairer. But

in youth all are so promising. They look so fine. And in a small town like this, they buzz about so ecstatically, dreaming and planning.

Seeing young boys walking through the streets of Napoleon and greeting each other and looking at the girls—sidewise or with a debonair security—brought back all the boys of my youth—all those who had been so promising and of such high hopes in my day. Where are they? Well, I do not need to guess. In most cases I know. They would make gloomy or dull tales. Why bother? In spring the sun-god breeds a new crop. Each autumn a new class enters school. Each spring time, at school's end, a group break away to go to the city.

Oh bright young hopes! Oh visions! visions!—mirages of success that hang so alluringly in amethyst skies!

CHAPTER XXXIII

As we were looking in this same window, I saw a man who looked exactly like a man who used to be a lawyer politician in Warsaw, a small town lawyer politician, such as you find in every town of the kind, pettifogging their lives away, but doing it unconsciously, you may well believe. This one had that peculiar something about him which marks the citizen who would like to be a tribune of the people but lacks the capacity. His clothes, nondescript, durable garments, were worn with the air of one who says "It is good to dress plainly. That is what my clients expect. Besides, I am a poor man, a commoner, and proud of it. I know that my constituents are proud of it too." He was standing at the foot of a law office stairs from which quite plainly he had just descended. This was not quite enough to confirm me in my idea that he was a country lawyer—he might have been a client—but I went further and asked him, in a roundabout way.

"What is the best road to Defiance?"

"Well," he replied, with quite an air, as who should say, "now here is a pleasant opportunity and diversion" —"There are two of them. One runs to the north of here, a hard, macadam road, and the other follows the canal and the river most of the way. Personally, I would choose the canal. It isn't quite as good a road, but the scenery is so much better. You have the river nearly always in view to your left. To the right the scenery is very attractive." He raised his hand in a slightly oratorical way.

"By the way, if you will pardon me, you are a lawyer, aren't you?"

"Well, yes, I suppose I might lay claim to that distinction," he replied, with a faintly dry smile. "I practice law here."

His coat was as brown as old brass, nearly, his shoes thick and unpolished, his trousers baggy. The soft hat he wore was pulled down indifferently over his eyes.

"I ask," I said, "because years ago, in Warsaw, Indiana, I knew a lawyer who looked very much like you."

"Indeed! I've never been in Warsaw, but I've heard of it. We have people here that go to Winona Lake. That's right near there, isn't it?"

"Practically the same place," I replied.

"Well, when there are so many people in the world, I suppose some of us must look alike," he continued.

"Yes," I replied, "I've met my counterpart more than once."

He began to expatiate on the charms of this region, but seeing that we were plainly rather anxious to be off, finally concluded and let us go. I could not help thinking, as he looked after us, that perhaps he would like very much to be going himself.

From here on the scenery was so simple and yet so beautiful that it was like a dream—such a land as Goldsmith and Gray had in mind when they wrote. This little stream, the Maumee, was delightful. It was, as he said, paralleled by a canal nearly all the way into Defiance and between canal and river were many little summer cottages, quaint and idle looking.

It had become excessively hot, so much so that I felt that now, at last, I was beginning to sunburn badly, but in spite of this we had no thought of putting up the top or of seeking shelter by lingering in the shade. It was so hot that I perspired sitting in the car, but even so it was too lovely, just moving along with what breeze the motion provided. At Napoleon, Booth had bought a light rubber ball, and with this, a few miles out, we stopped to play. The automobile gave us this freedom to seek ideal nooks and secluded places, and thus disport ourselves. The grass and trees were still green, not burned. Wheat fields newly shorn or still standing had that radiant gold hue which so pleases the eye at this season of the year. It was so hot and still that even all insects seemed to have taken to cover. We tossed our ball in a green field opposite a grove and looking up I could see a lonely buzzard soaring in the sky. Truly this is my own, my native land, I said to myself. I have rejoiced in hundreds of days just like this. All the middle West is like it—this dry heat, these clear skies, this sleepy baking atmosphere. For hundreds of miles, in my mind's eye, I could see people idling on their porches or under their trees, making the best of it. The farmer's wain was creaking along in the sun, the cattle were idling in the water, swishing their tails. Girls and boys home from school for the summer were idling in hammocks, reading or loafing. Few great thoughts or turmoils were breeding in this region. It was a pleasant land of drowsy mind and idle eye—I could feel it.

By winding ways, but always with a glimpse of this same Maumee or its parallel canal, we arrived at Defiance, and a little while later, at dusk, at Hicksville. Both of these towns, like Napoleon, were of the temperament of which I am most fond—nebulous, speculative, dreamy. You could tell by their very looks that that definite commercial sense which was so marked in places farther East was not here abounding. They were still, as at Warsaw in my day, outside the keen, shrill whip of things. Everyone was not strutting around with the all-too-evident feeling that they must get on. (I hate greedy, commercial people.) Things were drifting in a slow, romantic, speculative way. Actually I said to Franklin, and he will bear witness to it, that now we were in the exact atmosphere which was most grateful to me. I looked on all the simple little streets, the one and a half story houses with sloping roofs, the rows of good trees and unfenced lawns, and wished and wished and wished. If one only could go back—supposing one could—unreel like a film, and then represent one's life to oneself. What elisions would we not make, and what extensions! Some incidents I would make so much more perfect than they were—others would not be in the film at all.

In Defiance we all indulged in shaves, shoe shines, drinks. As we were nearing Hicksville we overtook two farmers—evidently brothers, on a load of hay. It was so beautiful, the charm of the land so great, that we were all in the best of spirits. To the south of us was a little town looking like one of those villages in Holland which you see over a wide stretch of flat land, a distant church spire or windmill being the most conspicuous object anywhere. Here it was a slate church steeple and a red factory chimney that stood up and broke the sky line. It was fairyland with a red sun, just sinking below the horizon, the trees taking on a smoky harmony in the distance. Spirals of gnats were in the air, and we were on one of those wonderful brick roads I have previously mentioned, running from Defiance to Hicksville, as smooth and picturesque to view as an old Dutch tile oven. Once we stopped the car to listen to the evening sounds, the calls of farmers after pigs, the mooing of cows, the rasping of guinea hens, and the last faint twitterings of birds and chickens. That evening hush, with a tinge of cool in the air, and the fragrant emanation of the soil and trees, was upon us. It needed only some voice singing somewhere, I thought, or the sound of a bell, to make it complete. And even those were added.

As we were idling so, these two farmers came along seated on a load of hay, making a truly Ruysdaelish picture in the amethyst light. We made sure to greet them.

"What town is that one there?" Franklin inquired, jovially.

"Squiresburg," the driver replied, grinning. His brother was sitting far back on the hay.

"This is the road to Hicksville all right, isn't it?" I put in.

"Yes, this is the road," he returned.

"How large a place is Squiresburg, anyhow?" I queried.

"Oh, seven or eight hundred."

"And how big is Hicksville?"

"Oh, two or three thousand."

"But Squiresburg's a better place than Hicksville," put in the brother, who sat behind, chewing a stalk of hay and smiling broadly.

"How's that?" inquired Franklin.

The fellow's manner was contagious.

"Oh, they're not as hard on yuh over in Squiresburg as they are in Hicksville." He munched his straw suggestively. "Y' kin have a better time there."

He smiled again, most elusively.

"Oh, this," said Speed, quickly, forming his fingers into a cup and upending it before his lips.

"That's it," said the man. "There ain't no license in Hicksville."

"Alas!" I exclaimed. "And we're bound for Hicksville."

"Well, tain't too late," said the man in front. "There's Squiresburg right over there."

"I'm afraid, I'm afraid," I sighed, and yet the thought came to me what a fine thing it would be to turn aside here and loaf in Squiresburg in one of its loutish country saloons, say, until midnight, seeing what might happen. The Dutch inns of Jan Steen were somehow in my mind. But just the same we didn't. Those things must be taken on the jump. An opportunity to be a success must provoke a spontaneous burst of enthusiasm. This suggestion of theirs, if it appealed to the others, provoked no vocal acquiescence. We smiled at them approvingly, and then rode on, only to comment later on what an adventure it might have proved—how rurally revealing.

As we entered Hicksville the lamps were being trimmed in a cottage or two, and I got a sense once more of the epic that life is day after day, year after year, century after century, cycle after cycle. Poets may come and poets may go, a Gray, a Goldsmith, a Burns in every generation, but this thing which they seek to interpret remains forever. A Daubigny, a Corot, a Ruysdael, a Vermeer, all American born, might well interpret this from generation to generation. It would never tire. Passing up this simple village street, with its small cottages on every hand, I could not help thinking of what a Monticelli or an Inness would make it. The shadows at this hour were somewhat flamboyant, like those in "The Night Watch." A sprinkling of people in the two blocks which comprised the heart of things was Rembrandtish in character. Positively, it was a comfort now to know that Franklin was with me, and that subsequently he would register this or something like it either in pen and ink or charcoal. It was so delightful to me in all its rural naïveté and crudity, that I wanted to sing about it or sit down in some corner somewhere and rhapsodize on paper. As it was, after exchanging a few words with a farmer who wanted to hear the story of our tour, we went to look for some picture postcards of Hicksville, and then to get something to eat.

It would seem at times as if life needed not so much action as atmosphere—certainly not action of any vigorous character—to make it transcendently pleasing. Insofar as I could see, there was no action in this town worthy of the name. Indeed, the people seemed to me to be of a lackadaisical turn, rurals of a very simple and unpretentious character, and, for the most part, as to the men, of an uncouth and workaday aspect. Many of them were of the stuff of which railroad hands are made, only here with the farm lands and the isolation of country life to fall back on, they were not so sophisticated.

The country lunch room which we encountered amused us all from one point of view and another. It was so typically your male center of rural life, swarming with all the wits and wags of the community and for miles around. Here raw yokels and noisy pretenders were eating, playing cards, pool, billiards, and indulging in rural wit, and we heard all the standard jests of country life. I gained the impression that the place had once been a barroom before the no-license limitation had descended upon it, and that many of its former patrons were making the best of the new conditions.

And here it was that for the first time in my life I tasted banana pie. Did you ever eat banana pie? Well! The piece I had here, in lieu of apple for which I inquired, a quarter section, with a larger layer of meringue on top, filled a long felt want and a void. It made up for the fact that I had to content myself with a ham sandwich and two fried eggs. It was thick—all of an inch and a half—and very pastryish. I asked the clerk (I cannot conscientiously call him a waiter) if he knew how to make it, but he did not. And I have been seeking ever since for a recipe as good as that from which this pie was made.

Next door to this restaurant was the Hotel Swilley— mark the name—and farther up the street, "Mr. and Mrs. C. J. Holmes, Undertaker." In the one drug and book and stationery store, where the only picture postcards we could find were of the depot and the "residence of N. C. Giffen," whoever he might be, several very young girls, "downtown for a soda," were calling up some other girl at home.

"Hello, Esther! Is this you, Esther? Well, don't you know who this is, Esther? Can't you tell? Oh, listen, Esther! Listen to my voice. Now can't you tell, Esther? I thought you could. It's Etta, of course. Wait a minute, Esther, Mabel wants to speak to you. Well, goodbye, Esther." (This last after Mabel had spoken to much the same effect as Etta.)

After idling about in what seemed an almost Saturday night throng, so chipper and brisk was it, we made our way to Fort Wayne. It was a brisk, cool ride. The moon was on high, very clear, and a light wind blowing which made overcoats comfortable. Just outside Hicksville we encountered another detour, which shut us off from our fine road and enraged us so that we decided to ignore the sign warning us to keep out under penalty of the law and to go on anyhow. There seemed a good road ahead in spite of the sign, and so we deliberately separated the boards on posts which barred the way and sped on.

But the way of the transgressor—remember! Scarcely

a mile had gone before the road broke into fragments, partially made passable by a filling of crushed stone, but after that it swiftly degenerated into mud, rubble and ruts, and we began to think we had made a dreadful mistake. Supposing we were stalled here and found? What would become of my trip to Indiana! Fined and detained, Franklin might get very much out of sorts and not care to go on. Oh, dear! Oh, dear!

We bumped along over rocks and stumps in the most uncomfortable fashion. The car rocked like a boat on a helter-skelter at Coney Island. Finally we came to a dead stop and looked into our condition, fore and aft. Things were becoming serious. Perspiration began to flow and regrets for our sinful tendencies to exude, when, in the distance, the fence at the other end appeared.

Immediately we cheered up. Poof! What was a small adventure like this?—a jolly lark, that was all. Who wouldn't risk a car being stuck in order to achieve a cutoff like this and outwit the officers of the law? One had to take a sporting chance always. Why certainly! Nevertheless, I secretly thanked God or whatever gods there be, and Franklin and Speed looked intensely relieved. We jogged along another eight hundred feet, tore down the wire screen at the other end, and rushed on—a little fearfully, I think, since there was a farm house near at hand with a lot of road-making machinery in the yard. Perhaps it was the home of the road foreman! I hope he doesn't ever read this book, and come and arrest us. Or if he does I hope he only arrests Franklin and Speed. On reflection a month or so in jail would not hurt them any, I think.

And then, after an hour or so, the city of Fort Wayne appeared in the distance. It does not lie on high ground, or in a hollow, but the presence of some twenty or thirty of those antiquated light towers which I mentioned as having been installed at Evansville, Indiana, in 1882, and which were still in evidence here, gave it that appearance. It seemed at first as though this town must be on a rise and we looking up at it from a valley; as we drew nearer, as though it were in a valley and we looking down from a height. We soon came to one of those pretentious private streets, so common in the cities of the West in these days—a street with a great gate at either end, open and unguarded and set with a superfluity of lights; which arrangement, plus houses of a certain grade of costliness, give that necessary exclusiveness the newly rich require, apparently. It was quite impressive. And then we came to a place where, quite in the heart of the city, two rivers, the St. Mary and the St. Joseph, joined to make the Maumee; and here, most intelligently, I thought, a small park had been made. It was indeed pleasing. And then we raced into the unescapable Main Street of the city, in this instance a thoroughfare so blazing with lights that I was much impressed. One would scarcely see more light on the Great White Way in New York.

CHAPTER XXXIV

THOUGH a city of seventyfive thousand, or thereabouts, Fort Wayne made scarcely any impression upon me. Now that I was back in Indiana and a few miles from my native heath, as it were, I expected, or perhaps I only half imagined, that I might gain impressions and sensations commensurate with my anticipations. But I didn't. This was the city, or town, as it was then, to which my parents had originally traveled after their marriage in Dayton, Ohio, and where my father worked in a woolen mill as foreman, perhaps, before subsequently becoming its manager. It had always been a place of interest, if not happy memory, to my mother, who seemed to feel that she had been very happy here.

When our family, such as it was (greatly depleted by the departure of most of the children), came north to Warsaw, Fort Wayne, so much nearer than Chicago and a city of forty thousand, was the Mecca for the sporting youth of our town. To go to Fort Wayne! What a week end treat! For most of our youth who had sufficient means to travel so far, it was a city of great adventure. The fare was quite one dollar and seventyfive cents for the round trip, and only the bloods and sports, as we knew them, attempted it. I never had money enough to go, as much as I wanted to, nor yet the friends who were eager for my companionship.

But what tales did I not hear of restaurants, saloons, theatres, and other resorts of pleasure visited, and what veiled hints were not cast forth of secret pleasures indulged in—flirtations, if not more vigorous escapades. Life was such a phantasm of delight to me then. Nameless and formless pleasures danced constantly before my eyes. Principally, not quite entirely, they were connected with the beauty of girls, though money and privilege and future success were other forms. And there were a few youths and some girls in Warsaw, who to my inexperienced judgment, possessed nearly all that life had to offer!

At this late date, however, Fort Wayne, looking at it in the cold, practical light of a middle-aged automobile tourist, offered but few titillations, either reminiscent or otherwise. Here it was, to me, sacred ground, and here had these various things occurred, yet as I viewed it now it seemed a rather dull, middle West town, with scarcely anything save a brisk commerce to commend it. Abroad one finds many cities of the same size of great interest, historically and architecturally—but here! By night and day it seemed bright enough, and decidedly clean. All that I could think of as Franklin and I drifted about it on this first night was that it was a very humble copy of every other larger American city in all that it attempted —streets, cabarets, high buildings and so on. Every small city in America desires to be like Chicago or New York or both, to reproduce what is built and done in these places—the most obvious things, I mean.

After dining at a cabaret Hofbräu House and sleeping in a very comfortable room which admitted the clangor of endless street car bells, however, I awoke next morning with a sick stomach and a jaded interest in all material things, and I had neither eaten nor drunk much of anything the night before—truly, truly! We had sought out the principal resort and sat in it as a resource against greater boredom, nothing more. And now, being without appetite, I wandered forth to the nearest drug store to have put up the best remedy I know for a sick stomach —nux vomica and gentian, whatever that may be.

It was in this drug store that the one interesting thing in Fort Wayne occurred—at least to me. There were, as it was still early, a negro sweeping the place, and one clerk, a lean apothecary with roached and pointed hair, who was concealed in some rear room. He came forward after a time, took my prescription, and told me I would have to wait ten minutes. Later another man hobbled in, a creature who looked like the "before" picture of a country newspaper patent medicine advertisement. He was so gaunt and blue and sunken-seamed as to face that he rather frightened me, as if a corpse should walk into your room and begin to look around. His clothes were old and brown and looked as though they had been worn heaven knows what length of time. The clerk came out, and he asked for something the name of which I did not catch. Presently the clerk came back with his prescription and mine, and going to him and putting down a bottle and a box of pills, said of the former, holding it up, "Now this is for your blood. You understand, do you? You take this three times a day, every day until it is gone." The sick man nodded like an automaton. "And these"—he now held up the pills—"are for your bowels. You take two o' these every night."

"This is for my blood and these are for my bowels," said the man slowly.

The nostrums were wrapped up very neatly in grey paper, and tied with a pink string. The corpse extracted out of a worn leather book sixtyfive cents in small pieces, and put them down. Then he shuffled slowly out.

"What ails him, do you suppose?" I asked of the dapper, beau-like clerk.

"Oh, chronic anæmia. He can't live long."

"Will that medicine do him any good, do you think?"

"Not a bit. He can't live. He'll all worn out. But he goes to some doctor around here and gets a prescription and we have to fill it. If we didn't, someone else would."

He smiled on me most genially.

What a shame to take his money, I thought. He looks as though food or decent clothes would be better for him, but what might one say? I recalled how when I was young and chronically ailing, how eagerly I clung to the thought of life, and would I not now if I were in his place? Here was I with a prescription of my own in my hand which I scarcely touched afterwards. But how near to his grave that man really was. And how futile and silly that advice about his blood sounded!

Without any special interest in Fort Wayne to delay us, and without any desire to see or do anything in particular, we made finally that memorable start for Warsaw toward which I had been looking ever since I stepped into the car in New York. Now in an hour or two or three, at the best, I would be seeing our old home, or one of them, at least, and gazing at the things which of all things identified with my youth appealed to me most. Here I had had my first taste of the public school as opposed to the Catholic or parochial school, and a delightful change it was. Warsaw was so beautiful, or seemed to me so at the time, a love of a place, with a river or small stream and several lakes and all the atmosphere of a prosperous and yet homey and home-loving resort. My mother and father and sisters and brothers were so interesting to me in those days. As in the poem of Davidson's,

> "The sounding cities, rich and warm
> Smouldered and glittered in the plain."

I was thirteen, fourteen, fifteen, sixteen. The sun and the air and some responsive chemistry which I do not understand were making my blood into wine. Would I now be dreadfully disappointed?

Our way lay through a country more or less familiar as to its character, though I had never actually been through it except on a train. All about were small towns and lakes which I had heard of but never visited. Now it was my privilege to see them if I chose, and I felt very much elated over it all. I was interested, amused, curiosity stirred.

But it was not until we reached Columbia City, only twenty miles from Warsaw, that my imagination was keenly aroused. Columbia City, small as it was, say fifteen or eighteen hundred at that time, and not much larger now, was another spot to which our small-town life-seeking gadabouts were wont to run on a Saturday night—for what purpose I scarcely know, since I never had sufficient means to accompany them. At that time, in that vigorously imaginative period, I conjured up all sorts of sybaritic delights, as being the end and aim of these expeditions, since the youths who comprised them were so keen in regard to all matters of sex. They seemed to be able to think of nothing else, and talked girls, girls, girls from morning to night, or made sly references to these jaunts which thereby became all the more exciting to me. Warsaw at that time was peculiarly favored with a bevy of attractive girls who kept all our youths on the *qui vive* as to love and their favor. With an imagination that probably far outran my years, I built up a fancy as to Columbia City which far exceeded its import, of course. To me it was a kind of Cairo of the Egyptians, with two horned Hathor in the skies, and what breaths of palms and dulcet quavers of strings and drums I know not.

These youths, who were quite smart and possessed of considerable pocket money, much more than I ever had or could get, would not have me as a companion. I was a betwixt and between soul at that time, not entirely debarred from certain phases of association and companionship with youths somewhat older than myself, and yet never included in these more private and intimate adventures to which they were constantly referring. They kept me on tenter hooks, as did the ravishing charms of so many girls about us, without my ever being satisfied. Besides, from this very town had come a girl to our Warsaw High School whom I used to contemplate with adoring eyes, she was so rounded and pink and gay. But that was all it ever came to, just that—I contemplated her from afar. I never had the courage to go near her. In the presence of most girls, especially the attractive ones, I was dumb, frozen by a nameless fear.

So this place, now we reached it, had interest to this extent, that I wanted to see what it was like although I really knew—courthouse, courthouse square, surrounding stores, and then a few streets with simple homes and churches. Exactly. It was like all the others, only somewhat poorer—not so good as Napoleon, Ohio, or even Hicksville.

But there was something that was much better than anything we had encountered yet—an Old Settler's Day, no less—which had filled the streets with people and wagons and the public square with tents, for resting rooms, had spread table cloths out on the public lawn for eating, while a merry-go-round whirled in the middle of one street, and various tents and stands on several sides of the square were crowded with eatables and drinkables of sorts. I believe they have dubbed these small aisles of tents a "Broadway," in the middle West. Of course, there were popcorn, candy, hot "weenies," as sausages are known hereabouts, and lemonade. I never saw a more typically rural crowd, nor one that seemed to get more satisfaction out of its modest pleasures.

But the very old farmers and their wives, the old settlers and settleresses and their children and their grandchildren, and their great grandchildren! Life takes on at once comic and yet poetic and pathetic phases the moment you view a crowd of this kind in the detached way that we were doing it. Here were men and women so old and worn and bent and crumpled by the ageing processes of life that they looked like the yellow leaves of the autumn. Compared with the fresh young people who were to be seen spinning about on the merry-go-round, or walking the streets in twos and threes, they were infinitely worn. Such coats and trousers, actually cut and sewn at home! And such hats and whiskers and canes and shoes! I called Franklin's attention to two stocky, pinky rustics wearing Charlie Chaplin hats and carrying Charlie Chaplin canes, and then to group after group of men and women so astonishing that they seemed figures out of some gnome or troll world, figures so distorted as to seem only fit fancies for a dream. We sat down by one so weird that he seemed the creation of a genius bent on depicting age. I tried to strike up a conversation, but he would not. He did not seem to hear. I began to whisper to Franklin concerning the difference between a figure like this and those aspirations which we held in our youth concerning "getting on." Life seems to mock itself with these walking commentaries on ambition. Of what good are the fruits of earthly triumph anyhow?

Nearly all of the older ones, to add to their picturesqueness, wore bits of gold lettered cloth which stated clearly that they were old settlers. They stalked or hobbled or stood about talking in a mechanical manner. They rasped and cackled—"grandthers," "gaffers," "Polichinelles," "Pantaloons." I had to smile, and yet if the least breath of the blood mood of sixteen were to return, one would cry.

And then came the younger generations! I wish those who are so sure that democracy is a great success and never to be upset by the cunning and self-interestedness of wily and unscrupulous men, would make a face to face study of these people. I am in favor of the dream of democracy, on whatever basis it can be worked out. It is an ideal. But how, I should like to ask, is a proletariat such as this, and poorer specimens yet, as we all know, to hold its own against the keen, resourceful oligarchs at the top? Certainly ever since I have been in the world, I have seen nothing but Americans who were so sure that the people were fit to rule, and did rule, and that nothing but the widest interests of all the people were ever really sought by our statesmen and leaders in various fields. The people are all right and to be trusted. They are capable of understanding their public and private affairs in such a manner as to bring the greatest happiness to the greatest number—but are they? I was taught this in the adjacent schools of Warsaw, quite as I was taught that the Christian ideal was right and true, and that it really prevailed in life, and that those who did not agree with it were thieves and scoundrels. Actually, I went into life from this very region believing largely in all this, only to find by degrees that this theory had no relationship to the facts. Life was persistently demonstrating to me that self-interest and only self-interest ruled—that strength dominated weakness, that large ideas superseded and ruled small ones, and so on and so forth, *ad infinitum*. It was interesting and even astonishing to find that we were not only being dominated mentally by a theory that had no relationship to life whatsoever, but that large, forceful brains were even then plotting the downfall of the republic. Big minds were ruling little ones, big thoughts superseding little ones. The will to power was in all individuals above the grade of amoeba, and even there. All of us were mouthing one set of ideas and acting according to a set of instincts entirely opposed to our so called ideas. I, for one, was always charging individuals with failing to live up to the Christian idea and its derived moral code, whereas no detail of the latter affected my own conduct in the least.

Looking at this crowd of people here in the streets of Columbia City, I was more affected by their futility and pathos—life's futility and pathos for the mass—than by anything else so far. What could these people do, even by banding together, to control the giants at the top? Here they were, entertained like babies by the most pathetic toys—a badge, a little conversation, a little face-to-face contemplation of other futilitarians as badly placed as themselves. The merry-go-round was spinning and grinding out a wheezy tune. I saw young girls sitting sidewise of wooden horses, lions and the like, their dresses (because of the short skirt craze) drawn to the knee, or nearly so. Imagine the storm which would have ensued in my day had any girl dared to display more than an ankle! (Custom! Custom!) About it were small boys and big boys and big girls, for the most part too poor to indulge in its circular madness very often, who were contenting themselves with contemplating the ecstasy of others.

"Franklin," I said, "you were raised out in this region about the time I was. How would such a spectacle as that have been received in our day?" (I was referring to the exhibition of legs, and I was very pleased with it as such, not quarreling with it at all.)

"Oh, shocking," he replied, smiling reminiscently, "it just wouldn't have occurred."

"And how do you explain its possibility now? These people are just as religious, aren't they?"

"Nearly so—but fashion, fashion, the mass love of imitation. If the mass want to do it and can find an excuse or permission in the eyes of others, or even if they don't want to do it, but their superiors do, they will suffer it. I haven't the slightest doubt but that there is many a girl sitting on a wooden horse in there who would rather not have her skirt pulled up to her knees, but since others do it she does it. She wants to be 'in the swim.' And she'd rather be unhappy or a little ashamed than not be in the swim. Nothing hurts like being out of style, you know, especially out in the country these days —not even the twinges of a Puritan conscience."

"Franklin," I said, "I'll tell you. You were raised on a farm and know farmer boys at sight. Pick me out a farmer's boy here and now, who hasn't money enough to ride in this thing, and I'll give him a dime. We'll see how he takes it."

Franklin smiled and looked around carefully. The thing interested him so much that he finally circled the merry-go-round and lighted on one youth whose short pants and ungainly shoes and cheap but clean little dotted shirt and small fifteen or twentyfive cent hat and pink cheeks, as well as his open mouth and rapt attention, indicated that here was a wonder with which he was thoroughly unfamiliar. I waited to see if he would step aboard at the next stop of the car, or the next, but no, he was merely an onlooker. At the next start of the car or platform I watched his eager eyes follow those who got on. It was pathetic, and when the merry-go-round started again he gazed aloft at the whirling thing in an ecstasy of delight. As it was slowing down for the second or third time, preparatory to taking on a new load, I reached over his shoulder and quite unheeded, at first, put a quarter before his eyes. For a moment he stopped quite dazed and looked at it, then at me, then at the quarter, then at me.

"Go on! Ride!" I commanded. "Get on!" The carousel was almost still.

Suddenly, with a mixture of reverence, awe, and a world of surprise in his eyes, he seemed to comprehend what I meant. He looked at his shabby father who had been standing near him all this while, but finding him interested in other things, clambered aboard. I watched him take his place beside a horse, not on it. I watched it start with almost as much pleasure as came to him, I think. Then as the speed increased, I turned to urge Franklin to photograph two old men, who were near. They were so wonderful. We were still at that when the machine stopped, only I did not notice. I was watching the two old men. All at once I saw this boy making his way through the crowd. He had his hand out before him, and as he reached me he opened it and there were the four nickels change.

"Oh, no," I said. "I didn't mean you to give them back. Run quick! Ride again! Get on before it starts again."

I can see those round, surprised blue eyes with the uncertain light of vague comprehension and happiness in them. He could scarcely make it out.

"Run quick," I said. "Ride four times, or do anything you please."

His eyes seemed to get rounder and bigger for a second, then his hand wavered, and the hungry fingers shut tight on the money. He ran.

"How's that for getting a thousand dollars' worth of fun for a nickel, Franklin?" I inquired.

"Right-o," he replied. "We ought to be ashamed to take it."

And it was literally true, so subtle are the ways by which one can come by what does not belong to him, even though partially paid for.

CHAPTER XXXV

GETTING to Warsaw was a matter of an hour or so at most from here. I think my principal sensation on entering Indiana and getting thus far was one of disappointment that nothing had happened, and worse, nothing could happen. From here on it was even worse. It is all very well to dream of revisiting your native soil and finding at least traces, if no more, of your early world, but I tell you it is a dismal and painful business. Life is a shifting and changing thing. Not only your own thoughts and moods, but those of all others who endure, undergo a mighty alteration. Houses and landscapes and people go by and return no more. The very land itself changes. All that is left of what you were, or of what was, in your own brain, is a dwindling and spindling thing.

Not many miles out from Warsaw, we passed through the town of Pierceton, where lived two girls I barely knew at school, and here we picked up a typical Hoosier, who, because we asked the road of the principal storekeeper, volunteered to ride along and show us. "I'm going for a couple of miles in that direction. If you don't mind I'll get in and show you."

Franklin welcomed him. I objected to the shrewd type, a cross between a country politician and a sales agent, who manages his errands in this way, but I said nothing. He made himself comfortable alongside Speed and talked to him principally the small change of country life.

As we sped along I began to feel an ugly resentment toward all life and change, and the driving, destroying urge of things. The remorselessness of time, how bitterly, irritatingly clear it stood out here! We talk about the hardness and cruelty of men! Contrast their sharpest, most brutal connivings with the slow, indifferent sapping of strength and hope and joy which nature practices upon each and every one of us. See the utter brutality with which every great dream is filched from the mind, all the delicate, tendril-like responsiveness of youth is taken away, your friends and pleasures and aspirations slain. I looked about me, and beginning to recognize familiar soil, such as a long stretch of white road ending in an old ice house, a railroad track out which I had walked, felt a sudden, overpowering, almost sickening depression at the lapse of time and all that had gone with it. Thirty years, nearly, had passed and with them all the people and all the atmosphere that surrounded them, or nearly so, and all my old intimacies and loves and romantic feelings. A dead world like this is such a compound—a stained-glass window at its best; a bone yard at its worst.

Approaching Warsaw after thirty years, my mind was busy gathering up a thousand threads long since fallen and even rotting in the grass of time. Here was the place, I said to myself, where we, the depleted portion of our family that constituted "we" at the time, came to stabilize our troubled fortunes and (it was my mother's idea) to give the three youngest children, of whom I was one, an opportunity to get a sensible American free school education. Hitherto our family (to introduce a little private history) had been more or less under the domination of my dogmatic father, who was a Catholic and a bigot. I never knew a narrower, more hidebound religionist, nor one more tender and loving in his narrow way. He was a crank, a tenth rate Saint Simon or Francis of Assisi, and yet a charming person if it had been possible to get his mind off the subject of religion for more than three seconds at a time. He worked, ate, played, slept and dreamed religion. With no other thought than the sanctity and glory and joy of the Catholic Church, he was constantly attempting to drive a decidedly recalcitrant family into a similar point of view.

In the main (there were ten of us living) we would

none of it. The majority, by some trick of chemistry which produces unheard of reactions in the strangest manner (though he and, to a much less extent, my mother, were religiously minded) were caught fast by the material, unreligious aspect of things. They were, one and all, mastered by the pagan life stream which flows fresh and clean under all our religions and all our views, moralistic and otherwise. It will have none of the petty, narrowing traps and gins wherewith the mistaken processes of the so-called minds of some would seek to enslave it. Life will not be boxed in boxes. It will not be wrapped and tied up with strings and set aside on a shelf to await a particular religious or moral use. As yet we do not understand life, we do not know what it is, what the laws are that govern it. At best we see ourselves hobbling along, responding to this dream and that lust and unable to compel ourselves to gainsay the fires and appetites and desires of our bodies and minds. Some of these, in some of us, strangely enough (and purely accidentally, of that I am convinced) conform to the current needs or beliefs of a given society; and if we should be so fortunate as to find ourselves in that society, we are by reason of these ideals, favorites, statesmen, children of fortune, poets of the race. On the other hand, others of us who do not and cannot conform (who are left-over phases of ancient streams, perhaps, or portentous striæ of new forces coming into play) are looked upon as horrific, and to be stabilized, or standardized, and brought into the normal systole-diastole of things. Those of us endowed with these things in mind and blood are truly terrible to the mass—pariahs, failures, shams, disgraces. Yet life is no better than its worst elements, no worse than its best. Its perfections are changing temporalities, illusions of perfection that will be something very different tomorrow. Again I say, we do not know what life is —not nearly enough to set forth a fixed code of any kind, religious or otherwise. But we do know that it sings and stings, that it has perfections, entrancements, shames— each according to his blood flux and its chemical char-

acter. Life is rich, gorgeous, an opium eater's dream of
something paradisiacal—but it is never the thin thing
that thin blood and a weak, ill nourished, poorly responding brain would make it, and that is where the majority
of our religions, morals, rules and safeguards come from.
From thin, petered out blood, and poor, nervous, non-
commanding weak brains.

Life is greater than anything we know.

It is stronger.

It is wilder.

It is more horrible.

It is more beautiful.

We need not stop and think we have found a solution.
We have not even found a beginning. We do not know.
And my patriotic father wanted us all to believe in the
Catholic church and the infallibility of the Pope and
confession and communion!

Great Pan of the Greeks, and you, Isis of the Egyptians, save me! These moderns are all insane!

.   .   .   .

But I was talking of the effect of the approach of
Warsaw upon me. And I want to get back to my mother,
for she was the center of all my experiences here. Such
a woman! Truly, when I think of my mother I feel that
I had best keep silent. I certainly had one of the most
perfect mothers ever a man had. Warsaw, in fact, really
means my mother to me, for here I first came to partially understand her, to view her as a woman and to
know how remarkable she was. An open, uneducated,
wondering, dreamy mind, none of the customary, conscious principles with which so many conventional souls
are afflicted. A happy, hopeful, animal mother, with a
desire to live, and not much constructive ability wherewith to make real her dreams. A pagan mother taken
over into the Catholic Church at marriage, because she
loved a Catholic and would follow her love anywhere.
A great poet mother, because she loved fables and fairies
and half believed in them, and once saw the Virgin Mary
standing in our garden (this was at Sullivan), blue robes,

crown and all, and was sure it was she! She loved the trees and the flowers and the clouds and the sound of the wind, and was wont to cry over tales of poverty almost as readily as over poverty itself, and to laugh over the mannikin fol de rols of all too responsive souls. A great hearted mother—loving, tender, charitable, who loved the ne'er do well a little better than those staid favorites of society who keep all laws. Her own children frequently complained of her errors and tempers (what mortal ever failed so to do?) and forgot their own beams to be annoyed by her motes. But at that they loved her, each and every one, and could not stay away from her very long at a time, so potent and alive she was.

I always say I know how great some souls can be because I know how splendid that of my mother was. Hail, you! wherever you are!

In drawing near to Warsaw, I felt some of this as of a thousand other things which had been at that time and now were no more.

.   .   .   .   .   .

We came in past the new outlying section of Winona, a region of summer homes, boat houses and casinos scattered about a lake which in my day was entirely surrounded by woods, green and still, and thence along a street which I found out later was an extension of the very street on which we had originally lived, only now very much lengthened to provide a road out to Winona. Lined on either side by the most modern of cottages, these new style verandaed, summer resorty things hung with swings and couch hammocks which one sees at all the modern American watering places, it was too new and smart to suit me exactly and carried with it no suggestion of anything that I had been familiar with. A little farther on, though, it merged into something that I did know. There were houses that looked as though they might have endured all of forty years and been the same ones I had known as the houses of some of my youthful companions. I tried to find the home of Loretta Brown, for instance, who was killed a few years later in a wreck in the West, and of Bertha Stillmayer, who used to hold my youthful fancy, at a distance. I could not find them. There was a church, also, at one corner, which I was almost sure I knew, and then suddenly, as we neared another corner, I recognized two residences. One was that of the principal lumber dealer of our town, a man who with his son and daughter and a few other families constituted the élite, and next to it, the home of the former owner of the principal dry goods store; very fine houses both of them, and suggesting by their architecture and the arrangement of their grounds all that at one time I thought was perfect—the topmost rung of taste and respectability!

In my day these were very close to the business heart, but so was everything in Warsaw then. In the first and better one, rather that of the wealthier of the two men, for they were both very much alike in their physical details, was, of all things, an automobile show room—an interesting establishment of its kind, made possible, no doubt, by the presence of the prosperous summer resort we had just passed. On the porch of this house and its once exclusive walk were exhibition tires and posters of the latest automobiles. In the other house, more precious to me still because of various memories, was the present home of the local Knights of Pythias, an organization I surely need not describe. In front of it hung a long, perpendicular glass sign or box, which could be lighted from within by incandescent globes. The lettering was merely "K. of P."

In years and years I cannot recall anything giving me a sharper wrench. I was so surprised, although I was fully prepared not to be—not that I cared, really, whether these houses had changed or not—I didn't. But in one of them, the present home of the K. of P., had lived in my time the Yaisley family, and this family was endeared to me, partly by its wealth (qualify this by the inexperience of youth and our personal poverty) and partly by the presence of Dora Yaisley, the youngest daughter, who was a girl of about my own age, possibly younger, and who, to me, was so beautiful that I used to dream about her all the time. As a matter of fact, from my fourteenth to my sixteenth year, from the first time I saw her until a long time after I had seen her no more, she was the one girl whose perfection I was sure of. Perhaps she would not be called beautiful by many. No doubt, if I could see her today, she would not appeal to me at all. But then——

CHAPTER XXXVI

WARSAW IN 1884-6

AND right here I began to ponder on the mystery of association and contact, the chemistry and physics of transference by which a sky or a scene becomes a delicious presence in the human brain or the human blood, carried around for years in that mystic condition described as "a memory" and later transferred, perhaps, or not, by conversation, paint, music, or the written word, to the brains of others, there to be carried around again and possibly extended in ever widening and yet fading circles in accordance with that curious, so-called law (is it a law?) of the transmutation of energy. That sounds so fine, that law of transmutation, and yet it makes such short work of that other fine palaver about the immortality of the soul. How many impressions have you transferred in this way? How much of you has gone from you in this way and died? A thin and pathetic end, I say, if all go on, being thinned and transmuted as they go.

Warsaw was an idyllic town for a youth of my temperament and age to have been brought to just at that time. It was so young, vigorous and hopeful. I recall with never-ending delight the intense sense of beauty its surrounding landscape gave me, its three lakes, the Tippecanoe River, which drained two of them, the fine woods and roads and bathing places which lay in various directions. People were always coming to Warsaw to shoot ducks in the marshes about, or to fish or summer on the lakes. Its streets were graced with many trees—they were still here in various places as we rode about today, and not so much larger, as I could see, than when I was here years before. The courthouse, new in my day, standing in an open square and built of white Indiana limestone, was as imposing as ever, and, as we came upon it now turning a corner, it seemed a really handsome building, one of the few in towns of this size which I had seen which I could honestly say I liked. The principal streets, Centre, Buffalo and South, were better built, if anything, than in my time, and actually wider than I had recalled them as being. They were imbued with a spirit not different to that which I had felt while living here. Only on the northwest corner of Centre and Buffalo Streets (the principal street corner opposite this courthouse) where once had stood a bookstore, and next to that a small restaurant with an oyster counter, and next to that a billiard and pool room, the three constituting in themselves the principal meeting or loafing place for the idle young of all ages, the clever workers, school boys, clerks and what not of the entire town, and I presume county—all this was entirely done away with, and in its place was a stiff, indifferent, exclusive looking bank building of three stories in height, which gave no least suggestion of an opportunity for such life as we had known to exist here.

Where do the boys meet now, I asked myself, and what boys? I should like to see. Why, this was the very center and axis of all youthful joy and life in my day. There is a kind of freemasonry of generations which binds together the youths of one season, plus those of a season or two elder, and a season or two younger. At this corner, and in these places, to say nothing of the village post office, Peter's Shoe Repairing and Shine Parlor, and Moon's and Thompson's grocery stores, we of ages ranging from fourteen to seventeen and eighteen— never beyond nineteen or twenty—knew only those who fell within these masonic periods. To be of years not much less nor more than these was the *sine qua non* of happy companionship. To have a little money, to be in the high or common school (upper grades), to have a little gaiety, wit, and intelligence, to be able to think and talk of girls in a clever, flirtatious (albeit secretly nervous manner), were almost as seriously essential.

A fellow by the name of Pierre (we always called him Peary) Morris ran this bookstore, which was the most popular meeting place of all. Here, beginning with the earliest days after our arrival, I recognized a sympathetic atmosphere, though I was somewhat too young to share in it. My mother (my father was still working in Terre Haute) placed us in what was known as the West Ward School. It adjoined an old but very comfortable house we had rented; the school yard and our yard touched. Here we dwelt for one year and part of another, then moved directly across the street, south, into an old brick house known as the Thralls Mansion, one of the first— as I understood it, actually *the* first—brick house to be built in the county years and years before. Here, in these two houses, we spent all the time that I was in Warsaw. From the frame or "old Grant house," I sallied each day to my studies of the seventh grade in the school next door. From the Thralls house I accompanied my sister Tillie each day to the high school, in the heart of the town, not far from this court house, where I completed my work in the eighth grade and first year high. I have (in spite of the fact that I have been myself all these years) but a very poor conception of the type of youth I was, and yet I love him dearly. For one thing, I know that he was a dreamer. For another, somewhat cowardly, but still adventurous and willing, on most occasions, to take a reasonable chance. For a third, he was definitely enthusiastic about girls or beauty in the female form, and what was more, about beauty in all forms, natural and otherwise. What clouds meant to him! What morning and evening skies! What the murmur of the wind, the beauty of small sails on our lakes, birds a-wing, the color and flaunt and rhythm of things!

Walking, playing, dreaming, studying, I had finally come to feel myself an integral part of the group of youths, if not girls, who centered about this bookstore and this corner. Judson Morris, or Jud Morris, as we called him, a hunchback, and the son of the proprietor, was a fairly sympathetic and interesting friend. Frank Yaisley, the brother of Dora, and two years older; George Reed, since elevated to a circuit judgeship somewhere in the West; "Mick" or Will McConnell, who died a few years later of lockjaw contracted by accidentally running a rusty nail into his foot; Harry Croxton, subsequently a mining engineer who died in Mexico and was buried there, and John and George Sharp, sons of the local flour mill owner and grandnephews of my mother; Rutger Miller, Orren Skiff, and various others were all of this group. There were still others of an older group who belonged to the best families and somehow seemed to exchange courtesies here and, in addition, members of a younger group than ourselves, who were to succeed us, as freshman class succeeds freshman class at college.

My joy in this small world and these small groups of youths, and what the future held in store for us, was very great. As I figured it out, the whole duty of men was to grow, get strong, eat, drink, sleep, get married, have children and found a family, and so fulfill the Biblical injunction to "multiply and replenish the earth." Even at this late date I was dull to such things as fame, lives of artistic achievement, the canniness and subtlety of wealth, and all such things, although I knew from hearing everyone talk that one must and did get rich eventually if one amounted to anything at all. A perfect, worldly wise dogma, but not truer, really, than any other dogma.

But what a change was here, not so much materially as spiritually! Have you ever picked up an empty beetle shell at the end of the summer—that pale, transparent thing which once held a live and flying thing? Did it not bring with it a sense of transmutation and lapse—the passing of all good things? Here was this attractive small town, as brisk and gay as any other, no doubt, but to me now how empty! Here in these streets, in the two houses in which we had lived, in this corner bookstore and its adjacent restaurant, in the West Ward and Central High Schools, in the local Catholic Church where mass was said only once a month, and in the post office, swimming holes, and on the lakes which surrounded us like gems, had been spent the three happiest years of my boyhood.

Only the year before we came here I had been taken out of a Catholic school at Evansville, Indiana. The public school was to me like a paradise after the stern religiosity of this other school. Education began to mean something to me. I wanted to read and to know. There was a lovely simplicity about the whole public school world which had nothing binding or driving about it. The children were urged, coaxed, pleaded with—not driven. Force was a last resort, and rarely indulged in. Can't you see how it was that I soon fell half in love with my first teacher, a big, soft, pink-cheeked, buxom blonde, and with our home and our life here?

But I was concerned now only with this corner book store and how it looked today. Coming out from New York, I kept thinking how it would look and how the square would look and whether there would be any of the old atmosphere about the schools or the lakes, or our two houses, or the houses of my friends, or the Catholic Church or anything. I wanted to see our ex-homes and the schools and all these things. Turning into the square after passing the first two houses mentioned, I looked at this corner, and here was this new bank building and nothing more. It looked cold and remote. A through car of a state-wide trolley system, which ran all the way from Michigan City and Gary on Lake Michigan to Indianapolis, Evansville, Terre Haute, and other places in the extreme south, stood over the way. There had been no street car of any kind here in my day. The court house was the same, the store in which Nueweiler's clothing store used to be (and because of Frank Nueweiler, an elderly figure in "our crowd," one of our rendezvous) was now a bookstore, the successor, really, to the one I was looking for. The post office had been moved to a new store building erected by the government. (I think in every town we passed we had found a new post office erected by the government.) The Harry Oram wagon works was in exactly the same position at the northwest corner of the square, only larger. There was no trace of Epstein's Wool, Hide and Tallow Exchange, which had stood on another corner directly across the way from the bookstore. A new building had replaced that. All Epstein's children had gone to Chicago, so a neighboring hardware clerk told me, and Epstein himself had died fifteen years before.

But what of the Yaisleys? What of the Yaisleys? I kept asking myself that. Where had they gone? To satisfy myself as to that, before going any farther, I went into this new bookstore in Nueweiler's old clothing emporium, and asked the man who waited on me while I selected postcards.

"What became of the Nueweilers who used to run this place as a clothing store?" I asked as a feeler, before going into the more delicate matter of the Yaisleys.

"Nueweiler?" he replied, with an air of slight surprise. "Why, he has the dry goods store at the next corner—Yaisley's old place."

"Well, and what has become of Yaisley, then?"

"Oh, he died all of twenty years ago. You must be quite a stranger about here."

"I am," I volunteered. "I used to live here, but I haven't been here now for nearly thirty years, and that's why I'm anxious to know. I used to know Frank and Will and Dora Yaisley, and even her elder sister, Bertha, by sight, at least."

"Oh, yes, Will Yaisley. There was an interesting case for you," he observed reminiscently. "I remember him, though I don't remember the others so well. I only came here in 1905, and he was back here then. Why, he had been out West by then and had come back here broke. His father was dead then, and the rest of the family scattered. He was so down and out that he hung around the saloons, doing odd jobs of cleaning and that sort of thing—and at other times laid cement sidewalks."

"How old was he at that time, do you think?" I inquired.

"Oh, about forty, I should say."

This unhappy end of Will Yaisley was all the more startling when I contrasted it with what I had known of him (1884-1886). Then he was a youth of twenty or twentyone or two, clerking in his father's store, which was the largest in town, and living in this fine house which was now a K. of P. Club. He was brisk and stocky and red-headed—his sister Dora had glints of red in her hair—and, like the rest of this family, was vain and supercilious.

Aphrodite had many devotees in this simple Christian village. The soil of the town, its lakes and groves, seemed to generate a kind of madness in us all. I recall that during the short time I was there, there was scandal after scandal, and seemingly innocent sex attractions, which sprang up between boys and girls whom I knew, ended disastrously after I had departed. One of the boys already referred to was found, after he was dead, to have left a pretty, oversexed school girl, whom I also knew, enceinte. The son of one of the richest land owners and a brother of a very pretty school girl who sat near me in first year high, was found, the year after I left, to have seduced a lovely tall girl with fair hair and blue eyes, who lived only two blocks from us. The story went round (it was retailed to me in Chicago) that she got down on her knees to him (how should anyone have seen her do that?) and on his refusing to marry her, committed suicide by swallowing poison. Her death by suicide, and the fact that he had been courting her, were true enough. I personally know of three other girls, all beauties, and all feverish with desire (how keen is the natural urge to sex!) who were easily persuaded, no doubt, and had to be sent away so that the scandal of

having a child at home, without having a husband to
vouch for it, might be hushed up.

Poor, dogma-bound humanity!   How painfully we
weave our way through the mysteries, once desire has
trapped us!

CHAPTER XXXVII

THE OLD HOUSE

DORA YAISLEY and her sister, insofar as I could learn this day, had fared no better than some of the others. Indeed, life had slipped along for all and made my generation, or many of the figures in it, at least, seem like the decaying leaves that one finds under the new green shoots and foliage of a later spring. Dora had married a lawyer from some other town, so my gossip believed, but later, talking to another old resident and one who remembered me, I was told that she had run away and turned up married—to leave again and live in another place. As for another beauty of my day, it was said that she had been seen in hotels in Indianapolis and Fort Wayne with some man not her husband. The book man with whom I first talked volunteered this information.

"But she's working now right here in Warsaw," he volunteered a little later. "If you know her, you might go to see her. I'm sure she'd be glad to see you. She hasn't any relative around now."

"You don't say!" I exclaimed, astonished. "Is she as good looking as ever?"

"No," he replied with a faint wryness of expression, "she's not beautiful any more. She must be over forty. But she's a very nice woman. I see her around here occasionally. She goes regularly to my church."

After browsing here so long with this man, Franklin having gone to seek something else, I returned to the car and requested that we proceed out Centre Street to the second house in which we had lived—the Thralls Mansion—that having been the most important and the more picturesque of the two. On nearing it I was again surprised and indeed given a sharp, psychic wrench which endured for hours and subsequently gave me a splitting headache. It was not gone, oh, no, not the formal walls, but everything else was. Formerly, in my day, there had been a large grove of pines here, with interludes, in one of which flourished five chestnut trees, yielding us all the chestnuts we could use; in another a group of orchard trees, apples, pears, peaches, cherries. The house itself stood on a slope which led down to a pond of considerable size, on which of a moonlight night, when our parents would not permit us to go farther, we were wont to skate. On the other side of this pond, to the southeast of it, was a saw and furniture mill, and about it, on at least two sides, were scattered dozens upon dozens of oak, walnut and other varieties of logs, stored here pending their use in the mill. Jumping logs was a favorite sport of all us school boys from all parts of the town—getting poles and leaping from pile to pile like flying squirrels. It was a regular Saturday morning and week day evening performance, until our mother's or sister's or brother's warning voices could be heard calling us hence. From my bedroom window on the second floor, I could contemplate this pond and field, hear the pleasant droning of the saw and planes of the mill, and see the face of the town clock in the court house tower, lighted at night, and hear the voice of its bell tolling the hours regularly day and night.

This house found and has retained a place in my affections which has never been disturbed by any other— and I have lived in many. It was so simple—two stories on the north side, three on the south, where the hill declined sharply, and containing eleven rooms and two cellar rooms, most convenient to our kitchen and dining-room.

It was, as I have said, a very old house. Even when we took it age had marred it considerably. We had to replace certain window sashes and panes and fix the chimney and patch the roof in several places where it leaked. The stairs creaked. Being almost entirely surrounded by pines which sighed and whispered continually, it was supposed to be damp but it was not. In grey or rainy weather the aspect of the whole place was solemn, historic. In snowy or stormy weather, it took on a kind of patriarchal significance. When the wind was high these thick, tall trees swirled and danced in a wild ecstasy. When the snow was heavy they bent low with their majestic plumes of white. Underneath them was a floor of soft brown pine needles as soft and brown as a rug. We could gather basket upon basket of resiny cones with which to start our morning fires. In spring and summer these trees were full of birds, the grackle of blackbird particularly, for these seemed to preempt the place early in March and were inclined to fight others for possession. Nevertheless, robins, bluebirds, wrens and other of the less aggressive feathers built their nests here. I could always tell when spring was certainly at hand by the noise made by a tree full of newly arrived blackbirds on some chill March morning. Though snow might still be about, they were strutting about on the bits of lawn we were able to maintain between groups of pines, or hopping on the branches of trees, rasping out their odd speech.

But now, as we rolled out my familiar street, I noted that the sawmill was no longer. The furniture factory had been converted into an electrical supply works. Furthermore, the pond at the foot of our house was filled up, not a trace of it remaining, and all saw logs, of course, long since cleaned away. Worse and worse, the pine grove had disappeared completely. In the front or west part of our premises now stood two new houses of a commonplace character, with considerable lawn space about them, but not a tree. And there had been so many fine ones! Furthermore, the ground about the house proper was stripped bare, save for one lone crab apple tree which stood near our north side door. It was still vigorous, and the ground under it was littered with bright red-yellow crabs which were being allowed to decay. From the front door, which once looked out upon a long cobble and brick walk, which ran between double rows of pine trees to our very distant gate (all gone now) protruded a sign which read, "Saws Filed." A path ran from this door southward over the very pond on which we used to skate! Near at hand was the "old Grant house" in which we had lived before we moved into this one, and it was still there, only it had been moved over closer to the school and another house crowded in beside it, on what was once our somewhat spacious lawn. The old school lawn, which once led down to the street that passed its gate, was gone, and instead this street came up to the school door, meeting the one which had formerly passed our house and ended at a stile, giving on to the school lawn. The school yard trees were gone, and facing the new street made of the old school lawn were houses. Only our old Thralls house remained standing as it was, on the right hand side.

I can only repeat that I was psychically wrenched, although I was saying to myself that I felt no least interest in the visible scene. I had lived here, true, but what of it? There was this of it, that somewhere down in myself, far below my surface emotions and my frothy reasoning faculties, something was hurting. It was not I, exactly. It was like something else that had once been me and was still in me, somewhere, another person or soul that was grieving, but was now overlayed or shut away like a ghost in a sealed room. I felt *it* the while I bustled about examining this and that detail.

First I went up to the old house and walked about it trying to replace each detail as it was, and as I did so, restoring to my mind scene after scene and mood after mood of my younger days. What becomes of old scenes and old moods in cosmic substance? Here had been the pump, and here it was still, thank heaven, unchanged. Here, under a wide-armed fir which once stood here, Ed, Al, Tillie and I had once taken turns stirring a huge iron pot full of apple butter which was boiling over pine twigs and cones, and also gathered cones to keep it going. Here, also, to the right of the front door as you faced west, was my favorite lounging place, a hammock strung between two trees, where of a summer day, or when the weather was favorable at any time, I used to lie and read, looking up between times through the branches of the trees to the sky overhead and wondering over and rejoicing in the beauty of life. We were poor in the main, and, worse yet, because of certain early errors of some of the children (how many have I committed since!) and the foolish imaginings of my parents, my father in particular, we considered ourselves socially discredited. We hadn't done so well as some people. We weren't rich. Some of us hadn't been good!! But in books and nature, even at this age, I managed to find solace for all our fancied shortcomings, or nearly all, and though I grieved to think that we had so little of what seemed to give others so much pleasure, and the right to strut and stare, I also fancied that life must and probably did hold something better for me than was indicated here.

After I had made the rounds once, Franklin sitting in the offing in his car and sketching the house, I knocked at the front door and received no answer. Finally I went inside and knocked at the first inside door, which originally gave into our parlor. The place looked really very tatterdemalion, like an isolated Eleventh Avenue, New York, tenement. No one answered, but finally from what was formerly my sister Theresa's room, on the second floor, a stocky and somewhat frowsy woman of plainly Slavic origin put her head over the balustrade of the handsome old carved walnut staircase, and called, "Well?"

"I beg your pardon," I said, "but once, a number of years ago, our family used to live in this house, and I have come back to look it over. Can you tell me who occupies it now?"

"Well, no one family has it now," she replied pleasantly on hearing of my mission. "There are four families in it, two on this floor up here, one on that floor (indicating) and one in the basement. The people on the first floor rent that front room to a boarder."

"A tenement!" I exclaimed to myself.

"Well, there doesn't appear to be anyone at home here," I said to her. "Do you mind if I look at your rooms? The room at the end of the hall there was once my sleeping room."

"Oh, not at all. Certainly. Certainly. Come right up."

I mounted the stairs, now creakier than ever, and entered a room which in our day seemed comparatively well furnished. It was memorable to me because of a serious siege of illness which my sister, Theresa, had undergone there, and because of several nights in which I had tried to sit up and keep watch. Once from this room, at two in the morning, I had issued forth to find our family physician, an old, grey-bearded man, who, once I had knocked him up, came down to his door, lamp in hand, a long white nightgown protecting his stocky figure, his whiskers spreading like a sheaf of wheat, and demanded to know what I meant by disturbing him.

"But, doctor," I said timorously, "she's very sick. She has a high fever. She asked me to beg you to come right away."

"A high fever! Shucks! Wasn't I just there at four? Here I am, an old man, needing my sleep, and I never get a decent night's rest. It's always the way. As though I didn't know. Suppose she has a little fever. It won't hurt her."

"But will you come, doctor?" I pleaded, knowing full well that he would, although he had begun irritably to close the door.

"Yes, I'll come. Of course I'll come, though I know it isn't a bit necessary. You run on back. I'll be there."

I hurried away through the dark, a little fearful of the silent streets, and presently he came, fussing and fuming at the inconsiderateness of some people.

I always think of old Dr. Woolley as being one of the nicest, kindest old doctors that ever was.

But now this room, instead of being a happy combination of bed room and study, was a kitchen, dining room and living room combined. There were prints and pots and pans hung on the walls, and no carpet, and a big iron cook stove and a plain deal table and various chairs and boxes, all very humble and old. But the place was clean, I was glad to see, and the warm, August sun was streaming through the west windows, a cheering sight. I missed the sheltering pine boughs outside, and was just thinking "how different" and asking myself "what is time, anyhow" when there came up the stairs a Slavic workingman of small but vigorous build. He had on grey jean trousers and a blue shirt, and carried a bucket and a shovel.

"The gentleman once lived in this house. He's come back to see it," explained his wife courteously.

"Well, I suppose it's changed, eh?" he replied.

"Oh, very much," I sighed. "I used to sleep in this end bedroom as a boy."

"Well, you'll find another boy sleeping there if you look," he said, opening the door, and as he did so I saw a small, chubby, curly-haired boy of four or five snoozing on his pillow, his face turned away from the golden sun which poured into the room. The beauty of it touched me deeply. It brought back the lapse of time with a crash.

How nature dashes its generations of new childhood against the beaches of this old, old world, I thought. Our little day in the sun is so short. Our tenure of the things of earth so brief. And we fight over land and buildings and position. To my host and hostess I said, "beautiful," and then that whimpering thing in the sealed room began to cry and I hurried down the stairs.

CHAPTER XXXVIII

DAY DREAMS

BUT I could not bear to tear myself away so swiftly. I went round to the side door on the north side, where often of a morning, before going to school, or of an afternoon, after school, or of a Saturday or Sunday, I was wont to sit and rock and look out at the grass and trees. As I see it now, I must have been a very peculiar youth, a dreamer, for I loved to sit and dream all the while. Just outside this door was the one best patch of lawn we possessed, very smooth and green. In late October and early November days it was most wonderful to me to sit and look at the leaves falling from the trees and think on the recurrent spectacles of spring, summer, autumn and winter, and wonder at the beauty and fragrance and hope of life. Everything was before me then. That is the great riches and advantage of youth. Experience was still to come—love, travel, knowledge, friends, the spectacle and stress of life. As age creeps on one says to one's self, Well, I will never do that any more—or that—or that. I did it once, but now it would not be interesting. The joy of its being a new thing is gone once and for all.

And so now, as I looked at this door, the thought of all this came upon me most forcibly. I could actually see myself sitting there in an old rocking chair, with my books on my knees, waiting to hear the last school bell ring, which would give me just fifteen minutes in which to get to school. It was all so perfect. Knowledge was such a solution—were they not always telling me so? If one studied one could find out about life, I thought. Somebody must know. Somebody did know. Weren't there books here on every hand, and schools and teachers to teach us?

And there was my mother, slipping about in her old grey dress working for us, for me, and wishing so wistfully that life might do better for us all. What a wonderful woman she was, and how I really adored her—only I think she never quite understood me, or what I represented. She was so truly earnest in her efforts for us all, so eager for more life for each and every one. I can see her now with her large, round grey eyes, her placid face, her hopeful, wistful, tender expression! Dear, dear soul! Sweet dreamer of vagrom dreams! In my heart is an altar. It is of jasper and chalcedony and set with precious stones. Before it hangs a light, the lamp of memory, and to that casket which holds your poet's soul, I offer, daily, attar and bergamot and musk and myrrh. As I write, you must know. As I write, you must understand. Your shrine is ever fragrant here.

Inside this door, when I knocked, I found a two-room apartment not much better than that of my Slavic friends upstairs. Although the young married woman, a mere girl, who opened the door, spoke English plainly, she seemed of marked Hungarian extraction, an American revision of the European peasant, but with most of the old world worn off. I had never been familiar with this type in my day. There was a baby here and a clutter of nondescript things—colored calendars and chromos on the walls; clap-trap instalment-sold furniture and the like. I made my very best bow, which is never a very graceful one, and explained why I was here. The young woman was sympathetic. Wouldn't I come right in?

"So this is the room," I said, standing in the first one. "My mother used to use this as a living room, and this (I walked into the next one, looking south over the vanished pond to the courthouse tower) as a sewing room. There was always such a fine morning light here."

"Yes, there is," she replied.

As I stood here, a host of memories crowded upon me. I might as well have been surrounded by spirits of

an older day suggesting former things. There sat my
father by that window, reading, in the morning, when he
was not working, the Lives of the Saints; in the evening the Chicago *Daily News* or *Die Wahrheit's Freund,*
issued in Cincinnati, or *Die Waisenfreund,* issued in Dayton. A hardy, industrious man he was, so religious that
he was ridiculous to me even at that time. He carried
no weight with me, though he had the power and authority to make me and nearly all the others obey. I
was aways doubtful as to just how far his temper and
fuming rages would carry him. As for my mother, she
usually sat in a rocking chair close to this very north
door, which looked out on the grass, to read. Her
favorite publications were *Leslie's Magazine* and *Godey's
Lady Book,* or some of the newer but then not startlingly
brilliant magazines—*Scribner's* or *Harper's.* For my
part I preferred *Truth,* or *Life,* or *Puck,* or *Judge,* publications which had been introduced into our family by
my brother Paul when we were living in Evansville. At
this time I had found Dickens, Scott, Thackeray, Haw-
thorne, Fielding, Defoe, and a score of others, and had
been reading, reading, reading, swiftly and with enjoyment. Cooper, Irving and Lew Wallace ("Ben Hur" at
least) were a part of my mental pabulum. From the
public library I drew Dryden, Pope, Shakespeare, Herrick and a dozen other English and American poets, and
brought them here. I was so keenly interested in love
at this time—so inoculated with the virus of the ideal in
the shape of physical beauty—that any least passage in
Dryden, Herrick, Pope, Shakespeare, held me as in a
vise. I loved the beauty of girls. A face piquant in
its delicacy, with pink cheeks, light or dark eyes, long
lashes—how I tingled at the import of it! Girlhood ravished me. It set my brain and my blood aflame. I was
living in some ecstatic realm which had little if anything
in common with the humdrum life about me, and yet it
had. Any picture or paragraph anywhere which referred
to or hinted at love lifted me up into the empyrean. I
was like that nun in Davidson's poem to whom the

thought of how others sinned was so moving. I never tired of hauling out and secretly reading and rereading every thought and sentence that had a suggestive, poetic turn in relation to love.

I can see some asinine moralist now preparing to rise and make a few remarks. My comment is that I despise the frozen, perverted religiosity which would make a sin of sex. Imagine the torture, the pains, the miseries which have ensued since self immolation has been raised to a virtue and a duty. Think of it—healthy animals all of us, or we ought to be—and it is a crime to think of love and sex!

CHAPTER XXXIX

STANDING in this room, looking at the place where our open fire used to be, but which was now closed up and a cooking stove substituted, and at the window where I often sat of a morning "studying" history, physical geography, geography, physiology, botany, and waiting for breakfast, or if it were afternoon and after school, for dinner, I asked myself, if I could, would I restore it all —and my answer was unhesitatingly yes. I have seen a great many things in my time, done a lot of dull ones, suffered intense shames, disgraces and privations, but all taken into account and notwithstanding, I would gladly be born again and do it all over, so much have I loved the life I have been permitted to live. Here, at this time, I was suffering from a boyish bashfulness which made me afraid of every girl. I was following this girl and that, nearly every beautiful one of my own age, with hungry eyes, too timid to speak, and yet as much as I longed and suffered on that account, I now said to myself I would gladly have it all back. I asked myself would I have mother and father, and my sisters and brothers, and all our old relatives and friends back as I knew them here, and my answer was, if it would not be an injustice to them, and if I could be as I was then and stand in the same unwitting relationship, yes. Life was intensely beautiful to me here. For all its drawbacks of money and clothes and friends it was nearly perfect. I was all but too happy, ecstatic, drunk with the spirit of all young and new things. If I were to have even more pain than I had, I think I would undertake it all gladly again.

The woman who permitted me to linger in these two

rooms a few minutes informed me that the man who occupied the rooms just overhead—those back of the day laborer—was the same whose sign, "Saws Filed," protruded from the front door. "It's Mr. Gridley and his boy. He isn't in yet, I think. He usually comes in, though, about this time. If you want to wait, I'm sure he'll be glad to let you see his rooms."

She spoke as if she knew Mr. Gridley, and I had the feeling from her very assuring words that he must be a pleasant and accommodating character.

As I went out and around to the front door again to have one more look, I saw an old man approaching across the quondam pond, carrying a small saw, and I felt sure, at sight of him, that it was Mr. Gridley. He was tall, emaciated, stoop shouldered, a pleasant and even conciliatory type, whose leathern cheeks and sunken eyes combined with a simple, unaffected and somewhat tired manner seemed to suggest one to whom life had done much, but whose courage, gentleness and patience were not by any means as yet exhausted. As he came up I observed: "This isn't Mr. Gridley, is it?"

"Yes, sir," he smiled. "What can I do for you?"

"You live in the rear rooms upstairs, I believe. My family used to live here, years ago. I wonder if you would mind my looking in for a moment. I merely want to see—for old time's sake."

His face warmed sympathetically.

"Come right up, neighbor," he volunteered. "I'll be only too glad to let you see. You'll have to excuse the looks of the place. My son and I live here alone, bachelor style. I've been out in the country today with him hunting. He's only fifteen years old."

We ascended the stairs, and he unlocked the door to my old rooms and let me in—the rooms where Ed and I and Tillie (or whichever other brother or sister happened to be here at the time) were separately provided for. It was a suite of three rooms, one large and two small, opening out on the north, east, and south, via windows to the garden below. In summer, and even in winter, these rooms were always ideal, warmed as they were by an open fire, but in summer they were especially cool and refreshing, there being an attic above which broke the heat—delightful chambers in which to read or sleep. We never had much furniture (a blessing, I take it, because of the sense of space which results) but what we had was comfortable enough and ample for all our needs. In my day there was a bed and a dressing stand and mirror in each of these rooms, and then chairs, and in the larger room of the three, quite double the size of the other two, a square reading table of cheap oak by which I used to sit and work at times, getting my lessons. In the main it was a delight to sit here of a hot summer day, looking out on the surrounding world and the trees, and reading betimes. Here I read Shakespeare and a part of Macaulay's "History of England" and Taine's "History of English Literature" and a part of Guizot's "History of France." I was not an omnivorous reader— just a slow, idle, rambling one—but these rooms and these books, and the thought of happy days to come, made it all a wonder world to me. We had enough to live on. The problem of financing our lives was not as yet distracting me. I longed for a little money, but not much, and life, life, life—all its brilliant pyrotechnic meanings —was before me, still to come.

"It's not very tidy in here," said my host, apologetically, as he opened the door. "Take a chair, neighbor. We live as though we were camping out. Ever since my wife died and my oldest boy went into the navy, I stopped trying to keep house much. Me and Harry—that's my youngest boy—take pot luck here. We do our own housekeeping. I've just suffered a great blow in the death of my oldest boy over at the Dardanelles. When he left the navy he went into the Australian Army, and they made him a captain and then when this war broke out his company was sent to the Dardanelles and he went along and has just been killed over there."

"It's very sad," I said, looking about at the beggarly and disorderly furniture. In one room I could see a shabbily gotten up and unmade bed. In this room was an iron cook stove, pots and pans, a litter of guns, saws, fishing poles, and the like.

"Yes," went on my host heavily, and with a keen narrative sense which was very pleasing to listen to, "he was an extra fine boy, really. He graduated here at the high school before he went into the marines, and stood high in all his classes. Everybody liked him,—a nice, straight-talking young fellow, if I do say it."

He arose, crossed to an old yellow bureau, and took out a picture of a young fellow of about twentysix or twentyeight, in the uniform of an Australian captain of infantry.

"The way he came to get into the Australian Army," he went on, looking fondly at the picture, "was—he was over there with one of our ships and they took a liking to him and offered him more pay. He was always a great fellow for athletics and he used to send me pictures of himself as amateur champion of this or that ship, boxing. They got his regiment over there on that peninsula, and just mowed it down, I hear. You know," he said suddenly, his voice beginning to tremble and break, "I just can't believe it. I had a letter from him only three weeks ago saying how fine he was feeling, and how interesting it all was.—And now he's dead."

A hot tear fell on a wrinkled hand.

"Yes, I know," I replied, moved at last. I had been so interested in my own connection with this place and the memories that were swarming upon me that I had been overlooking his. I now felt very sorry for him.

"You know," he persisted, surveying me with aged and wrinkled eyes, "he wasn't just an ordinary boy. I have letters here"—and now he fumbled around for something else—"from Lord Kitchener and the King and Queen of England and the Colonel of his regiment." (His voice broke completely, but after a time he went on:) "They all said what a fine fellow he was and what a loss his death is. It's pretty hard when you're so fond of anybody."

He stopped, and I had difficulty in restraining a tendency to cry a little myself. When one gets so old and a boy is so precious——!

He rubbed his nose with the back of his hand, while I read the formal acknowledgments of Colonel Barclay Sattersley, D.S.O., of Field Marshal Earl Kitchener, K.G., Secretary of State for War, and of Their Majesties, the King and Queen, formal policy letters all, intended to assuage all brokenhearted contributors to the great war. But it all rang very futile and hollow to me. The phrases of the ruling classes of England rattle like whitening bones of dead souls, anyhow.

"You know," he added, after a time, "I can't help thinking that there's been an awful mistake made about that whole thing down there. His letters told me what a hard time they had landing, and how the trenches were just full of dead boys after every charge. It seems to me they might have found some other way. It looks terribly heartless to let whole regiments be wiped out."

I learned a great deal about Warsaw and its environs from this man, for he had lived in this county and near here all his life. This house, as he described it, had been here since 1848 or thereabouts. The original owner and builder had been a judge at one time, but a loss of fortune and ill health had compelled him to part with it. His oldest and most intelligent son had been a wastrel. He occasionally came to Warsaw to look at this very house, as he had once, in our day, and to my surprise he told me he was here now, in town, loafing about the place—an old man. The houses in front had been built only a year before, so if I had come a year earlier I would still have seen the ground space about as it was, all the old trees still standing. The trees had all been cut down thirteen months before! The Grant house, in which we had first lived here, had been moved over about five years before. The school yard had been cut away about seven years before, and so it went. I asked him about George and John Sharp, Odin Oldfather, Pet Wall, Vesta Switzer, Myrtle Taylor, Judson

Morris, and so on—boys and girls with whom I had gone to school. Of some he knew a little something; of others he imagined his youngest boy Harry might know. Through his eyes and his words I began to see what a long way I had come, and how my life was rounding out into something different and disturbingly remote from all I had ever known. I felt as though I were in a tomb or a garden of wraiths and shadows.

But if I was depressed here, I was even more so when I came to study the Grant house and the school itself. The former having been inhabited when my mind was in its most formative period, I was struck by the fact that nearly all its then pleasing traces had been obliterated. There was a tree outside the kitchen door from which a swing had once been suspended, and where of a morning or an evening I used to sit and meditate, admiring the skies, the schoolhouse tower, the trees, the freshness of the year. Swing and tree were gone, the house having been moved, and even a longish, parallel window through which, so often, I could see my mother cooking or working at something in the kitchen, had been done over into something else and was now no more. There had been a medium sized, handsome spear pine in the shade of which I used to lie and read of a summer ("Water Babies," "Westward Ho," "The Scarlet Letter" and "The House of the Seven Gables," to say nothing of much of Irving and Goldsmith). It was gone. It was around this tree that once, of a late November evening not long after we had arrived here and I had been placed in the public school, that I was chased by Augusta Nueweiler (the daughter of the clothier who now owned the dry goods store once owned by Yaisley) in a determined desire to kiss me; which she succeeded in doing. If you will believe it, although I was thirteen years of age, I had never been kissed before. Why she had been attracted to me I do not know. She was plump and pretty, with a cap of short, dark ringlets swirling about her eyes and ears, and a red and brown complexion, and an open, pretty mouth. I thought she was very beautiful.

Back of this house had been a large garden or truck patch, which we planted richly that first summer, and back of that again, a grove of tall ash trees two acres in extent. To this, during that first summer and winter, I had been wont to repair in order to climb the trees and look out upon a large marsh (it seemed large to me at that time) which contained, as its principal feature, the winding Tippecanoe River or creek, making silvery S's between the tall sedges and their brown cat tails. It was a delightful sight to me then. I used to climb so high (all alone and often) that the wind would easily rock the tall spear to which I was clinging, and then it seemed as though I were a part of heaven and the winds and all rhythmic and colorful elements above man—elements which had no part or share with him.

It was to this grove that my brother Ed and I once repaired of a Saturday morning after a Friday night party—our very first—at which a kissing game had been played and we had been kissed. Life was just dawning upon us as a garden of flowers, in which girls were the flowers. We had already been commenting on various girls at school during the past two or three months, learning to talk about and discriminate between them, and now, at this party, given at the house of one girl whom I thought to be the most perfect of all, we had been able to see twenty or thirty, decked in fineries so delicate and entrancing, that I was quite beside myself. All the girls, really, that we had come to single out as beautiful were there—wonderful girls, to my entranced eyes—and each of us, as it happened, had been called in to be kissed by girls to whom we had scarce dared to lift our eyes before. It was all in the game, and not to be repeated afterward. The moralists tell us that such games are pernicious and infective in their influence, but to memory they are entrancing. Whatever it is that is making life—throwing us on a screen of ether quite as moving pictures are thrown on canvas, to strut through our little parts—its supremest achievements, so far, are occasions such as I have been describing—moments in which the blood of youth in a boy speaks to its fellow atoms in the body of a girl and produces that astonishing reaction which causes the cheeks to mantle, the eyes to sparkle or burn, the heart to beat faster, the lungs to become suffocatingly slow in their labors.

On this particular morning, sitting in this grove now no longer present and sawing a log of wood which was ours, Ed and I tried to recall how wonderful it had been and how we felt, but it was scarcely possible. It could not be done. Instead, we merely glowed and shivered with the memory of intense emotions. And today it comes back as astonishing and perfect as ever—a chemical state, a rich, phantasmagoric memory, and never to be recaptured. I have changed too much. All of us of that day have changed too much.

I saw Ed on the street not long ago and his hair was slightly grey and he was heavy and mature. Having been here, I was tempted to ask him whether he remembered, but I refrained because I half fancied that he would not, or that he would comment on it from a lately acquired religious point of view—and then we might have quarreled.

CHAPTER XL

But the school next door gave me the cruellest shock of all. I went into it because, it being mid August, the preliminary autumn repairs were under way and the place was open. Workingmen were scattered about—carpenters, painters, glaziers. I had no idea how sound my memory was for these old scenes until I stepped inside the door and saw the closets where we used to hang our hats and coats on *our* nails and walked up the stairs to the seventh grade room, which is the one in which I had been placed on our arrival in Warsaw.

Here it was, just as I had left it, apparently—the same walls, the same benches, the same teacher's table. But how small the benches had grown, scarcely large enough for me to squeeze into now, even though I allowed for a tight fit! The ceiling and walls seemed not nearly so high or so far as they had once seemed. At that very table sat Mae Calvert, our teacher—dead now, so someone told me later—a blooming girl of nineteen or twenty who at that time seemed one of the most entrancing creatures in all the world. She had such fine blue eyes, such light brown hair, such a rounded, healthy, vigorous body. And she had been so fond of me. Once, sitting at my little desk (it was the fifth from the front in the second aisle, counting from the west side of the room), she paused and put her hand on my head and cheek, pinching my neck and ear, and I colored the while I thrilled with pleasure. You see, hitherto, I had been trained in a Catholic school, what little I had been, and the process had proved most depressing—black garbed, straight laced nuns. But here in this warm, friendly room, with girls who were attractive and boys who were for the larger part genial and companionable, and with a teacher who took an interest in me, I felt as though I were in a kind of school paradise, the Nirvana of the compulsorily trained.

Another time (it was in reading class) she asked me to read a paragraph and when I had and paused, she said: "I can't tell you how beautifully you read, Theodore. It is so natural; you make everything so real." I blushed again, for I felt for the moment by some odd transposition that she was making fun of me. When I looked up into her face and saw her eyes—the way in which she looked at me—I understood. She was actually fond of me.

At later times and in various ways during this year she drew me out of an intense dreamy shyness by watching over me, expending an affection which I scarcely knew how to take. She would occasionally keep me after school to help me with my grammar—a profound mystery, no least rudiment of which I ever mastered—and when she gradually discovered that I knew absolutely nothing concerning it, she merely looked at me and pinched my cheek.

"Well, don't you worry; you can get along without grammar for a while yet. You'll understand it later on."

She passed me in all my examinations, regardless I presume, though I have reason to believe that I was highly intelligent in respect to some things. At the end of the year, when we were clearing up our papers and I was getting ready to leave, she put her arms about me and kissed me goodbye. I remember the day, the warm, spring sunlit afternoon, the beauty and the haunting sense of the waning of things that possessed me at the time. I went home, to think and wonder about her.

I saw her a year or so later, a much stouter person, married and with a baby, and I remember being very shocked. She didn't seem the same, but she remembered me and smiled on me. For my part, not having seen her for so long a time, I felt very strange and bashful—

almost as though I were in the presence of one I had never known.

But the feeling which I had here today passed over this last unheeded. It concerned only the particular days in which I was here, the days of a new birth and freedom from horrific Spartan restraint, plus the overawing weight of the lapse of time. Never before I think, certainly not since my mother's death, was I so impressed by the lapse of time, the diaphanous nothingness of things. I was here thirtytwo years before and all that I saw then had body and substance—a glaring material state. Here was some of the same material, the same sunlight, a few of the same people, perhaps, but time had filched away nearly all our characteristics. That boy— was his spiritual substance inside of me still unchanged, merely overlaid by experience like the heart of a palm? I could not even answer that to myself. The soul within me could not say. And at least foursevenths of my allotted three score years and ten had gone.

Down the street from this school about five doors was another house which was very familiar. I went up the narrow brick walk and knocked. A tall, lean, sallow creature of no particular figure but with piercing black eyes and long, thin hands came to the door. Her hair, once jet black, was thinly streaked with grey. She must have been all of thirtyfive or forty when I knew her as a boy. That made her sixtyfive or seventy now; yet I could see no particular change, so vigorous and energetic was she.

"Well, Ed," she exclaimed, "or is it Theodore? Well, of all things! Come right in here. I'm glad to see you. Land o' goodness! And Nate will be pleased to death. Nate! Nate!" she called into an adjoining room. "Come in here. If here isn't Theodore—or is it Ed?" ("It's Theodore," I interjected quickly.) "You know it's been so long since I've seen you two I can scarcely tell you apart. But I remember both as well as if it were yesterday. And it's been—let me see—how long has it been? Nearly thirty years now, hasn't it? Well, of all things!

I do declare! And you're getting stout, too. And you've grown to be over six feet, at least. Well, I do declare! To think of your walking in on me like this. Just you sit right down here and make yourself comfortable. Well, of all things!"

By now I must have been smiling like a Cheshire cat. Nate, or Nathaniel, one-time carpenter and builder (and still such, for all I know), strolled in. It was late in the afternoon, and he was lounging about in a white cotton shirt and grey trousers, his suspenders down about his hips, a pipe in his mouth and an evening paper in his hand.

"Well, Dorse," he called, "where do you come from?"

I told him.

"Think of that, now," exclaimed Mrs. McConnell, "and a car! And you came all the way through from New York? Well, lots of them do that now. Charlie Biggers went through from here to Pennsylvania in a Ford not long ago."

She cackled stridently. I was fascinated by her vigor in age.

"Nate here," she went on, "says he thinks we ought to get a machine one of these days, but lawsie! I don't know whether I could learn to run it, and I'm certain *he* couldn't." Her keen birdlike eyes devoured me, and she smiled. "And so you're a writer? Well, what do you write? Novels?"

"Well, some people condescend to call them that," I answered. "I'd hesitate to tell you what some others call them."

"It's funny I never heard of any of 'em. What's the names of some of 'em?"

I enlightened her.

"Well, now, that's strange. I never heard of a one of them—I must get two or three and see how you write."

"That's good of you," I chuckled, in the best of spirits.

"Bertie Wilkerson—you remember Bertie, don't you? —he was the son of the justice of the peace here—well, he's on one of the Cleveland papers now, writing in some way. There's a woman over here in Wabash (I knew the name of the novelist coming now) has made a big reputation for herself with her books. They have whole stacks of 'em here in the stores, I see. I read one of 'em. They tell me she's worth four or five hundred thousand dollars by now. You've heard of her, haven't you?" She gave me her name.

"Yes," I replied very humbly, "I have."

"Well, I don't suppose you make that much, anyhow, do you?" she queried.

"No," I replied. "I'm very sorry, I don't."

I could see by the stress she laid on the four or five hundred thousand dollars and the stacks of books in the local store that my type of authorship would never appeal to her.

Be that as it may, we found other things equally interesting to both to talk about. The town had changed. She began to tell when and in what manner and why the old pond had been filled in; why the leading banker, whose wide verandahed house had been a subject of wonder and envy to me, had moved it off the old property and built an even more splendiferous home. Children and grand-children had come to live with him. I could see the old house in its new position on the other side of the pond—a poor affair compared to what I thought it was. Why do our memories lie so? Could anyone or anything be a greater liar than the average memory?

When I came out of there after a time and returned to the car Franklin was still patiently sketching, making good use of his time, whereas Speed was sitting with his feet on a part of his engine equipment cleaning a chain. They were partly surrounded now: (1) by old Mr. Gridley, he of my former room, who was retailing the story of his son's death; (2) by a short, dusty, rotund, rather oily-haired man who announced that he was the owner of the property which had formerly sheltered me, and who by virtue of having cut down all the trees and built the two abominable houses in front seemed to think that he was entitled to my friendship and admiration—a *non sequitur* which irritated me greatly; (3) by a small boy from somewhere in the vicinity who stood with his legs very far apart, his hands in his pockets, and merely stared and listened while Mr. Gridley related the moving details of his son's death and the futility of the campaign at the Dardanelles. The owner of the houses in front kept trying to interject bits of his personal history as carpenter, builder, land speculator, and the like. It was most entertaining.

"I was just saying to your friend here," said the latter, who had never met me until this moment, "that if you're in town long enough you must come and take dinner with me. We're just plain people, but we can give you plenty to eat. Anyone who lived here as long ago as you did——"

I felt no least desire to dine with him, largely because he had cut down all the fine trees and built such trashy houses.

He chattered on in an impossible fashion. I could see he was greatly impressed by our possession of this car. And to have come all the way from New York! I wanted to annihilate him for having destroyed the trees —the wretch!

But I felt that we ought to be getting on. Here it was after five and I still had various things to see—the old Central High School, where so long ago I finished my eighth grade common and my first year German and algebra; the lakes, Centre and Pike, where with many others I had been accustomed to row, swim, skate, fish, and camp; the old swimming hole out in the Tippecanoe (three miles out, I thought, at least); our old Catholic Church, where I regularly went to confession and communion; the woods where I had once found a dead peddler, lying face down, self-finished, at the foot of a great oak; and so on and so forth—endless places, indeed. Besides, there were various people I wanted to see, people who, like the wiry Mrs. McConnell, could tell me much —perhaps.

Alas for intentions and opportunities! I suppose I might have spent days browsing and communing, but now that I was here and actually seeing things, I did not feel inclined to do it. What was there really to see, I asked myself, aside from the mere exterior or surface of things? In one more hour I could examine exteriorly or in perspective all of these things—the lakes, the school, the swimming hole, the church—they were all near at hand—unless I wanted to linger here for weeks. Did I really want to stay longer than this dusk?

Franklin was eager to get on. When first he invited me he had planned no such extended tour as this, and these were not his sacred scenes. It was all very well—but——

Nevertheless, we did cruise (as Speed was wont to express it), first to Centre Lake, where many a moonlight when the ice was as thick as a beam and as smooth as glass Ed, Tillie and I, along with a half hundred town boys and girls, had skated to our hearts' content or fished through the ice. My, how wonderful it was! To see them cutting ice on the lake with horses and fishing through holes only large enough to permit the extraction of a small sized fish when one bit. To my astonishment the waters of the lake had receded or diminished fully a fifth of its original circumference, and all the houses and boathouses which formerly stood close to its edge were now fully two hundred feet inland. In addition, all the smartness and superiority which once invested this section were now gone—the region of the summer conferences at Winona having superseded this. Houses I was sure I would be able to recall, should they chance to be here—those of Maud Rutter, Augusta Nueweiler (she of the fir tree kiss), Ada Sanguiat, were not discernible at all. I knew they were here unchanged, but I could not find them.

We went out past an old bridge to the northeast of the town (scarcely a half mile out) and found to my astonishment that the stream it once spanned—the Tippecanoe, if you please—and that once drained Centre and

Pike Lakes, was now no more. There was only a new stone culvert here, not the old iron and plank wagon bridge of my day—and no water underneath it at all, only a seepy muck, overgrown with marsh grass!! The whole river, a clear sandy-bottomed stream, was now gone—due to the recession of the lake, I suppose. The swimming hole that I fancied must be all of two or three miles out was not more than one, and it had disappeared, of course, with the rest. There was not even a sign of the footpath that led across the fields to it. All was changed. The wild rice fields that once stood about here for what seemed miles to me, and overrun in the summertime (July, August, and September, in particular) with thousands upon thousands of blackbirds and crows, were now well plowed cornland! I could not see more than the vaguest outlines of the region I had known, and I could not recapture, save in the vaguest way, any of the boyish moods that held me at the time. In my heart was a clear stream and a sandy bottom and a troop of half-forgotten boys, and birds, and blue skies, and men fishing by this bridge where was now this culvert—Ed and I among them occasionally—and here was nothing at all —a changed world.

"Oh, it's all gone!" I cried to Franklin. "Why, an iron wagon bridge used to hang here. This was a beautiful fishing pool. A path went across here. Let's go back."

We went up to the old Central High School, looking exactly as it did in my day, only now a ward instead of a high school—a new high having been built since I left —and here I tried to recapture some of the emotions I have always had in my dreams of it and have still. I saw troops of boys and girls coming out of it at noon and at four in the afternoon—I and my sister Tillie among them. I saw Dora Yaisley and Myrtle Taylor (of the pale flower face and violet eyes), and Jess Beasley and Sadie and Dolly Varnum—what a company! And there were George and John Sharp—always more or less companionable with me, and "Jud" Morris and Frank Yaisley and Al Besseler and a score of others—interesting souls all and now scattered to the four corners of the earth.

But sitting in the car—suddenly I saw myself in my seat upstairs looking out the north window which was nearest me, and dreaming of the future. From where I sat in those days I could see up a long, clean alley, with people crossing at its different street intersections for blocks away. I could see far off to where the station was and the flour mill and where the trains came in. I could hear their whistles—distant and beckoning—feeling the tug and pull of my future life to come out and away. I could see clouds and trees and little houses and birds over the court house tower, and then I wanted to get out and fly too—to walk up and down the great earth and be happy.

I tell you, in those days, wonderful, amazing moods were generated in the blood of me. I felt and saw things which have never come true—glories, moods, gayeties, perfections. There was a lilt in my heart and my soul. I wanted, oh! I wanted all that Nature can breed in her wealth of stars and universes—and I found—what have I found——?

The frame of any man is an infinitesimal shell. The soul of him so small, a pale lamp which he carries in his hands! The passions of which we boast or from whose imagined horrors we flee are such little things—rush lights—scarcely able to glimmer in so great a dark. People rage at men and women for their passions! At best, granting a Hero, a Caligula, an Alexander, a Napoleon— what small, greedy insects indeed they were. They blazed and bestrode the earth. They fought, conquered, reveled. Against the vast illimitable substance and force of things, what pale flames they really were, after all; so trivial, so unimportant. As well seek out the captains and generals and emperors of ants. In the vast something or nothing of life they are as much worth recording personally. I have eaten and drunken, and thirsted after all, but should the curtain descend now, how little have I had! How little could any man ever have!

Oh, great, scheming, dreaming Prince of Life—what is that you are after? What blood moods in your soul is it that we, your atoms, hurry to fulfill? Do you love? Do you hate? By billions sweating, blazing, do we fulfill some quaint desire of yours? Drop you the curtain then on me. I do not care—I am very tired. Drop it and let me dream no more the endless wonders and delights that never, never, can be.

CHAPTER XLI

WEST of Warsaw about twelve miles lies the town of
Silver Lake, on a small picturesque lake of the same name
—a place to which, during our residence at Warsaw, Ed
and I more than once repaired to visit a ne'er-do-well
uncle and his wife, the latter my mother's half sister.
This family was so peculiar and so indifferent to all
worldly success and precedence, so utterly trifling and
useless, that I am tempted to tell about them even though
they do not properly belong in this narrative. William
or "Bill" Arnold, as he was called locally, was really the
cause of it all. He was the father, but little more than a
country wastrel. He had a fiddle on which he could play
a little. He had a slightly cocked eye and a nasal voice,
high and thin. He had no more education than a squirrel
and no more care for things of place and position than
any rabbit or woodchuck. His wife, a kindly, inarticu-
late and meditative woman, who looked like my mother,
was all out of sorts and down at heels in soul and body
because of his indifference to all things material or spiritual. They lived in an old tumble-down, paintless house,
the roof of which leaked and the eaves sagged, and here,
and in other houses like it, no doubt, they had had four
children, one of whom, the eldest, became a thief (but a
very clever one, I have heard); the second a railroad
brakeman; the third the wife of an idle country loafer as
worthless as her father; the fourth, a hunchbacked boy,
was to me, at least, a veritable sprite of iniquity, thinking
up small deviltries the whole day long. He was fond of
fighting with his sister and parents, shouting vile names
when angry, and so conducting himself generally that he
was an object almost of loathing to such of our family
as knew him.

Their home was a delightful place for me to come to, so fresh, so new, so natural—not at all like our ordered home. I felt as though I were housed with a kind of genial wild animal—a fox or prairie dog or squirrel or coyote. Old Arnold had no more morals than a fox or squirrel. He never bathed. He would get up in the morning and feed his pigs and two horses, the only animals he owned—and then, if the weather was suitable and he had no absolutely compelling work to do, he would hunt rabbits (in winter) or squirrel or "patridges," or go fishing, or go down to the saloon to fiddle and sing or to a dance. He was always driving off to some dance where he earned a few cents as a fiddler (it was his great excuse), and then coming home at two or three in the morning, slightly tipsy and genial, to relate his experiences to anyone who would listen. He was not afraid of his wife or children exactly, and yet he was not the master of them either, and it used to scandalize me to have him called a loafer and an "old fool," not by her so much as by them. My own father was so strict, so industrious, so moral, that I could scarcely believe my ears.

I used to love to walk west from Warsaw on a fine summer's day, when my mother would permit me, and visit them—walk the whole twelve miles. Once she empowered me to negotiate for a cow which this family owned and for which we paid twentyfive dollars. Ed and I drove the cow up from Silver Lake. Another time we bought three (or four) pigs, and drove them (Ed and I) the whole twelve miles on a hot July day. Great heavens! What a time we had to get them to come along straight! They ran into bogs and woods—wherever there was a fence down—and we had to chase them until they fell exhausted—too far gone to run us farther. Once they invaded a tangled, low growing swamp, to wallow in the muck, and we had to get down on our hands and knees—our bellies actually—to see where they had gone. We were not wearing shoes and stockings; but we took off our trousers, hung them over our arms, and went in after them. If we didn't beat those pigs when we got near enough! Say! We chased them for nearly a mile to exhaust and punish them, and then we switched them along the rest of the way to "get even."

I remember one hot July afternoon, when I was visiting here, how my Aunt Susan read my fortune in the grounds of a coffee cup. It was after a one o'clock farmhand dinner. Uncle Bill and one or two of the other children had come and gone. I was alone with her, and we sat in the shade of an east porch, comfortable in the afternoon. I can see the wall of trees over the way, even yet, the bees buzzing about an adjacent trumpet vine, the grass hot and dry but oh! so summery.

"Now, let's see what it says about you in your cup," and she took it and turned it round and round, upside down three times. Then she looked into it meditatively and after a while began: "Oh, I see cities, cities, cities, and great crowds, and bridges, and chimneys. You are going to travel a long way—all over the world, perhaps. And there are girls in your cup! I see their faces." (I thrilled at that.) "You won't stay here long. You'll be going soon, out into the world. Do you want to travel?" she asked.

"Yes, indeed I do," I replied.

"Well, you will. It's all here."

Her face was so grave! She looked like one of the three fates, so old, so wrinkled, so distant.

I thought nothing of her at the time, but only of myself. How beautiful would be that outside world! And I would be going to it soon! Walking up and down in it! Oh, wonderful, wonderful, wonderful!

.   .   .   .   .   .

When we were traveling toward Warsaw it had been my idea that we would visit Silver Lake and if I could find nothing more I could at least look at that body of water and the fields that surrounded it and the streets with which I had been fairly familiar. The lake had seemed such a glorious thing to me in those days. It was so sylvan and silent. A high growth of trees surrounded it like a wall. Its waters reflected in turn blue, grey, green, black. It was so still within its wall of trees that our voices echoed hollowly. A fish leaping out of the water could be heard, and the echo of the splash. Often I sat here gazing at the blue sky and the trees, and waiting for a small red and green cork on my line to bob.

But my aunt and my uncle were long since dead, I knew. The children had gone—where? There was probably no least trace of them anywhere here, and I was in no mood to hunt them down. Still, in coming West, I had the desire to come here, to look, to stand in some one of these old places and recover if I might a boyhood mood.

Now, as we were leaving Warsaw, however, I was too physically tired and too spiritually distrait to be very much interested. My old home town had done for me completely—the shadows of older days. For one thing, I had a splitting headache, which I was carefully concealing, and a fine young heartache into the bargain. I was dreadfully depressed and gloomy.

But it was a fine warm night, with a splendid half moon in the sky and delicious wood and field fragrances about. Such odors! Is there anything more moving than the odors, the suspirings of the good earth, in summer?

As we neared Silver Lake (as I thought) we ran down into a valley where a small rivulet made its way and under the darkling trees we encountered a homing woman, coming from a milking shed which was close to the stream. Five children were with her, the oldest boy packing the youngest, an infant of two or three years. It reminded me of all the country families I had known in my time—a typical mid-Western and American procession. The mother, a not unprepossessing woman of forty, was clothed in a shapeless grey calico print with a sunbonnet to match, and without shoes. The children were all barefooted and ragged but as brown and healthy and fresh looking as young animals should be. It so chanced that Speed had to do something here—look after the light or supply the motor with a cooling draught —and so we paused, and the children gathered around us, intensely curious.

"Gee, ain't it a big one!" exclaimed the eldest. "Look at the silver."

He was descanting on the lamp.

"I'll bet it ain't no bigger than that jackdigger that went through here yesterday," observed the second eldest boastfully.

"What's a jackdigger?" I inquired helplessly.

"Oh, it's a car," replied the eldest, one of the handsomest boys one would want to look at—beautiful, really —all the more so because of his torn shirt and trousers and his bare feet and head.

"Yes, but what kind of car? What make?"

"Oh, I can't think. We see 'em around here now and then—great big fellers."

And now the next to the youngest, a boy of five or six, had come alongside where I was sitting and was looking up at me—a fat little cherub in panties so small you could have made them out of a good sized handkerchief.

"There you are," I said to him helpfully. "Won't you come up and sit with me here—such a nice big boy as you are?"

He shook his head and backed away a little.

"Huhuh," he said, after a pause.

"Why not?" I queried, a little yearningly, for I wanted him to come and sit with me.

"I can't," he replied, eyeing me solemnly. "I'm 'fraid."

"Oh, no," I said, "not afraid of me, surely? Don't you know that no one would think of hurting a little boy like you—not a person in all the world? Won't you come now and sit with me? It's so nice up here."

I held out my arms.

"I'm 'fraid," he repeated.

"Oh, no," I insisted. "You mustn't say that, not of me? You couldn't be. Can't you see how much I like

you? See here"—and I reached into my pocket—"I
have pennies and picturecards and I don't know what all.
Won't you come now? Please do."

"Go on, Charlie," called a brother. "Whatcha 'fraid
of? Go on." This brother came around then and tried
to persuade him.

All the while he was staring at me doubtfully, his eyes
getting very round, but finally he ventured a step forward, and I picked him up and snuggled him in my
arms.

"There, now," I said. "Now, you see? You're not
afraid of me, are you? Up here in the nice, big car?
And now here's your other brother come to sit beside
us"—(this because the next oldest had clambered in)—
"and here's a nickel and here's a picturecard and———"

"Who's 'fraid!" he crowed, sitting up in my lap. "I
ain't 'fraid, am I?"

"Indeed not," I returned. "Big boys like you are not
afraid of anything. And now here's a fine big nickel"—
I went on because he had ignored the previous offer.
"And here's a card. Isn't that nice?"

"Huhuh," he replied.

"You mean you don't like it—don't want it?"

"Huhuh," he repeated.

"And why not?"

"My mother won't let me."

"Your mother won't let you take any money?"

"Huhuh."

"Is that right?" I asked of the eldest boy, rather
taken aback by the morals of this group—they were so
orderly and sweet.

"That's right," he replied, "she won't let us."

"Well, now, I wouldn't have you do anything to dis-
please mother—not for worlds—but I'm sorry just the
same," observing her in the distance. She was bending
over several full milk pails. Even as I looked she picked
them up and came trudging toward us.

"Well, anyhow, you can take a card, can't you?" I

continued, and I gave each several pictures of Warsaw scenes. "They won't hurt, will they?"

"Huhuh," answered the little one, taking them.

As the mother neared us I suffered a keen recrudescence of the mood that used to grip me when my mother would go out of an evening like this to milk or walk about the garden or look after the roses at Sullivan, and Ed and Tillie and I would follow her. She was so dear and gentle. Under the trees or about our lawn we would follow her, and here under these odorous trees, in the light of this clear moon, the smell of cattle and wild flowers about, my mother came back and took me by the hand. I held onto her skirt and rubbed against her legs self protectingly. She was all in all to us in those years —the whole world—my one refuge and strength.

How benign is the power that makes mothers—and mothers' love!

Soon we were off again, speeding under the shade of overhanging trees or out in the open between level fields, and after racing about fourteen miles or thereabouts, we discovered that we were not near Silver Lake any more at all—had passed it by seven miles or so. We were really within six miles of North Manchester, Indiana, a place where a half uncle of mine had once lived, a stingy, greedy, well meaning Baptist, and his wife. He had a very large farm here, one of the best, and was noted for the amount of hay and corn he raised and the fine cattle he kept. My brother Albert, shortly after the family's fortune had come to its worst smash—far back in 1878 —had been sent up here by mother to work and board. She was very distraught at the time—at her wits' ends— and her brood was large. So here he had come, had been reasonably well received by this stern pair and had finally become so much of a favorite that they wanted to adopt him. Incidentally he became very vigorous physically, a perfect little giant, with swelling calves and biceps and a desire to exhibit his strength by lifting everybody and everything—a trait which my sister Tillie soon shamed out of him. When we had finally settled in Sullivan, in 1880, for a year or two he rejoined us and would not return to his foster parents. They begged him but the family atmosphere at Sullivan, restricted and poverty stricken as it was, proved too much for him. He preferred after a time to follow us to Evansville and eventually to Warsaw. Like all the rest of us, he was inoculated with the charm of my mother. No one of us could resist her. She was too wonderful.

And now as we neared this city I was thinking of all this and speculating where Al might be now—I had not heard from him in years—and how my half-uncle had really lived (I had never seen him) and what my mother would think if she could follow this ramble with her eyes. But also my head was feeling as though it might break open and my eyes ached and burned dreadfully. I wanted to go back to Warsaw and stay there for a while—not the new Warsaw as I had just seen it, but the old Warsaw. I wanted to see my mother and Ed and Tillie as we were then, not now, and I couldn't. We rolled into this other town, which I had never seen before, and having found the one hotel, carried in our bags and engaged our rooms. Outside, katy-dids and other insects were sawing lustily. There was a fine, clean bathroom with hot and cold water at hand, but I was too flat for that. I wished so much that I was younger and not so sick just now. I could think of nothing but to undress and sleep. I wanted to forget as quickly as possible, and while Franklin and Speed sallied forth to find something to eat I slipped between the sheets and tried to rest. In about an hour or less I slept—a deep, dreamless sleep;—and the next morning on opening my eyes I heard a wood dove outside my window and some sparrows and two neighbor women gossiping in good old Indiana style over a back fence, and then I felt more at ease, a little wistful but happy.

CHAPTER XLII

IN THE CHAUTAUQUA BELT

THE centre of Indiana is a region of calm and simplicity, untroubled to a large extent, as I have often felt, by the stormy emotions and distresses which so often affect other parts of America and the world. It is a region of smooth and fertile soil, small, but comfortable homes, large grey or red barns, the American type of windmill, the American silo, the American motor car—a happy land of churches, Sunday schools, public schools and a general faith in God and humanity as laid down by the Presbyterian or the Baptist or the Methodist Church and by the ten commandments, which is at once reassuring and yet disturbing.

This day as we traveled through Wabash, Peru (the winter home of Hagenbeck's and Wallace's combined shows, b'gosh!), Kokomo, where the world very nearly came to an end for Speed and where James Whitcomb Riley once worked in a printer's shop (I understood he had no love for my work)—and so on through Westfield, an old Quaker settlement, and to Carmel (where Franklin lives), and really to Indianapolis, for Carmel is little more than a suburb of the former,—I was more and more struck with the facts as I have outlined them here. Certain parts of the world are always in turmoil. Across the rasping grasses of Siberia or the dry sands of Egypt blow winds cold or hot, which make of the people restless, wandering tribes. To peaceful Holland and Belgium, the lowlands of Germany, the plains of France and Italy, and indeed all the region of the ancient world, come periodic storms of ambition or hate, which make of those old soils burying grounds not only of individual souls but of races. Here in America we have already had proof that certain sections of our land are destined apparently to tempestuous lives—the Atlantic and Pacific seaboards, Texas, Colorado, Kentucky, various parts of the South and the West and the Northwest, where conditions appear to engender the mood dynamic. From Chicago, or Colorado, or San Francisco one may expect a giant labor war or social upheaval of any kind; from Boston or Pennsylvania or New Mexico new religious movements may come—and have; New York, Pennsylvania, Kansas, Nebraska and Illinois can and have contributed vast political upheavals. This is even true of Ohio, its next door neighbor.

But Indiana lies in between all this—simple, unpretentious, not indifferent but quiescent,—a happy land of farms and simple industries which can scarcely be said to have worked any harm to any man.

Its largest cities have grown in an unobtrusive and almost unheralded way. Its largest contributions to American life so far have been a mildly soporific love literature of sorts, and an uncertain political vote. Anyone could look at these towns—all that we saw—and be sure that the natives were of an orderly, saving, genial and religious turn. I never saw neater small towns anywhere, nor more imposing churches and public buildings, nor fewer saloons, nor cleaner streets, nor better roads. A happy land, truly, where the local papers give large and serious attention to the most innocuous of social doings and the farmers take good care that all their land is under cultivation and well looked after.

As we were passing through Wabash, for instance— or was it Peru?—we came upon a very neat and pleasing church and churchyard, the front lawn of which an old man of a very energetic and respectable appearance— quite your "first citizen" type—was mowing with a lawn-mower.

"Why should a man of that character be doing that work this weekday, do you suppose?" I inquired of Franklin.

"To get to heaven, of course. Can't you see? Heaven

is a literal, material thing to him.   It's like this church
building and its grass.   The closer he can identify himself with that here the nearer he will come to walking into
his heaven there.   I've noticed at home that the more
prosperous and well to do farmers are usually the leaders in the church.   They apply the same rules of getting
on in religion that they do to their business.   It is all a
phase of the instinct of a man to provide for himself and
his family.   I tell you, these people expect to find more or
less a duplication of what they have here—with all the
ills and pinches taken out and all the refinements of their
fancy, such as it is, added."

I felt as I thought of that old man that this was true.
He reminded me of my father, to whom to do the most
menial work about a Catholic church was an honor—such
as carrying in wood, building a fire, and the like.   You
were nearer God and the angels for doing it.   Actually
you were just outside the pearly gates.   And if one could
only die in a church—presto!—the gates would open and
there you would be inside.

Truly, this day of riding south after my depressing
afternoon in Warsaw was one of the most pleasant of
any that had come to me.   Now that I had recovered
from my mood of the night before—a chemic and psychic disturbance which quite did for me—I was in a very
cheerful frame of mind.   Long before either Franklin
or Speed had risen this morning—they had spent the
evening looking around the town—I was up, had a cold
bath, and had written various letters and visited the post
office and studied the town in general.

It was a halcyon morning, partly grey with a faint tint
of pink in the East, when I first looked out, and such an
array of house martins on five telegraph or telephone
wires over the way as I had not seen in a long time.   Birds
are odd creatures.   Their gregariousness without speech
always fascinates me.   These, ranged as they were on
the different wires, looked exactly like the notes of a
complicated and difficult fugue—so much so that I said to
a passing citizen who seemed to show an interest: "Now,

if you had a piano or an organ just how would you play that?"

He looked up at the wires which a wave of my hand indicated, then at me. He was a man of over forty, who looked as though he might be a traveling salesman or hotelkeeper.

"They do look like notes, don't they?" he agreed.

We both smiled, and then he added: "Now you make me wonder." And so we parted.

Towns of this size, particularly in the Middle West— and I can scarcely say why—have an intense literary and artistic interest for me. Whether it is because of a certain comic grandioseness which accompanies some of their characters or an ultra seriousness entirely out of proportion to the seeming import of events here—or whether one senses a flow of secret and subconscious desires hindered or trammeled perhaps by cluttering or suffocating beliefs or weaknesses, or a lightness and simplicity of character due to the soil and the air—I do not know; but it is so. In this region I am always stirred or appealed to by something which I cannot quite explain. The air seems lighter, the soil more grateful; a sense of something delicately and gracefully romantic is abroad.

Like children they are, these people, so often concerned with little things which do not matter at all— neighborhood opinions, neighborhood desires, neighborhood failures and contempts which a little more mind could solve or dissolve so readily. Whenever I see a town of this size in Indiana I think of our family and its relation to one or many like it. My mother and sisters and brothers suffered so much from conventional local notions. They made such a pathetic struggle to rid themselves of trammeling, minor local beliefs.

And did they succeed?

Not quite. Who does? Small life surrounds one like a sea. We swim in it, whether we will or no. In high halls somewhere are tremendous councils of gods and supermen, but they will not admit us. Zeus and Apollo will not suffer the feeble judgments of humble man. And so here we sit and slave and are weary—insects with an appointed task.

North Manchester, like all the small Indiana towns, appealed to me on the very grounds I have outlined. As I went up the street this early morning with my letters I encountered an old man, evidently a citizen of importance —present or past—being led down by his daughter (I took her to be). The latter was a thin, anæmic person who looked endless devotion—a pathetic, yearning solicitude for this man. He was blind, and yet quite an impressive figure, large, protuberant as to stomach, a broad, well-modeled face somewhat like that of the late Henry Ward Beecher, long, snow white hair, a silk hat, a swinging cutaway coat of broadcloth, a pleated soft-bosomed shirt ornamented with a black string tie, and an ivory-headed cane. Under his arm were papers and books. His sightless eyes were fixed on nothing—straight ahead. To me he looked like a lawyer or judge or congressman or politician—a local big-wig of some kind yet stricken in this most pathetic of all ways. The girl who was with him was so intent on his welfare. She was his eyes, his ears, his voice, really. It was wonderful—the resignation and self-effacement of her expression. It was quite moving.

"Who is that man?" I asked of a grocer clerk putting out a barrel of potatoes.

"That? Oh, that's Judge Shellenberger—or he was judge. He's a lawyer now for the Monon (a railroad that runs through here). He used to be judge of the circuit court."

I watched them down the street, and as they turned into a block of buildings where I suppose was his office, my mind was busy conjuring up the background which enmeshed them. Life is so full of great tales—every life in its way a masterpiece if seen in its entirety and against the vast background of life itself. Poor, fluttering, summer loving man! The bones of him make the chalk cliffs of time.

To the curb in front of another grocery store as I

was coming back to the hotel drew up a small, rickety buggy—so dilapidated and antique, scarcely worthy or safe to be hauled about rough country roads any longer. In it were "my Grandfather Squeers"—jackknife legs and all—and his wife, a most spare and crotchety female, in a very plain black dress, so inexpensive, a grey linseywoolsey shawl and a grey poke bonnet. She looked so *set* and fixed and yet humanly interesting in her way. I felt sorry for the two of them at once, as I always do for age and that limited array of thoughts which has produced only a hard, toilsome life. (We laugh at ignorance or dullness or condemn them so loudly, but sometimes they are combined with such earnestness and effort that one would rather cry.) "My Grandfather Squeers" was plainly a little rheumatic and crotchety, too. He reminded me of that Mr. Gridley who was occupying my old room in Warsaw, only he was much older and not quite so intelligent. He was having a hard time getting down between the wheels and straightening out some parcels under the seat, the while Aunt Sally stared on straight ahead and the horse looked back at them—a not overfed bay mare which seemed very much concerned in their affairs and what they were going to do next.

"Now, don't you forget about them seed onions," came a definite caution from the figure on the seat.

"No, I won't," he replied.

"And ast about the potatoes."

"Yes."

He cricketed his way into the store and presently came out with a small bag followed by a boy carrying a large bag—of potatoes, I assumed.

"I guess we can put them right in front—eh, mother?" he called.

"Yes, I suppose so," she assented, rather sharply, I thought, but not angrily.

The while the boy roughly bestowed the bag between them he went back for something, then came out and readjusted the potatoes properly.

"He didn't have any red tape," he called loudly, as though it was a matter of considerable importance.

"Well, all right," she said. "Come on and get in."

With much straining of his thin, stiff legs he got up and as he did so I noticed that his coat and trousers were home-made—cut, oh! most amazingly—and out of some old, faded wine colored cloth to begin with, probably worn years before by someone else. It made me think of all the old people I had known in my time, scrimping along on little or nothing, and of the thousands and thousands perhaps in every land for whom life is so hard, so meagre! If an artist takes a special case in hand and depicts it, one weeps, but no scheme has been devised to relieve the intense pressure on the many; and we forget so easily. I most of all. If I were a god, I have often said to myself, I would try to leaven the whole thing a little more evenly—but would I? Perhaps if I were a god I would see a reason for things as they are—a strangeness, a beauty, a requital not present to these mortal eyes.

. . . .

These streets of North Manchester were hung with those same triangular banners—red, white, blue, green, pink, orange—which we had seen in the East and which announced the imminence of a local Chautauqua. I do not know much about that organization, but it certainly knows how to advertise in country towns. In the store windows were quite striking pictures of Stromboli, the celebrated band leader, a chrysanthemum haired, thin bodied Italian in a braided white suit, who had been photographed crouching, as though he were about to spring, and with one thin hand raised high in the air holding a bâton. His appearance was that of one who was saying: "One more crash now and I have won all." And adjoining him in every window was the picture of Madame Adelina Scherzo, the celebrated soprano prima donna "straight from the Metropolitan Opera House, New York," who was shown photographed with manager and friends on the observation platform of her private car. Madame Scherzo was in black velvet, with bare arms, shoulders and throat, an entrancing sight. She was rather pretty too, and a line under the picture made it clear that she was costing the management "$800.00 a day," a charge which interested me, considering the size of the town and county and the probable audiences which could be got out to see anything.

"How large is the hall where the Chautauqua entertainments are held?" I asked of the local bookstore man where I was buying some picturecards.

"It isn't a hall; it's a tent," he replied. "They bring their own tent."

"Well, how many will it seat or hold?"

"Oh, about fifteen hundred people."

"And how many can they count on at any given performance?"

"Oh, about a thousand."

"Not more than that?" I queried.

"A thousand is a good crowd for a fair night," he persisted.

"And how much can they average per head?" I continued.

"Oh, not more than twentyfive cents. The seats run fifteen, twentyfive, thirtyfive and fifty cents."

"Then say they average forty cents," I said to myself. "That would mean that they took in four hundred dollars at a single performance—or if there are two a day, between seven and eight hundred dollars a day. And this one singer costs them eight hundred."

I saw the horns and hoofs of the ubiquitous press agent.

"Do you think that Madame Scherzo gets the sum they say she does?" I asked of this same bookstore man, wondering whether he was taken in by their announcement. He looked fairly intelligent.

"Yes, indeed! She comes from the Metropolitan Opera House. I don't suppose she'd come out here for any less than that."

I wondered whether he intended this as a reflection on

Indiana or a compliment to North Manchester. It was a little dubious.

"Well, that's a good deal for a tent that only seats fifteen hundred," I replied.

"But you don't want to forget that they play to two audiences a day," he returned solemnly, as though he had solved it all.

I thought it unkind to argue with him. Why shouldn't North Manchester have a celebrated prima donna costing eight hundred dollars a day? Think how the knowledge of that would add to the natives' enjoyment of her music!

"You're right," I said. "I hadn't thought of that." And out I went.

.   .   .   .

While we were trifling about getting ready to start, a singular combination of circumstances produced an odd case of repetition or duplication of a set of facts which had occurred the year before, which impressed me greatly, the more so as it corresponded exactly with a number of similar instances in my own life.

I might preface my remarks by saying that throughout my life experiences and scenes have to a certain extent tended to duplicate or repeat themselves. Nietzsche remarks somewhere that we all have our typical experiences. It is not a particularly brilliant deduction, considering the marked predilections of certain temperaments. But when we connect up the fact with chemical or physical law, as we are likely some day to do, it becomes highly significant. Personally, I am one who believes that as yet we have not scratched the surface of underlying fact and law. I once believed, for instance, that nature was a blind, stumbling force or combination of forces which knew not what or whither. I drew that conclusion largely from the fumbling nonintelligence (relatively speaking) of men and all sentient creatures. Of late years I have inclined to think just the reverse, i. e., that nature is merely dark to us because of her tremendous subtlety and our own very limited powers of comprehension; also that in common

with many other minor forces and forms of intelligence—
insects and trees, for example—we are merely tools or
implements—slaves, to be exact—and that collectively
we are used as any other tool or implement would be used
by us.

Thus there is a certain species of ant, the Dorylii,
which is plainly a scavenger so far as the surface of the
earth is concerned, appearing at the precise moment when
a dead body is becoming offensive and burying and
devouring it. This may be said to be equally true of
buzzards, jackals, carrion crows, creatures which a Dar-
winian naturalist would explain as the result of an unin-
tentional pressure—and natural selection. On the other
hand, current biology tends to indicate that all is fore-
shadowed, prearranged; that indications of what will be
are given ages before it is permitted to appear. Onto-
genetic Orthogenesis it is called, I believe. The creative
forces have an amazing way of working. They may use
strange means—races of men and insects, of no particular value to them—to accomplish certain results. Thus
man might well be a tool intended to release certain
forces in the soil—coal, iron, stone, copper, gold—and all
his social organization and social striving merely the
physico-legal aspects or expression of the processes by
which all things are done. Multiple unit forces must
work in some harmonious way, and all these harmonious
processes would therefore need to be provided for. They
may be the chemical and physical laws by which we are
governed. How otherwise can one explain the fact that
although there is apparently sufficient wisdom in the universe to sustain immense sidereal systems in order and
to generate all the complex organisms which we see and
can examine at our leisure, yet man remains blind and
dumb as to the processes by which he comes and goes?
He has examined a little. He has prepared a lexicon of
laws whose workings he has detected. Beyond these
must be additional laws, or so he suspects, but what are
they? In the meantime, instead of nature permitting
him to go on (once he has his mind prepared for thought

along these lines), it strikes him down and puts new, ignorant youth in his place—new, ignorant generations of youths.

Actually (I sincerely believe this) it is not intended that man should ever be permitted to know anything. The temperaments of the powers to whom we pray are not magnanimous. Man is a slave, a tool. The fable of Prometheus and the divine fire has more of fact than of poetry in it. At every turn of man's affairs he is arbitrarily and ruthlessly and mockingly confused. New generations of the dull and thick are put forth. False prophets arise. Religionists, warriors, dreamers without the slightest conception of the import of that which they seek or do, arise, slay, burn, confuse. Man stands confounded for a time, a slave to illusion, toiling with forces and by aid of forces which he does not understand, and effecting results the ultimate use of which he cannot possibly grasp. We burn gas! For ourselves alone? We generate electricity! For ourselves alone? We mine coal, iron, lead, etc.—release it into space eventually. For ourselves alone? Who knows, really? By reason of the flaming, generative chemistry of our bodies we are compelled to go on. Why?

At the critical moment when man becomes too inquisitive he may be once more chained to the rock, Prometheus-like, and the eagles of ignorance and duty set at his vitals. Why the astounding bludgeoning of each other by the nations of Europe? Cosmically—permanently— what can they gain?

CHAPTER XLIII

As we were starting for Wabash from here, a distance of twenty miles or so, and at ten o'clock in the morning, it began to sprinkle. Now the night before, as we were entering this place, Franklin had been telling me that as he had gone through here the year before about this time in the morning, homebound from a small lake in this vicinity, some defect in the insulation of the wiring had caused a small fire which threatened to burn the car. They detected it in time by smelling burning rubber. Incidentally, it had started to rain, and they had to go back to the local garage for repairs.

"I bet it rains tomorrow," Speed had observed as he heard Franklin's story.

"Why?" I asked.

"There's a ring around the moon."

"That always means rain, does it?" I chaffed.

He did not answer direct, but concluded: "I bet it will be raining by tomorrow noon."

Just as we were leaving town, and before we reached a bridge which spans the Eel River at this place, I detected the odor of burning rubber and called Franklin's attention to it. At the same time Speed smelt it too, and stopped the car. We got out and made a search. Sure enough, a rubber covering protecting and separating some wires which joined in a box was on fire, and the smoke was making a fine odor. We put it out, but as we did so Franklin observed, "That's funny."

"What?" I inquired.

"Why, this," he replied. "At this place last year, in a rain, this very spot, nearly, we got out because we smelled burning rubber and put out a fire in this same box."

"That is odd," I said, and then I began to think of my own experiences in this line and the fact that so often things have repeated themselves in my life, in little and in big, in such a curious way.

Once, as I told Franklin now—the only other time, in fact, that I took an important trip in this way—a certain Englishman whom I had not seen in years burst in upon me with a proposition that I go to England and Europe with him, offering to see that the money for the trip was raised and without my turning a hand in the matter—and quite in the same way, only a week before, Franklin himself had burst in upon me with a similar proposition, which I had accepted. Another time, at the opening of a critical period of my life, I was compelled to undergo an operation in the process of which, under ether, certain characters appeared to me, acting in a particular way and saying various things to me which impressed me greatly at the time; and later, at another critical period when, strangely enough, I was, much against my wishes, undergoing another operation, these same characters appeared to me and said much the same things in the same way.

One of the commonest of my experiences, as I now told Franklin, had been a thing like this. I would be walking along thinking of nothing in particular when some person, male or female, about whom I cared nothing, would appear, stop me, and chat about nothing in particular. Let us say he or she carried a book, or a green parasol, or a yellow stick, and congratulated me upon or complained to me concerning something I had or had not done. As for my part, at that particular moment I might be trying to solve some problem in relation to fiction or finance—a crucial problem. It would be raining or beautifully clear or snowing. A year or two later, under almost exactly the same circumstances, when I would be trying to solve a similar problem, in rain or snow or clear weather, as the case might be, I would meet the same person, dressed almost as before, carrying a book or a cane or green parasol, and we would talk about nothing in particular, and I would say to my-self, after he or she were gone, perhaps: "Why, last year, at just about this place, when I was thinking of just some such problem as this, I met this same person looking about like this."

I am not attempting to theorize concerning this. I am merely stating a fact.

This system of recurrence applies not only to situations of this kind, but to many others. The appearance of a certain person in my life has always been heralded by a number of hunchbacks who came forward, passed—sometimes touching my elbow—and frequently looking at me in a solemn manner, as though some subconscious force, of which they were the tool, were saying to me, "See, here is the sign."

For a period of over fifteen years in my life, at the approach of every marked change—usually before I have passed from an old set of surroundings to a new —I have met a certain smug, kindly little Jew, always the same Jew, who has greeted me most warmly, held my hand affectionately for a few moments, and wished me well. I have never known him any more intimately than that. Our friendship began at a sanatorium, at a time when I was quite ill. Thereafter my life changed and I was much better. Since then, as I say, always at the critical moment, he has never failed. I have met him in New York, Chicago, the South, in trains, on shipboard. It is always the same. Only the other day, after an absence of three years, I saw him again. I am not theorizing; I am stating facts. I have a feeling, at times, as I say, that life is nothing but a repetition of very old circumstances, and that we are practically immortal, only not very conscious of it.

Going south from North Manchester, we had another blowout in the right rear tire and in connection with this there was a discussion which may relate itself to what I have just been saying or it may not. The reader may recall that between Stroudsburg and Wilkes-Barré, in Pennsylvania, we had had two blowouts in this same right rear wheel, or tire, and in connection with the last of these two blowouts just east of Wilkes-Barré, Franklin had told me that hitherto—ever since he had had the car, in fact—all the trouble had been in the same right rear wheel and that, being a good mystic, he had finally to realize for himself that there was nothing the matter with the perfect idea of this car as it existed before it was built or, in other words, its psychic unity, and hence that there couldn't be anything wrong with this right rear wheel. You see? After that, once this had been clearly realized by him, there had been no more trouble of any kind in connection with this particular quarter or wheel until this particular trip began.

"Now see here, Speed," I heard him say on this particular occasion. "Here's a psychic fact I want you to get. We'll have to get that right hand tire off our minds. This car is an embodiment of a perfect idea, an idea that existed clear and sound before this car was ever built. There is nothing wrong with that idea, or that tire. It can't be injured. It is in existence outside this car and they are building other cars according to it right now. This car is as perfect as that idea. It's a whole— a unit. It's intact. Nothing can happen to it. It can't be injured. Do you get me? Now you're going to think that and we're not going to have any trouble. We're going to enjoy this trip."

Speed looked at Franklin, and I felt as though something had definitely been "put over," as we say—just what I am not quite able to explain myself. Anyhow we had no more tire trouble of any kind until just as we were nearing Wabash or about half way between the two towns. Then came the significant whistle and we climbed down.

"There you have it!" exclaimed Franklin enigmatically. "You shouldn't have knocked on wood, Speed."

"What was that?" I inquired, interested.

"Well, you remember where we had the last blowout, don't you?"

"Yes," I said, "east of Wilkes-Barré."

"We haven't had any trouble since, have we?"

"Not a bit."

"Last night, after you had gone to bed, Speed and I went to a restaurant. As we were eating, I said: 'We've had some great tire luck, haven't we?' Perhaps I shouldn't have thought of it as luck. Anyhow he said, 'Yes, but we're not home yet,' and he knocked on wood. I said: 'You shouldn't knock on wood. That's a confession of lack of understanding. It's a puncture in the perfect idea of the car. We're likely to have a blowout in the morning.' And here it is."

He looked at me and smiled.

"What is this," I said, "a real trip or an illusion?"

He smiled again.

"It's a real trip, but it wants to be as perfect as the idea of it."

I felt my conception of a solid earth begin to spin a little, but I said nothing more. Anyhow, the wheel was fixed, as well as the psychic idea of it. And we didn't have any more tire trouble this side of Carmel, where Speed left us.

Going south from North Manchester, we came to Wabash, a place about as handsome as Warsaw, if not more so, with various charming new buildings. It was on the Wabash River—the river about which my brother Paul once composed the song entitled, "On the Banks of the Wabash Far Away" (I wrote the first verse and chorus!), and here we found a picture postcard on sale which celebrated this fact. "On the Banks of the Wabash Far Away," it said under a highly colored scene of some sycamore trees hanging over the stream. As my brother Paul was very proud of his authorship of this song, I was glad.

From here, since it was raining and we were in a hurry to reach Carmel before dark, we hustled west to Peru, about twenty miles, the cover up and the storm curtains on, for we were in a driving rain. I could not help noting how flat Indiana was in this region, how numerous were the beech and ash groves, how good the roads, and how Hollandesque the whole distant scene. Unlike Ohio, there was no sense here of a struggle between manufacture and trade and a more or less simple country life. The farmers had it all, or nearly so. The rural homes were most of them substantial, if not markedly interesting to look upon, and the small towns charming. There were no great factory chimneys cutting the sky in every direction, as farther east, but instead, windmills, and silos and red or grey barns, and cows, or horses, or sheep in the fields. At Peru I asked a little girl who worked in the five-and-ten-cent store if she liked living in Peru.

"Like it? This old town? I should say not."

"Why not?" I replied.

"Well, you ought to live here for a while, and you'd soon find out. It's all right to go through in a machine, I suppose."

"Well, where would you rather be, if not here?" I questioned.

"Oh, what's the use wishing—lots of places," she replied irritably, and as if desiring to end the vain discussion. "It never does me any good to wish."

She walked off to wait upon another customer, and I departed.

South of Peru were several county seats and towns of small size, which we might have visited had we chosen to take the time; but aside from passing through Kokomo, in order to see an enormous automobile works with which Speed had formerly been connected, and from whence, earlier in his life, he had attempted to flee at the approach of the end of all things, we avoided all these towns. It was raining too hard, and there would have been no pleasure in stopping.

At Kokomo, which appeared presently out of a grey mist and across a middle distance of wet green grass and small, far scattered trees, we had a most interesting experience. We met the man who made the first automobile in America, and saw his factory—the

Haynes Automobile Company, of which he was president and principal stockholder, and which was employing, at the time we were there, nearly three thousand men and turning out over two thousand cars a year, nearly a car apiece for every man and woman in the place. I saw no children employed.

The history of this man, as sketched to me beforehand by Franklin and Speed, was most interesting. Years before he had been a traveling salesman, using a light runabout in this very vicinity. Later he had interested himself in motors of the gas and steam variety and had entered upon the manufacture of them. Still later, when the problem of direct transmission was solved in France and the automobile began to appear abroad, he, in conjunction with a man named Apperson, decided to attempt to construct a car here which would avoid infringing all the French patents. Alone, really, without any inventive aid from Apperson, so to speak, Haynes solved the problem, at least in part. It was claimed later, and no doubt it was true, that he, along with many other mechanicians attempting to perfect an American car which would avoid French lawsuits, had merely rearranged, not improved upon, the French idea of direct transmission. At any rate, he was sued, along with others; but the American automobile manufacturers eventually beat the French patentees and remained in possession of their designs. Of all of these, Haynes was the first American to put an American automobile in the field.

We were shown over his factory before meeting him, however, and a fascinating spectacle it proved. We arrived in a driving rain, with the clouds so thick and low that you would have thought it dusk. All the lights in the great concern were glowing as though it were night. A friendly odor of smoke and hot mould sand and grease and shellac and ground metal permeated the air for blocks around. Inside were great rooms, three to four hundred feet long, all of a hundred feet wide, and glassed over top and sides for light, in which were droves of men, great companies of them, in jeans and jumpers, their faces and hands and hair stained brown or black with oil and smoke, their eyes alight with that keen interest which the intelligent workman always has in his work.

I never saw so many automobiles and parts of automobiles in all my life. It was interesting to look at whole rooms piled high with auto carriage frames or auto motors, or auto tops or auto bodies. I never imagined that there were so many processes through which all parts of a machine have to be put to perfect them, or that literally thousands of men do some one little thing to every machine turned out. We stood and gazed at men who were polishing the lacquered sides of automobile bodies with their thumbs, dipping them in oil and so rubbing down certain rough places; or at others hovering over automobile motors attached in rows to gasoline tanks and being driven at an enormous rate of speed for days at a time without ever stopping, to test their durability and speed capacity. It was interesting to see these test men listening carefully for any untoward sound or flash, however slight, which might indicate an error. We pay very little, comparatively, for what we buy, considering the amount of time spent by thousands in supplying our idlest wants.

And there were other chambers where small steel, or brass, or copper parts were being turned out by the thousand, men hovering over giant machines so intricate in their motions that I was quite lost and could only develop a headache thinking about them afterward. Actually, life loses itself at every turn for the individual in just such a maze. You gaze, but you never see more than a very little of what is going on about you. If we could see not only all the processes that are at work simultaneously everywhere, supplying us with what we use here, but in addition, only a fraction—that nearest us—of the mechanics and physics of the universe, what a stricken state would we be in! Actually, unless we were protected by lack of capacity for comprehension, I should think one might go mad. The thunder, the speed, the light, the shuttle flashes of all the process—how they would confuse and perhaps terrify! For try as we will, without a tremendous enlargement of the reasoning faculty, we can never comprehend. Vast, amazing processes cover or encircle us at every turn, and we never know. Like the blind we walk, our hands out before us, feeling our way. Like moths we turn about the autogenetic flame of human mystery and never learn—until we are burned, and not then—not even a little.

After inspecting the factory we came into the presence of the man who had built up all this enterprise. He was relatively undersized, quite stocky, with a round, dumpling-like body, and a big, round head which looked as though it might contain a very solid mass of useful brains. He had the air of one who has met thousands, a diplomatic, cordial, experienced man of wealth. I sensed his body and his mind to be in no very healthy condition, however, and he looked quite sickly and preoccupied. He had a habit, I observed, contracted no doubt through years of meditation and introspection, of folding both arms over his stout chest, and then lifting one or the other forearm and supporting his head with it, as though it might fall over too far if he did not. He had grey-blue eyes, the eyes of the thinker and organizer, and like all strong men, a certain poise and ease very reassuring, I should think, to anyone compelled or desiring to converse with him.

The story he told us of how he came to build the first automobile (in America) was most interesting.

Franklin had seemed to be greatly interested to discover whether as an Indiana pioneer this man had borrowed the all-important idea of transmission from either Daimler or Panhard, two Europeans, who in the early stages of the automobile had solved this problem for themselves in slightly different ways, or whether he had worked out for himself an entirely independent scheme of transmission and control. Franklin went after him on this, but he could get nothing very satisfactory. The man, affable and courteous, explained in a roundabout way that he had made use of two clutches, and then toward the end of the interview, when Franklin remarked, "You know, of course, that the idea of transmission was worked out some time before 1893" (the year Haynes built his first car), he replied, "You have to give those fellows credit for a great deal"—a very indefinite answer, as you see.

But to me the man was fascinating as a man, and I was pleased to hear him explain anything he would.

"I was already interested in gas and steam engines and motors of this type," he said, "and I just couldn't keep out of it."

"In other words, you put an old idea into a new form," I suggested.

"Yes—just that."

"Tell me—who bought your first car?" I inquired.

"A doctor up in Chicago," he smiled. "He has it yet."

"Of course, you thought you could make money out of it?"

"Well, I built my first car with the idea of having one for myself, really. I have a turn for mechanics. I borrowed enough money to begin manufacturing at once —took in a partner."

"And then what?"

"Well, the machine was a success. We just grew. In a few months we were behind on our orders, and always have been since."

He appeared too tired and weary to be actively at the head of any business at this time. Yet he went on telling us a little of his trade struggles and what he thought of the future of the automobile—in connection with farming, railroads and the like—then he suddenly changed to another subject.

"But I'm not nearly so interested in automobiles as I was," he observed smilingly, at the same time diving into his pocket and producing what looked like a silver knife. "My son and I"—he waved an inclusive hand toward an adjoining room built of red brick, and which seemed to be flickering romantically as to its walls with the flame reflections of small furnace fires—"have invented a thing which we call stellak, which is five hundred times harder than steel and cuts steel just as you would cut wood with an ordinary knife."

"Well, how did you invent that?" I asked.

"We had need of something of that kind here, and my son and I invented it."

"You just decided what to do, did you? But why did you call it stellak?" I persisted.

"After stella, star, because the metal turned out to be so bright. It has some steel in it, too."

He shifted his arms, sank his head into the palm of his left hand, and gazed at me solemnly.

"All the processes are patented," he added, with a kind of unconscious caution which amused me. I felt as though he imagined we were looking too curiously into the workshop, where the perfecting processes were still going on, and might desire to steal his ideas.

"There ought to be a real fortune in that," I said.

"Yes," he replied, with a kind of lust for money showing in his face, although he was already comfortably rich and daily growing richer as well as sicker, "we're already behind on our orders. Everybody wants to see it. We can use a lot ourselves if we can just make it fast enough."

There was a time in my life when I would have envied a man of this type, or his son, the mere possession of money seemed such an important thing to me. Later on, it became the sign manual of certain limitations of thought which at first irritated and then bored me. Now I can scarcely endure the presence of a mind that sees something in money as money—the mere possession of it. If the mind does not race on to lovelier or more important things than money can buy, it has no import to the world, no more, at least, than is involved in the syphoning of a clam. We must have grocers and brewers and butchers and bakers—but if we were never to have more than these or anything different or new!!

CHAPTER XLIV

THE run to Carmel, Franklin's home, was not long —say, forty miles—and we made it in a downpour and were silent most of the way. It was so dark and damp and gloomy that no one seemed to want to talk, and yet I took a melancholy comfort in considering how absolutely cheerless the day was. I could not help reflecting, as we sped along, how at its worst life persistently develops charm, so that if one were compelled to live always in so gloomy a world, one would shortly become inured to it, or the race would, and think nothing of it.

Once Speed called my attention to a group of cattle with their heads to wind and rain, and asked, "Do you know why they stand that way?"

"No," I replied.

"Well, all animals turn their fighting end to any trouble. If those were horses, now, their rump would be to the rain."

"I see," I said. "They fight with their heels."

"Like some soldiers," said Franklin drily.

In another place we saw another great stretch of beech woods, silvery in the rain, and Franklin commented on the characteristic presence of these groves everywhere in Indiana. There was one near his home, he said, and there had been one in every town I had ever lived in in this state.

At dusk we reached Westfield, only six miles from his home, where the Quakers lived. This was one of those typical community towns, with standardized cottages of grey-white wood and rather stately trees in orderly rows. Because of a difficulty here with one of the lamps, which would not light, we had to stop a while, until it grew quite dark. A lost chicken ran crying out of a neighboring cornfield, and we shooed it back towards its supposed home, wondering whether the rain and wind or some night prowler would not kill it. It was very much excited, running and squeaking constantly—a fine call to any fox or weasel. Chickens are so stupid.

Presently we came into Carmel, in the night and rain, but there being few lights, I could not make out anything. The car turned into a yard somewhere and stopped at a side door, or porch. We got out and a little woman, grey and small, cheerful and affectionate, as became a doting mother, came out and greeted us, kissing Franklin.

"What kept you so long?" she asked, in a familiar motherly fashion. "We thought you were going to get here by noon."

"So did we," replied Franklin drily. "I wired you, though."

"Yes, I know. Your father's gone to bed. He stayed up as long as he could. Come right in here, please," she said to me, leading the way, while Franklin stopped to search the car. I followed, damp and heavy, wondering if the house would be as cheerful as I hoped.

It was. It was the usual American small-town home, built with the number of rooms supposed to be appropriate for a given number of people or according to your station in life. A middle class family of some means, I believe, is supposed to have a house containing ten or twelve rooms, whether they need them or not. A veranda, as I could see, ran about two sides, and there was a lawn with trees. Within, the furnishings were substantial after their kind—good middle-west furniture. (Franklin's studio, at the back, as I discovered later, was charmingly appointed.) There were some of his early drawings on the wall, which love had framed and preserved. They reminded me of my family's interest in me. A tall, slim, dark girl, anæmic but with glistening black eyes, came in and greeted me. She was a sister,

I understood—a milliner, by trade, taking her vacation here. As she came, she called to another girl who would not come—why I could not at first comprehend. This was a niece to whom Franklin more than once on the way out had referred as being superiorly endowed temperamentally, and as possessing what spiritualists or theosophists refer to as an "old soul," she was so intelligent. He could not explain her natural wisdom save on the ground of her having lived before.

"Some people just insist on being shy," said the sister. "They are so temperamental."

She showed me to my room, and then went off to help get us something to eat.

Alone, I examined my surroundings, unpacked my things, opened a double handful of mail, and then came down and sat with the mother and sister at supper. It being late, bacon and eggs were our portion, and some cake—a typical late provision for anyone in America.

I wish I might accurately portray, in all its simplicity, and placidity, the atmosphere I found here. This house was so still—and the town. Mrs. Booth, Franklin's mother, seemed so essentially the middle West, even Indiana mother, with convictions and yet a genial tolerance of much. Making the best of a difficult world was written all over the place. There was a little boy here, adopted from somewhere because his parents were dead, who seemed inordinately fond of Franklin, as indeed Franklin seemed of him. I had had stories of this boy all the way out, and how through him Franklin was gaining (or regaining, perhaps, I had better say) a knowledge of the ethics and governing rules of boy-land. It was amusing to see them together now, the boy with sharp, bird-like eyes devouring every detail of his older friend's appearance and character—Franklin amused, fatherly, meditative, trying to make the most and best of all the opportunities of life. We sat in the "front room," or "parlor," and listened to the Victrola rendering pieces by Bert Williams and James Whitcomb Riley and Tchaikowsky and Weber and Fields and Beethoven

—the usual medley of the sublime and the ridiculous found in so many musical collections. Franklin had told me that of late—only in the last two or three years— his father had begun to imagine that there might or must be in music something which would explain the world's, to him, curious interest in it! Hitherto, on his farm, where there had been none, he had scoffed at it!

The next morning I arose early, as I thought—eight o'clock—and going out on the front porch encountered an old, grizzled man, who looked very much like the last portraits of the late General Sherman, and who seemed very much what he was, or had been—a soldier, and then latterly a farmer. Now he was all gnarled and bent. His face was grizzled with a short, stubby grey beard. The eyes were rather small and brown and looked canny. He got up with difficulty, a cane assisting him, and offered me a withered hand. I felt sympathy for all age.

"Well, ya got here, did ya?" he inquired shortly. There was a choppy brevity about his voice which I liked. He seemed very self sufficient, genial and shrewd, for all his years. "We expected ya last night. I couldn't wait up, though. I did stay up till eight. That's pretty late for me—usually go to bed at seven. Have a nice trip?"

We sat down and I told him. His eyes went over me like a swift feeling hand.

"Well, you're just the man I want to talk to," he said, with a kind of crude eagerness. "You from New York State?"

"Yes."

"Franklin tells me that Governor Whitman has got in bad, refusing to pardon that fellow Becker. He says he thinks it will hurt him politically. What do you think?"

"No," I replied. "I think not. I believe it will help him, if he doesn't injure himself in any other way."

"That's what I think," he exclaimed, with a kind of

defiant chuckle. "I never did think he knew what he was talking about."

On our way west, as I have indicated, Franklin had been telling me much of his father's and his own upbringing. They were types, as I judged, not much calculated either to understand or sympathize with each other—Franklin the sensitive, perceptive artist; his father the sheer, aggressive political soldier type. The one had artistic imagination, the other scarcely any imagination at all. I could see that. Yet both had a certain amount of practical understanding backed by conviction, which could easily bring them into conflict. I felt a touch of something here, as though this father would be rather gratified if he could prove his son to be in a false position. It amused me, for I knew from what I had heard that Franklin would be amused too. He was so tolerant.

More than that, I discovered a streak in the father which I think is to be found in thousands of countrymen the world over, in all lands, namely, that of pruriency, and that in the face of a rural conventionalism and even a religious bent which frowns on evidence of any tendency in that direction on the part of others, especially those most immediately related to them. Rural life is peculiar in this respect, somewhat different to that of the tribes of the city, who have so much more with which to satisfy themselves. Most isolated countrymen—or perhaps I had better modify that and say many confined to the silences of the woods and fields and the ministrations of one woman, or none—have an intense curiosity in regard to sex; which works out in strange, often naïve ways. In this instance it showed itself shortly in connection with some inquiry I made in regard to local politics—how the next election was coming out (I knew that would interest him) and who the local leaders were. Soon this resulted in the production of a worn and dingy slip of paper which he handed me, chuckling.

"What do you think of that?" he asked. I took it and read it, smiling the while.

It seemed that some local wag—the owner of the principal drug store—had written and circulated a humorous *double entendre* description of a golf game and someone's failure as a golfer, which was intended really to show that the man in the case was impotent. You can easily imagine how the thing was worked out. It was cleverly done, and to a grown-up person was quite harmless.

But the old gentleman was obviously greatly stirred by it. It fascinated and no doubt shocked him a little (all the more so since sex was over for him) and aroused in him a spirit of mischief.

"Well, it's very funny," I said. "Rather good. What of it?"

"What do you think of a man that'll get up a thing like that and hand it around where children are apt to get a hold of it?"

"As regards the children," I commented, "it's rather bad, I suppose, although I've seen but few children in my life that weren't as sexually minded, if not more so, than their elders. I wouldn't advise putting this in their hands, however. As for grownups, well, it's just a trivial bit of business, I should say," I concluded.

"You think so?" he said, restoring the paper to his vest pocket and twinkling his grey eyes.

"Yes," I persisted.

"Well, the fellow that got this up and handed it around here wants to head the republican county ticket this fall. I think I've got him, with this. I don't mean that he shall."

"Do you mean he's a bad character?" I smiled.

"Oh, no, not that exactly. He's not a bad fellow, but he's not a good leader. He's got too big a head. He can't win and he oughtn't to be nominated, and I don't mean that he shall be, if I can prevent it."

He was chewing tobacco as he talked, quite as a farmer at a fence corner, and now he expectorated solemnly, defiantly, conclusively.

"You don't like him personally, then?" I queried, curious as to the reason for this procedure.

"Oh, I like him well enough. He ain't no good as a leader, though—not to my way of thinking."

"Do you mean to say you intend to use this against him in the campaign?"

"I told him so, and some of the other fellows too, down at the post office the other day. I told him they'd better not nominate him. If they did, I'd circulate this. He knows it'll kill him if I do. I showed it to the Quaker minister here the other night, and he 'lowed it 'ud do for him."

"What's a Quaker minister?" I asked, suddenly interrupting the main theme of our conversation, curious as to the existence of such an official. "I never heard of the Quakers having a minister. I know they have elders and ministers in a general or democratic sense—men whose counsels are given more or less precedence over that of others, but no particular minister."

"Well, they have out here," he replied. "I don't know where or when they got 'em. This one lives right over there next the Quaker Church.

"So you have a Quaker Church instead of a meeting house, do you?" I commented.

"Yes, and they have congregational singing and an organ," observed the dark-eyed sister, who was just coming up now. "You don't hear of anything like that in a Friends' meeting house in the East, but you will here tomorrow." She smiled and called us in to breakfast.

It appeared that our host had eaten at six A. M., or five, but he came in with me for sociability's sake.

The discussion of the pornographic jocosity and its political use was suspended while we had breakfast, but a little later, the veranda being cleared and the old gentleman still sitting here, rocking and ruminating, I said:

"Do you mean to say you intend to use that leaflet against this man in case he runs?"

"I intend to use it," he replied definitely, but still with a kind of pleasant, chuckling manner, as though it were a great joke. "I don't think they'll nominate him, though, but if they do, it'll kill him sure."

He smiled enigmatically and went on rocking.

"But you're a republican?"

"Yes, I'm a republican."

"And he's a republican?"

"Yes."

"Well, politics must certainly be stirring things out here," I commented.

He chuckled silently, like an old rooster in a garden, the while he moved to and fro in his rocker, ruminating his chew of tobacco, and then finally he added, "It'll do for him sure."

I had to smile. The idea of stirring up a fight over so pornographic a document in a strictly religious community, and thus giving it a wider circulation than ever it could have in any other way, by a man who would have called himself religious, I suppose, had an element of humor in it.

At breakfast it was that I met the girl who refused to greet me the night before. As I looked at her for the first time, it struck me that life is constantly brewing new draughts of femininity, calculated to bewray or affright the world—Helens or Circes. The moralists and religionists and those who are saintly minded and believe that nature seeks only a conservative or coolly virtuous state have these questions to answer:

(1) How is it that for every saint born into the world there is also a cruel or evil minded genius born practically at the same time? The twain are ever present.

(2) That for every virtuous maid there is one who has no trace of virtue?—possibly many?

(3) That while an evil minded person may be reforming, or an immoral person becoming moral, nature itself (which religion is supposed to be reforming) is breeding others constantly, fresh and fresh, new types of those who, sex hungry or wealth hungry or adventure hungry, have no part or parcel with morality? The best religion or morals appear to be able to do is to contend with nature, which is constantly breeding the un- or immoral, and generating blood lusts which result in all the crimes

we know, and by the same token, all the religions. How is that?

These thoughts were generated, more or less, by my observation of this girl, for as I looked at her, solid and dimpling, I felt certain that here nature had bred another example of that type of person whom the moralists are determined to look upon as oversexed. She had all the provocative force that goes with a certain kind of beauty. I am not saying that she was so—merely that it was so she impressed me. Her mouth, for one thing, was full—pouty—and she was constantly changing its expression, as if aware of its import. Her eyes were velvety and swimming. Her neck and arms were heavy —rounded in a sensuous way. She walked with what to me seemed a distinct consciousness of the lines of her body, although as a matter of fact she may not have been. She was preternaturally shy and evasive, looking about as if something very serious were about to happen, as if she had to be most careful of her ways and looks, and yet really not being so. Her whole manner was at once an invitation and repulsion—the two carefully balanced so as to produce a static and yet an irritating state. I half liked and disliked her. If she had been especially friendly, no doubt I should have liked her very much. Since she was so wholly evasive, I fancied that I could dislike her quite as much.

And at that we got on fairly well. I made no friendly overtures of any kind, and yet I half felt as if she might be expecting something of the kind. She hung about for a time, came to and fro, and then disappeared. She changed her dress while we were down town, and seemed even more attractive. She came out and sat on the porch next to me for a time, and I tried to talk to her, but she made me feel uncomfortable, as though I were trying to force attentions on her.

Apparently she was as much a puzzle to some others as she was to me, for Franklin told me that she had once run away from the academy where she was being schooled, and had come here instead, her parents being dead and these being her nearest friends or relatives. Her guardian, appointed by law, was greatly troubled by her. Also, that she had quite a little money coming to her, and that once she had expressed a desire to be given a horse and gun and allowed to go west—a sixteen-year-old girl! She told me, among other things, that she wanted to go on the stage, or into moving picture work. I could not help looking at her and wondering what storms and disasters might not follow in the wake of such a temperament. She would be so truly fascinating and possibly utterly destructive.

In connection with this type of temperament or at any rate the temperament which is not easily fixed in one passional vise, I have this to say: that, in spite of all the theories which hold in regard to morals and monogamy, life in general appears to be chronically and perhaps incurably varietistic and pluralistic in its tastes and emotions. We hear much of one life, one love, but how many actually attain to that ideal—if it is one. Personally I have found it not only possible, but by a curious and entirely fortuitous combination of circumstances almost affectionately unavoidable, to hold three, four— even as many as five and six—women in regard or the emotional compass of myself, at one and the same time, not all to the same degree, perhaps, or in the same way, but each for certain qualities which the others do not possess. I will not attempt to dignify this by the name of love. I do not assume for a moment that it is love, but that it is a related state is scarcely to be questioned. Whether it is a weakness or a strength remains to be tested by results in individual cases. To some it might prove fatal, to others not. Witnes, the Mormons! As for myself I do not think it is. Some of my most dramatic experiences and sufferings, as well as my keenest mental illuminations, have resulted from intimate, affectionate contact with women. I have learned most from those strange, affectionately dependent and yet artistic souls who somehow crave physical and spiritual sympathy in the great dark or light in which we find ourselves—

this very brief hour here. Observing their moods, their vanities, their sanities, their affectional needs, I have seen how absolutely impossible it is to balance up the socalled needs of life in any satisfactory manner, or to establish an order which, however seemingly secure for the time being, will not in the end dry rot or decay.

I say it out of the depths of my life and observation that there is no system ever established anywhere which is wholly good. If you establish matrimony and monogamy, let us say, and prove that it is wholly ideal for social entertainment, or the rearing and care of children, you at once shut out the fact that it is the death of affectional and social experience—that it is absolutely inimical to the roving and free soul which must comb the world for understanding, and that the spectacles which entertain the sober and stationary in art, literature, science, indeed every phase of life, would never be if all maintained the order and quiet which monogamy suggests.

Yet monogamy is good—nothing better for its purpose. Two souls are entitled to cling together in affectional embrace forever and ever, if they can. It is wholly wonderful and beautiful. But if all did so, where, then, would be a story like Carmen, for instance, or an opera like Tristan and Isolde, or I Pagliacci, or Madame Butterfly, or Louise? If we all accepted a lock-step routine, or were compelled to—but need I really argue? Is not life at its very best anachronistic? Does it not grow by horrible alternatives—going so far along one line, on one leg, as it were, and then suddenly abandoning everything in that direction (to sudden decay and death, perhaps) and as suddenly proceeding in an entirely different direction (apparently) on the other leg? All those who find their fixed conditions, their orders and stable states suddenly crumbling about them are inclined to cry: "There is no God," "Life is a cruel hell," "Man is a beast—an insane egoist."

Friends, let me suggest something. Have faith to believe that there is a larger intelligence at work which

does not care for you or me at all—or if it does, only
to this extent, that it desires to use us as a carpenter
does his tools, and does use us, whether we will or no.
There is some idle scheme of entertainment (possibly
self-entertainment) which is being accomplished by some
power which is not necessarily outside man, but working
through him, of which he, in part, is the expression. This
power, in so far as we happen to be essential or useful
to it, appears beneficent. A great or successful person
might be inclined to look on it in that light. On the
other hand, one not so useful, a physical failure, for
instance—one blind or halt or maimed—would look upon
it as maleficent, a brooding, destructive demon, rejoicing in evil. Neither hypothesis is correct. It is as good
as the successful and happy feel it to be—as bad as the
miserable think it is bad—only it is neither. It is something so large and strange and above our understanding
that it can scarcely sense the pain or joy of one single
individual—only the pains or joys of masses.

It recognizes only a mass delight or a mass sorrow.
Can you share, or understand, the pains or delights of
any one single atom in your body? You cannot. Why
may there not be an oversoul that bears the same relationship to you that you bear to the individual atoms or
ions of your physical cosmos? Some undernourished,
partially developed ion in you may cry, "The power
which rules me is a devil." But you are not a devil. Nor
does it necessarily follow that the thing that makes you
is one. You really could not help that particular atom
if you would. So over us may be this oversoul which
is as helpless in regard to us as we are in regard to our
constituent atoms. It is a product of something else
still larger—above it. There is no use trying to find
out what that is. Let the religionist call it God if he
will, or the sufferer a devil. Do you bring all your forti-
tude and courage to bear, and do all that you can to
keep yourself busy—serenely employed. There is no
other answer. Get all you can that will make you or
others happy. Think as seriously as you may. Count

all the costs and all the dangers—or don't count them, just as you will—but live as fully and intelligently as you can. If, in spite of cross currents of mood and passion, you can make any other or others happy, do so. It will be hard at best. But strive to be employed. It is the only surcease against the evil of too much thought.

CHAPTER XLV

AN INDIANA VILLAGE

WHILE we were sitting on the veranda—Franklin's father and myself—Speed came by on his way down town, and Mr. Booth, having gathered a sense of approval, perhaps, for the pornographic document from my attitude, drew it out and showed it to him.

"Gee!" exclaimed Speed, after reading it. "I must get some of those."

Soon after, Franklin came out and, seeing the document and reading it, seemed troubled over the fact that his father should be interested in such a thing. I think he felt that it threw an unsatisfactory light on his sire, or that I, not understanding, might think so; but, after I made it clear that it was more or less of a Cervantesque bit of humor to me, he became more cheerful.

A little while thereafter we went downtown, Franklin and I, to inspect the village, and to see some of those peculiar natives of whom he had been talking. I think he must have a much better eye for rural and countryside types and their idiosyncrasies than I have, for I failed to gather any of those gay nuances which somehow he had made me feel were there. Little things in rural life which probably attract and hold his attention entirely escape me, as, for instance, the gaunt and spectacled old gentleman looking over his glasses into the troublesome works of his very small Ford. My own powers of observation in that direction, and my delight in them, are limited to a considerable extent by my sense of drama. Is a thing dramatic? Or at least potentially so? If not, it is apt to lose interest for me. As for Franklin, he was never weary of pointing out little things, and I enjoyed almost more of what was to be seen here and elsewhere because of his powers of indication than from my own observation.

Thus, on the way west, he had been telling me of one man who was almost always more or less sick, or thought he was, because, through one of the eccentricities of hypochondria, he discovered that one got more attention, if not sympathy, being sick than well. And when we came to the postoffice door here he was before it, complaining of a pain in his chest! It seemed to me, in looking at him, that by a process of thinking, if that were really true, he had made himself ill. He looked "very poorly," as he expressed it, and as though he might readily sink into a destructive illness. Yet Franklin assured me that there had really been nothing the matter with him to begin with, but that jealousy of sympathy bestowed upon a cripple, the one who was to run our car for us south from here, had caused him to resort to this method of getting some for himself!

Also, there was another young man who had been described to me as a village wag—one of three or four who were certain to amuse me; but when he now came forward to greet me, and I was told that this was the person, I was not very much interested. He was of the type that has learned to consider himself humorous, necessarily so, with a reputation for humor to sustain. "I must be witty," says such a one to himself, and so the eye is always cocked, the tongue or body set for a comic remark or movement. The stranger feels obliged by the very atmosphere which goes with such a person to smile anticipatorially, as who should say, something deliciously funny is soon to be said. I did not hear anything very humorous said, however.

Incidentally, I also met Bert, the crippled boy, who was to be our chauffeur south from this point. He was a youth in whose career Franklin seemed greatly interested, largely, I think, because other people of the village were inclined to be indifferent to or make sport of him. The boy was very bright and of a decidedly determined and characterful nature. Although both legs, below the hips, but not below the ankles, were practically useless, due to a schooltime wrestling bout and fall, he managed with the aid of a pair of crutches to get about with considerable ease and speed. There was no least trace of weakness or complaint or need of sympathy in his manner. Indeed, he seemed more self-reliant and upstanding than most of the other people I met here. How, so crippled, he would manage to run the car puzzled me. Franklin's father had already expressed himself to me as opposed to the idea.

"I can't understand what he sees in that fellow," he said to me early this morning. "He's a reckless little devil, and I don't think he really knows anything about machinery. Frank will stick to him, though. If it were my machine, I wouldn't have him near it."

Now that I looked at Bert, though, I felt that he had so much courage and hope and optimism—such an intriguing look in his eyes—that I quite envied him. He was assistant mail clerk or something at the post office, and when I came up and had been introduced through the window, he promptly handed me out several letters. When I told Franklin what his father had said, he merely smiled. "The old man is always talking like that," he said. "Bert's all right. He's better than Speed."

It takes a certain slow-moving type of intellect to enjoy or endure life in a small country town. To be a doctor in a place like this! or a lawyer! or a merchant! or a clerk!

In the main, in spite of many preliminary descriptions, Carmel did not interest me as much as I thought it would, or might. It was interesting—as one says with the wave of a hand or a shrug of the shoulders. Of more import to me was the Booth household, and the peculiar girl who would not come out to greet me at first, and Franklin's father and mother and sister. This day passed rather dully, reading proofs which had been sent me and listening to passing expresses which tore through here northward and southward, to and from Indianapolis, only fifteen miles away—never even hesitating, as the negro said—and listening to the phonograph, on which I put all the records I could find. Three recitations by James Whitcomb Riley, "Little Orphant Annie," "The Raggedy Man" and "My Grandfather Squeers," captured my fancy so strongly that I spent several hours just listening to them over and over, they were so delightful. Then I would vary my diet with Tchaikowsky, Mendelssohn, Beethoven and Bert Williams.

During the afternoon Franklin and I went for a walk in a nearby woods—a beech and oak grove—the beeches occupying one section and the oaks another. Truly, grey and lowery described this day. It was raining, but in addition the clouds hung so low and thick and dark that they were almost smothery in their sense of closeness. And it was warm and damp, quite like a Turkish bath. I had arrayed myself in great thigh-length rubber boots borrowed from Franklin's father, and my raincoat and a worthless old cap, so that I was independent of the long, dripping wet grass and the frequent pools of water.

"I know what I'll do," I exclaimed suddenly. "I'll go in swimming. It's just the day. Fine!"

When we reached the stream in the depth of the woods I was even more enchanted with the idea, the leafy depth of the hollow was so dark and wet, the water so seething and yellow, a veritable whirlpool, made so by the heavy rains everywhere about. Franklin would not come in with me. Instead, he stood on the shore and told me local tales of growths and deaths and mishaps and joys to many.

My problem was how to undress without getting my clothes wet and my feet so muddy when I came out that I could not put on my boots. By thought I solved it. I took off my raincoat, spread it down on the shore as a floor, then took off my boots and stood on it, dry and clean. Under one corner of it I tucked all my clothes to protect them from the rain; then, naked, I plunged into the swirling, boiling flood. It nearly swept me away, so terrific was the onslaught of the waters. I caught a branch hanging low, and, with my feet braced

against a few rocks below, lay flat and let the water rush
over me. It was wonderful to lie in this warm, yellow
water, a bright gold color, really, and feel it go foaming over my breast and arms and legs. It tugged at me
so, quite like a wrestling man, that I had to fight it to
keep up. My arms ached after a time, but I hung on,
loving the feel of it. Sticks and leaves went racing past.
I would kick up a stone and instantly it would be swept
onward toward some better lodging place farther down.
I figured an angle finally by which I could make shore,
letting go and paddling sidewise, and so I did, coming
up bumped and scratched, but happy. Then I dipped
my feet in the water, stood on my raincoat, drying myself with my handkerchief, and finally, dressed and refreshed, strode up shore.

Then we went off flower gathering, and made a big
bouquet of iron weed. He told me how for years he
had been coming to this place, how he loved the great
oaks and the silvery beeches, huddled in a friendly company to the north, and how he had always wanted to
paint them and some day would. The mania people have
for cutting their names on beech trunks came up, for here
were so many covered with lover's hearts—their names
inside—and so many inscriptions, all but obliterated by
time that I could not help thinking how lives flow by
quite like the water in the stream below.

Then we went back, to a fine chicken dinner and a
banana pie made especially for me, and the phonograph
and the rushing trains, the whistles of which I was never
tired hearing—they sounded so sad.

Another black, rainy night, and then the next morning the sun came up on one of the most perfect days
imaginable. It was dewy and glistening and fragrant
and colorful—a wonder world. What with the new wet
trees and grass as cool and delightful as any day could
be, it was like paradise. There was a warm south wind.
I went out on the lawn and played ball with Franklin,
missing three fourths of all throws and nearly breaking
my thumb. I sat on the porch and looked over the morn-

ing paper, watching the outing automobiles of many natives go spinning by and feeling my share in that thrill and tingle which comes over the world on a warm Sunday morning in summer. It was so lovely. You could just feel that everybody everywhere was preparing to have a good time and that nothing mattered much. All the best Sunday suits, all the new straw hats, all the dainty frocks, all the everything were being brought forth and put on. Franklin disappeared for an hour and came back looking so spick and span and altogether Sunday—summery—and like Ormonde and Miami Beach, that I felt quite out of it. I had a linen suit and white shoes and a sport hat, but somehow I felt that they were a little uncalled for here, and my next best wasn't as good as his. Curses! He even had on perfect, glistening, glorious patent leather shoes, and a new blue suit.

It was while I was sitting here inwardly groaning over my fate that a young girl came swinging up, one of the most engaging I had seen anywhere on this trip—a lithe, dancing figure, with bright blue eyes, chestnut hair and an infectious smile. I had observed her approaching some seventy feet away, and beside her Speed, and I was wondering whether she was merely a town girl of his acquaintance or by any chance that half sister of whom I had heard Franklin and Speed speaking on the way west, saying that she was very talented and was hoping to come to New York to study music. Before I had time to do more than compliment her in my mind, she was here before me, having tripped across the grass in a fascinating way, and was holding out a hand and laughing into my eyes.

"We've been hearing about your coming for several days now. Speed wrote us nearly a week ago that you might come."

It flattered me to be so much thought of.

"I've been hearing nice things of you, too," I said, studying her pretty nose and chin and the curls about her forehead. In any *apologia pro vita sua* which I may ever compose, I will confess frankly and heartily to a weakness for beauty in the opposite sex.

She seemed inclined to talk, but was a little bashful. From her general appearance I gathered that she was not only of a gay, lightsome disposition, but a free soul, spiritually as yet not depressed by the local morality of the day—the confining chains of outward appearances and inward, bonehead fears. I had the feeling that she was beginning to be slightly sex conscious without having solved any of its intricacies as yet—just a humming bird, newly on the wing. She hung about, answering and asking questions of no import. Presently Speed had to leave and she went along, with a brisk, swinging step. As she neared the corner of the lawn she turned just for a second and smiled.

.   .   .   .

Apropos of this situation and these two girls who curiously and almost in spite of myself were uppermost in my mind—the second one most particularly, I should like to say—that of all things in life which seem to me to be dull and false, it is the tendency of weak souls in letters and in life to gloze over this natural chemical action and reaction between the sexes, to which we are all subject, and to make a pretence that our thoughts are something which they are not—sweet, lovely, noble, pure. It has become a duty among males and females, quite too much so, I think, to conceal from each other and from themselves, even, the fact that physical beauty in the opposite sex stirs them physically and mentally, naturally leading to thoughts of union.

What has come over life that it has become so superfine in its moods? Why should we make such a puritanic row over the natural instincts of man? I will admit that in part nature herself is the cause of this, the instinct to restrain being possibly as great as the instinct to liberate, and that she demands that you make a pretence and live a lie, only it seems to me it would be a little better for the mental health of the race if it were more definitely aware of this. Certainly it ought not be connected with religious illusion. It may not be possible, because of the varying temperaments of people, for anyone to express what he feels or thinks at any precise moment—its reception is too uncertain—but surely it is permissible in print, which is not unakin in its character to the Catholic confessional, to say what one knows to be so.

All normal men crave women—and particularly beautiful women. All married men and priests are supposed, by the mere sacrament of matrimony or holy orders, thereafter to feel no interest in any but one (or in the case.of the priest none) of the other sex—or if they do, to rigidly suppress such desires. But men are men! And the women—many married and unmarried ones—don't want them to be otherwise. Life is a dizzy, glittering game of trapping and fishing and evading, and slaying and pursuing, despite all the religious and socalled moral details by which we surround it. Nature itself has an intense love of the chase. It loves snares, pitfalls, gins, traps, masks and mummeries, and even murder and death —yes, very much murder and death. It loves nothing so much as to build up a papier-mâché wall of convention, and then slip round or crash through it. It has erected a phantasmagoria of laws which no one can understand, and no one can strictly adhere to without disaster, and to which few do strictly adhere. Justice, truth, mercy, right are all abstractions and not to be come at by any series of weights or measures. We pocket our unfair losses or unearned gains and smile at our luck. Curiously, in finance and commercial affairs men understand this and accept it as a not altogether bad game. It has the element in it which they recognize as sport. When it comes to sex, the feeling becomes somewhat more serious. A man who will smile at the loss of a hundred, a thousand, or even a million dollars, will pull a grim countenance over the loss of a wife or a daughter. Death is the price in the judgment of some temperaments. In others it is despair. Why? And yet nature plans these traps and pitfalls. It is the all mother who schemes the

Circe and Hellenic temperaments—the fox, the wolf, the lion. A raging, destroying bull, which insists on gormandizing all the females of a herd, is the product of nature, not of man. Man did not make the bull or the stallion, nor did they make themselves. Is nature to be controlled, made over, by man, according to some theory which man, a product of nature, has discovered?

Gentlemen, here is food for a dozen schools of philosophy! Personally, I do not see that any theory or any code or any religion that has yet been devised solves anything. All that one can intelligently say is that they satisfy certain temperaments. Like those theorems and formulæ in algebra and chemistry, which aid the student without solving anything in themselves, they make the living of life a little easier—for some. They are not a solution. They do not make over temperaments which are not adapted to their purposes. They do not assist the preternaturally weak, or restrain the super-strong. They merely, like a certain weave of mesh in fishing, hold some and let others get away—the very big and the very little.

What sort of moralic scheme is that, anyhow, which governs thus? And why is poor, dull man such a universal victim of it?

CHAPTER XLVI

A SENTIMENTAL INTERLUDE

As we had planned it, we were to stay in Carmel only three days—from Friday until Monday—and then race south to Indianapolis, Terre Haute, Sullivan, Evansville, French Lick, Bloomington, back to Indianapolis, and after a day or night at Carmel for preparation, I might depart as I had planned, or I could stay here. Franklin suggested that I make his home my summering place—my room was mine for weeks if I cared to use it.

Actually up to now I had been anxious to get on and have the whole trip done with, but here in Carmel I developed a desire to stay and rest awhile, the country about was so very simple and homey; but I concluded that I must not.

Franklin had prepared a trip for Sunday afternoon which interested me very much. It was to be to the home of a celebrated automobile manufacturer, now dead, whose name, incidentally, had been in the papers for years, first as the President of the American Manufacturers Association, a very noble organization of materialists, I take it, and secondarily as the most strenuous opponent of organized labor that the country up to his day had produced. I hold no brief for organized labor any more than I do for organized manufacturers, being firmly convinced that both are entitled to organize and fight and that to the victors should belong the spoils; but at the present writing I would certainly sympathize with organized labor as being in the main the underdog, and wish it all the luck in the world. Personally, I believe in equilibrium, with a healthy swinging of the pendulum of life and time to and fro between the rich and the poor—a pendulum which should cast down the rich of today and elevate them again tomorrow, or others like them, giving the underdog the pleasure of being the overdog quite regularly, and vice versa. I think that is what makes life interesting, if it *is* interesting.

But as to this manufacturer, in spite of the entirely friendly things Franklin had to say of him, I had heard many other stories relating to him—his contentiousness, his rule of underpaying his labor, the way he finally broke down on a trip somewhere and forgot all the details of it, a blank space in his mind covering a period of two years. Franklin told me of his home, which was much more pleasant to hear about—a place down by a river near Indianapolis. According to Franklin, a good part of the estate was covered with a grove of wonderful trees, mostly beech. As you came to the place there was a keeper's lodge by the gate which made you feel as if you were entering the historic domain of some old nobleman. The house was along a beautiful winding drive, bordered with a hedge of all sorts of flowers usually in bloom all through the summer. The house was very much hidden among the beech trees, a large red brick structure with many windows and tall chimneys; the lower story constructed of large field boulders, such as are found here. At the front and at the left of the main entrance this masonry projected to make an immense porch, with wide massive arches and posts of the same great boulders.

"The first time I ever saw it," Franklin explained, "I stepped out of the car and went up to ring the bell. It was a warm day, and Mrs. ——— was sitting alone at the left end of this great porch, quietly observing a colored man servant who was playing a hose on the vines and the main inside wall of the porch, apparently to partly cool the atmosphere. She is a little, sweet, quiet woman, and as she rose to greet me, something in the great house and the boulders and in the quietness of the forest air about us, and perhaps in the gentle humility of the woman herself, came to me and impressed me with the utter futility of building houses at all; and of any man building a house beyond the ability of a woman to touch lovingly with her hands and to care for and make a home of. Some time later when I entered the house she was sitting alone in the great hall in the sort of dusk that pervaded it. I somehow felt that the house opposed her; that it was her enemy. I don't know; I may be wrong; it was only an impression."

I have reproduced Franklin's description as near as I can.

Of course I was interested to go. It promised a fine afternoon; only when the hour struck and we were off in our best feathers, two tires blew up and we were lucky to get to a garage. We limped back to Carmel, and I returned to my rocking chair on the front porch, watching cars from apparently all over the state go by, and wondering what had become of the two girls I had met —they had disappeared for the day, apparently—and what could I do to amuse myself. I listened to stories of local eccentricities, freaks of character, a man who had died and left a most remarkable collection of stuffed birds and animals, quite a museum, which he had elaborated while running a bakery, or something of that sort—and so on and so forth. Local morality came in for its usual drubbing—the lies which people live—the things which they seem and are not. Personally, I like this subtlety of nature—I would not have all things open and aboveboard for anything. I like pretence when it is not snivelling, Pecksniffery, calculated to injure someone for the very crimes or deceits which you yourself are committing. Such rats should always be pulled from their holes and exposed to the light.

Sitting on the veranda—Franklin felt called upon to do some work in his studio, a very attractive building at the rear of the lawn—I grew lonely and even despondent! It is a peculiarity of my nature that I suffer these spells out of a clear sky and at a moment's notice. I can be having the best time in the world, apparently (I am often amused thinking about it), and then

of a sudden, the entertainment ceasing, the situation
changing, I find myself heavily charged with gloom. I
am getting old! (I had these same spells at nineteen and
twenty.) Life is slipping on and away! Relatives and
friends are dying! Nothing endures! Fame is a
damned mockery! Affection is insecure or self-destroy-
ing! Soon I am in the last stages of despair and looking
around for some means (speculatively purely) to end it
all. It is really too amusing—*afterwards.*

While I was so meditating the first young girl came
back, with that elusive, enigmatic smile of hers, and two
underdone striplings of about eighteen or nineteen, and
another girl, intended largely as a foil. She was most
becomingly and tantalizingly dressed in something which
defies description, and played croquet—with the two
youths who were persistently seeking her favor and ignoring the other maiden. I watched her until I became irritated by her coy self sufficiency, and the art with which
she was managing the situation,—a thing which included
me as someone to disturb, too. I got up and moved
round to the other side of the house.

That night after dinner, Franklin and I went to Indianapolis on the trolley, and ignoring all the sights
went to a great hotel grill, where, entirely surrounded
by onyx and gilt and prism-hung candelabra, we had beer
in a teapot, with teacups as drinking vessels, it being
"against the law" to serve beer on Sunday. For the
same reason it cost seventy cents—two humble "schoon-
ers" of beer—for of course there was the service and
the dear waiter with his itching palm.

By ten-thirty the next morning the car, overhauled and
cleaned, was at the door, our new chauffeur at the wheel,
ready for the run south.

I carried my bags down, put them into the car, and
sat in it to wait. Franklin was off somewhere, in the
heart of the village, arranging something. Suddenly I
heard a voice. It had the tone I expected. Actually, I
had anticipated it, in a psychic way. Looking up and

across a space of lawn two houses away, I saw the second girl of this meeting place standing out under an apple tree, with a little boy beside her, an infant the Speed family had adopted.

She was most gay in her dress and mood—something eery and sylph-like.

"Aren't you coming over to say goodby?" she called.

I jumped up, ashamed of my lack of gallantry, and yet excusing myself on the ground that I was too timid to intrude before, and strolled over. She received me with a disturbed cordiality which was charming.

"It's right mean of you," she said.

"I was coming," I protested, "only I expected to put it over until Thursday—on my way back. That sounds rather bad, doesn't it, but really I wanted to come, only I was a little bit afraid."

"You—afraid?"

"Yes. Don't you think I can be?"

"Yes, but not of us, I should think. I thought maybe you were going away for good without saying goodby."

"Now, how could you?" I protested, knowing full well to the contrary. "How nice we look today. Such a pretty dress and the clean white shoes—and the ribbon."

She was as gay and fluffy as a bit out of a bandbox.

"Oh, no, I just put these on because I had to wear them about the house this morning." She smiled in a simple, agreeable way, only I fancied that she might have dressed on purpose.

"Well, anyhow," I said—and we began to talk of school and her life and what she wanted to do. Just as I was becoming really interested, Franklin appeared, carrying a package. "Alas, here he is. And now I'll have to be going soon."

"Yes," she said, quite simply, and with a little feeling. "You'll be coming back, though."

"But only for a day, I'm afraid."

"But you won't go away the next time without saying goodby, will you?"

"Isn't that kind of you," I replied. "Are you sure you want me to say goodby?"

"Indeed I do. I'll feel hurt if you don't." She held out her hand. There was a naïve simplicity about it all that quite disarmed me and made it all innocent and charming.

"Don't you think I won't?" I asked, teasingly. And then as I looked at her she blanched in an odd, disturbed way, and turning to the boy called, "Come on, Billy," and ran to a side porch door, smiling back at me.

"You won't forget," she called back from that safe place.

CHAPTER XLVII

INDIANAPOLIS, the first city on our way south and west, was another like Cleveland, Buffalo, Toledo, only without the advantage of a great lake shore which those cities possess. It is boasted as one of the principal railroad centers of America, or the world. Good, but what of it? Once you have seen the others, it has nothing to teach you, and I grow tired of the mere trade city devoid of any plan or charm of natural surroundings. The best of the European cities, or of later years, Chicago and New York—Chicago from the lake, vast, frowning giant that it is, and New York, like a pearly cloud lying beyond her great green wet meadows on her sea—ho, Americans, there are two pictures! Travel far and wide, see all that the earth has to show, view Delhi, Venice, Karnak, the sacred temples of the Ganges—there are no such scenes as these. Already one beholds them with a kind of awe, conscious that they may not be duplicated within a thousand or two thousands of years. What could be more astounding than New York's financial area, or Chicago's commercial heart!

All that these minor American cities like Indianapolis (and I do not wish to belittle my own state or its capital) have to show is a few high buildings in imitation of New York or Chicago. If any one of them had any natural advantages which would suggest a difference in treatment, they would not follow it. No, no, let us be like Chicago or New York—as like as we may. A few artistic low buildings might have more appeal, but that would not be like New York. A city may even have been laid out perfectly, like Savannah, but do you think it appreciates its difference sufficiently to wish to remain so? Never! Destroy the old, the different, and let's be like New York! Every time I see one of these tenth-rate imitations, copying these great whales, I want to swear.

Yet, aside from this, Indianapolis was not so bad—not unpleasing in places, really. There is a river there, the White, with which nothing seems to have been done except to build factories on it at one place; but, on the other hand, a creek called Broad Ripple—pretty name, that—has been walled and parked and made most agreeable to look upon.

One or two streets, it seemed to me, were rather striking, lined as they were with pretentious dwellings and surrounded by gardens and enclosed in walls—but, oh, the little streets, the little streets!

"Here is where Senator Fairbanks lives."

"There is where Benjamin Harrison lived before he became President."

Quite so! Quite so! But I am thinking of the little streets just the same, and the great, inordinate differences between things at times.

Franklin pointed out the First and Second Churches of Christ, Scientist—large, artistic, snow-white buildings—and a little later, at my request, the home of James Whitcomb Riley, laureate of all that perfect company of Hoosiers to be found in his sympathetic, if small, volumes. I revere James Whitcomb with a whole heart. There is something so delicate, so tender, so innocent not only about his work but about him. His house in Lockerbie Street was about as old and homely as it could be, as indeed was Lockerbie Street itself—but, shucks, who cares. Let the senators and the ex-presidents and the beef packers have the big places. What should the creator of "Old Doc Sifers" be doing in a great house, anyhow? Think of "Little Orphant Annie" being born in a mansion! Never. Only over my dead body. We didn't go in. I wanted to, but I felt a little bashful. As I say, I had heard that he didn't approve of me. I suggested that we might come another time, Franklin knowing him quite well; but I knew I wouldn't. Yet all my loving thoughts went out to him—most sympathetic and pleasing wishes for a long life and a happy life.

The run to Terre Haute was more or less uninteresting, a flat and lifeless country. We arrived there at nearly dusk, entering along a street whose name was changed to Wabash shortly after my brother's song became so popular. Among the first things I saw were the buildings and grounds of the Rose Polytechnic Institute—an institution which, famous though it is, was only of interest to me because the man who founded it, Chauncey Rose, was once a friend and admirer of my father's. At the time my father's mill burned in Sullivan and he was made penniless, it was this man who came forward and urged him to begin anew, offering to advance him the money. But my father was too much of a religious and financial and moral coward to risk it. He was doubtful of success—his nerve had been broken—and he feared he might not be able to repay Mr. Rose and so, in event of his dying, his soul would be in danger of purgatory. Of such is the religious mind.

. . . .

But this city of my birth! Now that I was in it, it had a strong and mournful fascination for me. Nothing that I was doing or being was altered thereby, but——

Suppose, once upon a time in a very strange wonderland, so wonderful that no mere earthborn mortal could tell anything about it or make you feel how wonderful it was, you had been a very little boy who had gotten in there somehow (how, he could not tell) and after a very few years had been taken out again, and never after that saw it any more. And that during that time many strange and curious things happened—things so strange and curious that, though you lived many years afterward and wandered here and there and to and fro upon the earth, still the things that happened in that wonderland, the colors of it and the sounds and the voices and the trees, were ever present, like a distant mirage or a background of very far off hills, but still present.

And supposing, let us say, that in this strange land there was once a house, or two or three or four or five houses, what difference? In one of them (someone later said it stood at Twelfth and Walnut in a city called Terre Haute, but if you went there now you could not find it) there was a cellar, damp and dark. The mother of the little boy, to whose skirts he used to cling when anything troubled or frightened him, once told him that in the cellar of this house lived a Cat-man, and that if he went near it, let alone down into it, the Cat-man might appear and seize him and carry him off.

The small boy firmly believed in the Cat-man. He listened at times and thought he heard him below stairs, stirring about among the boxes and barrels there. In his mind's eye he saw him, large and dark and toothy, a Hottentot's dream of a demon. Finally, after meditating over it awhile, he got his brother Ed and conferred with him about it. They decided that Prince, the family dog, might help to chase the Cat-man out, and so rid them of this evil. Prince, the dog, was no coward; a friendly, gay, and yet ferocious animal. He was yellow and lithe, a fighter. He plainly believed in the Cat-man too (upon request, anyhow), for the cellar stairs door being opened and the presence of the Cat-man indicated, he sniffed and barked and made such an uproar that the mother of the children came out and made them go into the yard. And then they heard her laughing over the reality of the Cat-man, and exclaiming: "Yes, indeed, you'd just better be careful and not go down there. He'll catch Prince too!"

But then there was a certain tree in this same yard or garden where once of a spring evening, at dusk, there was a strange sound being made, a sawing and rasping which in later years the boy was made quite well aware was a locust. But just at that time, at that age, in that strange land, with the soft, amethystine shadows pouring about the world, it seemed as though it must be the Cat-man come at last out of the cellar and gotten into the tree. The child was all alone. His mother was in the house. Sitting on the back porch meditating over the childish interests of the day, this sound began—and then the next minute he was frantically clasping his mother's knees, burying his face in her skirts and weeping. "The Cat-man! The Cat-man!" (Oh, what a horror! sawing there in that tree and leering! The child saw his eyes!)

And then the mother said: "No, there isn't any Cat-man; it is all a foolish fancy. There, there!" But to the child, for a long time, he was real enough, just the same.

And then there was "Old Mr. Watchman," an old man with one arm who used to come by the house where the small boy lived. He was a watchman somewhere at a railroad crossing, a solid, weary, brown faced white haired man who in winter wore a heavy great coat, in summer a loose, brown jacket, the pockets of which, or one pocket, at least, always, and every day, nearly, contained something which, if the little boy would only hurry out each morning or evening and climb on the fence and reach for, he might have.

"Mr. Watchman! Mr. Watchman!" I can hear him crying yet.

And somehow I seem to see a kindly gleam in the old blue eyes, and a smile on the brown face, and a big, rough hand going over a very little head.

"Yes, there we have it. That's the nice boy."

And then someone would call from the house or the gate, a father or mother, perhaps, "And now what do we say?"

"Oh, thank you, Mr. Watchman. Thank you."

And then the old watchman would go trudging onward with his bucket on his arm, and the boy would munch his candy or his peanuts or his apple and forget how kind and strange old Mr. Watchman really was— and how pathetic.

Then one day, some time later, after a considerable

absence or silence on the part of Mr. Watchman, the small boy was taken to see him where he was lying very still in a very humble little cottage, in a black box, with nickels on his eyes—and the little boy wanted to take the nickels, too.

Don't you suppose Mr. Watchman must have smiled, wherever he was, if he could?

And then one last picture, though I might recall a hundred from fairyland—a thousand. It is a hot day and a house with closed shutters and drawn blinds, and in the center of a cool, still room a woman sitting in a loose negligée, and at her feet the child playing with the loose, worn slippers on her feet. The boy is very interested in his mother, he loves her, and for that reason, to his small mind her feet and her worn slippers are very dear to him.

"See poor mama's shoes. Aren't you sorry for her? Think how she has to wear such poor torn shoes and how hard she has to work."

"Yes, poor shoes. Poor mummy."

"When you grow up are you going to get work and buy poor mother a good pair—like a nice, strong, big man?"

"Yes, work. Yes, I get mummy shoes."

Suddenly, something in the mother's voice is too moving. Some mystic thread binding the two operates to convey and enlarge a mood. The child bursts into tears over the old pattens. He is gathered up close, wet eyed, and the mother cries too.

.   .   .   .

At the same time, this city of my birth was identified with so much struggle on the part of my parents, so many dramas and tragedies in connection with relatives and friends, that by now it seemed quite wonderful as the scene of almost an epic. I might try to indicate the exact character of it as it related to me; but instead, here at any rate, I will only say that from the time the mill burned until after various futile attempts to right ourselves, at Sullivan and Evansville, we finally left this part of the country for good, it was one unbroken stretch of privation and misery.

In that brilliant and yet defective story entitled "The Turn of the Balance," by Brand Whitlock, there is narrated the career of an unfortunate German family which might almost have been ours, only in order to deal with so many children as there were in our family, the causes would necessarily have been further enlarged, or the data greatly condensed. In addition, there was no such complete collapse involved. The more I think of my father, and the more I consider the religious and fearful type of mind in general, the more certain I am that mere breeding of lives (raising a family without the skill to engineer it through the difficulties of infancy and youth) is one of the most pathetic, albeit humanly essential, blunders which the world contains. Yet, and perhaps wisely so, it is repeated over and over, age in and age out, *ad infinitum*. Governments love large families. These provide population, recruit large armies and navies, add the necessary percentage to the growth of cities and countries, fill the gaping maws of the factories. The churches love large families, for they bring recruits to them and give proof of that solid morality which requires that sex shall result in more children and that these shall be adequately raised in the fear of God, if not in the comforts of life. Manufacturers and strong men generally like large families. Where else would they get the tools wherewith they work—the cheap labor— and the amazing contrasts between poverty and wealth, the contemplation of which gives them such a satisfaction in their own worth and force? Nature loves large families, apparently, because she makes so many of them. Vice must love large families because from them, and out of their needs and miseries, it is principally recruited. Death must love them too, for it gathers its principal toll there. But if an ordinary working man, or one without a serene and forceful capacity for toil and provision, could see the ramifications and miseries of birth in poverty, he would not reproduce himself so freely.

My father was of that happy religionistic frame of mind which sees in a large family—a very large family indeed, for there were thirteen of us—the be all and the end all of human existence. For him work, the rearing of children, the obligations of his religion and the liberal fulfilling of all his social obligations, imaginary or otherwise, were all that life contained. He took life to be not what it is, but what it is said to be, or written to be, by others. The Catholic volumes containing that inane balderdash, "The Lives of the Saints," were truer than any true history—if there is such a thing—to him. He believed them absolutely. The pope was infallible. If you didn't go to confession and communion at least once a year, you were eternally damned. I recall his once telling me that, if a small bird were to come only once every million or trillion years and rub its bill on a rock as big as the earth, the rock would be worn out before a man would see the end of hell—eternal, fiery torture—once he was in it. And then he would not see the end of it, but merely the beginning, as it were. I recall invoking his rather heated contempt, on this occasion, by asking (or suggesting, I forget which) whether God might not change His mind about hell and let somebody out after a time. It seemed to him that I was evidently blasphemously bumptious, and that I was trifling with sacred things!

Unfortunately for him, though really not for us, I think, in the long run, his children were differently minded. Owing to an arrogant and domineering disposition, he insisted on the first ten, or first five, let us say, being educated in the then Catholic parochial schools, where they learned nothing at all. Just before his failure, or the fire which ruined him, he gave the ground on which the church and school of St. Joseph in Terre Haute now stand, to the rector of that parish. Priests and bishops had the run of our home in the days when we were prosperous. After that they did not come so much, except to demand to know this, that, or the other, or to complain of our conduct. After my father's failure, and because he did not feel himself courageous enough to venture on a new enterprise with the aid of the wealthy Mr. Rose, the then sufficiently grown children were supposed to go to work, the girls as housemaids, if necessary (for their education having been nothing, they had no skill for anything else), the boys as "hands" in the mill, the one thing my father knew most about, if they would (which they wouldn't), in order to learn a trade of some kind.

Instead there was a revolt. They broke out into the world to suit themselves. To save expenses, my mother had taken the three youngest, Ed, Clair (or Tillie, as we always called her) and myself, first to a friend at Vincennes, Indiana, for a few weeks' stay, then to Sullivan, where we remained two years trying to maintain ourselves as best we could; thence to Evansville, where, my brother Paul having established himself rather comfortably, we remained two more; thence to Warsaw (via Chicago), where we remained three years and where I received my only intelligent schooling; thence out into the world, for the three youngest of us, at least, to become, as chance might have it, such failures or successes as may be. The others, too, after one type of career and another, did well enough. Paul, for one, managed to get a national reputation as a song writer and to live in comfort and even luxury. All of the girls, after varying years and degrees of success or failure, married and settled down to the average troubles of the married. One of these, the third from the eldest, was killed by a train in Chicago in her thirtysecond year, in 1897. One brother—the youngest (two years younger than myself) —became an actor. The brother next older than myself became an electrician. The fourth eldest, and one of the most interesting of all, as it seemed to me, a railroad man by profession, finally died of drunkenness (alcoholism is a nicer word) in a South Clark Street dive in Chicago, about 1905. So it goes. But all of them, in their way, were fairly intelligent people, no worse and no better than the average.

I can see the average smug, conventional soul, if one such should ever chance to get so deep into this book, chilling and sniffing over this frank confession. My answer is that, if he knows as much about life as I do or has the courage to say what he really knows or believes, he would neither be chilling or sniffing. If any individual in this dusty world has anything to be ashamed of, it is certainly not the accidents, ignorances and stark vicissitudes with which we are all more or less confronted. These last may be pathetic, but they have the merit nearly always of great and even beautiful drama; whereas, the treacheries, shams and poltrooneries which make for the creation and sustenance of the sniffy and the smug are really the things to be ashamed of. I can only think of Christ's scathing denunciation of scribes, hypocrites and pharisees and his reference to the mote and the beam.

. . . .

In Terre Haute, not elsewhere, we moved so often for want of means to pay our rent, or to obtain cheaper places, that it is almost painful to think of it in retrospect, though at the time I was too young to know anything much about it. There was so much sickness in the family, and at this time a certain amount of ill feeling between my mother and father. Several of the girls ran away and (in seeming, only in so far as the beliefs of my father were concerned) went to the bad. They did not go to the bad actually as time subsequently proved, though I might disagree with many as to what is bad and what good. One of the boys, Paul, got into jail, quite innocently it seems, and was turned out by my father, only to be received back again and subsequently to become his almost sole source of support in his later years. There was gloom, no work, often no bread, or scarcely any, in the house. Strange shifts were resorted to. My mother, and my father, for that matter, worked and slaved. Both, but she in particular, I am sure, because of her ambitious, romantic temperament, suffered the tortures of the damned.

Alas, she never lived to see our better days! My father did.

But Terre Haute! Terre Haute!

Here I was entering it now for the first time since I had left it, between seven and eight years of age, exactly thirtyseven years before.

CHAPTER XLVIII

THE SPIRIT OF TERRE HAUTE

ASIDE from these perfervid memories in connection with it, Terre Haute was not so different from Fort Wayne, or even Sandusky, minus the lake. It had the usual main street (Wabash Avenue) lighted with many lamps, the city hall, postoffice, principal hotel, and theatres; but I will say this for it, it seemed more vital than most of these other places—more like Wilkes-Barré or Binghamton. I asked Franklin about this, and he said that he felt it had exceptional vitality—something different.

"I can't tell you what it is," he said. "I have heard boys up in Carmel and Indianapolis who have been down here say it was a 'hot town.' I can understand now something of what they mean. It has a young, hopeful, seeking atmosphere. I like it."

That was just how it seemed to me, after he had expressed it—"a seeking atmosphere." Although it claimed a population of only sixtyseven thousand or thereabouts, it had the tang and go of a much larger place. That something which I have always noticed about American cities and missed abroad, more or less, unless it was in Rome, Paris and Berlin, was here,—a crude, sweet illusion about the importance of all things material. What lesser god, under the high arch of life itself, weaves this spell? What is it man is seeking, that he is so hungry, so lustful? These little girls and boys, these half-developed men and women with their white faces and their seeking hands—oh, the pathos of it all!

Before going to an hotel for dinner, we drove across the Wabash River on a long, partially covered bridge, to what I thought was the Illinois side, but which was only a trans-Wabash extension of Vigo County. Coming back, the night view of the city was so fine—tall chimneys and factories darkling along the upper and lower shores with a glow of gold in the center—that Franklin insisted he must make a memory note, something to help him do a better thing later, so we paused on the bridge while he sketched the lovely scene by arc light. Then we came back to the Terre Haute House (or the Terrible Hot House, as my brother Paul used to call it), where, for sentimental reasons, I preferred to stop, though there was a newer and better hotel, the Deming, farther up the street. For here, once upon a time, my brother Rome, at that time a seeking boy like any of those we now saw pouring up and down this well lighted street—(up and down, up and down, day after day, like those poor moths we see about the lamp)—was in the habit of coming, and, as my father described it, in his best suit of clothes and his best shoes, a toothpick in his mouth, standing in or near the doorway of the hotel, to give the impression that he had just dined there.

"Loafers! Idle, good-for-nothings!" I can hear my father exclaiming even now.

Yet he was not a loafer by any means—just a hungry, thirsty, curious boy, all too eager for the little life his limited experience or skill would buy. He was the one who finally took to drink and disappeared into the maelstrom of death—or is it life?

And here, once in her worst days, my mother came to look for work, and got it. In later years, Paul came here to be tendered a banquet by friends in the city because of his song about this river—"a tribute to the state"—as one admirer expressed it.

Not that I cared at all, really. I didn't. It wouldn't have made any vast difference if we had gone to the other hotel—only it would have, too! We arranged our belongings in our adjoining rooms and then went out for a stroll, examining the central court and the low halls and the lobby as we passed. I thought of my mother—and Rome, outside on the corner—and Paul at his sentimental banquet, and then—well, then I felt "very sad like," as we would say in Indiana.

Up the street from our hotel was the Deming, the principal hotel of this city—"our largest," as the average American would say—just like every other hotel in America which at this day and date aspires to be "our largest" and to provide the native with that something which he thinks is at once *recherché* (curse that word!) and "grand," or "gorgeous." Thus, there must be (1) a group of flamboyantly uniformed hall boys and porters, all braids and buttons, whose chief, if not sole duty, is to exact gratuities from the unwilling and yet ecstatic visitor; (2) an hotel clerk, or three or five, who will make him feel that he is a mere upstart or intruder, and that it is only by the generosity of a watchful and yet kindly management (which does not really approve of him) that he is permitted to enter at all; (3) maids, manicuresses, and newsstand salesladies, who are present solely to make him understand what he has missed by marrying, and how little his wife knows about dress, or taste, or life; (4) a lobby, lounging room, shoeshining parlor and barber shop, done entirely in imitation onyx; (5) a diningroom in imitation of one of the principal chambers of the Palace of Vairsigh; (6) a grill or men's restaurant, made to look exactly like a western architect's dream of a Burgundian baronial hall; (7) a head waiter who can be friends only with millionaires or their equivalent, the local richest men; (9) a taxi service which can charge as much if not more than any other city's. This last is absolutely indispensable, as showing the importance of the city. But nevertheless we went here, after prowling about the city for some time, to enjoy a later supper—or rather to see if there were any people here who were worth observing at this favorite American midnight pastime. There were—in their way.

Those that we saw here—in the grill—suggested at once the aspirations and the limitations of a city of this size and its commercial and social predilections. For here, between eleven and one, came many that might be called "our largest" or "our most successful" men, of a solid, resonant, generative materiality. The flare of the cloth of their suits! The blaze of their skins and eyes! The hardy, animal implication of their eyes!

And the women—elder and younger! wives and daughters of those men who have only recently begun to make money in easy sums and so to enjoy life. They reminded me of those I had seen in the Kittatinny at Delaware Water Gap. What breweries, what wagon works, what automobile factories may not have been grinding day and night for their benefit! Here they were, most circumspect, most quiescent, a gaudy and yet reserved company; but as I looked at some of them I could not help thinking of some of the places I had seen abroad, more especially the Abbaye Thélème in Paris and the Carlton at Monte Carlo, where, freed from the prying eyes of Terre Haute or Columbus or Peoria in summer or winter, the eager American abroad is free to dance and carouse and make up, in part, for some of the shortcomings of his or her situation here. Yes, you may see them there, the sons and daughters of these factory builders and paint manufacturers, a feverish hunger in their faces, making up for what Indiana or Illinois or Iowa would never permit them to do. Blood will tell, and the brooding earth forces weaving these things must have tremendous moods and yearnings which require expression thus.

But what interested me more, and this was sad too, were the tribes and shoals of the incomplete, the botched, the semi-articulate, all hungry and helpless, who never get to come to a place like this at all—who yearn for a taste of this show and flare and never attain to the least taste of it. Somehow the streets of this city suggested them to me. I know the moralists will not agree with me as to this, but what of it? Haven't you seen them of a morning—very early morning and late evening, in their shabby skirts, their shapeless waists, their messes of hats, their worn shoes, trudging to and from one wretched task and another, through the great streets and the splendid places? And are you content always to dismiss them as just dull, or weak, or incapable of understanding those finer things which you think you understand so well? Are there not some possibly who are different? Oh, you brash thinkers who dismiss them all so lightly—Not so fast, pray! Do not lean too heavily upon the significance of your present state. Tonight, tomorrow, may begin the fierce blasts that will sweep away the last vestige of what was strength, or pride, or beauty, or power, or understanding. Even now the winds of disaster may be whining under your door. A good body is something, a brain is more. Taste, beauty, these are great gifts, not achievements. And that which gave so generously can as certainly take away again. When you see them trudging so hopelessly, so painfully, their eyes riveted by the flashing wonders of life, let it be not all contempt or all pride with which you view them. Hold to your strength if you will, or your subtlety; but this night, in your heart, on your knees, make obeisance. These are tremendous forces among which we walk. With their powers and their results we may have neither part nor lot. What, slave, do you strut and stare and make light of your fellow? This night may you be with them, not in paradise, but in eternal nothingness—voiceless, dreamless, not even so much as a memory of anything elsewhere. Nothing!

Even so! Even so!

HICKSVILLE

A Rembrandt effect

WITH THE OLD SETTLERS AT COLUMBIA CITY, INDIANA

CENTRAL INDIANA
A Farm and Silo

IN CARMEL
Franklin's Home Town

THE BEST OF INDIANAPOLIS

THE STANDARD BRIDGE OF FIFTY YEARS AGO
Reelsville, Indiana

FRANKLIN'S IMPRESSION OF MY BIRTHPLACE

TERRE HAUTE FROM WEST OF THE WABASH

MY FATHER'S MILL
Sullivan, Indiana

VINCENNES
The Knox County Fair

THE FERRY AT DECKER

THE OHIO AT EVANSVILLE

A BEAUTIFUL TREE ON A VILE ROAD
Warwick County, Indiana

A CATHEDRAL OF TREES
Jasper, Indiana

FRENCH LICK
The Hotel and Fresh Water Spring

CHAPTER XLIX

FOR good, bad, or indifferent, whether it had been painful or pleasant, the youth time that I had spent in Terre Haute had gone and would never come back again. My mother, as I remembered her then—and when is a mother more of a mother than in one's babyhood?—was by now merely a collection of incidents and pains and sweetnesses lingering in a few minds! And my father, earnest, serious-minded German, striving to do the best he knew, was gone also—all of thirteen years. Those brothers and sisters whose ambitions were then so keen, whose blood moods were so high, were now tamed and sober, scattered over all the eastern portion of America. And here was I walking about, not knowing a single soul here really, intent upon finding one man perhaps who had known my father and had been kind to him; for the rest, looking up the houses in which we had lived, the first school which I had ever attended, the first church, and thinking over all the ills we had endured rather than the pleasures we had enjoyed (for of the latter I could scarcely recall any), was all with which I had to employ myself.

In the first place, the night before coming in, because it was nearly dark and because neither Franklin nor I cared to spend any more time in this southern extension than we could help, I wanted to find and look at as many of the old places as was possible in the summer twilight, for more than look at them once I could scarcely, or at least, would not care to do. It was not a difficult matter. At the time we lived there, the city was much smaller, scarcely more than one-third its present size, and the places which then seemed remote from the business heart were now a five-minute walk, if so much. I could see, in coming in, that to get to Ninth and Chestnut, where I was born, I would have to go almost into the business section, or nearly so. Again, the house at Twelfth and Walnut, where the first few years of my life were spent— say from one to five—was first on our route in, and it was best to have Bert turn in there, for the street labelings were all very plain and it was easy to find our way. It was very evident that Terre Haute was another manufacturing city, and a prosperous one, for smoke filled the air and there was a somewhat inspiriting display of chimneys and manufacturing buildings in one direction and another. The sound of engine bells and factory whistles at six o'clock seemed to indicate a cheerful prosperity not always present in larger and seemingly more successful cities. Franklin, as I have said, noted a temper or flare of youth and hope about the town, for he spoke of it.

"I like this place. It is interesting," he said. "I had no idea Terre Haute was so fine as this."

As for me, my mind was recurring to old scenes and old miseries, commingled with a child's sensations. Once in this town, in company with Ed and Al, I picked coal off the tracks because we had no coal at home. Somewhere here Ed and I, going for a sack of cornmeal, lost the fifty cents with which to buy it, and it was our last fifty cents. In a small house in Thirteenth Street, as I have elsewhere indicated, the three youngest of us were sick, while my father was out of work, and my mother was compelled to take in washing. In some other house here—Seventh and Chestnut, I believe—there was a swing in a basement where I used to swing all alone by the hour, enjoying my own moods even at that time. From a small brick house in Fourteenth Street, the last I ever knew of Terre Haute, I carried my father's dinner to him in a pail at a woolen mill, of which he was foreman or manager or something. He was never exactly a day laborer for anyone. I remember a "carder" and a "fuller" and a "blower" and a "spinning jenny" and his explaining their functions to me. Somewhere in this town

was the remainder of St. Joseph's School, or its site, at
least, where at five years of age I was taken to learn my
A B C's, and where a nun in a great flaring white bonnet
and a black habit, with a rattling string of great beads,
pointed at a blackboard with a stick and asked us what
certain symbols stood for. I recall even now, very faintly,
it is true, having trouble remembering what the sounds
of certain letters were.

I remember the church attached to this school, and a
bell in a tower that used to get turned over and wouldn't
ring until some one of us boys climbed up and turned it
back—a great treat. I remember boating on a small,
muddy pool, on boards, and getting my feet very wet, and
almost falling in, and a serious sore throat afterwards. I
remember a band—the first I ever heard—(Kleinbind's
Terre Haute Ringold Band as my father afterwards explained was its official title)—marching up the street, the
men wearing red jackets with white shoulder straps and
tall black Russian shakos. They frightened me, and I
cried. I remember once being on the Wabash River with
my brother Rome in a small boat—the yellow water
seemed more of a wonder and terror to me then than it
does now—and of his rocking the boat and of my scream-
ing, and of his wanting to whip me—a brotherly bit of
tenderness, quite natural, don't you think? I remember,
at Twelfth and Walnut, a great summer rainstorm, when
I was very young, and my mother undressing me and telling me to run out naked in the great splattering drops
making bubbles everywhere—an adventure which seemed
very splendid and quite to my taste. I remember my
brothers Paul and Rome as grownups—men really—
when they were only boys, and of my elder sisters—girls
of thirteen, fifteen, seventeen, seeming like great strong
women.

Life was a strange, colorful, kaleidoscopic welter then.
It has remained so ever since.

Here I was now, and it was evening. As we turned
into Walnut Street at Twelfth I recognized one of the
houses by pictures in the family and by faint memories

and we stopped to give Franklin time to sketch it. It was a smoky, somewhat treeless neighborhood, with a number of children playing about, and long rows of one-story workingmen's cottages receding in every direction. Once it had a large yard with a garden at the back, apple, pear and cherry trees along the fence, a small barn or cow shed, and rows of gooseberry and currant bushes bordering several sides. Now all that was gone, of course. The house had been moved over to the very corner. Small houses, all smoky, had been crowded in on either hand so tightly that there were scarcely sidewalks between them. I asked a little girl who came running over as the car stopped and Franklin began sketching, "Who lives over there?"

"Kifer," she replied.

"What does he do?"

"He works. They keep boarders. What are you making?"

"A picture."

"Of that house?"

"Yes."

"What for?"

"Well, I used to live there and I've come back all the way from New York to see it."

"Oh!" And with that she climbed up on the running board to look on, but Franklin shooed her off.

"You mustn't shake the car," he said.

She got down, but only to confer with six or seven other children who had gathered by now, and all of whom had to be enlightened. They ran back for a moment or two to inform inquisitive parents, but soon returned, increased in number. They stood in a group and surveyed the house as though they had never seen it before. Obviously, it had taken on a little luster in their eyes. They climbed up on the running boards and shook the car until Franklin was compelled to order them down again, though it was plain that he was not anxious so to do. Bats were circling in the air overhead—those fine, ricocheting winged mice. There were mosquitoes about, annoying numbers of them—horrible clouds, in fact, which caused me to wonder how people endured living in the neighborhood. People walked by on their way home from work, or going out somewhere, young men in the most dandified and conspicuous garbs, and on porches and front steps were their fathers in shirt sleeves, and women in calico dresses, reading the evening paper. I studied each detail of the house, getting out and looking at it from one side and another, but I could get no least touch of the earlier atmosphere, and I did not want to go in. Interiorly it held no interest for me. I could not remember how it looked on the inside anyhow.

After leaving this house, I decided to look up Ninth and Chestnut, where I was born, but not knowing the exact corner (no one in our family having been able to tell me) I gave it up, only to notice that at that moment I was passing the corner. I looked. There were small houses on every hand. Which one was ours, or had been? Or was it there at all any more? Useless speculation. I did not even trouble to stop the car.

But from here I directed the car to Eighth and Chestnut, a corner at which, in an old red brick house still standing, my mother, as someone had informed me, had once essayed keeping borders. I was so young at the time I could scarcely remember—say six or seven. All I could recall of it was that here once was a little girl in blue velvet, with yellow hair, the daughter of some woman of comparative (it is a guess) means, who was stopping with us, and who, because of her blue velvet dress and her airs, seemed most amazing to me, a creature out of the skies. I remember standing at the head of the stairs and looking into her room—or her mother's, and seeing a dresser loaded with silver bits, and marveling at the excellence of such a life. Just that, and nothing more, out of a whole period of months. Now I could only recall that the house was of brick, that it had a lawn and trees, a basement with a brick floor, and a sense of abandonment and departed merit. Finding it at this late date was not likely, but we ran the car around there and stopped and looked. There was a brick house there, old but improved. Was it the same? Who can tell, or what matter, really? The difference was to me.

We think of life as a definite, enduring thing, some of us; but what a thin shadow, or nothingness, it must be, really, when the past and your youth and all connected with it goes glimmering thus like smoke. I always think of that passage in Job (XIV: 1-2) "Man that is born of a woman is of few days, and full of trouble. He cometh forth like a flower and is cut down; he fleeth also as a shadow, and continueth not." When I think of that, and how ideas and notions and fames and blames go glimmering, I often ask myself what is it all about, anyhow, and what are we here for, and why should anyone worry whether they are low or high, or moral or immoral. What difference does it really make? And to whom? Who actually cares, in the long run, whether you are good, bad or indifferent? There is much talk and much strutting to and fro and much concealment of our past ills and shames, and much parading of our present luxuries and well beings. But, my good friends, the wise know better. You cannot talk to a man or woman of capacity or insight or experience of any of these sharp distinctions. To them they do not exist. We are all low or high according to our dynamic energy to get and keep fame, money, notoriety, information, skill—no more. As for the virtuous, and those supposedly lacking in virtue— the honest and those who are dishonest—kind heaven, we haven't the first inklings of necessary data wherewith to begin even to formulate a theory of difference! We do not know, and I had almost said we cannot know, though I am not one to be cocksure of anything—not even of the impossibility of perfection.

Allons! Then we moved the car to Seventh and Chestnut Streets, where had stood another house near a lumber yard. In this house was the swing in the basement where I used to swing, the sunlight pouring through a low cellar window, such days as I chose to play there. Outside was a great yard or garden with trees, and close at hand a large lumber yard—it seemed immense to me at the time—pleasingly filled with odoriferous woods, and offering a great opportunity for climbing, playing hide and seek, running and jumping from pile to pile, and avoiding the watchman who wanted to catch us and give us a good beating for coming into it at all.

And beyond that was a train yard full of engines and cars and old broken down cabooses and a repair shop. When I was most adventurous I used to wander even beyond the lumber yard (there was a spur track going out into this greater world), staring at all I saw, and risking no doubt my young life more than once. At one time I fell off a car on which I had adventurously climbed and bruised my hand quite seriously. At another time I climbed up into a worn out and discarded engine, and examined all the machinery with the utmost curiosity. It all seemed so amazing to me. Engineers, firemen, brakemen, yard men—how astonishing they all seemed—the whole clangorous, jangling compact called life.

But this house was now a mere myth or rumor—something that may never have existed at all—so unreal are our realities. It had gone glimmering. There was no house here anything like that which I had in mind. There was a railroad yard, quite a large one, probably greatly enlarged since my day. There was a lumber yard adjoining it, very prosperous looking, and enclosed by a high board fence, well painted, and a long, old, low white house with green shutters. We stopped the car here and I meditated on my mother and sisters and on some laughing school teachers who took meals with us here at this time. Then we moved on. I was glad to go. I was getting depressed.

The last place we tried for was that much mentioned in Thirteenth Street, Thirteenth between Walnut and Chestnut, as some one of my relatives had said, but I could not find it. When we reached the immediate vicinity we found a hundred such houses—I had almost said a thousand—and it was a poor, sorrowful street, the homes of the most deficient or oppressed or defeated. I wanted to hurry on, and did so, but musingly and romantically, in passing, I picked out one which stood next to an alley —an old, small, black, faded house, and said to myself, that must be ours. But was it? Because of uncertainty my heart could not go out to it. It went out only to that other house back in the clouds of memory, where my mother and my sisters and brothers were all assembled.

And this street—yes, my heart went out to it—oh, very much. I felt as though I would be willing to trade places with and take up the burden of the least efficient and most depressed of all of those assembled here, in memory of—in memory of——

CHAPTER L

A LUSH, EGYPTIAN LAND

THE next morning, after purchasing our customary picture cards, we were about to achieve an early start when I suddenly remembered that I had not tried to find the one man I really wanted to see—a man for whom my father had worked in years gone by, the son of a mill owner who after his father's death with a brother had inherited this mill and employed my father to run it. Although he was very much younger than my father at that time, there had always been a bond of sympathy and understanding between them. But even in my father's lifetime the woolen industry in this region had fallen on hard lines—the East and some patents on machinery held by Massachusetts manufacturers crowding these westerners to the wall—so that this boy and his brother, who had been such good friends to my father, had been compelled to abandon their woolen properties entirely and Adam Shattuck had gone into the electric lighting business, and had helped, I understand, to organize the local electric light plant here and for a while anyhow was its first vice-president and treasurer. After that I heard nothing more.

I had never seen him, but as is always the case with someone commercially connected with a family—a successful and so helpful a personality—I had heard a great deal about him. Indeed, in our worst days here, the Shattuck family had represented to me the height of all that was important and durable, and to such an extent that even now, and after all these years, I hesitated whether to inflict myself on him, even for so laudable a purpose as ·inquiring the exact site of the old mill or whether he recalled where my father first lived, on moving to Terre Haute from Sullivan, and which was the house where I was born. Nevertheless, I looked him up in the city directory and could find only one Adam B. Shattuck, "hay, grain, and feed, 230 South Fourth Street," a region and a business which did not seem likely to contain so important a person. Nevertheless, because I was anxious to see the old mill which my father had managed under his ownership (I knew it stood somewhere down near the river's edge), I ventured to go to this address, to find perchance if he could tell me where the true Adam B. Shattuck was to be found.

And on the way, because it was only a few blocks at most in any direction, I decided to look up the old St. Joseph's Church and school which I had attended as a child, my first school, to see if possibly I could recognize anything in connection with that. A picture postcard which I had found showed a quite imposing church on the site my father had given, but no school.

Imagine my surprise on reaching it to be able to recognize in a rear building to which a new front had, in years gone by, been added, the exact small, square red brick building in which I had first been drilled in my A B C's. Owing to a high brick wall and the presence of an encroaching building it was barely visible any longer from the street, but stripped of these later accretions I could see exactly how it looked—and remember it! As I gazed, the yard, the pond, the old church, the surrounding neighborhood, all came back to me. I saw it quite clearly. As at Warsaw, Indiana, I now suffered a slight upheaval in my vitals. A kind of nostalgia set in. The very earth seemed slipping out from under my feet. I looked through the small paned windows into one of the old rooms and then, because it was exactly the same, I wanted to get away. I went round by the church side and seeing a funeral train in front walked through the door into this newer building. Before the altar rail, surrounded by tall candles, lay a coffin. And I said to myself: "Yes, it is symbolic. Death and change have taken much, so far. They will soon take all."

Then I climbed back into the car.

It was only a few blocks to the hay, grain and feed emporium of this bogus Adam Shattuck, and when I saw it, a low, drab, one story brick building, in a very dilapidated condition, I felt more convinced than ever that this man could have nothing to do with my father's quondam employer. I went through the dusty, hay strewn door and at a small, tall, dusty and worn clerical desk saw an old man in a threadbare grey alpaca coat, making some entries in a cheap, reddish paper backed cashbook. There was a scale behind him. The shadowy, windowless walls in the rear and to the sides were lined with bins, containing sacks of oats and bran, bales of hay and other feed. Just as I entered a boy from the vicinity followed me, pushing a small truck, and laid a yellow slip on the desk.

"He says to make it four half sacks of bran."

"Can you tell me where I will find a Mr. Adam B. Shattuck, who used to own the Wabash Woolen Mills here?" I inquired.

"I'm the man—Adam B. Shattuck. Just excuse me a minute, will you, while I wait on this boy."

I stared at him in rude astonishment, for he seemed so worn, so physically concluded. His face was seamed and sunken, his eyes deep tired, his hands wrinkled.

"You're Mr. Shattuck, are you? Well, I'm the son of Paul Dreiser, who used to work for you. You don't remember me, of course—I was too young——"

"This isn't by any chance Theodore, is it?" he commented, his eyes brightening slightly with recognition.

"Yes, that's me," I said.

"Your brother Paul," he said, "when he was out here a few years ago, was telling me about you. You write, I believe——"

"Yes."

"Well, of course, I've never known of you except indirectly, but—how long are you going to be in town?"

"Only this morning," I replied. "I'm just passing through. This isn't my car. I'm traveling in it with a friend. I'm visiting all the old places just for the fun of it. I was just coming to you to ask if you could tell me where the old mill stood—whether it's still standing."

"Right at the foot of the street here," he commented very cheerfully, at the same time bustling about and getting out the half sacks of bran and other things. "It's just as it was in your father's day, only it is a wagon company now. All the woolen mills in this section died out long ago. Your father foresaw that. He told me they would. I went into the electric lighting business afterward, but they crowded me out of it—consolidation and all that. Then I got into this business. It isn't much but it's a living. One seventyfive," he said to the boy, who put the money on the desk and went out.

"Yes, indeed, I knew your father. He was a fine man. He worked for us off and on for pretty near fifteen year, after his own mill went up. This was no country for woolen manufacture, though. We couldn't compete with the East. Why, I read here not long ago that two hundred mills in Indiana, Ohio and Illinois had closed up in twenty years—two hundred! Well, that's all over. So you're Theodore! You couldn't stay and have lunch with me, could you?"

"Thank you, I couldn't possibly," I replied. "I'm only a guest in this car and I can't detain them too long. I did want to see you, though, and so I came."

"That's right; that's right," he said. "It's good of you. Times have changed with me some, but then, I've lived a long time. I've a son in New York. He's with . . . (he mentioned a large and successful company). You ought to call on him some time. He'd be glad to see you, I'm sure."

He rambled on about one thing and another and followed me . . . to the door.

"You couldn't tell me, by any chance, where the first house my father ever occupied in Terre Haute stands?" I said idly.

"Yes, I can. It's right around here in Second Street, one block south, next to a grocery store. You can't miss it. It's a two story brick now, but they added a story a long time ago. It was a one story house in his time, but then it had a big yard and lots of trees. I remember it well. I used to go there occasionally to see him. . . . Right down there at the foot of the street," he called after me.

I climbed into the car and down we went to the old mill to stare at that, now whirring with new sounds and looking fairly brisk and prosperous; then back to the old brick house, looking so old and so commonplace that I could well imagine it a fine refuge after a storm. But I had never even heard of this before and was not expecting to find it. Then we raced forth Sullivan-ward and I was heartily glad to be gone.

. . . .

The territory into which we were now passing was that described in the first chapter of this book—of all places that I ever lived in my youth the most pleasing to me and full of the most colorful and poetic of memories. Infancy and its complete non-understanding had just gone. For me, when we arrived here, adolescence—the inquisitive boy of twelve to sixteen—had not yet arrived. This was the region of the wonder period of youth, when trees, clouds, the sky, the progression of the days, the sun, the rains, the grass all filled me with delight, an overpowering sense of beauty, charm, mystery. How eager I was to know, at times—and yet at other times not. How I loved to sit and gaze just drinking it all in, the sensory feel and glory of it. And then I had gone on to other ideas and other places and this had never come back— not once in any least way—and now I was to see it all again, or the region of it——

Sullivan, as we found on consulting our map, lay only twentyfive miles south, or thereabouts. Our road lay through a perfectly flat region, so flat and featureless that it should have been uninteresting and yet it was not. I have observed this of regions as of people, that however much alike they may appear to be in character there is, nevertheless, a vast difference in their charm or lack of it. This section in which I had been partially reared had charm—not the charm of personal predisposition, as others will testify, but real charm. The soil was rich—a sandy loam. The trees were shapely and healthy—peaceful trees, not beaten by angry winds and rains. The fields were lush with grass or grain—warm bottom lands these, composed of soil carried down by ancient rivers—now, in the last hundred years or so, given names. As we came out of Terre Haute I turned and looked back at it, a prosperous, vigorous town. East of it, in a healthy, fruitful region, in that hill country around Reelsville and Brazil, there had been coal mines—soft coal mines, providing work and fuel. Here on our route to Sullivan were other mines, at Farmersburg, seven miles out, a town by the way which I recalled as being somehow an outpost of the priest who read mass at Sullivan, at Shelburne and other places still farther south. You could see the black, dirty breakers across flat green fields in which stood round healthy trees.

As we went south, one of those warm sudden rains sprang up, or came down—one of those quick, heavy rains which I recognized as characteristic of the region of my infancy. We saw it coming in the distance, a thickening of smoke clouds over some groves in the west. Then a green fog seemed to settle between us and the trees, and I knew it was raining.

"Here it comes," I called. "Had we better get the top up?"

Bert, who was now the master of motion and a radically different temperament to Speed, paid no heed. He was very taciturn or meditative at times, but equally gay at others, and much more self sufficient and reliant, if anything. I had been most interested by the quiet, controlling way in which he had gone about getting himself housed and fed at night and at other times. Porters and garage managers gave no least care to Bert. He managed them and suggested ways and means to us occasionally. Whenever anything happened to the car he leisurely extracted himself with the aid of his crutches and set about adjusting it as though there were not the least thing defective about him. It was interesting, almost amusing.

But now, as I say, he paid no heed and soon a few heavy drops fell, great, splattering globules that left inch size wet spots on our clothing, and then we were in the storm. It gushed.

"Now, will you listen?" I observed as we jumped down. Franklin and I bustled about the task of getting the hood up. Before we could do it, though—almost before we could get our raincoats on—it was pouring—a torrent. It seemed to come down in bucketfuls. Then, once we had the hood up and the seats dried and our raincoats on and were suffocating of heat, the storm was gone. The sun came out, the road looked golden, the grass was heavenly. In the distance one could see it raining elsewhere, far across the fields.

"Yes," I observed feelingly and tenderly, " 'this is me own, me native land;' only I wish it wouldn't make its remembered characteristics quite so obvious. I can be shown that it is just as it used to be, without being killed."

The land smiled. I'm sure it did. Aren't there such things as smiling lands?

And a little farther on, without any suggestion from me, for I am well satisfied that he would never be so influenced, Franklin was commenting on the luxurious character of the region. The houses were all small and simple, very tasteless little cottages, but very good and new and seemingly comfortable, sheltering no doubt the sons and daughters of people who had been here when I was. Excellent automobiles were speeding along the roads, handsome western makes of cars—not so many Fords. The cattle in the fields looked healthy, fat. Timothy and corn were standing waist high. It was hot, as it should be in a fat riverland like this. We had not gone far before we had to get out to examine a hay baling machine— the first hay baler (for the use of individual farmers) I had ever seen. There had been a haypress at Sullivan, a most wonderful thing to me to contemplate in my day— a horse going round in a ring and so lifting and dropping a great weight which compressed the hay in a box; but this was different. It was standing out in an open field near three haystacks and was driven by a gasoline motor, a force which made short work of the vast quantities of hay piled on the feeder. Three men operated it. The horses that drew it stood idle to one side.

"How much hay can you bale in a day?" I asked of one of the farmers.

"Depends on the number working," he replied. "We three men can do up a couple of stacks like that." He was referring to two goodly mounds of sweet brown hay that stood to the left.

"Do you call it hard work?" I asked.

"No, not very," he answered. "Pitching hay from the stacks down onto it and pulling the bales away."

"What will the farmer not get next?" I inquired of Franklin. "It seems that nearly all the heavy labor of the old days is gone."

"It's true," he said. "I never saw a machine like this before. I've heard of them. All that they need now is a good, cheap traction plow and farming will be a weak man's job—like golf—and twice as healthy."

We climbed back.

Scudding along under green trees and through stretches of meadow and under a hot, almost baking sun, we came at last to various signs reading: "For Fine Dry Goods Visit Squibbs, South Side Square," or "If You Want The Best Hardware In Sullivan Go To Beach & Gens."

"Ha! then someone of the Beach family has gone into the hardware business," I commented.

Presently a huge sign appeared hanging across the road. It read:

"Sullivan Welcomes You."

"Imagine 'dirty old Sullivan' venturing to welcome anyone!" I commented, quoting my sister. "If she could only see that!" I added.

"There's another name I recognize, anyhow," I commented to Franklin, as another sign came into view. "Some member of that family owned the clover field back of our house in my time. Good luck to him, if it's in good condition."

In a few minutes we were rolling up a street which would have taken us to the public square if we had followed it; instantly I was on the *qui vive* to see what if anything I could remember. This was a section, the northwest corner of Sullivan, which I recalled as having been a great open common in my time, filled principally with dog fennel and dandelion and thistles and containing only one house, a red one, occupied by an Irish section boss, whose wife (my mother having befriended her years before when first she and her husband came to Sullivan) had now, at the time my mother was compelled to make this return pilgrimage, befriended us by letting us stay—mother and us three youngsters—until she could find a house. It was a period of three or four days, as I recall it. The father of this family, Thomas Brogan, was a great, heavy handed, hulking, red faced Irishman who knew only work and Catholicism. On Sunday in some weird, stiff combination of Sunday clothes and squeaky shoes, he was accustomed to lead in single file procession his more or less recalcitrant family through weeds and along the broken board walks of this poorly equipped region to mass. I saw him often, even in my day. His youngest son, Harry Brogan, often played with Ed and me and once he instigated some other, older boys, to lick us—a tale too long and too sad to be told here. His second youngest son, Jim—alias Red Brogan and subsequently known to fame as "Red Oliphant," a bank robber (finally electrocuted by the state of New York at Sing Sing for murder—he and three or four others shot a night watchman, or so the police said)—was often beaten by his father with a horsewhip because he would not work in the local coal mine or perhaps do other drudging about his home. This coal mine, by the way, had killed his elder brother Frank some three or four years before by explosion, a tragedy which you might have thought would

have ended coal mining in that family. Not at all. Far
from it. These beatings had continued until the boy ran
away, uneducated of course, and became the character he
subsequently was or was alleged to have been. I do not
know. If you want to know of a fairly good boy who died
a criminal in the chair owing to conditions over which he
had no least control or certainly very little, this was one.
If I were Red Brogan and were summoned before the
eternal throne—would that there were one—I would
show Him the stripes on my back and my neglected brain
and ask Him why, if He were God, He had forsaken me.

I have heard my mother tell how she was present at
the time this older brother's body was brought up out of
the mine (eight men were killed at the time) and how
tragic seemingly was the grief of both Mr. and Mrs.
Brogan. Later on, after we left Sullivan, the family became somewhat more prosperous and it is likely that the
youngest son was not compelled to work as the others had.

CHAPTER LI

BE that as it may, it was much of this and related matters that I was ruminating as I came through this region. But I could find no traces of what had formerly been. There was no red house anywhere—repainted probably. The coal mine, which I had remembered as being visible from this section, was not to be seen. Later I learned that it had been worked out and abandoned. The coal had all been dug out. Many new small houses in orderly, compact rows now made streets here. We had Bert follow this road a few blocks and then turn discreetly to the east until we should cross the railroad tracks, for I recalled that it was across these tracks or track facing another weed-grown square, and what was then a mildly industrious institution of the town, the hay press, that our house stood.

This square had always seemed a fascinating thing to me, for despite the fact that it was on the extreme outskirts of the town and in a district where (a little farther out) stood the village slaughterhouse, emitting uncomfortable odors when the wind was blowing right, still it was near the town's one railroad station and switching yards—there was a turntable near the hay press—and we could see the trains go by and watch the principal industry of the place, switching, the taking on or dropping off of cars. Every morning at ten-thirty and every afternoon at two there was a freight train—the one in the morning from the south, the other in the afternoon from the north —which stopped and switched here. As an eight to ten-year-old boy how often I have sat on our porch, playing "engine" or "freight" with empty cigar boxes for cars (an extra big one for a caboose) and a spool for a smokestack, and imitated the switching and "making up" which I saw going on across the common. A delicious sense of wonder and delight always lingered in my mind in connection with Sullivan, for although we were apparently desperately poor there were compensations which the inscrutable treasure of youth trebled and quadrupled—nay multiplied an hundred and a thousand fold.

This indeed, I said to myself, as I looked at it now trying eagerly to get it all back and failing so dismally in the main, was that Egyptian land of which I have spoken. Here were those blue skies, those warm rains. Back of this house which I am now to see once more perhaps will be that perfect field of clover—only remembered in the summer state, so naturally optimistic is the human soul. In the sky will be soaring buzzards, surely. Over a field of green will stand a tall, gnarled dead tree trunk, its gauntness concealed by a cape of wild ivy. On its topmost level will sit a brown hawk or a grey headed eagle calculating on methods of capture. Across the street, up the road a little way, will be the brown home of "crazy old Bowles," who used to come to our well for water singing and sometimes executing a weird step, or gazing vacantly and insanely at the sky. He was an ex-army man, shot in the head at Lookout Mountain and now a little daffy. He had been pensioned and was spending his declining years here. "Crazy old Bowles" was his local name.

A few steps farther out this same road, the last house but one (which was ours) would be the house of Mrs. Hudson, a lonely and somewhat demented old widow whose children had long since gone and left her to live here quite alone. We children thought her a witch. Down in a hollow, beyond our house, where lay the whitening skulls and bones of many an ox and cow, stood the tumbledown slaughterhouse, to me a fearsome place. I always imagined dead cows prowling about at night. Over the way from our house had been a great elm, in which Ed and I used to climb to swing on its branches. In its shade, in summer time, Tillie, Ed and I played house. I can hear the wind in the leaves yet. Beyond the slaughterhouse eastward was a great cornfield. In autumn, when the frost was whitening the trees, I have seen thousands of crows on their way southward resting on the rail fences which surrounded this field, and on the slaughterhouse roof and on a few lone trees here and there, holding a conference. Such a cawing and chattering!

Beyond the clover field again, in a southeasterly direction, was the fine farm of Mr. Beach, his white house, his red barn, his trees sheltering peacocks that in summer "called for rain." In the fields all about were blackberries, raspberries, dewberries, wild plums, wild crabapple trees—a host of things which we could gather free. If either Ed or I had had the least turn of ingenuity we might have trapped or shot enough wild animals to have kept us in meat—possibly even in funds, so numerous were various forms of small game. In summer we could have picked unlimited quantities of berries and helped mother preserve them against dark days. We did—some. But in the main all we did was to fish a little—as the thought of pleasure moved us.

But oh, this pleasing realm! Once here I could not see it as it really was at the moment, nor can I now write of it intelligently or dispassionately. It is all too involved with things which have no habitat in land or sea or sky. The light of early morning, the feet of youth, dreams, dreams, dreams—— Yes, here once, I told myself now, we carried coal in winter, Ed and Al and I, but what matter? Was not youth then ours to comfort us? My father was gloomy, depressed, in no position or mood to put right his disordered affairs. But even so, oh Sullivan! Sullivan! of what wonders and dreams are not your poorest and most commonplace aspects compounded!

As we crossed the tracks by the railroad station, only two long blocks from "our house" in the old days, I began to recognize familiar landmarks. At the first corner beyond the station where I always turned north had been four young trees and here now were four quite large ones.

I was convinced they were the same. Looking up the street north I recognized the open common still intact, and as we neared the house the identical hay press, if you please, newly covered with tin and perhaps otherwise repaired, but standing close to the tracks, where formerly the hay was loaded onto cars. By the sounds issuing from it, it must have been busy indeed. At the spot where we now were at the moment should have been Bowles' house, a low, one story yellow affair, but now only a patch of weeds and a broken well top indicated that a house had once stood there. Looking quickly for "our house" I distinguished it, one of a row of seemingly new and much poorer ones, but this older house was still the best of them all. Beyond, where Mrs. Hudson's house should have been and the great elm, and the Poe-like slaughter-house, was nothing but a railroad track curving Y-fashion and joining another which ran where once the slaughter-house hollow had been. There was no hollow any more, no tree, no nothing. Only a right-angled railroad track or switching Y.

My field of clover!

It was an unkempt weed patch, small, disreputable, disillusionizing—a thing that had never been large at all or had shrunk to insignificant proportions. My tree—the column of the brooding hawk—it was gone. There was no fine fecund truck patch alongside our house, where once we had raised corn, potatoes, peas, onions, beans— almost our total summer and winter fare. Three other small shabby houses and their grounds occupied the field we had cultivated. I realized now in looking at this what an earnest, industrious woman my mother must have been.

A band of ragamuffin children were playing out in front, children with bare legs, bare arms, in most cases half bare bodies, and so dirty! When they saw our car they gathered in a group and surveyed us. One of the littlest of them had a sore-eyed puppy elevated to his loving breast. It was a "poor white trash" neighborhood.

"My brother's got tabuckalosis of the bones," one little girl said to me, nodding at a skimpy, distrait looking youth who stood to one side, rather pleased than not that his ailment should attract so much attention.

"Oh, no," I said, "surely not. He doesn't look as though he had anything but a good appetite, does he, Franklin?"

"Certainly not," replied the latter cheerfully.

The youth gazed at me solemnly.

"Oh, yes, he has," continued his sister, "the doctor said so."

"But don't you know that doctors don't know everything?" put in Franklin. "Doctors just imagine things, the same as other people. Why, look at him—he's nice and healthy."

"No, he ain't either," replied this protector argumentatively. "If he don't get better he'll haff to go to the 'ospital. Our doctor says so. My mother ain't got the money or he'd go now."

"Dear! Dear!" I exclaimed, looking at the youth sympathetically. "But there, he looks so well. You feel all right, don't you?" I asked of the contemplative victim, who was staring at me with big eyes.

"Yes, sir."

"You're never sick in bed?"

"No, sir."

"Well, now here's a nickel. And don't you get sick. You'll be well so long as you think so."

"Ooh, let's see it," commanded the advertising sister, drawing near and trying to take the hand with the coin.

"No."

"Well, let's see how it looks."

"No."

"Well, then, keep it, smarty! You'll have to give it to maw, anyhow."

I began to wonder whether "tabuckalosis" of the bones was not something developed for trade purposes or whether it was really true.

The house was in exactly the same position and physically unchanged save that in our day the paint was new and white; whereas, now, it was drab and dirty. The yard, or garden as the English would call it, had all been cut away, or nearly so, leaving only a dusty strip of faded grass to the right as one looked in. In "our" time there was a neat white picket fence and gate in front. It was gone now. Inside, once, were roses in profusion, planted by mother, and a few small fruit trees—a peach, a cherry, an apple tree. Now there were none. The fence on which I used to sit of a morning—the adored back fence —and watch the swallows skimming over the clover and the yellow humble bees among the blooms was gone also. Not a trace of all the beauty that once was mine. I stood here and thought of the smooth green grass that I had rejoiced in, the morning and evening skies, the cloud formations, the bluebird that built a nest under one corner of our roof, the swallows that built their hard bony nests in our chimneys and lost them occasionally—they and their poor naked young tumbling to ruin on our cool hearthstones. Had it been in fact or only in my own soul?

I thought of my mother walking about in the cool of the morning and the evening, rejoicing in nature. I saw her with us on the back porch or the front—Tillie, Ed, myself, and some of our elders gathered about her— listening to stories or basking in the unbelievable comfort of her presence.

Here, at dusk, I said, Ed and I used to throw cinders and small rocks at the encircling bats, hoping, as Ed used to say, to "paralyze" them. From our doorstep at night we could hear the whistle of incoming and outgoing trains and see the lighted coaches as they passed. An old grist mill a half mile "down the track," as we always referred to the region due south, ground grain all night and we could hear the poetic rumble of the stones. Here, occasionally, my brooding father would come from Terre Haute, to sit with us and bring a little money—the money that he could spare from past accumulated debts.

My brother Rome came here once—"to get drunk and disgrace us," as my sister said. My elder sisters came, to avoid their father and have the consoling counsel and love of their mother. My brother Al came from my Uncle Martin's fruit farm at North Manchester, if you please, to lord it over us with his rustic strength, to defeat and terrorize all our accumulated enemies (Ed and I had a genius for storing up enemies for him) and to elicit our contempt for his country bumpkin manners. And here finally when my mother was distrait as to means of weathering the persistent storm and we were actually cold and hungry, my brother Paul, now a successful minstrel man and the author of "The Paul Dresser Comic Songster" (containing all the songs sung in the show) and now traveling in this region, came to her aid and removed us all to Evansville—the spring following this worst of winters.

In addition to all this my father's first mill was still here at that time—and even now as I later discovered— only two blocks away, behind the station—burned once but restored afterward—and also an old house which he had built and owned but had been compelled to sell. In those days these were the signs and emblems of our former greatness, which kept our drooping spirits from sinking too low and made us decide not to be put upon forever and ever by life.

As I stood looking at this I had once more that sinking sensation I experienced in Warsaw and Terre Haute. Life moves so insensibly out from under you. It slips away like a slow moving tide. You look and the box or straw that once was at your doorstep is far down stream —or rather you are the box, the straw. Your native castle is miles removed. I went in and knocked at the door while Franklin, without, sketched and photographed to suit himself. A slattern of a woman, small, young, stodgy, greasy, but not exactly unattractive, came to the door and stared at me in no particularly friendly way. Why are some animals so almost unconsciously savage?

"I beg your pardon," I said. "I lived here once, years ago. Would you let me come in and look over the house?"

As I spoke a tall, gaunt yokel of not over twentysix ambled out from an inner room. He was an attractive specimen physically but so crude and ignorant. He looked me over superficially. I might have been a policeman or an enemy.

I repeated my question.

"Yes, I guess you kin look it over," he said distantly. "It ain't quite made up yet. The boarders don't keep their rooms just as spick as might be."

Boarders! In this unkempt house! It was a litter. The best pictures were flyspecked lithographs or chromos. The floors when they were laid with anything were covered with earthy looking rag carpets—creaky, yellow, nondescript furniture. A litter and crush of useless things —tin and glass lamps, papers, cheap pamphlets—a red tablecloth or two—and there were flies and odors and unmade beds.

I went through, looking into each room, restoring it to my mind as it had been. We had not had much—the rooms in our day were sparely and poorly furnished, tastelessly so no doubt—but there is an art in spareness and bareness and cleanliness, and still more in a pervasive personality like my mother's. What we had, thanks to her, was clean and neat, with flowers permitted to approach as near as summer and soil and pots made possible. I realized now that it was her temperament which like a benediction or a perfume had pervaded, surrounded, suffused this whole region and this home for me. It was my mother and myself and my brothers and sisters in part whom I was remembering—not just the house and the grounds.

Aside from this house there was not much that I wanted to see—not much with which I was intimately identified. A Catholic church to which a priest came once a month and in which the Catholic school was held—an institution which, fortunately, I was not permitted to attend very long, for want of shoes to wear; the old mill which my father built and which after a fire was restored, and in the mill pond of which Ed and I were wont to fish, on occasion; the courthouse square and postoffice, in the latter of which I have often waited eagerly for the distribution of mail—not that it meant anything to me personally, but because my mother was so pathetically eager for word of some kind; the Busseron river or creek, which I knew we would see as we left town. We left this group of chattering children, one of whom, a girl, wanted to sell us the small dog in order, as she said, to buy herself a new riding whip. I could not decide whether she was indulging in a flight of fancy—so poverty stricken was her home—or whether on some farm near by was a horse she was actually permitted to ride. She was brisk and stodgy—a black eyed, garrulous little creature with a fondness for great words, but no real charm.

With one backward glance on my part we were off to the mill, which stood just as it was in my day, only instead of running full time as it did then there was an assignee's sign on the door saying that all the stock and fixtures of the Sullivan Woolen Mills Company would be sold under the hammer at a given date to satisfy certain judgments— a proof I thought of Mr. Shattuck's assertions. The small white Catholic Church, still at hand, was no longer a Catholic Church but a hall, the Catholics having moved to a more imposing edifice. The county courthouse was entirely new, a thing in the usual fashion and scarcely so attractive as the old. The little old postoffice in its brown shell was replaced by a brick and glass structure, owned no doubt by the government. There was a Carnegie Library of sorts—what town has been skipped? A new central public school, various new churches, Baptist, Methodist, Presbyterian, showing where a part of the savings of the American people are being put. We stopped for lunch and picture postcards—and found only sleepy, lackadaisical merchants and clerks, a type of indolence befitting a hot, inter-river region. For to the east of this town about twenty miles was the White river (which we crossed at Indianapolis), and to the west about ten miles the Wabash, and all between was low, alluvial soil—a wonderful region for abundant crops—a region frequently overflowed in the springtime by the down rushing floods of the north.

CHAPTER LII

HAIL, INDIANA!

GOING out of Sullivan I made an observation, based on the sight of many men and women, sitting on doorsteps or by open windows or riding by in buggies or automobiles, or standing in yards or fields—that a lush, fecund land of this kind produces a lush, fecund population—and I think this was well demonstrated here. There was a certain plumpness about many people that I saw—men and women—a ruddy roundness of flesh and body, which indicated as much. I saw mothers on doorsteps or lawns with kicking, crowing children in their arms or youngsters playing about them, who illustrated the point exactly. The farmers that I saw were all robust, chunky men. The women—farm girls and town wives—had almost a Dutch stolidity. I gazed, hardly willing to believe, and yet convinced. It was the richness of this soil —black, sandy muck—of which these people partook. It made me think that governments ought to take starving populations off unfertile soils and put them on land like this.

Going south from here Franklin and I fell into a very curious and intricate discussion. The subtlety of some people's private speculations at times astonishes me. Not that our conversation was at all extraordinary from any point of view, but it was so peculiar in spots. I am not wildly intoxicated by the spirit of my native state, not utterly so at any rate; yet I must admit that there is something curiously different about it—delicate, poetic, generative—I hardly know what I want to say. On the way there I had been saying to Franklin that I doubted whether I should find the West still the same or whether it was as generative and significant as I had half come to make

myself believe it was. After leaving Warsaw I had remarked that either I or the town had changed greatly,
and since the town looked the same, it must be me. To
this he assented and now added:

"You should go sometime to a Speedway race at Indianapolis, as I have often, year after year since it was
first built. There, just when the first real summer days
begin to take on that wonderful light, and a kind of lumi-
nous silence over things suggests growing corn and ripen-
ing wheat and quails whistling in the meadows over by
the woods, you will find an assemblage of people from
all over this country and from other countries—cars by
the thousands with foreign licenses; which make you feel
that this is the center of things. I've been there, and getting a bit tired of watching the cars have gone over into
the woods inside the grounds and lain down on the grass
on my back. There would be the same familiar things
about me, the sugar and hickory trees, the little cool
breeze that comes up in the middle of the day, through
the foliage, the same fine sky that I used to look up into
when a boy; but, circling around me continuously for
hours, coming up from the south and along the great
stretches, and from the north bank of the track, were
the weird roar and thunder of an international conflict.
Then I would get up and look away south along the
grandstands and see flying in the Indiana sunlight the
flags of all the great nations, Italy and England, France
and Belgium, Holland and Germany. So I sometimes
think the spirit that has been instrumental in distinguish-
ing this particular section from other sections of the country is something still effective; that it does not always lead
away from itself; that it has established its freedom from
isolation and mere locality and accomplished here a quite
vital contact with universal thought."

"That's all very flattering to Indiana," I said, "but do
you really believe that?"

"Indeed I do," he replied. "This is a most peculiar
state. Almost invariably, on socalled clear days in July
and August out here, an indescribable haze over every-

thing leaves the horizons unaccounted for and the distance a sort of mystery. This, it has always seemed to me, is bound to produce in certain types of mind a kind of unrest. In such light, buzzards hanging high above you or crows flying over the woods are no longer merely the things that they are but become the symbols of a spiritual, if I may use the word, or æsthetic, suggestiveness that is unescapable. The forests here also, or such as used to be here, must have had their influence. Temples and cathedrals, all works of art, are designed to impress men's minds, leading them into varying conditions of consciousness. The forests of sugar and beech and poplar and oak and hickory about here originally, it has been said, were the most wonderful on the face of the earth. No one had ever experimented with the action of such things as these on people's minds, to determine specific results, but I fancy they have them. In fact I sometimes think there is something about soil and light, a magnetism or creative power like the electric generative field of a dynamo, which produces strange, new, interesting things. How else can you explain the fact that 'Ben Hur' was written out here at Crawfordville, under a beech tree, or why the first automobile course, after Brooklands, England, was built here at Indianapolis, or why La Salle, with a company of adventurers, should come canoeing down the St. Joseph and the Maumee into this region? I believe thoroughly in the presence of a great resource of relative truth, constituted of the facts of all human things; that this resource is available to anyone whoever or wherever he may be, who can, in his mind, achieve a clear understanding of his own freedom from the necessities of mere physical communication. This may seem to be getting a little thin but it is not beside the actual point if you trouble to think of it."

"That's rather flattering to dear old Indiana," I repeated, "but still I'm not sure that I'm absolutely convinced. You make out a fairly plausible case."

"Look at the tin plate trust," he continued, "one of the first and most successful. It originated in Kokomo and expanded until it controlled the Rock Island Railway, Diamond Match, and other corporations. Look at the first American automobile—it came from here—and James Whitcomb Riley and George Ade and Tarkington, and other things like that."

"Yes, 'and other things like that,'" I quoted. "You're right."

I did not manage to break in on his dream, however.

"Take this man Haynes, for instance, and his car. Here is a case where the soil or the light or the general texture of the country generated a sense of freedom, right here in Indiana in a single mind, and to a great result; but instead of his going away or its taking that direction, Haynes developed his own sense of freedom right here by building his motor car here. He rose above his local limitations without leaving. Through his accomplishment he has made possible a fine freedom for some of the rest of us. After all, individual freedom is not simply the inclination and the liberty to get up and go elsewhere; nor is it, as people seem to think, something only to be embodied in forms of government. I consider it something quite detached from any kind of government whatever, a thing which exists in the human mind and, indeed, is mind."

Franklin was at his very best, I thought.

"This is getting very esoteric, Franklin," I commented, "very, very esoteric."

"Just the same," he continued, "the automobile is a part of this same sense of freedom, the desire for freedom made manifest; not the freedom of the group but the freedom of the individual. That's about what it amounts to in the ultimate. Here we have been traveling across country, not limited in our ability to respond as we chose to the 'call of the road' and of the outdoors in general; and we have been bound by no rule save our own, not by the schedule of any organization. That same freedom was in Haynes' mind in the first instance, and right here, stationary in Indiana,—and it was generated by Indiana,—the conditions here."

"Yes," I agreed.

"Well, to me Indiana is noteworthy in having done and in still doing just that sort of thing. It stands unique in having produced a great many celebrated men and women in all departments of work, not only those who have departed from the state but those who have remained and gained a publicity for their achievements far outside its boundaries. It was, I'm confident, primarily this soil-generated call that came to you. It came to me. It must have come the same to many others, or to all I should say who have accomplished things, those who have grasped at or struggled for, if you wish to speak of it that way, universal standards and scope. You felt it and picked up and went away some years ago; now on your return you do not feel the old generative impulse any more; everything seems miserably changed and the beauty to a large extent faded. But it is not. I also do not find things the same any more. Yet I am convinced the old call is still here; and when I return I have a feeling that out here on the farms, driving the cows in the morning and at evening, in the small towns, and hanging around the old watergaps along the creeks, are boys just like we used to be, to whom the most vital thing in life is this call and the longing—to be free. Not to be free necessarily or at all, of these local experiences, but to achieve a working contact with universal things."

"That sounds very well, at least," I commented.

"There's something in it, I tell you," he insisted, "and what's more, though I'm not inclined to make so very much of that, Indiana was originally French territory and La Salle and his companions coming down here may have brought a psychic sprig of the original French spirit, which has resulted in all these things we have been discussing."

"You surely don't believe that?" I questioned.

"Well, I don't know. Certainly Indiana is different—inquisitive, speculative, constructive—the characteristics which have most distinguished the French. And, by the way," he added, returning to Haynes and his car for a moment, "a short time before Haynes developed his automobile, though not long enough, I'm sure, or to such an extent that he could have known much of its progress, the same problem was being studied and worked out in France by Levasser."

He looked at me as though he thought this was significant, then continued: "But I'm really not inclined to think that all this stuff is true or that there is a deep laid spiritual connection between France and Indiana. I don't. It's all amusing speculation, but I do believe there is something in the soil and light idea."

He leaned back and we ceased talking.

CHAPTER LIII

IT was just outside of Sullivan, a mile or two or three, that we encountered the Busseron, the first stream in which, as a boy, I ever fished. The strangeness of that experience comes back to me even now—the wonder, the beauty of a shallow stream, pooled in places, its banks sentineled by tall trees, its immediate shoreline ornamented by arrogant weeds and bushes blooming violently.

The stillness of the woods, the novelty of a long bamboo pole and a white line and a red and green cork; a hook, worms, the nibble of the unseen creature below the yellow surface of the stream. Even now I hear a distant gun shot—hunters prowling after birds. I see a dragon fly, steely blue and gauze of wing, fluttering and shimmering above my cork (why should they love cork floats so much?). My brother Ed has a nibble! Great, kind heaven, his cork is gone—once! twice!!

"Pull him out, Ed."

"For God's sake, pull him out!"

"Gee, look at that!"

Oh, a black and white silvery fish—or a dark, wet, slippery cat—as lovely and lustrous as porcelain. Oh, it's on the grass now, flipping here and there. My nerves are all a-tingle, my hair on end, with delight. I can scarcely wait until I get a bite—hours perhaps—for my brother Ed was always a luckier fisherman than I, or a better one.

And then late in the afternoon, after hours of this wonder world, we trudge home, along the warm, dusty, yellow country road; the evening sun is red in the West, our feet buried in the dust. Not a wagon, not a sound, save that of wood doves, bluejays, the spiritual, soulful, lyric thrush. On a long, limp twig with a

fork at the end is strung *our* fish, so small and stiff now—
so large, glistening, brilliant, when we caught them. On
every hand are field fragrances, the distant low of cows
and the grunts of pigs. I hear the voice of a farmer—
"Poo-gy! Poo-gy! Poogy! Poogy!"

"Gee, ma kin fry these—huh?"

"You bet."

Brown-legged, dusty, tired, we tramp back to the
kitchen door. There she is, plump, tolerant, smiling—a
gentle, loving understanding of boys and their hungry,
restless ways written all over her face.

"Yes, they're fine. We'll have them for supper. Wash
and clean them, and then wash your hands and feet and
come in."

On the grass we sit, a pan between us, cleaning those
penny catches. The day has been so wonderful that we
think the fish must be perfect. And they are, to us. And
then the after-supper grouping on the porch, the velvety
dusk descending, the bats, the mosquitoes, the smudge
carried about the house to drive out the mosquitoes, tales
of Indians and battle chiefs long dead, the stars, slumber.

I can feel my mother's hand as I lean against her knee
and sleep.

By just such long, hot yellow roads as Ed and I traversed as boys Franklin and I came eventually to Vincennes, Indiana, but only after traversing a region so flat
and yet so rich that it was a delight to look upon. I had
never really seen it before—or its small, sweet simple
towns—Paxton, Carlisle, Oaktown, Busseron. The fields
were so rich and warm and moist that they were given
over almost entirely to the growing of melons—water
and cantaloupe, great far flung stretches of fields. Large,
deep-bodied, green-painted wagons came creaking by,
four, five, and six in a row, hauling melons to the nearest
siding where were cars. There were melon packing
sheds to be seen here and there, where muskmelons were
being labeled and crated. It was lovely. At one point
we stopped a man and bought two watermelons and sat
down by the roadside to eat. Other machines passed and

the occupants looked at us as though we had stolen them.

"Here we are," I said to Franklin, "three honest men, eating our hard-earned melons, and these people believe we stole them."

"Yes, but think of our other crimes," he replied, "and anyhow, who wouldn't—three men eating melons by a roadside, the adjoining fields of which are dotted with melons."

The man who had passed in the buggy had leered at us in such a convicting way.

And yet I have Franklin and Bert to witness we paid ten cents each for two of the best melons we ever tasted.

At Paxton and at Carlisle again we came upon coal mines—that vein of soft coal which seems to underlie this whole region. Miners in droves were to be seen walking along the roads as at Wilkes-Barré, their faces smudgy, their little lamps standing up from their caps, their big tin buckets hanging on or tucked under their arms. We stopped at one town and examined the exterior of a mine because it was so near the road. Every few seconds out of its subterranean depths (three hundred and fifty feet, the man told me) up a deep, dripping shaft would come a small platform carrying several small cars of coal, which would be shunted onto a runway and "empties" pushed in to take their places. I asked the man who ran the engine in the nearby shed how many tons of coal they would take out in a day. "Oh, about four hundred," he said.

"Any men ever killed here?"

"Yes, occasionally."

"Recently?"

"Well, there was an explosion two years ago."

"Many men killed?"

"Eight."

"Were there any before that?"

"Two, about three years before."

He wiped his sweaty forehead with a grimy hand.

"Wouldn't like to go down, would you?" he asked genially, after a time—quite unconscious of our earlier conversation, I think.

"No, thanks," I replied.

I had a sicky feeling, conveyed by that dark, dripping shaft. Three hundred and fifty feet—not me!

But I said to myself as I looked at all the healthy, smiling miners we met farther on, "If I were a prince or a president and these were my subjects, how proud I would be of a land that contained such—how earnest for their well being"—I had so little courage to do what they were doing.

But in spite of these mines, which were deep and far-reaching, as we learned, in many districts stretching for miles in different directions, the soil manifested that same fertility and the land grew flatter and flatter. All the towns in here were apparently dependent upon them. There were no rises of ground. Interesting groves of trees crowded to the roadside at times, providing a cooling shade, and excessively marshy lands appeared, packed with hazel bushes and goldenrod, but no iron weed as in the East. The roads were sped over by handsome automobiles—much finer in many instances than ours—and I took it that they were representative of the real farmer wealth here, a wealth we as a family had never been permitted to taste.

In about two hours we entered Vincennes—a front tire having blown up just outside Sullivan on the banks of the Busseron. At its edge we came upon a fairgrounds so gaily bedecked with tents and flags that we parked our car and went in—to see the sights. The Knox County Fair. It seemed to me that this farmers' show supported my belief in their prosperity, for to me at least it turned out to be the most interesting county fair I had ever seen. The animals displayed—prize sows and boars, horses and sheep of different breeds, chickens and domestic animals of various kinds,—were intensely interesting to look at and so attractively displayed. I never saw so many fat sheep, dams and rams, nor more astonishing hogs, great, sleek rolling animals that blinked at us with their little eyes and sniffed and grunted. Great white pleasant tents were devoted to farm machinery and automobiles and by these alone one could tell that here was a prosperous and buying population, else the manufacturers had never troubled to send so much and such expensive machinery. All that the farmer could use—machines for ploughing, planting, cutting, reaping, binding, fertilizing, baling (I think I counted a score of separate machines of this kind), to others intended for use around the home—kerosene cook stoves, well pumps, cream separators, churns, washing machines—a whole host of these—to the latest inventions in motor ploughs and motor driven farm wagons—were here. The display of automobiles was lavish—really all the important makes were represented and in addition there was a racetrack with races going on and a large number of tented amusements—the wild men from Boola-Boola; Calgero, the mindreader, several moving picture shows, a gypsy dancer, and the like.

Franklin and I browsed around at our leisure. On so fine and so hot an afternoon it was amusing to idle under these great trees and study the country throng. A hungry boy was treated to "weenies" (the Indiana version of "hot dog") and coffee by him—a treat he was very backward about accepting. Hundreds, judging by the parked cars outside, possessed automobiles. Various church congregations of the region had established restaurant booths to aid one or other of their religious causes. At a table in the booth of the Holy Trinity Roman Catholic Church of Vincennes I ate a dish of chicken dumplings, a piece of cherry pie, and drank several glasses of milk, thereby demonstrating, I think, that no inalienable enmity existed between myself and the Catholic Church, at least not on the subject of food. At this booth, besides the several becalicoed and bestarched old ladies who were in attendance, I noticed a tall Bernhardtesque girl of very graceful and sinuous lines who was helping to wait on people. She had red hair, long delicate tapering fingers, a wasplike but apparently uncorseted waist, and almond shaped greenish grey eyes. No edict of the Church prevented her from wearing hip tight skirts or one that came lower than perhaps four or five inches below the knee. She had on rings and pins and, quite unconsciously I think, took graceful and dreamful attitudes. There was a kind of high scorn—if not rebellion—in her mood, for one aiding a religious cause——

I wondered how long Vincennes and the sacred precincts of the Church would retain her.

CHAPTER LIV

Is it an illusion of romance, merely, or is it true that, in spite of the fact that the French, governmentally speaking, have been out of old Vincennes—the very region of it—for over a hundred and fifty years, and that nearly all we know of the town of twenty thousand has come into existence in the last fifty years, there still exists in it, hovers over it, the atmosphere of old France? Do we see, always, what we would like to see, or is there something in this matter of predisposition, the planting of a seed, however small, which eventually results in a tree of the parent stock? I was scarcely prepared to believe that there was anything of old France about this town—it seemed quite too much to ask, and yet rolling leisurely through these streets, it seemed to me that there was a great deal of it. The houses, quite a number of them, had that American French Colonial aspect which we have all come to associate with their forbears, the palaces and decorative arts of the high Louis! France, the modifier of the flamboyant dreams of the Renaissance! France, the mother, really, of the classic styles of England! The cooler, more meditative and Puritan spirit took all that was best in the dreams and supergrand taste of the France of the Kings and Emperors and gave us Heppelwhite and Sheraton, and those charming architectural fancies known as Georgian. Or am I wrong?

And here in Vincennes, in the homes at least, there was something reminiscent of this latter, while in the principal streets—Third and Second—and in the names of some of the others, there was a suggestion of such towns or cities as Rouen and Amiens—a mere suggestion, perhaps, some might insist, but definite enough to me. As a matter of fact, tucked away in this southern river region of Indiana, it seemed very French, and I recalled now that my first and only other connection with it had been through a French woman, a girl protégé of my mother, who had married (she was a wild, pagan creature, as I can testify) the manager or captain of the principal fire station in the then city of twelve thousand. Before her marriage, at Terre Haute, she had done sewing for my mother, in our more prosperous days, and when conditions grew so bad that my mother felt that she must get out of Terre Haute, instead of going to Sullivan direct (I do not think her original intention was to go to Sullivan at all) she wrote this French woman of her troubles, and upon her invitation visited her there. For a period of six weeks, or longer, we lived in the apartment which was a part of the fire captain's perquisites, and a part of the central fire station itself—the rear half of the second floor. There must have been some unimportant connection between this and the county jail or central police station, or both, for in a building adjoining at the rear I remember there was a jail, and that I could go back, if I chose, downstairs and out, and see some of the incarcerated looking out through the bars. It was a pleasant enough place as such things go, and my mother must have had some idea of remaining in Vincennes, for not long after we arrived my sister and brother and I were put in another Catholic School,—the bane of my youthful life. This did not last very long, however, for shortly thereafter we were taken out and removed to Sullivan. Eleven years later, at the time of my mother's death in Chicago, this woman, who was then and there a dressmaker, came to cry over her coffin and to declare my mother the best friend she ever had.

My youthful impressions of Vincennes, sharp as they may have been at the time, had by now become very vague. I remember that from the fire tower, where hung an alarm bell and to which we were occasionally permitted to ascend, the straight flowing Wabash River was to be seen; also that northward, toward Sullivan, were Merom Bluffs, where pleasure seekers from Vincennes were accustomed to drive. My mother went once. Also, that certain tow headed and dark girls seemed very numerous about the fire station at night. Also that once, during our stay, there was a big fire, and that we all arose and went out to join the great throng watching it. Our host, the captain, was seen to mount a ladder and break in a window and disappear in a red glow, much to my mother's and my own horror. But he came back alive.

In ambling about, I found the exact firehouse, enlarged and improved, "where it has always been," as one of the neighboring tradesmen told me—new automobile engines and trucks in it—and then I was ready to go. I had seen all I could hope to remember, even dimly. We hurried to a neighboring garage, took on a store of oil and gasoline, and were off in the twilight and the moonlight, for Evansville.

. . . .

Uncertain is the outcome of all automobilists' plans forever and ever, as with all other plans. Although we had inquired and inquired, getting the exact way (and Franklin's conferences on these matters were always extended and minute) we were soon safely on the wrong road. We had been told to make for a place called Decker, via a town called Purcell, but soon in the shades of a fast falling night we were scuttling up a cowpath, under dark and ghostly trees.

"How would it do to call on some squirrel or chipmunk and pay our respects?" suggested Franklin. "They appear to be about the only people living here."

We decided to go back.

Once more on a fairly good road again, a mile or so back, we met a charming milkmaid, with fine arms, pink cheeks, and two brimming buckets of milk. Modestly, she told us we were on the wrong road.

"You should have kept the macadam road to Purcell. This goes to St. Francisville across the river. But if you go up here a mile or two and take the first road to your left, it will bring you to St. Thomas, and there's a road on from there to Decker. But it would be better if you went back."

"Back? Never!" I said to Franklin, as the girl went on, and thinking of the miles we had come. "It's a fine night. Look at the moon." (There was an almost full moon showing a golden tip in the eastern sky.) "Soon it will be as bright as day. Let's ride on. We'll get to Evansville by morning, anyhow. It's only sixty miles or so."

"Yes, if we could go straight," amended Bert, pessimistically.

"Oh, we'll go straight enough. She says St. Thomas is only eight miles to our left."

So on we went. The moon rose. Across flat meadows in the pale light, lamps in distant houses looked like ships at sea, sailing off a sandy coast. There were clumps of pines or poplars gracefully distributed about the landscape. The air was moist, but so fragrant and warm! These were the bottom lands of the White and Wabash Rivers, quite marshy in places, and fifteen miles farther south we would have to cross the White River on a ferry.

We sped on. The road became sandy and soft. Now and then it broke into muddy stretches where we had to go slow. From straggling teamsters we gathered characteristic and sometimes amusing directions.

"Yuh go up here about four miles to Ed Peters' place. It's the big white store on the corner—yuh can't miss it. Then yuh turn to yer left about three miles, till yuh come to the school on the high ground there (a rise of about eight feet it was). Then yuh turn to yer right and go down through the marsh to the iron bridge, and that'll bring yer right into the Decker Road."

We gathered this as we were leaving St. Thomas, a lonely Catholic outpost, with a church and sisters' school of some kind.

On and on. Riding is delightful in such a country. In lovely cottages as we tore past I heard mellifluous voices singing in some archaic way. You could see lighted lamps on the family tables,—a man or woman or both sitting by reading. On doorsteps, in dooryards now and then were loungers, possibly indifferent to the mosquitoes. The moon cleared to a silvery perfection and lighted all the fields and trees. There were owl voices and bats. In Ed Peters' place a crowd of country bumpkins were disporting themselves.

"Har, har, har! Whee-oh!"

You should have heard the laughter. It was infectious.

A man outside directed us further. We came to the school, the iron bridge in the marsh, and then by a wrong road away from Decker, but we found it finally.

It was a railroad town. On the long steps of a very imposing country store, lighted by flaring oil lamps, a great crowd of country residents (all men) were gathered to see the train come in,—an event soon to happen, I gathered. They swam in a Vierge or Goyaesque haze, —a full hundred of them, their ivory faces picked out in spots by the uncertain light. We asked of one the road to Evansville, and he told us to go back over the bridge and south, or to our left, as we crossed the bridge.

"The ferry hain't here. It may be as ye can't get across t'night. The river's runnin' purty high."

"That would be a nice note, wouldn't it?" commented Bert.

"Well, Decker looks interesting to me," observed Franklin. "What's the matter with Decker? I'd like to sketch that crowd anyhow."

We went on down to the ferry to see.

En route we encountered a perfectly horrible stretch of road—great, mucky ruts that almost stalled the car —and in the midst of it an oil well, or the flaring industry of driving one. There was a great towering well frame in the air, a plunger, a forge, an engine, and various flaring torches set about and men working. It was so attractive that, although up to this moment we had been worrying about the car, we got out and went over, leaving it standing in inches and inches of mud. Watching the blaze of furnaces for sharpening drills and listening to the monotonous plunging of the drill, we sat about here for half an hour basking in the eerie effect of the torches in the moonlight and against the dark wood. It was fascinating.

A little later we came to the waterside and the alleged ferry. It was only a road that led straight into the river—a condition which caused Franklin to remark that they must expect us to drive under. At the shore was a bell on a post, with a rope attached. No sign indicated its import, but since far on the other side we could see lights, we pulled it vigorously. It clanged loud and long. Between us and the lights rolled a wide flood, smooth and yet swiftly moving, apparently. Small bits of things could be seen going by in the pale light. The moon on the water had the luster of an oyster shell. There was a faint haze or fog which prevented a clear reflection.

But our bell brought no response. We stood here between bushes and trees admiring the misty, pearly river, but we wanted to get on, too. On the other side was a town. You could hear laughing voices occasionally, and scraps of piano playing or a voice singing, but the immediate shore line was dark. I seized the rope again and clanged and clanged "like a house afire," Bert said.

Still no response.

"Maybe they don't run at night," suggested Bert.

"He said the water might be too high," commented Franklin. "It looks simple enough."

Once more I pulled the bell.

Then after another drift of moments there was a faint sound as of scraping chains or oars, and after a few moments more, a low something began to outline itself in the mist. It was a flat boat and it was coming, rigged to an overhead wire and propelled by the water. It was coming quite fast, I thought. Soon it was off shore and one of the two men aboard—an old man and a young one—was doing something with the rear chain, pulling the boat farther upstream, nearer the wire.

"Git that end pole out of the way," called the older of the two men, the one nearer us, and then the long, flat dish scraped the shore and they were pushing it far inland with poles to make it fast.

"What's the matter? Couldn't you hear the bell?" I inquired jocundly.

"Yes, I heard the bell, all right," replied the older man truculently. "This here boat ain't supposed to run nights anyhow in this here flood. Y'can't tell what'll happen, logs and drifts comin' down. We've lost three automobiles in her already as it is."

I speculated nervously as to that while he grumbled and fussed.

"Hook 'er up tight," he called to his assistant. "She might slip out yet."

"But up at Decker," I added mischievously, "they said you ran all night."

"They said! They said! Whadda they know about this here ferry? I'm runnin' this, I guess. Havin' to git out here nights, tar-erd (he was meaning tired) as I am, an' take this thing back an' forth. I'm gittin' sick on it. I hain't got to do it."

"I know," observed Franklin, "but we're very anxious to get across tonight. We have to be in Evansville by morning anyhow."

"Well, I don't know nothin' about that. All I know is everybody's in a all-fired hurry to git across."

"Well, that's all right now, doctor," I soothed. "We'll fix this up on the other side. You just take us over like a good sort."

The aroma of a tip seemed to soothe him a little.

"Be keerful how you run that car," he commented to Bert. "One feller ran his car on an' up-ended this thing an' off he went. We never did get the machine out. She was carried on down stream."

Bert manœuvred the car very gingerly. Then we poled off in the moonlight, and I could see plainly that there was a flood. We were slow getting out to where the main current was, but once there its speed shocked me.

A vast, sullen volume of water was pouring down—on and away into the Wabash, the Ohio, the Mississippi, the Gulf. I was thinking how wonderful water is anyhow—out of the unknown, into the unknown, like ourselves, it comes and goes. And here, like petty actors in a passing play, we were crossing under the moon— the water as much a passing actor as any of us.

"Better pay out more at the stern there," called the old man to his helper. "She's pushin' her pretty hard."

The water was fairly boiling along the upstream side.

"At any minute now," he continued, "a bundle of drift or logs or weeds is like to come along and foul us, and then if that there wire gave way, where'd we be?"

I felt a little uncomfortable at the thought, I confess —Franklin's good machine, his inability to swim, the eddying swiftness of this stream.

Fortunately, at this rate, the center was soon passed and we began to near the other shore. The current drove us up into a deep-cut shallow inlet, where they poled the punt close to shore and fastened it.

Then Bert had to make a swift run with the machine, for just beyond the end of the boat was a steep incline up which we all had to clamber.

"Don't let 'er slip back on yer," he cautioned. "If yer do, she's like to go back in the water" . . . and Bert sent "her" snorting uphill.

We paid the bill—fifty cents—(twentyfive of that being tacked on as a penalty for routing him out "tar-erd as he was" and fifteen cents extra for disturbing observations about drifts, lost automobiles, and the like). Then we bustled up and through an interesting, cleanly looking place called Hazleton (population twentyfive hundred) and so on toward Evansville, which we hoped surely to reach by midnight.

CHAPTER LV

BUT we didn't reach Evansville, for all our declaration and pretence of our need. A delightful run along a delightful road, overhung with trees (and now that we were out of the valley between the two rivers, cut between high banks of tree shaded earth), brought us to Princeton, a town so bright and clean looking that we were persuaded, almost against our wishes, to pass the night here. Some towns have just so much personality. They speak to you of pleasant homes and pleasant people—a genial atmosphere. Here, as elsewhere, indeed, in all but the poorest of these small midwestern towns, the center of it was graced by the court house, a very presentable building, and four brightly lighted business sides. The walks about the square were outlined, every fifty feet or less, by a five-lamp standard. The stores were large and clean and bright. A drug store we visited contained such an interesting array of postcards that I bought a dozen—pictures of great grain elevators, four or five of which we had seen on entering the town, sylvan scenes along the banks of the Patoka, a small lake or watering place called "Long Pond," and scenes along tree sheltered roads. I liked the spirit of these small towns, quite common everywhere today, which seeks out the charms of the local life and embodies them in colored prints, and I said so.

Walk into any drug or book store of any up to date small town today, and you will find in a trice nearly every scene of importance and really learn the character and charms of the vicinity. Thus at Conneaut, Ohio, but for the picture postcards which chronicled the fact, we would never have seen the giant cranes which emptied steel cars like coalscuttles. Again, except for the picture postcards displayed, I would never have sensed the astonishing charms of Wilkes-Barré, Sandusky, or even my native Terre Haute. The picture cards told all, in a group, of what there was to see.

We discovered a most interesting and attractive quick lunch here, quite snowy and clean, with a bright, open grill at the back, and here, since we now were hungry again, we decided to eat. Franklin saw cantaloupes in the window and I announced that I had bought a picture card of a cantaloupe packing scene in a town called Cantaloupe, which, according to my ever ready map, was back on the road we had just come through.

"They ought to be good around here," he commented, rather avidly, I thought. "Nice, fresh cantaloupe right out of the field."

We entered.

I did not know, really, how seriously Franklin craved fresh, ripe, cold muskmelon in hot weather until we got inside.

"We'll have muskmelon, eh?" he observed eagerly.

"All right. I'll divide one with you."

"Oh, no," he returned, with the faintest rise in his inflection. "I'd like a whole one."

"Delighted, Franklin," I replied. "On with the dance. Let muskmelon, etc."

He went to the counter and persuaded the waiter maid to set forth for him two of the very largest—they were like small watermelons—which he brought over.

"These look like fine melons," he observed.

"They're splendid," said the girl. "This is a melon country."

A traveling salesman who was eating over at another table exclaimed, "I can vouch for that."

Franklin and I began. They were delicious—fragrant, a luscious product of a rich soil. We ate in silence, and when his was consumed, he observed, eyeing me speculatively, "I believe I could stand another one."

"Franklin!" I exclaimed reproachfully.

"Yes, I could," he insisted. "They're great, don't you think so?"

"As good as ever I have eaten—better even."

"That settles it. I'm going to have one more."

He brought it over and ate it alone, while I sat and talked to him and marveled. Once more, when he was finished, he fixed me with his eye.

"Well, now, how do you feel?" I inquired.

"Fine. You know—you'll think it's funny—but I could eat another—a half anyhow."

"Franklin!" I exclaimed. "This is too much. Two whole melons and now a third!"

"Do you think it's too much?"

There was a sort of childish naïveté about the inquiry which moved me to laughter—and firmness. Franklin achieves this quite unconsciously, at times—a certain self-abnegating shyness.

"I certainly do. Here it is after eleven. We are supposed to be up early and off—and here you sit eating muskmelons by the crate. This is shameful. Besides, you can get more tomorrow. We are in the land of the muskmelon."

"Oh, all right," he consented, quite crestfallen.

I did not realize at the time that I was actually stopping him, and before he had enough. It was a joke on my part.

The next day was Wednesday, a bright, sunny day, and pleasantly cool. The sun streaming under my black shades at six and earlier awoke me, and I arose and surveyed the small town, as much of it as I could see from my window and through encircling trees. It was as clean and homey and pleasing as it had seemed the night before. By now Franklin, hearing me stirring, was up too, and we awakened Bert, who was still asleep. If we were to get to Evansville and on to Indianapolis and Carmel again in this one day, it would have to be a long and speedy run, but even now I began to doubt whether we should make it. Evansville was too interesting to me, as one of my home towns. It was all of fifty miles away as we would ride, and after that would come a cross-country run of one hundred and fortyfive miles as the crow flies, or counting the twists and turns we would make, say one hundred and seventyfive miles—a scant calculation. There were, as my map showed, at least seven counties to cross on returning. In our path lay French Lick and West Baden—the advertised Carlsbads of America. North of that would be Bedford, the home of the world's supply of Indiana limestone, and beyond it Bloomington, the seat of the State University, where I had spent one dreamy, lackadaisical year. After that a run of at least sixtyfive miles straight, let alone winding, before we could enter Carmel.

"It can't be done, Franklin," I argued, as we dressed. "You said three days, but it will be four at the earliest, if not five. I want to see a little of Evansville and Bloomington."

"Well, if we have decent roads, we can come pretty near doing it," he insisted. "Certainly we can get home by tomorrow night. I ought to. I have a lot of things to do in town Friday."

"Well, you're the doctor," I agreed, "so long as I see what I want to see."

We bustled downstairs, agreeing to breakfast in Evansville. It was six thirty. Those favored souls who enjoy rising early in the morning and looking after their flowers were abroad, admiring, pinching, cutting, watering. It was a cheering spectacle. I respect all people who love flowers. It seems to me one of the preliminary, initiative steps in a love and understanding of beauty. Evansville came nearer at a surprising rate. I began to brush up my local geography and list in my mind the things I must see—the houses in which we had lived, the church and school which I was made to attend, the Ohio River, at the foot of Main Street—where once in January, playing with some boys, I fell into the river, knocked off a floating gangway, and came desperately near being swept away by the ice. Then I must see Blount's Plow Works, and the chair factory of Messrs. Nienaber and

Fitton, where my brother Al worked for a time, and where of a Saturday I often went to help him. And the Evansville Ironstone Pottery Company must be found, too, at whose low windows I was wont to stand and delightedly watch the men form cups, plates, pitchers, etc., out of grey, wet clay. This seemed to me the most wonderful manufacturing process of all those witnessed by me in my youth. It was so gracefully and delicately accomplished. There was only one other thing that compared in interest, and that was the heating and melting of iron in great furnaces in an enormous iron foundry on the same street with the Catholic School which I used to pass every day and where the pouring of the glistening metal into cauldrons and the pouring of that into wondrously intricate moulds of sand, whereby were shaped iron fences, gratings, culvert tops, had always been of the intensest interest to me.

The essential interest of Evansville to me, however, was that at that particular time in my youth, and just at the time when seemingly things had reached a crisis for my mother—whose moods were invariably my own —Evansville had appeared like a splendid new chapter in our lives, and resolved all of our difficulties, for the time being, into nothing. How was this done? Well, as I have indicated somewhere, I believe, our oldest brother, the oldest living member of the family of children, had come to my mother's rescue in the nick of time. By now he was a successful, though up to this time wandering, minstrel man—an "end man," no less. But, more recently still, he had secured a position with a permanent or stock minstrel company located in the Evansville Opera House, where he was honored with the position of interlocutor and end man, as the mood prompted him, and where nightly he was supposed to execute a humorous monologue. Incidentally, he was singing his own songs. Also, incidentally he was conducting a humorous column in a local paper, the Evansville *Argus*. The fences and billboards of the city attested to his comparative popularity, for a large red and yellow single sheet print of his face was conspicuously displayed in many windows.

His life so far had proved a charming version of the prodigal son. As a boy of seventeen, for errors which need not be recounted here, he was driven out of the home. As a man of twentyseven (or boy) he had now returned (the winter previous to our moving) adorned with a fur coat, a high silk hat, a gold-headed cane.

My mother cried on his shoulder and he on hers. He really loved her so tenderly, so unwaveringly, that this in itself constituted a fine romance. At once he promised to solve all her difficulties. She must come out of this. He was going to Evansville now. There is a bit of private history which should be included here, but which I do not wish to relate, at present. The result was that thereafter a weekly letter containing a few dollars—three or four—arrived every Monday. (How often have I gone to the postoffice to get it!) Then there was some talk of a small house he was going to rent, and of the fact that we were soon to move. Then one summer day we did go, and I recall so well how, arriving in Evansville at about nine o'clock at night (my mother and we three youngest), we were met at the station by the same smiling, happy brother, and taken to the house at 1413 East Franklin Street; where on seeing her new home and its rather comfortable equipment, my mother stood in the doorway and cried—and he with her. I cannot say more than that. It all seems too wonderful—too beautiful, even now.

CHAPTER LVI

BUT I cannot possibly hope to convey the delicious sting life had in it for me at this time as a spectacle, a dream, something in which to bathe and be enfolded, as only youth and love know life. Not Evansville alone but life itself was beautiful—the sky, the trees, the sun, the visible scene. People hurrying to and fro or idling in the shade, the sound of church bells, of whistles, a wide stretch of common. Getting up in the morning, going to bed at night. The stars, the winds, hunger, thirst, the joy of playing or of idly musing.

In Evansville I was just beginning to come out of the dream period which held for me between the years of seven and eleven. The significance of necessity and effort were for the first time beginning to suggest themselves. Still, I was not awake, only vaguely disturbed at times, like a silky, shimmery sea, faintly touched by vagrom winds. The gales and storms were to come fast enough. I was really not old enough to understand all or even any of the troublesome conditions affecting our family. Like my companionable brother and sister, I was too young, undaunted, hopeful. Sometimes, in my dreams, a faint suggestion of my mood at the time comes back, and then I know how I have changed—the very chemistry of me. I do not respond now as I did then, or at any rate, I think not.

As we neared the city we could see the ground elevating itself in the distance, and soon we were riding along a ridge or elevated highroad, suggestively alive with traffic and dotted with houses.

.   .   .   .   .   .

Evansville is a southern city, in spite of the fact that

it is Indiana, and has all the characteristic marks of a southern city—a hot, drowsy, almost enervating summer, an early spring, a mild winter, a long, agreeable autumn. Snow falls but rarely and does not endure long. Darkies abound, whole sections of them, and work on the levee, the railroad, and at scores of tasks given over to whites in the north. You see them ambling about carrying packages, washing windows, driving trucks and autos, waiting on table. It is as though the extreme south had reached up and just touched this projecting section of Indiana.

Again, it is a German city, strangely enough, a city to which thousands of the best type of German have migrated. Despite the fact that Vincennes and Terre Haute were originally French, and then English, except for small sections through here, the German seems to predominate. We saw many German farmers, the Americanized type, coming up from Terre Haute, and here in Evansville German names abounded. It was as true of my days as a boy here as it is now—even more so, I believe. There are a number of purely German Catholic or Lutheran churches controlled by Bavarian priests or ministers.

Again it is a distinctly river type of town, with that floating population of river squatters—you can always tell them—drifting about. I saw a dozen in the little while I was there, river nomads or gypsies bustling about, dark, sallow, small, rugged. I have seen them at St. Louis, at Memphis, in Savannah, where the boats come up from the sea and down from Augusta. I can always tell them.

Once inside the city, I was interested to note that most cities, like people, retain their characteristics permanently. Thus in my day, Evansville was already noted as a furniture manufacturing city. Plainly it was so still. In half a dozen blocks we passed as many large furniture companies, all their windows open and the whir and drone of their wheels and saws and planes pouring forth a happy melody. Again, it was already at that time establishing a reputation for the manufacture of cheap pottery; and here, to our left, was a pottery crowded in among other things, not large, but still a pottery. If there was one, we might expect others.

At the edge of the town, making its way through a notable gorge, was Pigeon Creek, a stream in which Ed, Al and I had often bathed and fished, and to the shore of which we had been led, on divers occasions, by a stout German Catholic priest, or three or four of them, giving an annual or semiannual picnic. The fact that the land rises at this section was probably what attracted the first settlers here, and gives to this creek and the heart of the city a picturesque and somewhat differentiated character.

Not far from the center of the city, in a region which I once considered very remote, we passed the double-steepled church of St. Anthony, an institution which, because I was taken to its dedication by my father, I had retained in memory as something imposing. It was not at all—a rather commonplace church in red brick and white stone, such as any carpenter and builder of Teutonic extraction might design and execute. A little farther on, facing my much beloved Vine Street, where stood Holy Trinity Catholic Church and School, and along which, morning and evening, I used to walk, I discovered the Vanderburg County Court House, filling a space of ground which had once been our public school playground. It was very large, very florate, and very like every other court house in America.

Friends, why is it that American architects can design nothing different—or is it that our splendidly free and unconventional people will not permit them? I sometimes feel that there could not exist a more dull witted nation architecturally than we are. In so far as intelligence is supposed to manifest itself in the matter of taste, we give no evidence of having any—positively none. Our ratiocinations are of the flock, herd or school variety. We run with the pack. Some mountebank Simon in art, literature, politics, architecture, cries "thumbs up," and up goes every blessed thumb from the Atlantic to the Pacific. Then some other pseudoratiocinating ass calls "thumbs down," and down go all thumbs—not a few, but all. Let a shyster moralist cry that Shakespeare is immoral and his plays are at once barred from all the schools of a dozen states. Let a quack nostrum peddling zany declare that the young must not be contaminated, and out go all the works of Montagne, Ibsen, Hauptmann, Balzac, on the ground, forsooth, that they will injure the young. Save the sixteen year old girl, if you must make mushheads and loons, absolute naturals, of every citizen from ocean to ocean!

I despair, really. I call for water and wash my hands. A land with such tendencies can scarcely be saved, unless it be by disaster. We need to be tried by fire or born again. We do not grasp the first principles of intellectual progress.

But our breakfast! Our breakfast! Before getting it I had to take Franklin to view the Ohio River from Water Street (I do believe they have changed the name to Riverside Drive, since New York has one) for I could not rest until he had seen one of the most striking American river scenes of which I know anything. I know how the Hudson joins the ocean at New York, the Missouri the Mississippi at St. Louis, the Moselle the Rhine, at Coblenz, the New and Big Kanawha in the picturesque mountains of West Virginia, and the Alleghany the Monongahela to make the Ohio in Pittsburg—but this sweep of the Ohio, coming up from the South and turning immediately south again in a mighty elbow which pushes at the low hill on which the city stands, is tremendous. You know this is a mighty river, bearing the muddy waters of half a continent, by merely looking at it. It speaks for itself.

Standing on this fronting street of this purely commercial city, whose sloping levee sinks to the water's edge, you see it coming, miles and miles away, this vast body of water; and turning, you see it disappearing around a lowland, over whose few weak and yellow trees the water frequently passes. In high water, whole towns and valleys fall before it. Houses and cabins go by on its flood.

On it ride those picturesque sternwheelers, relics of an older order of navigation, and here on this bright August morning were several anchored at our feet. They were fastened to floating wharves, chained to the shore. On the long, downward slope of cobble stones were lying boxes and bales, the evidence of a river traffic that no inimical railroad management can utterly kill. A river capable of bearing almost all the slow freight of a half score of states is left to distribute the minor shipments of perhaps four or five. Franklin and Bert were struck with it, which pleased me greatly, for it is pleasant to bring another to a great view. They exclaimed over its scope and beauty.

Then we went looking for a restaurant. Although the killing of game was still out of season, we found one where broiled squirrels were being offered for the humble sum of sixty cents. We feasted. Our conservative chauffeur declared, as we sat down, that he did not care for anything much, and then ordered a steak, three eggs, a pot of coffee, a bowl of wheatena, muffins and hashed brown potatoes, topped off with a light plate of waffles and maple syrup.

"Bert," exclaimed Franklin, "you really aren't as strong as you might be this morning. You *must* look after yourself."

He scarcely heard. Lost in a sea of provender, he toiled on, an honest driver worthy of his hire.

And here it was that the question of muskmelons once more arose—this time to plague me—melons which, as we have seen, were as plentiful as manna in the desert.

"Now," Franklin observed with unction as we sat down, "I'm going to have another muskmelon."

"Right," I congratulated him, with the air of a generous host, "now's the time."

"Give me a nice large, cold muskmelon," he observed to the darky who now appeared, napkin on arm.

"Sorry, boss," replied that worthy, "we ain't got no mushmelers dis mawnin. Dey ain't none to be had in de maaket."

"What's that?" I demanded, looking up and getting nervous, for we were in the very best restaurant the city afforded. "No muskmelons! What are you talking about? We saw fields of them—miles of them—between here and Vincennes and Sullivan."

"Da's right, boss. Da's where dey grows. You see 'um dere all right. But dey don't allus bring 'um down here. Dis ain't no maaket. Dey go noth and east—to New Yawk and Chicago. Da's what it is."

"You mean to say you can't get me a single melon?" queried Franklin feebly, a distinct note of reproach in his voice. He even glanced my way.

"Sorry, boss. If dey wuz to be had, we'd have 'um. Yessir—dis is de place. We cain't git 'um—da's it."

Franklin turned upon me coldly.

"That's what comes of not eating all that I wanted to when I wanted to. Hang it all."

"Franklin," I said. "I am stricken to the earth. I crawl before you. Here is dust and here are ashes." I gesticulated with my arms. "If I had thought for one moment———"

"And all those fine melons up there!"

"I agree," I said.

He buried his face in the bill of fare and paid no attention to me. Only Bert's declining state of health restored him, eventually, and we left quite cheerful.

.   .   .   .   .   .

Only a block or two from our restaurant was the St. George Hotel, my brother's resort, unchanged and as old fashioned as ever, white, with green lattices, rocking-chairs out in front, an airy, restful, summery look about it. How, once upon a time, he loved to disport himself here with all the smart idlers of the town! I can see him yet, clothed to perfection, happy in his youth, health and new found honors, such as they were. Then came Holy Trinity (church and school), at Third and Vine, an absolutely unchanged institution. It had shrunk and lost quality, as had everything else nearly with which I had been connected. The school fence, the principal's red brick house at the back (how I used to dread it), the church next door, with the rear passage by which, when we were extra good, we went to receive colored picture cards of the saints or Jesus or Mary, and when we were bad—to be warned by the priest.

The latter adventure was terrible. It had never befallen me, but other boys had experienced it.

I cannot possibly convey to you, I fear, how very definitely this particular school and church impressed me at the time. Although I had started in several schools, this was really my first. By this time my mother was beginning to doubt the efficacy of Catholic schools in general (how they would have condemned her for that!), but as yet she was not quite positive enough in her own mind to insist on a change. When I found it was another Catholic school I was to attend I was very downhearted. I was terrorized by the curriculum, the admixture of priests, nuns and one bewhiskered Herr Professor, very young and as he seemed to me very terrible, a veritable ogre, who ruled the principal school room here. Really he was a most amazing person in his way. He had blazing eyes, heavy black eyebrows, black hair, a full black beard, and he walked with a dynamic stride which, as it seemed to me, was sufficient to shake the earth. He controlled the principal or highest grade, and I, now eleven years of age and with a tendency to read a little of everything, was deemed fit to be put there—why I never can tell.

Oh, those two terrible years! The best I can say for them or the worst is this, that outside the school and at home was heaven; inside was hell. This young professor had the German idea of stern, vigorous control; in which he was supported by the parish rector. He whipped boys vigorously, and possibly for the type of youth under him this was just the thing. They were unquestionably a tough, thick-bottomed lot, and they made my life a nightmare into the bargain. It seems to me now as I look back on it that I learned nothing at all, not even catechism. The school rooms were always being prowled over by the rector and various nuns and sisters superior, whose

sole concern seemed to be that we should learn our catechism and be "graduated," at twelve years of age,
whether we knew anything or not.   Think of it!   I am
not grossly lying or exaggerating about the Catholic
Church and its methods.   I am telling you what I felt,
saw, endured.

During these two years, as it seems to me, I never
learned anything about anything.   There was a "Bible
history" there which entertained me so much that I read
in it constantly, to the neglect of nearly everything else;
and some of the boys brought "Diamond Dick" or its
that day equivalent, and these we read under the seats, I
among others, though I liked my "Bible history" and my
geography (such as it was) better.   On several occasions
I had my hands severely marked by a ruler, wielded by
the Herr Professor Falk—great red welts put across
both my palms, because I whispered or laughed or did not
pay attention.   And once he pulled my ear so hard that I
cried.   He had a "habit" (shall I call it) of striking disorderly boys across the cheek so hard and so fiercely that
their faces blazed for an hour; or of seizing them, laying
them over a bench and beating them with a short rawhide
whip.   Once I saw a boy whom he intended so to whip
turn on him, strike him across the face, and run and jump
out the window to the ground, say seven feet below.   To
me, at that time, with my viewpoint on life, it was dreadful.   My heart used to beat so I thought I would faint,
and I lived in constant dread lest I be seized and handled
in the same way.   Whenever we met him or the Catholic
priest or any other dignitary connected with the school
or church we were supposed (compelled is the right word)
to take off our hats.   And if it was a priest we had to
say, in German, "praised be Jesus Christ," to which he
would reply "Amen."   When school was over, at four
P. M., I would creep away, haunted by the thought that
on the morrow I would have to return.

Next to the school was the Church, and this also had
been more or less of a torture to me, though not quite
so much so.   Here the Reverend Anton Dudenhausen (I

am not inventing his name) was supreme, and here I
made my first confession (no real sins at all, really—
fibbing to my mother was the worst), and received my
first communion. It was not a very striking church, but
then with its gilt altars, the candles, the stained glass windows, the statues and stations of the cross, it seemed quite
wonderful—only I was always afraid of it all! It seemed
alien to the soul of me.

Entering it this day I found it just the same, not quite
as large as I had fancied but still of good size as such
churches go.

I recalled now with a kind of half pleasure, half pain,
all the important functions that went on in this church,
the celebrations of Easter, Christmas (the whole Christ-
child manger fable set forth life size and surrounded by
candles), Palm Sunday, Good (or Black) Friday, when
everything in the church was draped in black, the forty
days of Lent, and the masses, high or low, sung on every
great saint's day or when bishops or missionaries (the
latter to billysunday us) or other dignitaries came to visit
us. My father was always much wrought up about these
things when he was at home and the church always seemed
to blaze with banners, candles and crowds of acolytes in
red and white or visiting priests in white and gold. I
always felt as though heaven must be an amazing and difficult place to reach if so much fuss over the mere trying
for it here was necessary.

Then, in addition, there were the collections, commun-
ions, church fairs, picnics, raffles—a long line of amazing
events, the chief importance of which was, as it seemed
to me, the getting of money for the church. Certainly
the Catholics know how to keep their communicants busy,
and even worried. My recollection of school and church
life here is one confused jumble of masses, funerals, pro-
cessions, lessons in catechism, the fierce beating of recalcitrant pupils, instructions preparatory to my first confession and communion, the meeting of huge dull sodalities
or church societies with endless banners and emblems—

(the men a poor type of workingmen)—and then marching off somewhere to funerals, picnics and the like out of
the school or church yard.

Inside (and these were partly what I was coming to
see today) were the confessional, where I once told my
sins to the Reverend Anton, and the altar rail and the
altar, where once I had been received in Holy Communion
and was confirmed by the Bishop, sitting on a high throne
and arrayed in golden canonicals of the church. I can
see him now—a pale, severe German, with a fine nose and
hard blue eyes. I can feel his cool fingers anointing my
forehead. Think of the influence of such formulas and
all gorgeous flummery on the average mind! Is it any
wonder that so many succumb permanently to theories
and isms so gloriously arrayed? The wonder to me is
that any child should ever be able to throw off the oppressive weight—the binding chains thus riveted on him.

Today, because it was so near September, they were
cleaning the schoolrooms and preparing them for a new
batch of victims. Think of the dull functioning of dogma,
century after century, age after age. How many millions and billions have been led—shunted along dogmatic
runways from the dark into the dark again. They do not
fell them with an axe as at the stockyards, nor open their
veins with a knife as befalls the squealing swine, but they
fell and bleed them just the same. I am not ranting
against Catholicism alone. As much may be said of Mo-
hammedanism, Confucianism, Shintoism, Brahmanism,
Buddhism—the Methodist, Presbyterian, Baptist yokes.
It is possible that for the latter it may be said that the
chains are not so difficult to break. I don't know. But
here they come, endless billions; and at the gates dogma,
ignorance, vice, cruelty seize them and clamp this or that
band about their brains or their feet. Then hobbled, or
hamstrung, they are turned loose, to think, to grow if
possible. As well ask of a eunuch to procreate, or of an
ox to charge. The incentive to discover is gone.

Says the dogmatist, "See, this is the manner of it. If

you dare to think otherwise, you are damned. Your soul will grill in hell—and here is the nature of that hell."

Poor life! I wonder that ever an Athens came to pass or a Rome arose, to have so glorious a fall!

CHAPTER LVII

THE BACKWOODS OF INDIANA

STOPPING to look at the old school door I went in. I recalled how, once upon a time, when we were first starting to school here, we tried to induce Ed to enter, he being the youngest and very shy as to education. But he refused to go and ran back home. The next day my sister Sylvia and I and Tillie took him, but at the gate he once more balked and refused to enter. It was a dreadful situation, for already we others had found the discipline here to be very stern. Perhaps it was Ed's subconscious realization of what was about to be done to his soul that terrified him. At any rate, when pressed to come he cried and even screamed, making such an uproar that that same Herr Professor Ludwig Falk, ogreific soul that he was, came rushing out, grabbed him, and carried him, squalling, within. For a time he was not to be dealt with even there, but finding eventually that no one harmed him, he sat down and from that day to the time he left, two years later, learned nothing at all, not even his catechism —for which same I am truly grateful. But the formalism of the church caught him, its gold and colors and thunderings as to hell, and now he is as good a Catholic as any and as fearful of terrific fires.

Once inside, in the same room in which I used to sit and fear for my life and learned nothing, I encountered a black-garbed sister, her beads dangling at her waist, the same kind that used to overawe and terrify me in my youth. Because she looked at me curiously I bowed and then explained: "Once I went to school here—over thirty years ago." (I could see she assumed I was still a good Catholic.) I went on: "I sat in this seat here. It was the third row from the wall, about six seats back.

A Mr. Falk was my teacher here then, and a Father Dudenhausen the pastor."

"Yes," she said simply, "I have heard of Mr. Falk— but he has not been here for years. He left many years ago. Father Dudenhausen died fifteen years ago."

"Yes, so I heard," I replied, "and Father Livermann —do you know of him?"

"No, I never heard of him, but if you will go to the pastor in the house back of the church, he can tell you. He would be pleased to see someone who had been here so long ago."

I smiled. I was only fortyfour, but how old I really was, after all.

Then Franklin came in with his camera.

"Do you mind if we take a picture of it?" I asked.

"Not at all," she replied. "It would be nice."

"How would you like to sit at the desk there? I have sat in rooms where a sister was my teacher."

"Oh, I think I'd better not," she replied. "I'm not sure if it's permissible. I——"

Just then another, an older, nun came in, and she put the matter to her in soft whispers.

She was dying to do it. I could see that.

"Well, the rules," I heard the other say aloud.

There was more whispering, and then she mounted the platform and turned her head sidewise so that her bonnet concealed her face. Franklin snapped her.

"Would you like a copy of it, if it turns out well?" I inquired.

"Oh, it would please me very much."

"And your name?"

"Sister Mary Caroline—316 Vine Street."

I took one last look and went out.

Outside was the yard in which we had always played. As an eleven and twelve-year-old boy, this had seemed a dreadful place to me—one of brawls and arguments. I was not a fighter nor tough enough physically to share in the rough sports that went on here—leap frog, snap the whip, and bean bag. I did, but I was always getting the worst of it and in addition, for some unaccountable reason, I was always finding myself involved in fights. Suddenly, out of a clear sky, without my having said a word to anybody, I would be the object of some bucky little American's or German-American's rage or opposition—a fist would be shaken in my face. I would be told to "wait till after school." After school a crowd would gather. I would be led, as it were, like a lamb to the slaughter. The crowd would divide into "sides." I would be urged to take off my coat and "go for him." But I was never much on the go. Somehow I did not know how to fight; even when at times I thought I ought to, or might win. A chance blow once won me a victory and great applause. I knocked my opponent flat—and all the fight out of him apparently—but quite by accident. I hadn't intended to at all. At other times I received undeserved beatings, which left me wondering what I had done and why life was so fierce. It made me shy of other boys. I kept out of trouble by keeping away from them, wandering about by myself and rejoicing in the beauty of life as a whole—its splendid, spectacular reality.

Inside the Church was nothing to disturb me or cause me to alter my point of view. It was just the same. There was the Reverend Anton Dudenhausen's confessional, front, left; and here were all the altars, statues, stations, windows, just as I had left them. I looked up at the organ loft where I had pumped air for the organ, weekdays and Sundays. It was apparently as I had left it. Kind heaven, I exclaimed to myself, standing in here, what a farce life is anyhow. Here is this same Church, from the errors and terrors of which I managed by such hard straits of thought to escape, and here is a city and a school pouring more and more victims into its jaws and maw year after year, year after year! Supposing one does escape? Think of all the others! And if this were the middle ages I would not even dare write this. They would burn me at the stake. As it is, if any attention is paid to me at all I will be denounced as a liar, a maligner, a person with a diseased brain, as one of my dear relatives (Catholic of course) condescended to remark. Yet at my elbow as I write stands the Encyclopedia Britannica and Van Ranke's "History of The Papacy," and a life of Torquemada, to say nothing of scores of volumes demolishing the folly of religious dogma completely— and yet—and yet—the poor victims of such unbelievable tommyrot as this would be among the first to destroy me and these things—the very first.

A little way down Vine Street from the school was the old foundry, now enlarged and doing a good business in old metal melting and recasting. We turned into Main, where it joined Vine, and there a block away was Blounts Iron Works unchanged. Thirtythree years had not made a particle of difference. The walls were as red and dusty, the noise as great. I went along the windows, looking in, and so interesting were the processes that Franklin joined me. In exactly the same positions, at the same windows, were seemingly the same men at the exact machines, heating, welding, shaping and grinding shares. It was astonishing. I felt young for the moment. At these windows, with my books under my arm, I had always lingered as long as I dared, only I recalled now that my eyes then came just above the window sills, whereas now the sills touched my middle chest. It was almost too good to be true.

And there, up Main Street, quite plainly was the railroad station we entered the night we came from Sullivan, and whence we departed two years later for Chicago and Warsaw—only it had been rebuilt. It was a newer, a grander affair—a Union Station, no less. Then we had slipped in, my mother and her helpless brood, and were met by Paul and put on a little one horse street car which had no conductor at the rear but only a small step, and in which, after depositing coins in a case where a light was, we rode a few blocks to Franklin Street. I recalled the night, the stars, the clang of summer engine bells, the city's confusing lights. It seemed so wonderful, this city; after Sullivan, so great. It had forty or fifty thousand people then (seventyfive thousand today). On the train, as we came in, it seemed as if we were coming into fairyland.

"Mister," I said to a passing Southern water type, a small, gypsyish, swarthy little man, "can you tell us where Franklin Street is?"

"Why, sweetheart, right they it is—right they at the conoh."

The eyes poured forth a volume of gentle sunny humor. I smiled back. It was like being handed a bouquet of roses.

We turned into Franklin Street and rode such a little way—two blocks say. The house was easy to identify, even though the number had now been made 1415. It was now crowded in between a long row of brick and frame houses, of better construction, and the neighborhood had changed entirely in physical appearance though not in atmosphere. Formerly, save for our house, all was open common here. You could see from our house to the station at which we had arrived—from our house to the interesting potteries which I still hoped to find, east or toward the country. You could see north to the woods and an outlying Catholic Orphan Asylum.

Now all that was changed. It was all filled with houses. Streets that in my time had not even been platted now ran east and west and north and south. Our large yard and barn were gone. The house had no lawn at all, or just a tiny scrap in front. The fine commons at the back where all the neighborhood boys gathered to play ball, circus, top, marbles, was solidly built over with houses. I remembered how I used to run, kicking my bare toes in clover blooms in the summer. Once a bee stung me and I sat down and cried; then getting no aid, I made a paste of mud and saliva and held that on—instructions from big Ed Fisher, one of our neighborhood gang. I recalled how Ed and I played one old cat here with Harry Trochee, the gypsy trader's son, up the street, and how we both hated to have to run up the street to Main Street to the grocer's or butcher's for anything. Here I could stand and see the steeple of Holy Trinity, clear across the city at Third and Pine, and hear the Angelus tolled, morning, noon and night. It was beautiful to me—I have often paused to listen—and to feel. Across the common of a Saturday I have wandered to the potteries to look in at the windows at so many interesting things that were being made.

"Shall we stop?" asked Franklin, as we neared the door.

"Please don't. I don't want to go in."

Some little children were playing on our small front porch.

And next came the potteries themselves, over in the exact region where they should have been, but now swollen to enormous proportions. The buildings extended for blocks. Hundreds, if not thousands, of men and women must have been at work here. You could see them at all the windows, turning cups, saucers, plates, bowls, pitchers, tureens—thousands in a day. The size and the swing of it all was like a song. We got out and wandered about up and down the low red walls, looking at windows and doors, seeing the thousands upon thousands of bits of clay being shaped into the forms which they retain for a little while only to be returned to their native nothingness again. So may we be shaped and cast back broken—to be used some day for something else.

"The methods have changed," said one man, talking to me through a window. "Twenty years ago a lot of the work was still done by hand, but now we do it all by machinery. We have forms like this"—and he held up one. "You see we put just so much clay in and press this down and that makes the exact thickness. It can't be more or less. I make a hundred and twenty plates an hour."

He made twenty while we looked on.

Another man, at the next window, was putting handles on cups.

After this there was nothing of interest to see, so we consulted the map and decided that our best plan was to go first to Boonville in Warwick County, the next county east; then northeast to Huntingberg and Jasper in Dubois

County, and then still northeast through Kellerville and Norton into Orange County, and so reach French Lick and West Baden.

Neither of us had ever been there. It was of some slight interest to me as being famous—a great cure and the quondam resort of my brother Paul, who was fond of places of this kind. Indeed, he was a kind of modern Falstaff, roystering with drinkers and women and having a gay time of it wherever he was—a vigorous animal soul, with a world of sentiment and a capacity for living which was the admiration and the marvel of all beholders.

So we were off.

In so far as this part of the trip was concerned, I can truthfully say the attraction was off. There was still Bloomington, my one year university town, but beside Warsaw and Terre Haute and Sullivan and Evansville— how it paled! Chicago was really of much more interest to me, the Chicago that I visited between Evansville and Warsaw, but this trip did not include that. Besides, I had been to Chicago so often since.

We followed hot, wet bottom lands to Boonville, a poorer town even than Sullivan, with unpaved streets and a skimpy county fair not to be compared with the one of Knox County, in which Vincennes was situated. Then we struck northeast through a region where the roads were so bad that it seemed we should never come through with the car. Water puddles, and streams even, blocked the way. At one place we shot over a bridge the far end of which sank as we crossed, and a ditch of nine feet of depth yawned beside the track, separated by but one foot of earth! Death seemed to zip close to my ear at that moment. We saw poor homes, poor stores, wretched farms, shabby, almost ragged people. At one town, Selvin, on the road to Huntingberg, a pretty country girl "tending" the general store there asked us if we were coming from Boonville, and when we said yes, asked if we had seen the fair.

"Yes," replied Franklin.

"It's fine, isn't it?" she commented.

"Yes," he replied gently.

You can imagine the isolation of this region when I tell you that our automobile attracted universal attention; that we saw only one other between Boonville and Huntingberg; that dogs and horses ran away frightened at the horn; and that children ran out to see. This did not seem quite possible.

At Holland, however, in the southwest corner of Dubois County, we encountered a splendid road, smooth and white, along which we tore. Indeed, this whole county proved a revelation, for whereas the two preceding ones were poor, wretched even, this was prosperous and delightful to look upon. Great meadows of emerald were interspersed with splendid forests of ash and beech. One saw sheep and Jersey and Holstein cattle in the fields, and for a novelty, new for me in America, repeated flocks of snow white geese, great droves of them,—a region, no doubt, given to feather raising.

Huntingberg was alive and clean—a truly handsome little town with well built houses, wide streets, attractive stores, a brisk, businesslike atmosphere. It was really charming, romantically so. Beyond it was an equally fine road leading to Jasper, the county seat. On this we encountered a beech grove so noble and well planned that it had the sanctity and aroma of a great cathedral. Through the columns of trees one could see the sun sinking—a great red ball of fire. The sky was sapphire and the air cool. Those lowings and bleatings and callings and tinklings of evening were just beginning. We ran the car into a fence pocket, and letting down the bars of a gate walked into this great hall. I was deeply impressed—moved really. I put my arms behind my back and gazed aloft into the silvery branches. I laid reverent hands on their smooth, silvery trunks—and my cheek. I almost asked them to bless me—to help me grow strong, natural, frank—all that a struggling mind in a mystic world should become. I spoke to the red sun in the West and bade it adieu for another night. I looked into the small still pools of water to be found here, wherein stars would see their faces latterly, and begged of all wood sprites and water nymphs, nixies and pixies, that some day, soon perhaps, they would make me one in their happy councils and revels. I looked up through the trees to the sky, and told myself again, as I do each day, that life is good, that in spite of contest and bitterness and defeated hopes and lost ambitions and sickness and envy and hate and death—still, still, there is this wondrous spectacle which, though it may have no part or lot with us, or we with it, yet provides all we know of life. The sigh of winds, the lap of waters, the call of birds—all color, fragrance, yearning, hope, sweet memory—of what old mysteries are these compounded!

.   .   .   .   .   .

Jasper, the county seat, was another town of which I most heartily approved. It was beautiful, like the rest of this striking county. The court house, like most of those in this region and elsewhere, was new, but in this instance built with considerable taste and individuality—not a slavish copy—and set in a square at the intersection of four wide streets on a slight rise of ground, so that coming townward from any direction, and from a long way off, one could see it commanding one of these striking approaches. What a charming place in which to grow up, I thought!

Again, there was a river here, that selfsame Patoka of Princeton, and as we entered from the south, it provided some most interesting views, sylvan and delicate. Still once more there was a church here—St. Joseph's Roman Catholic—which was a triumph of taste. Most Roman Catholic Churches, and for that matter every other denominational church in America, have enough spent on them to insure originality and charm in design, if only taste were not wanting—but taste, that priceless, inexpensive thing, is rarely ever present. They build and build, slavish copies of European models, usually of cathedrals, so that when one sees an original design it is like a breath of fresh air entering a stuffy room. This Church was built of a faintly greenish gray stone, and possessed a soaring, yet delicate bell tower at one corner. It stood on a considerable rise, in an open space and at right angles with a low flat brown convent or school, which gave its entrance way a plaza-like atmosphere. But for the fact that it was late and we were in a hurry, and it was locked, we would have entered, but we would have had to go for a key.

CHAPTER LVIII

AFTER passing through Jasper and Dubois Counties, where we had seen more good automobiles, good roads and brisk life than we had since the very best sections of northern Indiana and Ohio, our luck in roads left off. Around the courthouse square at Jasper we had seen machines of the best make, and parties of well to do people driving; but on our road to Kellerville and Norton and French Lick we passed nothing but rumbling wagons and some few, not very good, cars.

And now the landscape changed rapidly. I had always heard that Brown County, east of Monroe (the seat of our state university), was the roughest and most picturesque in the state, containing a hill, the highest in Indiana, of over five hundred feet! As a student I had walked there with a geologizing party, but if my memory served me correctly, it did not compare in picturesqueness with the region through which we were now making our way. Heights and depths are variable matters anyway, and the impression of something stupendous or amazingly precipitous which one can get from a region of comparatively low altitude depends on the arrangement of its miniature gorges and crevasses. Here in Orange County I had an impression of great hills and deep ravines and steep inclines which quite equalled anything we had seen. It suggested the vicinity of Stroudsburg in Pennsylvania, and as we sped along there were sudden drops down which we ground at breakneck speed, which quite took my breath away. It was a true and beautiful mountain country, becabined, lonely, for the most part bridgeless—and such roads! We bumped and jounced and floundered along. Now and again we were at the

very bottom of a ravine, with lovely misty hills rising
sheer above us. Again, we were on some seeming mountain side, the valleys falling sharply away from the road
and showing some rocky rivulet at the bottom. More
than once we shot the machine through a tumbling, spark-
ling, moonlit stream.

At the bottom of one ravine I saw a light, and we being
very uncertain of our way, I climbed out at the gate and
went up under some vines and bushes to knock at the
door. Inside, since it was open, I beheld a quite metropolitan interior—craftsman furniture, a wall of well-
built shelves loaded with books, a table strewn with magazines and papers, and the room lighted by a silk shaded
lamp. When I knocked a short, stocky, legal looking
youth of most precise manners and attire and a large pair
of horn glasses on his nose, arose from a small secretary
and came over.

"French Lick?" I inquired.

"About eighteen miles," he replied. "You are on the
right road."

I felt quite reduced. I had expected to find a picturesque, ambling, drawling mountaineer.

Between bounces and jounces and "holding back"
against declivities to which Bert seemed amazingly indifferent, I sat and dreamed over those moonlit hills.
What a possession for a state like Indiana, I thought—a
small, quaint, wonderful Alpine region within its very
center. As time went on and population increased, I
thought, this would afford pleasure and recreation to
thousands, perhaps hundreds of thousands, who knows,
who could not afford to go farther. Plainly it had already
evinced its charm to the world, for were we not on the
very outskirts of two of the most remarkable curative
spring resorts in America, if not in the world? Who had
not heard of French Lick—West Baden? And yet when
I went to school at the state university, these places had
not been heard of locally, let alone nationally.

I recall a long, lanky student from this very county
who was studying law at "our college," who told me of

French Lick, and that "a lot of people around there thought the waters were good for rheumatism." I expected, somehow, as we rode along, to see some evidence in the way of improved mountain conditions—better houses, more of them, possibly—now that we were in the vicinity of such a prosperous resort, but not a sign was there. Ten o'clock came and then eleven. We were told that we were within nine miles, seven miles, four miles, two miles—still no houses to speak of, and only the poorest type of cabin. At one mile there was still no sign. Then suddenly, at the bend of a road, came summer cottages of the customary resort type, a street of them. Bright lamps appeared. A great wall of cream colored brick, ablaze with lights, arose at the bottom of the ravine into which we were descending. I was sure this was the principal hotel. Then as we approached gardens and grounds most extensive and formal in character appeared, and in their depths, to the left, through a faint pearly haze, appeared a much larger and much more imposing structure. This was THE hotel. The other was an annex for servants!

All the gaudy luxury of a Lausanne or Biarritz resort was here in evidence. A railroad spur adjoining a private hotel station contained three or four private cars, idling here while their owners rested. A darkened Pullman train was evidently awaiting some particular hour to depart. At the foot of a long iron and glass awning, protecting a yellow marble staircase of exceedingly florate design, a liveried flunky stood waiting to open automobile doors. As we sped up he greeted us. Various black porters pounced on our bags like vultures. We were escorted through a marble lobby such as Arabian romances once dreamed of as rare, and to an altar like desk, where a high priest of American profit deigned to permit us to register. We were assigned rooms (separate quarters for our chauffeur) at six dollars the day, and subsequently ushered down two miles of hall on the fifth or sixth floor to our very plain, very white, but tastefully furnished rooms, where we were permitted to pay the various slaves who had attended us.

"George," I said to the robustious soul who carried my bag, "how many rooms has this hotel?"

"Eight hundred, suh, Ah believe."

"And how many miles is it from here to the dining-room?"

"We don't serve no meals aftah nine o'clock, suh, but Ah expects if you wanted a lil' sumfin sent up to yo room, de chef would see you done got it."

"No, George, I'm afraid of these chefs. I think I'll go out instead. Isn't there a restaurant around here somewhere?"

"Nothin' as you-all'd like to patronize, suh, no suh. Dey is one restaurant. It keeps open most all night. It's right outside de grounds here. I think you might get a lil' sumfin dayah. Dey has a kinda pie countah."

"That's it, George," I replied. "That's me. A plain, humble pie counter. And now good night to you, George."

"Good night, suh."

And he went out grinning.

I may seem to be exaggerating, but I say it in all seriousness. These enormous American watering place hotels, with their armies of servants, heavy, serious-faced guests, solemn state diningrooms, miles of halls and the like, more or less frighten me. They are so enormous. Their guests are so stiff, starchy, captain-of-industry-like. And they are so often (not always) accompanied by such pursy, fussy, heavily bejeweled or besilked and velveted females, whose very presence seems to exude a kind of opposition to or contempt for simple things, which puts me on tenter hooks. I don't seem quite to belong. I may have the necessary money to pay for all and sundry services such as great hostelries provide—for a period anyhow—but even so, I still feel small. I look about me furtively and suspect every man I see of being at least a millionaire. I feel as though I were entirely surrounded by judges, merchant princes, eminent doctors, lawyers, priests, senators and presidents, and that if I dare say a word, some one might cry—"That man! Who is he, anyhow? Put him out." And so, as I say, I "kinda-sorta" slip along and never make any more noise or fuss or show than I have to. If a head waiter doesn't put me in exactly the place I would like to be, or the room clerk doesn't give me just the room I would like, I always say, "Ah, well, I'm just a writer, and perhaps I'd better not say anything. They might put me out. Bishops and doctors and lawyers ought to have all the center tables or window seats, and so——" It's really uncomfortable to be so humble—just nothing at all.

.   .   .   .   .   .

But notwithstanding this rather tragic state, my room was a good one, and the windows, once opened to the moonlight, commanded a fine view of the grounds, with the walks, spring pavilions and artificial grottoes and flower beds all picked out clearly by the pale, ethereal light. The restaurant over the way was all that George said it was and more—very bad. The whole town seemed to be comprised of this one great hotel and an enormous annex for servants and chauffeurs, and then a few tatter-demalion resorts and the town cottages. The springs in the grounds were four or five in number, all handsomely hooded with Moorish pavilions. In each case these latter were floored with colored marbles, and you went down steps into them, carrying your own glass and drinking all of the peculiar tasting fluid you could endure. Resident physicians prescribe treatments or methods, for a price. The very wealthy visitors or patients often bring their own physicians, who resent, no doubt, all local medical advice. The victims, or lovers of leisure, idle about these far-flung grounds, enjoying the walks, the smooth grass, the views, the golf links and the tennis courts. The hours for meals are the principal hours—and dinner from seven to nine is an event—a dress affair. The grand parade to the diningroom seems to begin at six fortyfive or six fifty. At that time you can sit in the long hall leading to that very essential chamber and see the personages go by.

For this occasion, at breakfast the next morning and luncheon, which here is a kind of an affair of state, Franklin and I did well enough. We were given tables with a pleasant view, walked over the grounds, drank at all the springs, bought picture postcards, and after idling and getting thoroughly refreshed, decided to be on our way. West Baden, as it proved, was directly on our route out of town, not more than three quarters of a mile off; and to this we repaired, also, merely to see.

If anything, it was more assuming in its appearance than French Lick. The principal hotel, an enormous one of cream brick and white stone, with a low, flat, red oval dome, Byzantine or Moroccan in spirit, was almost of the size and the general appearance of the Trocadero in Paris. As in the case of the hotel at French Lick, the grounds were very extensive and gardened to within an inch of their life. Pagodas and smart kiosks indicated the springs. A great wide circular driveway admitted to the entrance of the principal hotel. Banked and parked with stone, there was a stream here which ran through the principal grounds, and there were other hotels by no means humble in their appearance.

Satisfied at having at least seen these twin resorts, I was content to make short work of the rest of the journey. At Paoli (what a rural sounding midwestern name), the county seat of this poor and rather backwoods county, we found a courthouse so small and countrified that we could not resist the desire to pause and observe it—it was so nondescript—a cross between a Greek temple and a country school. The Greek temple was surmounted by a small, somewhat German looking belfry. About it, on all sides, ran the old time hitching rail for wagons, an unpretentious note which indicated the nonarrival of the automobile: To it were fastened a collection of nondescript wagons, buggies, and buckboards, intermingled with three or four small automobiles. I got out and walked through it only to see the county treasurer, or someone in his office, sawing away on a fiddle. The music was not exactly entrancing, but jolly. Outside stood a rather gaunt and malarial looking farmer in the poorest of crinkly jeans, threadbare and worn at the elbows. "Tell me," I said. "I see on the map here a place called Lost River. Is there a river here and does it disappear underground?"

"That's just what it does, mister," he replied most courteously, "but thar ain't nothin' to see. The water just sorta peters out as it goes along. You can't see nothin' but just dry stones. I don't know exactly where it does come up again. Out here Orangeville way, I think. There are a lot of underground caves around here."

We went on, but on discovering a splendid stretch of road and speeding on it, we forgot all about Lost River.

Throughout this and the next county north, the roads seemed to attain a maximum of perfection, possibly due to the amazing quarries at Bedford, beyond. We traveled so fast that we ran down a hen and left it fluttering in the road, a sight which gave me the creeps and started a new train of speculation. I predicted then, to myself privately, that having run down one thing we would run down another before the trip was over, for, as I said before, this is the sort of thing that is always happening to me—what Nietzsche would call my typical experience. If I should stop at one pretentious hotel like the Kittatinny, on a trip like this, I would be sure to stop at another, like French Lick, before I was through, or if I lost a valuable ring on Monday, I would be sure to lose a valuable pin on Thursday or thereabouts. Life goes on in pairs for me. My one fear in connection with this chicken incident was that the loss might prove something much more valuable than a chicken, and the thought of death by accident, to others than myself, always terrifies me.

Through the region that suggested the beauty and sweep of western New York, we now sped into Bedford City, a city that seemed to have devoted hundreds of thousands of dollars to churches. I never saw so many large and even quite remarkable churches in so small a town. It only had twelve thousand population, yet the churches looked as though they might minister to thirty thousand.

Just at the edge of this town, north, we came to quarries, the extent and impressiveness of which seemed to me a matter of the greatest import. Carrara, in Italy, is really nothing compared with this. There some of the pure white stone is mined—cut from tunnels in the sides of the hills. Here the quarries are all open to the sky and reaching for miles, apparently, on every hand. Our road lay along a high ridge which divided two immense fields of stone, and sitting in our car we could see derricks and hear electrically driven stone drills on every hand for miles. There were sheer walls of stone, thirty, forty, and as it seemed to me, even fifty feet high, cut true to plummet, and which revealed veins of unquarried stone suggesting almost untold wealth. At the bottom of these walls were pools of dull green water, the color of a smoky emerald, and looking like a precious stone. In the distance, on every hand, were hills of discarded stone, or at least stone for which there was no present use. I fancy they were veined or broken or slightly defective blocks which are of no great value now, but which a more frugal generation may discover how to use. In every direction were car tracks, spurs, with flat cars loaded or waiting to be loaded with these handsome blocks. As we went north from here, following a line of railroad that led to Bloomington, Indiana, the ways seemed to be lined with freight trains hauling this stone. We must have passed a dozen such in our rapid run to Bloomington.

.   .   .   .

In approaching this town my mind was busy with another group of reminiscences. As I thought back over them now, it seemed to me that I must have been a most unsatisfactory youth to contemplate at this time, one who lacked nearly all of the firm, self-directive qualities which most youths of my age at that time were supposed to have. I was eighteen then, and all romance and moonshine. I had come down from Chicago after these several years at Warsaw and two in Chicago, in which I had been trying to connect commercially with life, and as I may say now, I feel myself to have been a rather poor specimen. I had no money other than about three hundred dollars loaned to me, or rather forced upon me, by an ex-teacher of mine (one who had conducted the recitation room in the high school at Warsaw) who, finding me working for a large wholesale hardware company in Chicago, insisted that I should leave and come here to be educated.

"You may never learn anything directly there, Theodore," she counseled, "but something will come to you indirectly. You will see what education means, what its aim is, and that will be worth a great deal. Just go one year, at least, and then you can decide for yourself what you want to do after that."

She was an old maid, with a set of false upper teeth, and a heavenly, irradiating smile. She had led a very hard life herself, and did not wish me to. She was possessed of a wondrously delicate perception of romance, and was of so good a heart that I can scarcely ever think of her without a tendency to rhapsodize. She was not beautiful, and yet she was not unattractive either. Four years later, having eventually married, she died in childbirth. At this time, for some reason not clear to myself, she yearned over me in a tender, delicate, motherly way. I have never forgotten the look in her eyes when she found me in the wholesale hardware house (they called me down to the office and I came in my overalls), nor how she said, smiling a delicate, whimsical, emotional smile:

"Theodore, work of this kind isn't meant for you, really. It will injure your spirit. I want you to let me help you go to school again."

I cannot go into the romance of this—it is too long a story. I forget, really, whether I protested much or not. My lungs and stomach were troubling me greatly and I was coughing and agonizing with dyspepsia nearly all the while. After some conferences and arrangements made with my mother, I came—and for an entire college year dreamed and wondered.

I know now for a fact that I never learned, all the time I was there, quite what it was all about. I heard much talk of -ologies and -tries and -isms without quite grasping the fundamental fact that they were really dealing with plain, ordinary, everyday life—the forces about us. Somehow I had the vague uncertain notion that they did not concern ordinary life at all. I remember one brisk youth telling me that in addition to law, which he was studying, he was taking up politics, taxation, economics, and the like, as aids. I wondered of what possible use those things could be to him, and how much superior his mind must be to mine, since he could grasp them and I, no doubt, could not.

Again, the professors there were such a wondrous company to me, quite marvelous. They were such an outré company, your heavy-domed, owl-like wiseacres, who see in books and the storing up of human knowledge in books the sum and substance of life's significance. As I look back on them now I marvel at my awe of them then, and at that time I was not very much awestricken either— rather nonplussed.

Suffice it to say that the one thing that I really wanted to see in connection with this college was a ground floor parlor I had occupied in an old, rusty, vine-covered house, which stood in the center of a pleasing village lawn and had for a neighbor a small, one-story frame, where dwelt a hoyden of a girl who made it her business to bait me the first semester I was there. This room I had occupied with a law student by the name of William or Bill Wadhams, center rush and almost guiding spirit of the whole college football team, and afterwards county treasurer of and state senator from an adjacent Indiana county. He was a romping, stamping, vigorous, black-haired, white-faced pagan, who cursed and drank a little and played cards and flirted with the girls. He could be so mild and so engaging that when I first saw him I liked him immensely, and what was much more curious he seemed to take a fancy to me. We made an agreement as to expenditures and occupying the same room. It did not seem in the least odd to me, at that time, that he should occupy the same bed with me. I had always been sleeping with one or the other of my brothers. It was more odd that, although he at once surrounded himself with the crême-de-la-crême of the college football world, who made of our humble chamber a conference and card room, I got along well enough with them all to endure it, and even made friends out of some of them. They were charming —so robust and boisterous and contentious and yet genial.

Through his personality or my own—I can never quite make out which—I was drawn into a veritable maelstrom of college life. I had no least idea what I wanted to study, but because I had been deficient in certain things in high school, I took up those,—first-year Latin, geometry, English literature, history and Old English. How I ever got along I do not know. I think I failed in most things because I never mastered grammar or mathematics. However, I staggered on, worrying considerably and feeling that my life, and indeed my character, was a failure. Between whiles, I found time and the mood for associating with and enjoying all sorts of odd personalities—youth of the most diverse temperaments and ambitions, who seemed to find in me something which they liked,—a Michigan law student, an Indiana minister's son, a boy who was soon to be heir to a large fortune and so on and so on. I was actually popular with some, after a fashion, and if I had known how to make use of my abilities in this line—had I really craved friendship and connections—I might have built up some enduring relationships which would have stood me in good stead, commercially and socially, later. As it was, my year ended, I left college, dropping all but half a dozen youths from my list of even occasional correspondents, and finally losing track of all of them, finding in different scenes and interests all that I seemed to require in the way of mental and social diversion.

CHAPTER LIX

A COLLEGE TOWN

BLOOMINGTON, as we sped into it, did not seem much changed from the last time I had laid eyes upon it, twentyfive years before, only now, having seen the more picturesque country to the south of it, I did not think the region in which it lay seemed as broken and diversified as it did the year I first came to it. Then I had seen only the more or less level regions of northern and southern Indiana and the territory about Chicago, and so Bloomington had seemed quite remarkable, physically. Now it seemed more or less tame, and in addition, it had grown so in size and architectural pretentiousness as to have obliterated most of that rural inadequacy and backwoods charm which had been its most delightful characteristic to me in 1889.

Then it was so poor and so very simple. The court house square had been a gem of moss-back simplicity and poverty, more attractive even, rurally speaking, than that court house I just mentioned as being the charm of Paoli. Here, also, the hitching rail had extended all around the square. I saw more tumble-down wagons, rheumatic and broken-down men, old, brown, almost moss covered coats and thin, bony, spavined horses in the Bloomington of 1889 than I ever saw anywhere before or since. In addition to this, in spite of the smallness of the college, many of the six hundred students had considerable money, for Indiana was a prosperous state and these youths and girls were very well provided for. Secret or Greek letter societies and college social circles of different degrees of import abounded. There were college rakes and college loafers and college swells. At that time the university chanced to have a faculty which, because of force and brains, was attracting considerable attention. David Starr Jordan, afterwards President of Leland Stanford, was president here. William Gifford Swain, afterwards President of Swarthmore, was professor of mathematics. Rufus L. Green, a man who made considerable stir in mathematics and astronomy in later years, was associate in the chair of mathematics. Jeremiah Jenks, a man who figured conspicuously in American sociological and political discussion in after life and added considerable luster to the fame of Cornell, was occupying the chair of sociology and political economy. Edward Howard Griggs, a man who has carried culture, with a large C, into all the women's clubs and intellectual movements of one kind and another from ocean to ocean, was occupying an assistant professorship in literature. There was Von Holst, called to the chair of history at the University of Chicago, and so on—a quite interesting and scintillating galaxy of educative minds.

The student body, of which I was such an unsatisfactory unit, seemed quite well aware of the character and import of the men above them, educationally. There was constant and great talk concerning the relative merits of each and every one. As Miss Fielding, my sponsor and mentor, had predicted, I learned more concerning the seeming import of education, the branches of knowledge and the avenues and vocations open to men and women in the intellectual world than I had ever dreamed existed —and just from hearing the students argue, apotheosize, anathematize, or apostrophize one course or one professor or another. Here I met my first true radicals— young men who disagreed vigorously and at every point with the social scheme and dogma as they found it. Here I found the smug conventionalists and grinds seeking only to carve out the details of a profession and subsequently make a living. Here I found the flirt, the college widow, and the youth with purely socializing tendencies, who found in college life a means of gratifying an intense and almost chronic desire for dancing, dressing, spooning, living in a world of social airs and dreams.

There were, oddly enough, hard and chronic religionists even among the incoming class, who were bent upon preaching "the kingdom of God is at hand" to all the world. They seemed a little late to me, even at that day and date, though I was still not quite sure myself.

Catholicism had almost made heaven and hell a reality to me. And here were attractive and intellectual women —the first I had ever seen, really—who in those parliamentary and social discussions incidental to student class and social life as represented by professorial entertainments and receptions, could rise and discuss intelligently subjects which were still more or less nebulous to me. They gave me my first inkling of the third sex. Indeed, it was all so interesting, so new, so fascinating, that I was set agape and remained so until the college year was over.

I regained my health, which I had thought all but lost, and in addition began to realize that perhaps there were certain things I might intelligently investigate over a period of years, with profit to myself. I began to see that however unsuited certain forms of intellectual training and certain professions might be to me, they offered distinct and worthy means of employment to others. Though I had been aroused at first, now I began to be troubled and unhappy. I felt distinctly that I had wasted a year, or worse yet, had not been sufficiently well equipped mentally to make the most of it. I began to be troubled over my future, and while I was not willing to accept my sponsor's kind offer and return the following year (I realized now that without some basic training it would do me no good), still, I was not willing to admit to myself that I was intellectually hopeless. There must be some avenue of approach to the intellectual life for me, too, I said to myself,—only how find it? I finally left unhappy, distrait, scarcely knowing which way to turn, but resolved to be something above a mere cog in a commercial machine. This proved, really, one of the most vitalizing years of my life.

During my stay here, what novel sensations did I not experience! It was all so different from the commercial life from which I had been extricated in Chicago. There I had been rising at five thirty, eating an almost impossible breakfast (often the condition of my stomach would not permit me to eat at all), taking a slow, long distance horse car to the business heart, working from seven to six with an hour for lunch, in a crowded, foreman bossed loft, and then taking the car home again to eat, and because I was always very tired, to go to bed almost at once. Only Saturday afternoons in summer (the Saturday half holiday idea was then becoming known in America) and Sunday in winter offered sufficient time for me to recuperate and see a little of the world to make life somewhat endurable for me,—a situation which I greatly resented. It was most exasperating.

In college all that was changed. From the smoky, noisy city, I was transported once more to the really peaceful country, where all was green and sweet, and where owing to the peculiarly equable climate of this region, flowers bloomed until late December. The college curriculum necessitated my presence in class only from nine until twelve thirty or so. After that I was free to study or do as I chose. Outside my window in this lovely old house where I had a room were flowers and vines and a grape arbor heavy with blue grapes, and a stretch of grass that was like balm to my soul. The college campus, while it contained but a few humble and unattractive buildings, was so strewn with great trees and threaded through one corner of it (where I entered by a stile) with a crystal clear brook, that I was entranced. Many a morning on my way to class or at noon on my way out, I have thrown myself down by the side of this stream, stretched out my arms and rested, thinking of the difference between my state here and in Chicago. There I was so unhappy in the thing that I was doing. The Irish superintendent who was over my floor despised me— very rightly so, perhaps,—and was at no pains to conceal it, threatening always to see that I was discharged at the end of the year. Our home life was now not so unpleasant, only I found no time to enjoy it; my work was too arduous.

Here were no pots and kettles to pile in bins, no endless loads of tinware and woodenware to unpack out of straw or crates and store away, only to get them out again on orders. There I felt myself a pointless, unimportant bondslave. Here I was a free, intellectual agent, to come or go as I chose. I could even attend classes or not as I chose. Study was something I must do for myself or not. There was no one present to urge me on. Various youths, as I have said, at once gathered about me. Prospective lawyers, doctors, politicians, preachers, educators in embryo, walked by my side or sat by me at the club boarding table, or dropped in between four and six of an afternoon, or walked with me in the country, or played cards on Saturday afternon or Sunday, or proposed an evening at church or at a debating society to discuss philosophy or read, or even a call upon a girl. I was not very well equipped materially, but neither was I absolutely unpresentable, and aside from the various Greek letter and social fraternities, it did not make so much difference. I was never actually tapped for membership in one of these latter, and yet I was told afterwards that two different fraternities had been seriously divided over the question of my eligibility—another typical experience of mine. But I went out a great deal nevertheless, dreamed much, idled, rested; and if at the end of the year I was mentally disgruntled and unhappy, physically I was very much improved. There can be no question of that. And my outlook and ambitions were better.

. . . .

It was during this winter that I experienced several of those early, and because I was young and very impressionable, somewhat memorable love affairs which, however sharp the impression they made at the time, came to nothing. Owing to a very retiring and nervous disposition I could never keep my countenance or find my tongue in the presence of the fair. If a girl was pretty and in the least coquettish or self conscious, I was at once stricken as if with the palsy, or left rigid and played over by chills and fever.

Adjoining this house, in the cottage previously mentioned, was a young, tow headed hoyden, who no sooner saw that I was in this house as a guest, than she plotted my discomfiture and unrest.

It was my custom, because there was a space between two windows outside of which were flowers, to study in the east side of my room, looking out on the lawn. In the cottage adjoining were several windows through which, on divers occasions during the first and second week, I saw a girl looking at me, at first closing the shutters when she saw me looking; but later, finding me bashful, no doubt, and inclined to keep my eyes on my books, leaving them open and even singing or laughing in a ringing, disturbing way. On several occasions when our eyes met, she half smiled, or seemed to, but I was too terrified by the thought of a possible encounter on the strength of this to be able to continue my gaze, or to do what would seem the logical thing to most, to speak, or nod, or smile. Nevertheless, in spite of my inability to meet her overtures in the spirit in which they were made, she was apparently not discouraged. She continued to half smile— to give me the shaking realization that some day soon I might have to talk to her whether I would or not—and then where would I find words?

One afternoon, as I was brooding over my Latin, attempting to unravel the mysteries of conjugations and modifications, I saw her come out of her back door and run across the lawn to the kitchen of the old widow lady who kept this house. I was not at all disturbed by this, only interested, and keenly so, even jealous of the pleasure the old lady was to have in the girl's company. She was exceedingly pretty, and by now there were other male students in the house, though not on my floor. I thought of her graceful body and bright hair and pink cheeks, when suddenly there was a knock at my door, and opening it I encountered the feeble old lady who kept the place, very nervous and bashful herself, but smiling amusedly in a sly, senile way.

"The young lady next door wants to know if you won't help her with her Latin. There's something she can't quite understand," she said weakly.

Actually my blood ran cold. My hair writhed and rose, then wilted. I felt shooting pains in my arms and knees.

"Why certainly," I managed to articulate, not knowing anything about Latin grammar, but being dizzard enough to imagine that any educational information was required on this occasion.

I followed into the old fashioned diningroom, with its table covered with a red cotton cloth, and there was the girl simpering and mock-shy, looking down after one appealing glance at me, and wanting to know if I wouldn't please show her how to translate this sentence!

We sat down in adjoining chairs. It was well, for my knees were rapidly giving way. I was dunce enough to look at her book instead of her, but at that her head came so close that her hair brushed my cheek. My tongue by then was swollen to nine times its normal proportions. Nevertheless I managed to say something—God only knows what. My hands were shaking like leaves. She could not have failed to notice. Possibly she took pity on me, for she looked at me coyly, laughed off her alleged need, inquired if I was taking Latin, and wanted to know if I wasn't from Fort Wayne, Indiana. She knew a boy who had been here the year before who looked like me, and he was from Fort Wayne.

With all these aids I could do nothing. I couldn't talk. I couldn't think of a single blessed thing to say. It never occurred to me to tease her, or to tell her how pretty she looked, or frankly to confess that I knew nothing of Latin but that I liked her, and to jest with her about love and boys. That was years beyond me. I was actually so helpless that in pity, or disgust, she finally exclaimed, "Oh, well, I think I can get along now. I'm so much obliged to you"—and then jumped up and ran away.

I went back to my room to hide my head and to bemoan my cowardice and think over the things I should have said and done and the things I would do tomorrow or the next time I met her. But there never was any next time. She never troubled to look so teasingly out of her window. Thereafter when she passed the house she ran and seemed absorbed in something else. If, unavoidably, our eyes met, she nodded, but only in a neighborly way. And then in a few days, the aforesaid William Wadhams appeared upon the scene, gallant roysterer that he was, and made short work of her. One glance and there was a smile, a wave of the hand. The next afternoon he was leaning over her fence talking in the most gallant fashion. There was a gay chase a day or two later, in and out of bushes and around trees, in an attempt to kiss her, but she got away, leaving a slipper behind her which he captured and kept while he argued with her through her window. Later on there were other meetings. She went on a drive with him somewhere one Sunday afternoon. In my chagrined presence he discanted on having kissed her, and on what a peach she was. It was a pathetic, discouraging situation for me, but the race is to the swift, the battle to the strong, and so I told myself at the time. I really did not resent his victory. I liked him too much. But I developed a kind of horror of my own cowardice, a contempt for my ineptness, which in later years, year by year, finally built up a kind of courage.

. . . .

There was another girl, fifteen or sixteen, across the street from me, the daughter of a doctor, living in a low, graceful, romantic cottage, fronted by trees and flowers. She inspired me with an entirely different kind of passion. The first was heavily admixed with desire—the girl who approached me inspired it. In the second case it was wholly sexless, something which sprang like a white flame at the sight of a delicate, romantic face, and while it tortured me for years, never went beyond the utmost outposts of romance. Although later I often fell in love with others, still I could never quite get her out of my mind. And though she colored this whole year for me, desperately, I never even spoke to her.

I first saw her coming home from school, a slim, delicate, tenuous type, her black hair smoothed back from her brow, her thin, slender white hands holding a few books, a long cape or mackintosh hung loosely about her shoulders, and—I adored her at sight. The fictional representations of Dante's Beatrice are the only ones that have ever represented her to me. I looked after her day after day until finally she noticed me. Once she paused as she went into her home, her books under her arm, and picking a flower stood and held it to her face, glancing only once in my direction. Then she danced lightly up her steps and disappeared. At other times, as she would pass, she would glance at me furtively, and then seem to hurry on. She seemed terrorized by my admiration. I did my best to screw up my courage to the point of being able to address her, and yet I never did. There were so many opportunities, too! Daily she went to the post office or down town for something or other, nearly every afternoon she came home along the same street, and most often alone. With some girls, or her sister, who was learning to play the violin, she went to church of a Wednesday and Sunday evening. I followed her and attended that church—or waited outside. Once in January, right after the Christmas holidays, there was a heavy snow fall and we had sleighing on this very street. She came out with her sled one Saturday morning and looked over at me where I was sitting by my window, studying. I wanted to go forth and speak to her on this hill—there were so few there—but I was afraid. And she sledded alone!

Then as the year drifted toward spring, I wrote her a note. I composed fifteen before I wrote this one, asking her if she would not come down to the campus stile after she had put her books away—that I wanted to talk with her. It was a foolish note, quite an impossible proposition for a girl of her years—frightening. All I had to say I could have said, falling in step with her at some point, and beginning a friendly, innocent conversation. But I was too wrought up and too cowardly to be able to do the natural thing.

After days of preliminary meditation I finally met her in her accustomed path, and handed her the paper. She took it with a frightened, averted glance—there was a look of actual fear in her eyes—and hurried on. I went to the stile, but she did not come. I saw her afterward, but she turned away, not in opposition, I could see that, but in fright. That night I saw her come to the window and look over at my window, but when she saw me looking she quickly drew the blind. Thereafter she would look regularly, and one evening, after putting away her books, I saw her walk down to the stile, but now I was too frightened to follow. And so it went until the end of the second semester, when, because of room changes and most of the crowd I was familiar with moving to the district immediately south of the college, I felt obliged to move also. Besides, by now I had given up in despair. I felt that she must feel and see that I was without vitality—and as for my opinion of myself, it is beyond description.

I left, but often of an evening in the spring I used to come and look at her windows, the lighted lamp inside communicating a pale luster to them. I was miserably, painfully unhappy and sad. But I never spoke. The very last day of my stay but one, in the evening, I went again—just to see.

What better tribute could I pay to beauty in youth!

CHAPTER LX

"BOOSTER DAY" AND A MEMORY

ENTERING Bloomington this afternoon, the memories of all my old aches and pains were exceedingly dim. We say to ourselves at many particular times, "I will never forget this," or, "The pain of this will endure forever," but, alas! even our most treasured pains and sufferings escape us. We are compelled to admit that the memory of that which rankled so is very dim. Marsh fires, all of us. We are made to glow by the heat and radiance of certain days, but we fade—and we vanish.

Nevertheless, entering Bloomington now it had some charm, only as I thought the whole thing over the memory of my various sex failures still rankled. "I was not really happy here," I told myself. "I was in too transient and inadequate a mood." And perhaps that was true. At any rate, I wanted to see this one principal room I have previously mentioned, and the college and the court house, and feel the general atmosphere of the place.

As a whole, the town was greatly changed, but not enough to make it utterly different. One could still see the old town in the new. For although the old, ramshackle, picturesque attractive court house had been substituted by a much larger and more imposing building of red brick and white stone—a not uninteresting design—still a number of the buildings which had formerly surrounded it were here. The former small and by no means cleanly post office, with its dingy paper and knife marked writing shelf on one side, had been replaced by a handsome government building suitable for a town of thirty or forty thousand. A new city hall, a thing unthought of in my day, was being erected in a street just south of the square. New bank buildings, dry-goods stores, drug store, restaurants, were all in evidence. In my time there had been but two restaurants, both small, and one almost impossible. Now there were four or five quite respectable ones, and one of considerable pretensions. In addition, down the Main Street could be seen the college, or university, a striking group of buildings entirely different from those I had known. A picture postcard, referring to one of the buildings, spoke of five thousand population for the city, and a four thousand attendance for the University.

Feeling that too much had disappeared to make our stop of any particular import, still I was eager to see what had become of the old rooming house, and whether the little cottage next door and the home of Beatrice over the way were still in existence. Under my guidance we turned at the exact corner, and stopped the car at the curb. I was by no means uncertain, for on the corner diagonal from my old room was a quondam student's rooming house too obviously the same to be mistaken. But where was the one in which I had lived? Apparently it was gone. There was an old house on the corner looking somewhat like it, and the second from it on the same side was evidently the small house in which Miss T—— had lived; and over the way—yes, save for another house crowded in beside it, that was the same too. Only in the case of this house on the corner . . .

All at once it came to me. I could see what had been done.

"Willie," I said, to a boy who was playing marbles with two other boys, right in front of us, "how long has this second house been here—this one next to the corner?"

"I don't know. I've only been here since Booster Day."

"Booster Day?" I queried, suddenly and entirely diverted by this curious comment. "What in the world is Booster Day?"

"Booster Day!" He stared incredulously, as though

he had not quite heard. "Aw, gwann, you know what Booster Day is."

"I give you my solemn word," I replied, very seriously. "I don't. I never heard of it before. Believe it or not—I never did. I don't live anywhere around here, you know."

"Hey, Tozer," he called to another boy who was up in a tree in front of the house, and who up to this moment had been keeping another youth from coming near by striking at him with a stick, "here's a feller says he never heard of Booster Day. Aw, haw!"

"It's the truth," I persisted. "I'm perfectly serious. You think I'm teasing you, but I'm not. I never heard of it."

"Where dya live then?" he asked.

"New York," I replied.

"City?"

"Yes."

"Didya come out here in that car?"

"Yes."

"And they ain't got a Booster Day in New York?"

"I never heard of one before."

"Well, we have one here."

"Well, when does it come, then?" I asked, hoping to get at it in that way.

"In summer time," he replied, smiling, "now—about August."

"No, it don't," commented the boy in the tree. "It comes in the spring. I know because we were still in school yet last year, and they let us out that day."

"Well, what month was it in then?" I went on. "April, May, June?"

"May, I think," said the boy in the tree. "I know we were still in school anyhow."

"Well, what do they do on Booster Day?" I inquired of the boy on the ground. "What do you do?"

"Well," he said, kicking the bricks with his toes, "they, now, send up balloons and shoot off firecrackers and have a parade, and someone goes up in a flying machine, at least he did last year."

"Yes, what for, though?" I inquired.

"Because it's Booster Day," he insisted.

"But don't you see that isn't an answer?" I pleaded. "I want to know what Booster Day is for—why they have it, why they send up balloons and call it Booster Day. They didn't have a Booster Day when I lived out here."

"I know," called the boy in the tree gallantly. He had evidently been turning this problem over in his own mind, and now came to the other's rescue. "It's the day all the stores advertise to get people to come into town. It's to boost the town."

"Well, now, that sounds reasonable," I commented. "And does it come on the same day every year?"

"I don't know. I think so."

"Well, how long have you been here?"

"I was born here."

"And have you always had a Booster Day?"

"Yes, sir."

"Well now, there you have it," I said to the first boy. "Booster Day is the day you boost the town—advertising day. You think it's always been and yet you don't even know what day it comes on. I'll bet you haven't had such a day out here for more than ten years."

"Ooh!" chimed in one of the little ones, quite apropos of so great a flight of time. "I was born—now—three years ago."

"Were you?" I said. "Then you scarcely know of Booster Day, do you?"

"No."

"Ya do, too," put in the ground boy. "Ya said awhile ago ya saw the parade last summer."

"No, I never."

"Ya did too."

To prevent hostilities over this very important point, I said to another boy, drawn near, and who was standing by open-mouthed: "Where do you live?"

"In there," he pointed, indicating my old study. "We keep boarders."

"Then you can tell me maybe—did that house always have a porch?"

"No, sir. They put that one on two years ago."

"And was it always on the corner?"

"No, sir. They moved it over when they built this house in here. I know 'cause, now, we lived down there before we moved up here, and I seen 'em do it."

"That settles it," I said cheerfully. "Do you suppose your mother would let me go in and look at that corner room?"

"My mother's away to the country. It's only my sister's at home. But you can come in. The room ain't rented now."

He marched briskly up the steps and opened the door. I followed while Franklin, who had been idly listening to the conversation as he sketched, stood outside and watched me. It was quite the same, save for a new, smooth, hardwood floor and the porch. The window where I always sat commanded no view of any lawn, but, looking across the way and at the house diagonally opposite, I could get it all back. And it touched me in a way —like the dim, far-off echo or suggestion of something— a sound, an odor—one could scarcely say what. At best it was not cheerful, a slight pain in it,—and I was glad to leave.

Once outside I sat under the wide spreading elms waiting for Franklin to finish his sketch and thinking of old days. Over there, in the house diagonally opposite, on the second floor, had lived Thompson, the vain, in his delightfully furnished room. I always thought of him as vain, even in school. He was so tall, so superior, with a slight curl to his fine lips, with good clothes, a burning interest in football and hockey, and money, apparently, to gratify his every whim. He had a kindly, curious and yet supercilious interest in me, and occasionally stopped in to stare at me, apparently, and ask casually after my work.

And around the corner of the next block, in a large square house, but poorly provided with trees, lived one of the most interesting of the few who took an interest in me at the time. I could write a long and exhaustive character study of this youth, but it would be of no great import here. He was a kind of fox or wolf in his way, with an urbane and enticing way of showing his teeth in a smile which quite disarmed my opposition and interested me in him. He was a card sharp and as much a gambler as any young boy may be. He drank, too, though rarely to excess. All the mechanistic religious and moral propaganda of the college intended to keep the young straight were to him a laughing matter. He was his own boss and instructor. Evidently his family had some money, for they seemed to provide him freely. Once he came to me with the proposal that we take two girls, both of whom he knew and to whom he seemed perfectly willing to recommend me in the most ardent fashion, to Louisville over a certain holiday—Washington's Birthday, I think—he to arrange all details and expenses. At first I refused, but after listening to him I was persuaded and agreed to go. The result, as I feared, proved decidedly disastrous to my vanity.

His girl, whom he took me to see, was petite, dark, attractive, by no means shy or inexperienced; and at her house I was introduced to a plump, seductive blonde of about seventeen, who was quite ready for any adventure. She had been told about me, almost persuaded against her will, I fancy, to like me. But I had no tongue. I could not talk to her. I was afraid of her. Still, by reason of a superhuman effort on my part to seem at ease, and not dull, I got through this evening; how I don't know. At any rate, I had not alienated her completely.

The following Sunday we went, and had I had the least *sang froid* or presence, I might then and there have been instructed in all the mysteries of love. This girl was out for an adventure. She was jealous of the attention showered upon her friend by W——. Se-

cretly I think she admired him, only in this instance
loyalty to her friend and indifference on his part made
any expression of it a little difficult. I was a poor substitute—a lay figure—of which she was perfectly willing to make use.

On the way on the train we sat in the same seat and
I took her hand. A little later I gallantly compelled
myself to slip my arm around her waist, though it was
almost with fear and trembling. I could not think of
any witty, interesting things to say, and I was deadly conscious of the fact. So I struggled along torturing myself all the way with thoughts of my inadequacy.

Arrived at Louisville, we walked about to see the
sights. There had been a great tornado a few days
before, and the tremendous damage was still very much
in evidence. Then we went to the principal hotel for
dinner. My friend, with an effrontery which to me
passed over into the realm of the unbelievable, registered
for the four of us, taking two rooms. I never even saw
the form of registration. Then we went up, and my girl
companion, having by now concluded that I was a stick,
went into the room whither W—— and his sweetheart
had retired. W—— came to my room for me, and we
went down to dinner. He even urged more boldness
on my part.

After dinner, which passed heavily enough for me,
for I was conscious of failure, we had five hours before
our train should be due to return. That time was spent
in part by myself and this girl idling in the general parlors, because W—— and his mate had mysteriously
disappeared. Then after an hour or more they sought
us out and suggested a drive. Since we had brought
bags, we had to return to the hotel to get them and pay
the bill. There was still three quarters of an hour.
After perfecting her toilet in the room belonging to my
friend, my girl came downstairs to the parlor and, a
half hour later, just in time to make the train, W——
and his charmer appeared. The day was done. The

opportunity gone. As in the previous cases, I heaped
mounds of obloquy upon my head. I told myself over
and over that never again would I venture to make overtures to any woman—that it would be useless. "I am
doomed to failure," I said. "No girl will ever look at
me. I am a fool, a dunce, homely, pathetic, inadequate."

Back in Bloomington I parted from them in a black
despair, concealing my chagrin under a masque of pseudo-
gaiety. But when I was alone I could have cried. I
never saw that maiden any more. Afterwards W——
took me to see his girl again. He had no feeling of disappointment in me, apparently, or rather he was careful
to conceal it. He seemed to like me quite as much as
ever, but he proposed no more outings of that kind.

And there were C. C. Hall, who lived in a small hall
bedroom over me, and used to insist, for policy's sake,
I fancy, that he *thought* better in a small room, and that
too much heat was not very healthy; and Short Bill
Haughey, expert on the violin and a seeker after knowledge in connection with politics and taxation; Arthur
Pendleton, solemn delver into the intricacies of the law;
Russell Ratliff, embryo metaphysician and stoic—a long
company. I can see them now, all life before them, the
old, including men and women, merely so much baggage
to be cleared away—*their* careers, *their* loves, *their* hopes
all that was important in life. And life then felt so
fresh and good, so inviting.

After this came the university, wholly changed, but
far more attractive than it had been in my day—a really
beautiful school. I could find only a few things—Wylie
Hall, the brook, a portion of some building which had
formerly been our library. It had been so added to
that it was scarcely recognizable. I ran back in memory to all those whom I had known here—the young
men, the women, the professors. Where were they all?
Suddenly I felt dreadfully lonely, as though I had been
shipwrecked on a desert island. Not a soul did I know
any more of all those who had been here; scarcely one

could I definitely place. What is life that it can thus obliterate itself, I asked myself. If a whole realm of interests and emotions can thus definitely pass, what is anything?

CHAPTER LXI

THE END OF THE JOURNEY

WE sped north in the gathering dusk, and I was glad to go. It was as though I had been to see something that I had better not have seen—a house that is tenantless, a garden that is broken down and ravished and run to weeds and wild vines, naked and open to the moon—a place of which people say in whispers that it is haunted. Yes, this whole region was haunted for me.

I took small interest in the once pleasing and even dramatic ravine where, in my college year, I had so often rambled, and which then seemed so beautiful. Now I was lonely. If I were to add one chamber to Dante's profound collection in the Inferno, it would be one in which, alone and lonely, sits one who contemplates the emotions and the fascinations of a world that is no more.

For a little way the country had some of the aspects of the regions south of French Lick, but we were soon out of that, at a place called Gosport, and once more in that flat valley lying between the White and Wabash rivers. At Gosport, though it was almost dark, we could see an immense grassy plain or marsh which the overflowing river had made for itself in times past, a region which might easily be protected by dykes and made into a paradise of wheat or corn. America, however, is still a young and extravagant country, not nearly done sowing its wild oats, let alone making use of its opportunities, and so such improvements are a long time off.

At Gosport, a very poorly lighted town, quite dark, we were told that the quickest way to Martinsville, which was on our route to Indianapolis, was to follow the river road, and because the moon had not risen yet, we were halloing at every crossroads to find out whether we were on the right one.

"Hallo-o-o!"

"Hallo! What do you want?"

"This the right road to Martinsville?"

"Straight on!"

How often this little hail and farewell occurred outside houses set back far from the road!

And the night lights of machines coming toward us were once more as picturesque as those east of Warsaw, New York. From afar we could see them coming along this flat bottomland, like giant fireflies, their rays, especially when they swept about turns, seeming to stand out before them like the long feeling antennæ of insects, white and cautious. They were all headed in the direction of Gosport, though it did not seem quite possible that they were all going there.

In this warm, sensuous wind that was blowing here, it seemed as though nature must be about some fruitful labor. Sometimes a night achieves a quality of this sort, something so human and sympathetic that it is like a seeking hand. I sat back in the car meditating on all I had seen, how soon now we would be in Indianapolis and Carmel,—and then this trip would be over. Already with turns and twists and bypaths we had registered about two thousand miles. We had crossed four states and traversed this fifth one from end to end nearly. I had seen every place in which I had ever lived up to sixteen years of age, and touched, helplessly, on every pleasant and unpleasant memory that I had known in that period. The land had yielded a strange crop of memories and of characteristics to be observed. What did I think of all I had seen, I asked myself. Had the trip been worth while? Was it wise to disinter those shades of the past and brood over them? I recalled the comment of the poet to whom I had given the reception when I told him I was coming out here. "You won't get anything out of it. It will bore you." But had I been bored? Had I not gotten something out of it? Somehow the lines of the ghost in Hamlet kept repeating themselves:

"I am thy father's spirit, doomed for a certain time to walk the earth—"

Martinsville, about half way to Indianapolis, counting from Gosport, was another county seat, and in stopping there for a shave and a mouthful of something to eat, I learned that this, also, was a locally celebrated watering place, that there were not less than six different sanatoriums here, and always as many as fifteen hundred patients taking the baths and drinking the water for rheumatism and gout—and I had scarcely ever heard of the place. The center of the town looked as though it might be enjoying some form of prosperity, for the court house on all sides was surrounded by large and rather tasteful and even metropolitan looking shops. This portion of the city was illuminated by five-lamp standards and even boasted two or three small fire signs. I began to wonder when, if ever, these towns would take on more than the significance of just newness and prosperity. Or is it better that people should live well always, rather than that their haunts should be lighted by the fires of tragedy? Did Rome really need to be sacked? Did Troy need to fall?

Franklin seemed to consider that peace and human comfort were of more import than great tragic records, and I thought of this, but to no purpose. One can never solve the riddle, really. It twists and turns, heaves and changes color, like a cauldron that glows and bubbles but is never still.

And then we settled ourselves once more for the last run of thirtyfive miles to Indianapolis. It was after nine, and by eleven, anyhow, if not before, barring accidents, we should be there. The country north of here, so far as I could see, retained none of the interesting variations of the land to the south. It was all level and the roads, if one could judge by the feel, as smooth as a table. There were no towns, apparently, on this particular road, and not many houses, but we encountered market wagon after market wagon, heavily loaded with country produce, a single light swinging between their

wheels, all making their way north to the young, color-
less city of three hundred thousand or more.

And when we were still within ten miles of it occurred
the second of these psychic accidents which always come
in twos for me. South of Bedford we had killed a hen.
In the glow of our lamp, perhaps a hundred yards away,
there suddenly appeared out of the dark a brown pig,
young but quite as large as a dog, which at sight of the
lights seemed to make straight for us. It was squealing
plaintively, as though seeking human care, and yet we
bore down on it, quite unable, as Bert explained afterward, to turn quickly enough to save it.

There was a smash, a grunt, and then silence. We
were speeding along quite as swiftly as before.

"I tried to turn," Bert called back, "but the darn little
fool made straight for us. They always do for some
reason."

"Yes, it's odd about pigs that way," commented
Franklin.

"Number two," I said to myself.

And in a mile or two more the lights of Indianapolis
began to appear. It had clouded up, as I have said, as
we neared Martinsville, and now the heavens reflected
the glow of the city below. We passed those remote
houses which people seeking to make a little money out
of their real estate, or to live where rents are low, build
and occupy. I thought of the walled cities of the middle
ages, when people crowded together as compactly as
possible, in order to gain the feeling of comfort and
security. In these days we are so safe that the loneliest
cabin in the mountains fears no unfriendly intruder.

In a few moments more we were trundling up a rough
street, avoiding street cars, crossing railroad and car
tracks and soon stopping at the main entrance of one of
those skyscraper hotels which every American town of
any size must now boast or forever hang its head in
shame. Anything under nine stories is a failure—a sore
shame.

"We'll have a bite of something before we run out to Carmel, won't we?" commented Franklin.

"Let's end this historic pilgrimage with a drink," I suggested. "Only mine shall be so humble a thing as a Scotch and soda."

"Well, I think I'll have some tea!" said Franklin.

So in we went.

I was not at all tired, but the wind had made me sleepy. It had been a pleasant day, like all these days—save for the evoked spirits of dead things. We drank and smiled and paid and then sped out of Indianapolis's best street, north, and on to Carmel. We were within a mile and a half of Franklin's home when we had our last blowout in the front right wheel—the two rear ones carried new tires.

"I knew it!" exclaimed Bert crustily, reaching for his crutches and getting himself out. "I knew we'd never get back without one. I was just wondering where it was going to happen."

"That's funny, Bert!" exclaimed Franklin. "The last time we came north from Indianapolis, do you remember, we broke down right here."

"I remember all right," said Bert, getting out the tools and starting to loosen the tire clamps. "You'd better get out your note book, Mr. Dreiser, and make a note of this; the trip's not done yet."

Bert had seen me draw my deadly pencil and paper so often that he could not resist that one comment.

"I'll try and remember this, Bert, without notes, if you'll just get the wheel on," I commented wearily.

"This is what comes of thinking evil," called Franklin jocosely. "If Bert hadn't been thinking that we ought to have a breakdown here, we wouldn't have had one. The puncture was really in his psychic unity."

"What's that?" asked Bert, looking up.

"Well, it's something connected with the gizzard," I was about to say, but instead I observed: "It's your spiritual consciousness of well being, Bert. You're all right only you don't know it. You want to get so that you always know it."

"Uh huh!" he grunted heavily. "I see."

But I don't think he did.

Then we climbed in, and in about two more minutes we were carrying our bags up Franklin's front steps and dismissing the car for the night. Mrs. Booth came out and welcomed us.

"We thought you were going to get back last night. What delayed you?"

"Oh, we just took a little longer," laughed Franklin.

.   .   .   .

There were letters and a telegram, and instead of my being able to stay a few days, as I had hoped, it seemed necessary that I should go the next day. My train left at two, and to get various things left at Indianapolis on my way south, I would have to leave a little before one. Speed appeared the next morning to say he would like to accompany me as far as Indianapolis. Bert came to say goodby early. He was off to join a high school picnic, composed exclusively of ex-classmates of a certain high school year. I was beginning to think I should see no more of my charming friend of a few days before, when,—but that——

.   .   .   .

On my long, meditative ride back to New York, I had time to think over the details of my trip and the nature of our land and the things I had seen and what I really thought of them. I concluded that my native state and my country are as yet children, politically and socially— a child state and a child country. They have all the health, wealth, strength, enthusiasm for life that is necessary, but their problems are all before them. We are indeed a free people, in part, bound only by our illusions, but we are a heavily though sweetly illusioned people nevertheless. A little over a hundred years ago we began with great dreams, most wondrous dreams, really—impossible ideals, and we are still dreaming them.

"Man," says our national constitution, "is endowed

by his creator with certain inalienable rights." But is he? Are we born free? Equal? I cannot see it. Some of us may achieve freedom, equality—but that is not a right, certainly not an inalienable right. It is a stroke, almost, of unparalleled fortune. But it is such a beautiful dream.

As for the American people, at least that limited section of it that lies between New York and Indiana, the lakes and the Ohio River—what of them? Sometimes I think of America as a country already composed of or divided into distinct types or nationalities, which may merge or not as time goes on;—or they may be diverging phases of American life, destined to grow sharper and clearer—New England, the South, the Far West, the Middle West. Really, this region between New York and Indiana—New York and the Mississippi really—may be looked upon as a distinct section. It has little in common with New England, the South, or the Far West, temperamentally. It is a healthy, happy land in which Americans accept their pale religions and their politics and their financial and social fortunes with an easy grace. Here flourishes the harmless secret order; the church and the moving picture entertain where they do not "save"; the newspapers browbeat, lie, threaten, cajole; the plethoric trusts tax them of their last cent by high prices, rents, fares and interest on mortgages,—and yet they rarely, if ever, complain. It is still a new land—a rich one. Are they not free and equal? Does not the sacred American constitution, long since buried under a mass of decisions, say so? And have they not free speech to say what the newspapers, controlled by the trusts, will permit them to say? Happy, happy people!

Yet for the dream's sake, as I told myself at this time, and as against an illimitable background of natural chance and craft, I would like to see this and the other sections with which it is so closely allied, this vast republic, live on. It is so splendid, so tireless. Its people, in spite of their defects and limitations, sing so at their tasks.

There are dark places, but there are splendid points of light, too. One is their innocence, complete and enduring; another is their faith in ideals and the Republic. A third is their optimism or buoyancy of soul, their courage to get up in the morning and go up and down the world, whistling and singing. Oh, the whistling, singing American, with his jest and his sound heart and that light of humorous apprehension in his eye! How wonderful it all is! It isn't English, or French, or German, or Spanish, or Russian, or Swedish, or Greek. It's American, "Good Old United States,"—and for that reason I liked this region and all these other portions of America that I have ever seen. New England isn't so kindly, the South not so hopeful, the Far West more so, but they all have something of these characteristics which I have been describing.

And for these reasons I would have this tremendous, bubbling Republic live on, as a protest perhaps against the apparently too unbreakable rule that democracy, equality, or the illusion of it, is destined to end in disaster. It cannot survive ultimately, I think. In the vast, universal sea of motion, where change and decay are laws, and individual power is almost always uppermost, it must go under—but until then——

We are all such pathetic victims of chance, anyhow. We are born, we struggle, we plan, and chance blows all our dreams away. If, therefore, one country, one state dares to dream the impossible, why cast it down before its ultimate hour? Why not dream with it? It is so gloriously, so truly a poetic land. We were conceived in ecstasy and born in dreams.

And so, were I one of sufficient import to be able to speak to my native land, the galaxy of states of which it is composed, I would say: Dream on. Believe. Perhaps it is unwise, foolish, childlike, but dream anyhow. Disillusionment is destined to appear. You may vanish as have other great dreams, but even so, what a glorious, an imperishable memory!

"Once," will say those historians of far distant nations

of times yet unborn, perchance, "once there was a great republic. And its domain lay between a sea and sea— a great continent. In its youth and strength it dared assert that all men were free and equal, endowed with certain inalienable rights. Then came the black storms of life—individual passions and envies, treasons, stratagems, spoils. The very gods, seeing it young, dreamful, of great cheer, were filled with envy. They smote and it fell. But, oh, the wondrous memory of it! For in those days men were free, because *they imagined they were free——*"

Of dreams and the memory of them is life compounded.

THE END

Theodore Dreiser authored realistic portrayals of life in the United States. His two best-known works are *Sister Carrie* and *An American Tragedy*, but he also wrote more than fifteen other books—including fiction, autobiography, poetry, and plays, as well as writings on travel, politics, and science.

Franklin Booth studied at the Art Institute of Chicago and the Art Student's League in New York. Best known for his intricate and precise drawings, he was a founder of the commercial art movement. His drawings appeared in magazines ranging from *The Masses* to *Good Housekeeping*.

Douglas Brinkley, Director of the Eisenhower Center for American Studies and Professor of History at the University of New Orleans, is the author of award-winning books such as *Dean Acheson: The Cold War Years, 1953–1971*, *Driven Patriot: The Life and Times of James Forrestal* (with Townsend Hoopes), and *Majic Bus: An American Odyssey*.